# DEADLINE

# JAMES RESTON

# DEADLINE

*A*
*Memoir*

RANDOM HOUSE
NEW YORK

Library of Congress Cataloging-in-Publication Data

Reston, James
Deadline by James Reston
p.  cm.
Includes index.
ISBN 0-394-58558-5
1. Reston, James  2. Journalists—United States—
Biography. 3. New York Times—History. 4. United States—
History—20th century.  I. Title.
PN4874.R447A3  1991
070'.92—dc20    91-52679
[B]

Manufactured in the United States of America


Book design by Jo Anne Metsch

FOR SALLY

# Foreword

I STARTED TO write this book as a political memoir of my fifty years as a reporter, columnist, Washington correspondent, and executive editor of *The New York Times*, but it got away from me and turned into a personal memoir of love and hope. I wrote it because I happened to live through one of the great periods of American history and journalism, when "The New World came to the rescue of the Old," usually at the last minute before deadline. To have been a fortunate witness to this long transformation while many more talented and less fortunate colleagues lost their lives along the way seemed to justify and even to require that I add a few glimpses of my own. It contains no thumping revelations about the ten presidents who had the honor and agony of presiding over our affairs during my days on the Washington merry-go-round, for they were always on display or on guard when they let me in the door; but I have now lived in every decade of the twentieth century, and I wanted to tell a few stories about this long journey before my own last deadline. Besides, as an old sportswriter, I had always kept a box score of runs, hits, and errors at the end of the game.

From Pearl Harbor in 1941 to the Gulf War in 1991, these were years of merciless violence, which didn't always make sense but always made news. They began with a revolution in communications that led to a revolution in politics and changed the world. By good luck, I happened to be around the corner during many of these struggles, and I look back on them with pride in my country and with relief and gratitude, for many of the things we feared the most never happened.

Hitler didn't get the atom bomb before the United States; this for a time was the Allies' nightmare. The alliance between the Soviet Union and Communist China, which was supposed to run everything from the Sea of Japan to the Baltic Sea, fell apart. Communism wasn't a success in the Third World but a spectacular failure, even in the USSR. And in America, while the extremists of the Right and the Left made the most noise, the moderates made most of the laws.

The ideologues who dreamed of saving the mentally enfeebled world and the Washington wonder-workers who tried to spread democracy abroad by corrupting it at home couldn't even save themselves. No doubt many scoundrels got away with their tricky schemes, but a surprising number of them were caught. In 1914, Lord Grey, the British foreign secretary, said, "The lamps are going out all over Europe; we shall not see them lit again in our lifetime." But just as I came to the end of my journey, Uncle Sam came along and turned them on again.

In preparation for these events, and for convenience in writing these memoirs, I chose my parents carefully and planned my life in accordance with the calendar. I was born in Scotland at the end of the first decade of the century, in 1909, and thereafter counted my years by decades. My parents brought me to the United States in 1920. I met Sally Fulton of Sycamore, Illinois, the central figure in this love story, in 1930. We were married on Christmas Eve of 1935. Our first son, Richard, was born on Bastille Day, July 14, 1937; our second son arrived on Jim Reston Day, March 8, 1941; and our third son, Tom, was born on the Fourth of July, 1946. (This obviously took some careful policy planning.) I joined *The New York Times* in London, with an assist from Adolf Hitler, on the day the Second World War started, September 1, 1939, and retired from the *Times* fifty years later on my eightieth birthday.

All during this long period—a quarter of all the years of the Republic—I worked under the tyranny of the deadline, reporting on the fleeting problems and personalities of the moment, always with a sense of time running out. But someday, I promised Sally, I would be free of deadlines and would try to see this tumultuous period not in bits and pieces but as a whole, and write a love letter to America for its generosity to one of the immigrants of the world. This book is an attempt to keep that promise.

Three things have dominated my life: the stern teachings of my mother and father; the love and intelligence of Sally Fulton, my wife these past fifty-six years; and the influence of the integrity of *The New York Times*. These and the ideals of America have been my guides in reporting and commenting on the news, leading no doubt to many hard and insensitive judgments. But I see a different America now through an old man's eyes, recollecting in tranquillity the terrible predicaments of the past that I was so dogmatic about in my youth, and trying now to reconcile and understand them.

Like the immigrants who came here to transform their lives, the United States didn't have an easy passage. It had to smash a lot of idols. It had to join and even create the "entangling alliances" the Founders had warned against. It had to find common ground between the squabbling political parties, races, and nations, and it did all these things, not without a lot of staggering and blundering, but just better than any other nation on earth.

In considering this rosy judgment, the reader would do well to remember that I'm an unreconstructed Scotch Calvinist, and nothing makes us happier than misery. But during this long journey, starting the first night of the Second World War, when I watched the children and the old folks being evacuated from London in the blackout, I met few people who even imagined that by the end of the century the old empires would have vanished, that the United States would still have an army standing guard in Europe, that the United States and the USSR would be negotiating the control of nuclear weapons, that democracy and not dictatorship would be the dominant force in world politics, that doctrinaire nationalism, socialism, capitalism, and even communism would be adjusting to the realities of a computerized world economy, and—greatest paradox of all—that fear, which had led to so many wars in the past, became, in a world of nuclear weapons, the greatest barrier to a third world war.

"It is the first step in wisdom," Alfred North Whitehead wrote in a little book called *Symbolism,* "to recognize that the major advances in civilization are processes which all but wreck the society in which they occur. . . . The art of free society consists, first, in the maintenance of the symbolic code, and secondly, in fearlessness of revision. Those societies which cannot combine reverence for their symbols with freedom of revision must ultimately decay from anarchy or from slow atrophy." I believe the United States in these past fifty years sensed the truth of these remarks.

Nothing, of course, has been settled—certainly not in the Soviet Union, China, or the Middle East—and no doubt the arguments over the ideal society will go on until the Mississippi flows into the Pacific. America is still a land of extremes, ignoring the world one day and trying to run it the next, swinging from prohibition to hedonism, and confusing the pursuit of happiness with the pursuit of pleasure. But everything is under discussion in preparation for the twenty-first century: the control of nuclear weapons, terrorism, drugs, pollution, and even sex; the continuing plight of the hungry half of the human family; and even the exploration of the heavens by a new generation of Walt Whitman's pioneers.

I write about all this for many reasons. America filled my head with its dreams and my life with the love and companionship of my wife, and it opened the way, I believe, to a happier world for our children and grandchildren. I wanted to leave my darlings a glimpse of a world that is vanishing. Since I still can't quite believe the transformations I have witnessed, it must be hard for those born after the Second World War to remember that over 70 million people were killed in that struggle (and 17 million more in wars and rebellions since then), or to appreciate the work of many men and women, most of them now forgotten, who did so much to revive our hope.

I think the original architects of our postwar foreign policy were shortchanged not only by the journalists but by the historians; most of the progress in this murderous century came not from the famous names at the top in Washington but from their faithful and often vilified assistants down below. I look back on the ten presidents on my beat with amazement, and sometimes with pity. One of them (Kennedy) was murdered; another (Roosevelt) died in office; a third (Nixon) was forced to resign, as was his vice president (Agnew). Except for Roosevelt, they were not exceptional men, but they managed to make the system work, and for that, much credit belongs to the Founders, who didn't write a constitution for saints or giants.

I thought of calling this book *Scotty* on the theory that a lot of dog lovers would buy it, but instead I called it *Deadline*—defined in my old battered dictionary as "the latest time by which something must be completed"—because meeting deadlines is what I did most of my life. More important, deadlines are also what the United States has been facing for the last fifty years, dealing with the depression, beating the Nazis, containing the Communists, controlling the Bomb, always at the last minute or a little later.

In fact, one of the striking things about the U.S. record in this century is that the nation didn't seem to be able to take many necessary decisions without a crisis deadline. It didn't reform its failing economy until the alarming depression of the thirties; or rearm and defend itself against Hitler until it was struck at Pearl Harbor; or take the Soviet threat seriously until the Communists conquered Eastern Europe, threatened the eastern Mediterranean, blockaded Berlin, and sent nuclear missiles to Cuba; or think seriously about its reliance on Middle Eastern oil until Iraq invaded Kuwait; or deal with its racial problems until the blacks were rioting in the streets; or even worry about its budget deficit, let alone deal with it, until it became a world scandal.

My hope is that the United States will regard the end of the century as a deadline for reforming its priorities and its budgets to improve the education of its children, the health of its people, and the modernization of its industries and transportation facilities. All this will have to be done to meet the commercial challenge of Japan and a more united Europe. It would help as well if we reformed our present system of nominating top officials and reaching major government decisions. But that is not the main subject of this book. *Deadline* is merely one reporter's personal stories from the past— stories that might be relevant to a future that cannot be his. I wanted to write about this period from a reporter's viewpoint because, while we are in the communications business, we journalists have never, in my view, been good at communicating why our freedom was so protected by the First Amendment to the Constitution—with the result that reporters are almost as mistrusted as politicians.

I had trouble writing this book for, as my journalistic son Richard pointed out, I have always written from "the outside in," and my patient and understanding editor, Kate Medina, at Random House, insisted the time had come to write from "the inside out." Accordingly, the book is more personal than I intended. Most of it was composed without much help from the dozen or so diaries I started and stuck with diligently, sometimes for as long as a week. But I had the help of Sally, and of the young men and women who have assisted me in my office at the *Times* for over thirty years, and whose friendship I will take with me for the rest of my life.

On the whole, I believe in happy endings, and when I consider the achievements of this great country in the last fifty years, I have to believe that America—dear, yearning, still youthful America—will be even more faithful to its ideals in the century to come.

—JAMES RESTON
May 1991

# Contents

# PART ONE

## A SCOTTISH BOYHOOD

# CHAPTER 1

# *Character of the Scots*

*Scotland*

Yet do thy children
Honor and love thee.
Harsh is thy schooling,
Yet great is the gain:
True hearts and strong limbs,
The beauty of faces,
Kissed by the wind
And caressed by the rain.
　　　　　—Sir Alexander Gray
　　　　　(1882–1968)

ON NOVEMBER 3, 1909, when I was born in Clydebank, Scotland, just outside Glasgow, the long peace of the previous century was drawing to a close. Although I wasn't following the news at the time, I have it on hearsay that the Scots were demanding a Royal Commission to look into the poverty of the people. It did so and said, "We have seen conditions in Glasgow that can be described only as appalling. Families are condemned to live in atrocious conditions, which should shock the national conscience . . . heaps of uncollected garbage and rubbish, pools of stagnant and foul-smelling water." When I arrived in these surroundings, it was said that Glasgow had the highest infant mortality rate of any city in Western Europe, and it was my mother's oft-expressed conviction that my sister, Joanna, and I had been born only through the intercession of the Lord. This was not my father's favorite theory.

I venture here to say a few things about the Scots, for their Calvinism probably had more effect on my journalism than any other "ism," but the reader should beware. Newspaper legends tend to become more exaggerated and fantastic with the passage of the years. In memory, reporters are inclined to suggest that every scoundrel is punished, every saint exalted, every mystery solved—usually by the courage and genius of the press.

Even so, one of the excuses for preserving the story of this search for a home in America, I suppose, is that we owe our children, if nobody else, what in their earliest years they cannot acquire by themselves—the gift of memory. I have come to believe that one of the most amiable qualities of the American people is that, compared to other peoples, they are always looking forward and have no memory, except maybe in the South.

Yet we are fascinated by the personal sacrifices of our elders who founded and tamed this vast country, if *tamed* is the right word. We often wonder about the early lives of our own parents, for it's hard for us to imagine them when they were young and full of the love that brought us into the world. We usually think of them when they were in middle age, caught between their own rebellious children and their aging parents, or when they were too old to remember.

My mother was born in Scotland in 1873 during the Victorian era, when Benjamin Disraeli was prime minister of Britain and General Grant was president of the United States. She died in her ninety-eighth year in Santa Cruz, California, when Richard Nixon was still in the White House, at which time, being an adoring supporter of Franklin Roosevelt, she apparently decided there was no point in going on.

I wish I knew more about the struggles of her life. She lived for nearly half the life of the Republic, and she had a hard life, secure in her Presbyterian faith, and clear-minded almost to the end. On the whole, I think she enjoyed her trials in her Calvinist way. She was married for over sixty years to my father, who was a patient saint, and had to be to endure my mother's obstinate convictions.

In passing, I should say that I'm not interested in family trees, but sometimes you have to resort to them to be understood. My maternal grandmother was Annie McTier Gordon, who was manager of the Bristol Hotel in the village of Stranraer when she was nineteen. She married a talented but somewhat tipsy sculptor named Andrew Irving, and his modest monuments still stand in the graveyard in Stranraer. She produced eight daughters in a row (my mother, Johanna, was third in line), followed at last by a son, known in the family as "Wayward Johnnie," who apparently thought eight elder sisters were too many and ran away to New Zealand and was never heard from again. When Annie Gordon died at fifty-seven, Andrew Irving printed up a little card, inscribed as follows:

> A kinder heart ne'er ceased to beat
> In confines of the human breast—
> Her equal ne'er again I'll meet,
> Devoted mother, wife the best . . .

My other grandmother had the more familiar maiden name of Elizabeth Barrett. She married a Glasgow fishmonger, who had the misfortune to be hit on the head by a barrel of salt herring and never recovered.

I have no memory of my grandparents, for I never saw them, but it's interesting that most of our family stories are about the women. In Scotland, it is the women who tend to dominate the working-class families, control their meager finances, and impose the moral authority of the church.

Scotland, in the first decade of this century, did not enjoy many of the glories of the imperial wealth, even though at the time it was building over half the world's merchant ships. For a while, it had an inventive and flourishing engineering industry along the River Clyde—even for thirty years an innovative automobile industry—and plenty of cheap labor.

It built war vessels for the British and other governments and fast steam yachts, motor cruisers, and six-meter sailboats for the rich. These were marvels of mechanical ingenuity, well ahead of their time, with glistening and immaculate interior cabinetry, some with extravagant facilities. One yacht, built for a Glasgow merchant, had a pipe organ in its saloon. James Gordon Bennett, the owner of the New York *Herald,* commissioned in Clydebank the *Lysistrata,* which had a fancy bicycle track around its main deck. Later on, in John Brown's shipyard, where my father worked, the magnificent ocean Queens were built, and somehow launched miraculously sideways into the narrow channel of the Clyde.

Scotland was fortunate in some other ways, too. It had good stone for building and talented architects, who were not dominated by local tastes or subservient to the fashions of London. They built some beautiful squares and terraces and regular boulevards, but behind these symbols of opulence and the forests of shipbuilding cranes along the Clyde lived the people who did the work. They did not live well.

The country's most valuable export in those days was not whisky, but people. Boswell quotes Dr. Johnson as saying that the brightest prospect any Scotsman ever saw was "the high road to England," but my parents' more glittering dream was America, and they looked to the sea for escape as soon as I was born.

My father had a brother David, a molder by trade, who had a job at the National Cash Register Company in Dayton, Ohio, and he encouraged my parents to join him. My father went first by himself. How he scraped together enough money to go, or how my mother coped with two small children in his absence I have no way of knowing. This was in 1911, when I was two years old. At that time, the population of the United States was just over 91 million and the country was looking for cheap labor. William Howard Taft had just been elected president, all three hundred pounds of him. Henry Ford had just produced the Model T car, which could be purchased "in any color so long as it was black," and as I discovered later, *The New York Times* had reported on the day of my birth that the Honorable William J. Gaynor of Tammany Hall had been elected mayor of New York City.

When my father landed a job, my mother and my sister, Joanna, and I joined him in Dayton, and we all moved in with Uncle David and Aunt Alice. This proved to be a disaster. My mother was homesick for the Old Country and remembered crying then more than at any other time of her life. With the kindest intentions on both sides, there were simply too many children in the same house, too many women in the same kitchen. One day my mother is reported to have looked in Aunt Alice's closet and said, "David must be close [stingy]—Alice has so few clothes." This was apparently overheard and produced a storm. After the quarrel, my mother was determined to go back home, and what my mother decided to do in our family, we did. She regretted this decision later on, though she never admitted it. She resolved all illogical decisions on the ground that it was "the will of the Lord," and against the combination of her will and faith, no opposition could prevail. So back we went to Scotland, in 1911; it was a country then in the shadow of the First World War.

I never understood these domestic events. They were so uncharacteristic of my mother. It wasn't like her to pry into other people's business or gossip about them. She was a determined woman, but she was not flighty or impulsive. She was always telling me to think about the consequences of what I was saying and doing. ("Keep your eyes open, boy, and mind what you're saying.") And while my father was often openly homesick for the Old Country, my mother always denied that she longed for that dreary tenement life of poverty and unemployment.

After the family quarrel, we had taken rooms at Mrs. Eikenbarry's house on Wayne Avenue in Dayton, where my mother had plenty of time to calm down, but when she made up her mind to do something, not even the threat of war could stop her. I never forgot this incident all my life and lived in dread in my own house of ever saying anything that might cause a break in my own family.

My first memory of Scotland after our return was a view from a tenement house in Dalmuir outside Clydebank, of the big ships at anchor or under construction on the River Clyde. But we stayed there for only a few months before moving to Alexandria, where my father had another new job.

# CHAPTER 2

# Tales from the Kitchen

THE SCOTS, BY their own admission, are a contrary bunch and not excessively modest. One of their favorite toasts is "Here's to us; who's like us? Damn few, and they're all dead." They are always praising Scotland and leaving it, but it never leaves them. After over forty years in the United States, my father still had the Clydeside burr on his tongue, but he didn't go around dancing the Highland fling or longing for the Old Country. Yet it helps to know a little of Scottish history and geography to get an inkling of my parents' character.

The Gaels, who settled Scotland long before the Romans, were romantic wanderers and explorers, always getting run over by their enemies and dreaming of some splendid but unrecoverable past. Defeated by the English, imbued with Old Testament Presbyterianism, and cursed by poverty, whisky, and golf, they were, and are, a fatalistic people, patient, enterprising, proud, clannish, and a little bit dour.

"There is no special loveliness in that gray country," Robert Louis Stevenson wrote in *The Scot Abroad,* "with its rainy, sea-beat archipelago; its fields of dark mountains; its unsightly places, black with coal; its treeless, sour, unfriendly-looking cornlands; its quaint, gray, castled city, where the bells clash of a Sunday, and the wind squalls, and the salt showers fly and beat."

But even Stevenson couldn't quite make up his mind about Scotland. In one of his fanciful moods, he proclaimed that "the happiest lot on earth is to be born a Scotsman," but remembering the galloping consumption that almost took his life, he added later, "I do not even know if I desire to live there. You must pay for it in many ways, as for all advantages on earth." He went on to observe, "You have to learn the paraphrases and the shorter catechism; you generally take to drink; your youth, as far as I can find out, is a time of louder war against society, of more outcry and tears and turmoil, than if you had been born, for instance, in England. But somehow life is warmer and closer; the hearth burns more redly; the lights of home shine softer on the rainy street; the very names, endeared in verse and music, cling nearer round our hearts."

This, of course, is pure moonshine, but the Scots retain, with good reason, a reputation for being poor and proud, hardworking and hard drinking, sentimental, argumentative, part the Reverend John Knox and part the irreverent Robert Burns, joyless in their pleasures, partial to education and religion, with strong left-wing political opinions, most of them wrong.

They speak their minds and are at times tactlessly blunt. I remember once going with Sally for supper into a little inn on the Scottish coast near the Summer Isles, and finding in the after-dinner parlor two sturdy men, one old and one young, alone and dressed in the kilt. We greeted them with a remark about the sunny weather, unusual in those parts.

Upon hearing my voice, the older man said, "Ye're an American, are ye?" I said I was. He reflected on this and then asked abruptly, "Are ye a Christian country?" I said we were, among other things. "Then why do ye treat the black man the way you do?" he demanded. The younger man rescued us by saying, "We didn't always treat the black man so well in the Empire, did we, Father?" But the old gentleman wasn't to be put off. He didn't mean to be offensive but it wasn't his Scottish way to be evasive either.

Even the Scottish humor—and they have a lot of it—is sharp as a fishhook. They admire the quick retort. One of my favorite politicians in the thirties was Jimmy Maxton, a tall eloquent man with fierce deep-set eyes, and an alarming shock of long hair. Winding up a speech in Gourock one night, he roared, "Just think of it, just think of the wee weans [children]. There are," he announced with his hair waving below his shoulders, "over a million men out of work in this country!" Voice from the back of the hall: "Half of them are barbers!"

The English, of course, are the source of most of the canards against the Scots, who repay them by collecting or manufacturing anti-English stories in which the Scot is always the winner: Admiral

Nelson's famous signal to the fleet, "England expects every man to do his duty," irritated two Scottish sailors. "Not a word about puir old Scotland," said the first. "That's just a hint to the English." Said the second: "Nae Scotsman needs to be tel't tae dae his duty!"

Another story is of Dr. Johnson getting a bowl of porridge from a brisk Scottish waitress in London. "Very good for hogs," he remarked in disgust. "Then let me help you to a little more," replied the lady.

Old chestnuts about the Scots are passed down from generation to generation, and my father loved them, all the more for their retelling. For all their pose of moral rectitude, the Scots take out their humor on sex and the church. "I'm wet, drooked wet," said the preacher coming into the church out of the rain. The beadle comforted him. "Dinna vex yersel, Minister, ye'll be dry enough in the pulpit."

Robert Burns even composed some graveyard jingles:

> Ye mauchline bairns, as by ye pass
> To school in bands thegither,
> O tread but lightly on the grass,
> Perhaps he was your faither [father]

Burns on sex in Aberdeen:

> Here lie the bones of Elizabeth Charlotte,
> Born a virgin, died a harlot.
> She was aye a virgin at Seventeen,
> A remarkable thing in Aberdeen.

I cannot, indeed dare not, vouch for generalizations about the Scottish character, but recognize some glimmers from my own early experience. My parents were on good terms with the Lord and lived for the church and their children—nothing else. To them, life was an everlasting struggle—"a vale of tears" as they were always saying—but all would be rewarded "in the other world," provided we kept the faith.

There was, they believed, only one road to heaven, and they were sure it didn't run through Rome. My mother taught me to sing when I was a little boy, "King William slew the papish crew at the Battle of Boyne Water," but her bigotry didn't carry over into the next generation.

For our two elder sons married two wonderful young women of

the Roman Catholic faith, Jody O'Brien of Delavan, Wisconsin, and Denise Leary of New York City. I called my mother and urged her to come to our eldest son's wedding in Washington. She was then in her eighties, living in California and spry enough to make the trip. "The wedding would be in the Catholic church?" she asked suspiciously. I said it would. "Na, na," she said emphatically, "I wouldnie hold ma tongue!"

The place I remember best as a boy in Scotland was the village of Alexandria in Dumbartonshire on the River Leven, which flows out of Loch Lomond into the industrial pollution of the River Clyde and the Glasgow slums. Loch Lomond and the countryside around it seemed to me then, and still remain in my memory as, one of the most beautiful prospects in the world. The loch was dotted with islands and dominated by the heights of Ben Lomond at the top, and my father took me tramping there on the heather-purpled hills even before I was strong enough to make the grade.

Alexandria was a plain little town with a tiny square surrounded by small shops, my favorite being one that sold a little poke of chipped fruit for a penny. I have the happiest memories of our life in that village. The atmosphere in our family was one of intimidating piety, austerity, and authority, respectful of religion, education, and hard work. There was never a drop of whisky or a pinch of tobacco in our house, and while sex was tolerated as a necessary evil, I retain the impression that my folks thought anything so popular had to be dangerous if not downright wicked. My mother reluctantly conceded its temptations. "We're no made o' wax," she'd say.

We lived in a room and kitchen in a red stone tenement house at 29 Gray Street in Alexandria. It had running water but the toilet was out back through "the close" next to the midden where everybody dumped their garbage. We lived in the kitchen. It had a coal grate where everything was cooked on the hob. And it had a big bed recessed high in the wall where we all slept together after saying our prayers on a long wooden stool at the foot.

We had a kitchen sink where the dishes were washed, but no bathtub. Saturday night baths were taken in a big tin contraption, which was kept under the bed during the rest of the week, and it was also used for bobbing for apples at Hogmanay, or New Year's Eve. Each member of the family bathed alone and in turn, with the others temporarily banished to "the other room."

My mother was an aggressive cleaner. I can still see her with a duster around her head scrubbing the floor on her knees or polishing the brass around the fire or the gas lamps. She would look at me and say, "I love to work!" My cousin Ella from Glasgow recalls looking out the window and being rebuked by my mother. "Don't breathe on the window," she said, "ye'll get it dirty."

My father was under orders never to come in the outside door with his boots on, and in our house Mother's commands were not ignored. The other room was kept for "company" but we never had any company. The food was plain and nourishing. Bread and soup from the big pot on the hob, and of course, porridge every morning, which I hated. "Stop your boking [gagging]," my mother would say.

My mother was a strong, stern, brown-eyed woman, five or six inches taller than my father, and she looked down on him unfairly in more ways than one. She had had a year or so in a private school, and recited the Lord's Prayer in atrocious French to demonstrate her superior education. As chancellor of the exchequer, she took command of my father's brown pay envelope and gave him back half a crown when she was in a generous mood. She was, as is said of the religious Scots, "haunted by duty," and she was the strict moral disciplinarian of the family and the keeper of its conscience.

Every Sunday when I was a boy, Mother, Father, Joanna, and I walked to the Church of Scotland a mile and a half up the road in the village of Renton. We then walked back to a cold lunch. "There will be no cooking on the Sabbath," my mother would say. In the afternoon, putting a strain on religion, we would walk back again for the evening service, returning at last to climb gratefully into the big dark bed in the wall.

Every night she saw to it that I said my prayer by the side of the bed:

> Jesus tender shepherd hear me,
> Bless thy little lamb tonight,
> Through the darkness be thou near me,
> Keep me safe till morning light.
> All this day thy hand has led me,
> And I thank thee for thy care,
> Thou has warmed and clothed and fed me,
> Listen to my humble prayer:
> Let my sins be all forgiven,
> Bless the friends I love so well,
> Take me when I die to heaven,
> Happy there with thee to dwell.

I then climbed into bed and watched the flickering shadows on the ceiling and listened briefly while my father read aloud to my mother from the Bible. When I was asked at age six or seven what I was going to do when I was a man, my obedient reply was that I was "going to preach the gospel to the heathen," which, come to think of it, is what most columnists think they do.

My mother must have loved the church partly because it was her only escape from the kitchen. While the rest of us could get away to school or work, she was always there, shining things up or cooking or scrubbing our clothes on an old tin board. When she was really troubled, she would slip into the other room and pray on her knees for fifteen or twenty minutes, returning without a word. She was canny, shrewd, sometimes witty, but always true and always kind.

In 1938, my wife, Sally, and I went back to look at 29 Gray Street, and there was a little sign in the window, saying COMMUNIST PARTY OF ALEXANDRIA. We also went to the neighboring village of Renton where my Uncle Bob and Aunt Martha ran a fish-and-chip shop, but the shop was closed. "He took too much on tick [credit]," a candid neighbor explained. "You'll find him through the close and up the back stairs." Up we went, hand in hand, and knocked gently at the door. A little boy answered and I asked for Mr. McGown. This suspicious gentleman appeared in his trousers, long-sleeved underwear, and galluses.

"I'm Jim Reston's son from America," I said, "and this is my wife, Sally." He stood in the doorway and roared with laughter. "So you struck it rich!" he said, and finally shook our hands. We returned to the Vale of Leven in 1987, but the old church was closed, its lovely stained-glass windows blinded by cinder block, and the old school too had been demoted to a village grade school.

If any of this sounds excessively gloomy, I cannot remember the slightest resentment. We were careful with our meager provisions. If I objected to the food placed before me, it was taken away, no excuses and no substitutes. Once, coming home from the store, I dropped an egg on the landing outside our place, scooped it up in my two hands, and was lucky that I didn't get it for supper. My mother often threatened to box my ears, but never laid a hand on me, nor did my father, but if I argued with her, she would take me by the shoulders. "You're downright cheeky," she would say. "That's what you are!"

Out of the house, I was remarkably free. I went to the Vale of Leven Academy, which sounds fancy but wasn't. It was just the village school, presided over by an amiable old gentleman who reluctantly skelped us over the hand with a leather strap in cases of fecklessness or willful disobedience.

The school stood on the verge of Christie Park on the Balloch Road, close to the River Leven. I often daundered home from school along its banks, always stopping quietly at the railway bridge. For at certain times of the year, huge salmon as big as myself lay glittering and motionless in the shadow of the bridge. I could cast out to them with a white grub on a hook, almost tickling their noses, but never with so much as a nibble.

There were few books in our kitchen, other than the occasional tale of joy or woe my father brought home from the library. But when I think about the lessons of those days, it was there I learned many things of enduring value. For one thing, my mother and father hated pretense. They wanted and demanded straight answers to simple questions—"No nonsense, boy!"—only the plain truth. Many years later I realized that pretense was the enemy of good reporting and the curse of politics. Maybe my mother carried this too far. She had no room for childish imagination, and even denounced the royal family for "swanking around and wasting money."

Also, it was my parents' conviction that every lie left a drop of poison in its wake. To "get on"—always the Scottish ambition—you were to use your good qualities and not your bad. Maybe not now, but in the long run, they insisted, "every lie will be punished and every good deed rewarded." The evidence against this hopeful conclusion is monumental, but that was their belief and command.

Their emphasis was not on the intellect but on character, on simple things like keeping time and keeping promises. All this may sound Sunday-schoolish, and was meant to be. There was to be no restless routine of pleasures or entertainment such as confuse many children today. Life was concentrated in that kitchen—"a good place to start," as they say in the army TV ads.

Above all, there was a sense of security in this Spartan routine. If I came home late, my mother was always there demanding an account of the day's activities and wanting to know if I had got into any mischief. When I disobeyed, she predicted that I would end up in "the bad fire" if I didn't mend my ways. She had an endless store of Old Country maxims.

"Gang warily," she'd say as I went off to school. Later: "Keep a grip on yersel. . . . Be grateful for small mercies. . . . It's no sin to be poor but a shame to stay that way. . . . Make do and mend. . . . Remember, a little money put by is a great comfort." One of my

favorites was her unfailing remark when I complained about a frayed
shirt or a hole in my sock: "I'll mend it the night, but a man running
for his life would never notice." Patience was her watchword: "You
can get used to anything but hanging," she'd say.

My father was a gentler sort. He was a strong, handsome little
man—"five feet two in ma stocking feet," he'd say. At work he was
called Wee Jimmy. He had golden hair and light blue eyes. He was
a machinist and worked when there was work at John Brown's
shipyard, or at the Singer Sewing Machine Company, or at Beard-
more's auto factory, where they made munitions for the British army
during the war. In most of these jobs he was an inspector, and he took
great pride in measuring things down to a hair's breadth, and he was
very good at it. When I was older and played in golf tournaments,
he followed me around and would tell me almost precisely how many
yards there were to the hole, but he never suggested what club I
should use. When I complained that my putting was off, he'd say,
"You're a wee bit shaky inside."

He had a lovely clear voice, and sang in the church choir and went
up into the Carman Hill on Saturdays with other choir members to
practice the next day's hymns. All his life he would hum quietly to
himself as if he had no cares.

He had an uncertain life. An official report by the British government described the lot of the working man at that time in this way:
"Hire and fire were peremptory. Men could be laid off at a few hours'
notice. Craftsmen in the shipyards could be dismissed as soon as
their specific contribution had finished, and then reengaged a week
or so later. Joiners there and on construction sites carried large boxes
of tools on their shoulders as they hiked from one place to another
looking for employment, sometimes working for two or three different employers in a couple of months."

This was my father's lot, but he never shirked. He was an amiable
grumbler, not only against the factory owners, but against the shop
stewards and even against many of his fellow workers, whom he
denounced as "lazy louts." At times he would threaten to "chuck the
whole jing-bang," by which he meant going back to Ohio, but we
were trapped in Scotland by the First World War and had to listen
to my mother's endlessly repeated advice to grin and bear it.

Fortunately, my father had a wonderful gift for amusing and
improving himself. He was contentedly unhappy. When he couldn't
find work and there was tension in the kitchen—which was often—
he would take to the hills and go on what he called "the randan,"

a long hike of ten or even fifteen miles. Sometimes he took me along on these punishing tramps with a stout homemade brown paper kite as big as myself. We kept going until I cried from weariness. "Stop your greetin'," he'd order, "we'll soon be home."

He was an avid reader and a tireless gardener. He would spend hours on end at the public library reading *Spurgeon's Sermons* or scoring favorite passages in his Bible with a ruler and red ink. His garden was a little community plot in the village down by the banks of the Leven, where he grew vegetables and flowers. And always he would save some seeds from his flower packets, and, when he went walking through the lonely woods, he would plant them in some unexpected spot in the hope that some other wandering stranger would one day come across the blossoms and be mystified and delighted.

Mother was usually glad to have him out of the kitchen but complained that by walking so much "you're wearing out your boots." His remedy for this was to go to the Salvation Army and get another pair free. If they didn't fit, he'd put them on, soak them and his feet in a bucket of water, and go off on another long walk. "Now they fit fine," he'd announce when he came back.

He was one of the most nimble men I have ever seen. To amuse my sister and me, he would walk all over the kitchen on his hands, until my mother would say, "Stop this nonsense!" I can still hear him singing or saying the family blessing at the kitchen table. At the time, I thought his blessing unnecessarily long, so later we changed it to Burns's Selkirk blessing:

> Some hae meat that canna eat,
> And some hae none that want it.
> But we hae meat and we can eat,
> So let The Lord be thankit.

The first accident in my life occurred one night when I was seven. I was putting on my pajamas in front of the fire, when I staggered and fell toward the grate, grabbing the big black kettle swinging over the coals. The boiling water spilled out over my back and left arm and would have drenched my head, perhaps with fatal results, had my father not grabbed my right arm and swung me, dripping and screaming, into the middle of the room, hitting and burning my sister's leg on the way. I still carry the scars.

Though we lived in Alexandria all through the First World War,

I have no recollection of fear or even anxiety. The Germans, so far as I knew, never got that far north with their zeppelins. The Scots even joked about it. "If England falls," they said, "it may be a long war."

A long and murderous war it was for everybody, including the Scots. They lost 150,000 men, 20 percent of all the British dead. For our family, it was a time of waiting and planning and saving to escape once more to America. This determination was probably stiffened by an uprising of the workers in Glasgow near the end of the war. After the butchery of the trenches, Lloyd George, in one of his Welsh soliloquies, had promised that postwar Britain would be a "land fit for heroes." But the Scots got nothing but the Welsh Wizard's poetry and more unemployment.

Accordingly, on March 14, 1918, the Scottish Trades Union Congress called on the government to introduce the forty-hour workweek and on January 27, 1919, forty thousand Glasgow workers went on strike in support of this demand. On the following day, the crowd had doubled and the secretary of state for Scotland, Robert Munro, imagining a Bolshevik uprising (a few red flags had been flown), appealed in panic to Lloyd George for help.

Twelve thousand troops, a hundred army trucks, and six tanks appeared in the streets of Glasgow to prevent violence, but violence broke out on January 31 when another vast crowd gathered in George Square, around the corner from my Uncle Tom's flat. The police broke it up with nightsticks and the leaders of the strike were arrested and jailed. I knew nothing of all this, but it couldn't have encouraged my parents to stay in Scotland. Ernest Bevin, the former British foreign secretary, once said to me, "The problem with our people is their poverty of desire," that is to say, they were too contented with their hard lot. But that was not true of my mother and father. They wanted out, and one night my sister, Joanna, and I overheard my father telling a friend he had actually booked passage to New York. This was Harry MacKenzie, a locksmith from Clydebank and one of my favorites. Whenever he came to our kitchen in my early years, he always said to me: "Shout up the chimney, 'I'm ma mither's big tumshie [turnip],' and I'll gie ye a penny," which I did and he did.

In 1920, my father sailed off to America ahead of us, as he had done ten years before, to find work and make a place for us. When, a few months later, the good news came that he was ready, I announced with great pride to all my friends at school and church that

I was going to America, and I was presented by my Sunday school class with a little Bible wishing me well and marking the ninth verse of the first chapter of Joshua: "Be strong and of a good courage, be not afraid; neither be thou dismayed, for the Lord thy God is with thee whithersoever thou goest."

Mother, Joanna, and I sailed on the liner *Mobile* and we took along Harry MacKenzie's lovely twenty-four-year-old daughter, Maggie, who had a problem. She was a secretary to one of the top officials at John Brown's shipyard, and was engaged to a young Scottish engineer, who had taken a new job in Africa and jilted her. This was why she wanted to get away to the United States, and she planned the journey in ways we didn't know. At the time there was a wartime law in Britain that all gold had to be turned in to the British treasury, but Maggie somehow managed to trade her life's savings into gold sovereigns, and sewed them into her corset before she got on the ship.

You have to know the threat of sin and damnation preached by the Church of Scotland to understand the Scottish conscience and the fate of Maggie. Halfway across the Atlantic, still brooding over her broken engagement, she had a complete nervous collapse and my mother found her one day tearing the corset and its gold coins off her body and trying to stuff them out the porthole into the sea. This she did not manage, but she was restrained in the ship's hospital ward, and turned back when we arrived in New York.

I remember that voyage even now with the thrill of excitement. Most of the time the ship moved steadily with a gentle cradling motion, and I was allowed to go up from steerage at night to watch our long foaming trail under the stars. We had a guessing game every evening about how many miles the ship had covered in the preceding twenty-four hours, and there were foot races every day for the children on the upper deck, but after her collapse we were not allowed to see poor Maggie again, and this troubled my mother. There would be "great dangers" ahead in New York, she kept saying, and we were to "stay close to one another," and not to talk to strangers. Months later we learned that Maggie recovered, married another guy, and spent the rest of her life in Australia, but I cried when we couldn't go back to the *Mobile* to say good-bye to her, and still think on that sad day when we began our long and happy life in what my mother always called the Promised Land.

# PART TWO

## AMERICA: FIRST IMPRESSIONS

# CHAPTER 3

# Dayton, Ohio:
# Books and Sports

And I saw a new heaven and a new earth,
for the first heaven and the first earth were passed away.
—Revelations 21:1

ALL I REMEMBER about my first days in America was that it was a noisy place, and we prayed a lot. When we were all vaccinated on Ellis Island, my sister, Joanna, fainted. My mother took this as a bad omen and kept warning us to be wary. I don't remember much about the ride from New York to Dayton except that the train was bigger than the ones we had in Scotland. The houses seemed flimsy because they were made of wood, and we saw some signs on the roofs of the buildings saying MAIL POUCH, but they didn't look like post offices to me. They were, of course, advertising chewing tobacco of that name.

We could have been going to any one of the eighteen Daytons in the United States, but our destination was the one in Ohio. When we arrived, the place was in a joyful uproar. The reason, as I learned later, was that the owner of the local paper, James Middleton Cox, was running for president of the United States, along with a young man from New York named Franklin Delano Roosevelt. I don't know who arranges these lucky accidents, but they are the story of my life. For this was my introduction to politics, and Cox, the publisher of the *Dayton Daily News,* was later responsible for getting me into the newspaper business.

Dayton also numbered among its inhabitants at that time a number of other distinguished characters, and my mother was always pointing them out to me as examples of poor boys who made good because they learned their lessons and ate their porridge. Among them were the Wright brothers, who tinkered around in their bicycle shop and invented the airplane on the side; John H. Patterson, the head of the National Cash Register Company, which dominated the world money-machine market; and Boss Kettering, the inventive genius of the General Motors Corporation. I was ten when we settled there.

I remember our arrival in Dayton, for my father was there to meet us, waving and running along the platform. He had a job at the Dayton Scale Company and rooms for us at Mrs. Durkin's rooming house along the railroad tracks in the East End. These quarters had electric lights and, even more surprising, a toilet inside the house. I had, of course, seen these things before, but never with a chance to use them with such miraculous results.

I was taken to the Huffman grade school the following morning— over the railroad tracks and across Fifth Street with its big yellow streetcars—and presented to the principal by my mother in her black Sunday dress. She was worried about my rough Scottish speech. "Mind and try to speak a little better," she whispered to me as we waited our turn. She had my birth certificate, and also a plain bold certificate of approval from the Vale of Leven Academy. She waited wistfully as I disappeared into a noisy classroom. It was not a happy day.

I was dressed in my proper British suit with starched white shirt, tie, neat jacket and short pants, long stockings, and bare knees. This spectacle, the very symbol of a British sissy, created a scene at recess time, and I was laughed at and roughed around a little, and I came home in tears, blubbering that I would never go back there until I had a pair of knickers like everybody else. Mother was sympathetic but said never mind. "But you don't understand," I said, "they *laughed* at me!" But of course she understood, as always, and submitted to my ultimatum. She took me downtown on Saturday and bought me a pair of knickers, and I returned to school on Monday less conspicuously dressed but still timorous inside and still afraid of being different and apart.

Early on the following Saturday, my father took me, aged ten, on the Oakwood streetcar to the Dayton Country Club, where I got my first job as a caddy, and I came home that night in triumph with a new dollar bill—seventy-five cents for lugging the sticks and a twenty-five-cent tip. Sometimes a whole life is influenced by some small incident or accident, and so this introduction to golf proved to be for me. I thought I had never seen anything so beautiful as those rolling hills of the country club with their manicured green fairways, lined with trees and pockmarked by white sandy bunkers. The clubhouse, fringed with flowers, seemed to me like a palace, and the men I caddied for, amused by my Scottish brogue, treated me with the utmost kindness. One day, one of them even drove me to Middletown in the biggest car I had ever seen and made me a present of my first bicycle.

Every day in good weather I went back to the golf course after school when caddies were scarce, and on Saturday mornings from six till nine I earned two dollars for weeding the greens. Some weeks I brought home as much as fifteen dollars, a welcome addition to my mother's exchequer. Joanna went to night school to learn shorthand and typing, and my mother worked mornings cleaning other folks' houses, but was always home waiting for me after school or when I came back from the golf club.

She was wary about making friends with strangers, anxious that my sister and I might be put upon when we were out of her sight. She kept the rooms spotlessly clean and went to the grocery at the end of the day hunting for bargains. She saw to it that we were warm at night by putting the carpets over the beds, and before long we moved to a rented house farther out the East End on Jersey Street, where for the first time in our lives Joanna and I had bedrooms to ourselves.

This was, however, a stressful time. My father was in and out of work, and my mother fussed constantly with him, as if it were his fault. She was lonely, I think, and kept asking what was to become of us in this strange new land. She didn't have the companionship of my Uncle David and Aunt Alice, for she never forgave them for the old family quarrel during our first stay in Dayton, and they were never in our house. But she found solace at the St. Paul's Methodist Church on Huffman Avenue, and would always say on Sunday nights, "Come what may, the Lord will provide."

Dayton was and is an exceptional city. It was badly damaged by the flooding Miami River in 1913 but was greatly improved in the rebuilding by proud local leadership. Politically, mainly through the influence of Cox, it was a liberal enclave in contrast to the conservative cities of Cincinnati in the south, Columbus, the capital of the state to the north, and Indianapolis to the west over in Indiana.

After the election of 1920, apparently under the illusion that golf might be a consolation for his defeat, Governor Cox played every weekend at the Dayton Country Club and usually the old Scotch pro, Nipper Campbell, played favorites and let me caddy for him. The governor was a good politician and a wobbly golfer. His backswing was better than his follow-through, and he conceded himself putts longer than the rules allowed. Other than this serious flaw in character, he was kind to me. He encouraged me to learn the game, gave me a couple of old clubs and a free lesson from the assistant pro, and I began hacking around on the pitch-and-putt spread in a little swale in back of the caddy house.

This happy routine of school and the golf course was interrupted by the second accident of my boyhood. When I was about twelve, I was caddying for a man with the unlikely name of Lamar Fluhart, who was playing in a boozy foursome on a Wednesday evening. In those days, it was the fashion for boys to put Vaseline on their hair and train it straight back in a pompadour. To keep everything slick, we wore a little skullcap with a bright tassel on top. This apparently intrigued Fluhart, who said to me on the twelfth tee, "Let's see if I can knock that tassel off your cap." I thought he was joking and so did he, but he swung his driver and knocked me unconscious with a blow on the top of my head. They rushed me, covered with blood, to the Miami Valley Hospital, where they cauterized the cut and later took me home to my mother, who gave Mr. Fluhart a lecture on the evils of drink. "Ye might have killed the boy!" she said.

After the Huffman grade school, I went to Stivers Manual Training High School, which was well named. In addition to the normal courses, I took tailoring from a jovial old geezer named Mr. Begg, who taught me how to darn and sew and take the bags out of the knees of my pants with a big heavy steam iron. I met my first friend there, another "outsider" named Nathan Patterson, who had a wagon and introduced me to baseball and other games at the playground across from the school.

In those days, when I needed a haircut, I was instructed by my mother to have the deed done at the "Barber College" on Fifth Street, where I was obliged to sit in a chair by a big plate-glass window, where passersby could watch the students in this clip joint practicing on the innocent. At fifteen cents an operation, it was no doubt a bargain, but I saw no need to advertise our poverty and finally escaped from this indignity by adding my fifteen-cent lunch money and squandering it at a real man's barbershop.

In the winter, when there was no caddying to be done, I got other odd jobs—ushering at a downtown movie theater, putting on skates at an amusement park in the West End, and jerking soda in Gallagher's Drugstore at Fifth and Jefferson—but by the time I was sixteen, I was spending all my free time on weekends playing golf at the Hills and Dales public course. I hit practice balls until my hands were blistered and learned that my father was right: to be steady on the greens, I had to be steady inside. In my senior year at Oakwood High School, I won the state high school golf championship and went on to win the Dayton District Men's tournament and the Ohio Public Links title. This delighted my father but worried my mother. "Don't get all puffed up," she kept saying. The family meanwhile was making progress, and we bought our first house in a new development up among the swells at the end of the streetcar line in Oakwood.

It was success in these tournaments that got me into my first newspaper office. I made friends with the sportswriters during these events, particularly with Si Burick, the sports editor of the *Dayton Daily News,* a thoughtful and friendly teacher. In the wintertime after school, I would hang around his desk, and when the basketball scores came in by phone from the local schools, Si would let me take them down and write "shorts" that to my surprise and delight actually appeared in the paper exactly as written. My father collected these stammering beginnings and kept them in a big cardboard box all his life. He was a great admirer of Sir Walter Scott, who once wrote to a young aspiring newspaper reporter: "Your connection with any newspaper would be a disgrace and a degradation. I would rather sell gin to poor people and poison them that way." Apparently this advice escaped my father, for he encouraged my scribbling, and my mother, always stirring the melting pot, kept saying, "Nobody will understand you if you don't learn to speak better."

She was a little wary, however, of the atmosphere of newspaper offices and golf clubs. She thought they were a little "loose," so she decided they should be countered by strict attendance not only at Sunday school and church, but at revival meetings when itinerant evangelists came to Dayton. One of her favorites was Homer Rhodehever, who had a loud voice and a doleful message. I can still hear him singing: "Yield not to temptation / For temptation is sin / Look ever to Jesus / He will carry you in." At the word *temptation,* my mother would look at me with a knowing scowl to make sure I got the point, but she never mentioned sex to me, nor did my father. The closest she ever came to it was once at the end of high school when she said to me, "One day you may be tempted, and if you are, take to your heels and run!"

In 1927, when I was a junior in high school, my parents became American citizens, and my sister and I got in free as minor dependents. It was then that my mother began talking about my going to college, and she insisted on it every time I mentioned trying to be a golf professional. "All foolishness!" she would say. "Get a job and get yourself an education." In this she was undoubtedly right, for while I could fade or lean a ball into the wind, I wasn't long off the tees, and as a certified coward, I always got the yips on four-foot downhill putts. Accordingly, I did as I was told. I took a year off after high school and got my first full-time job, again through sports, in the employment department of the Delco Remy Corporation, where my father worked. I was editor of the factory house organ called the "Delco Doings," which reported the announcements of the management and the weddings and other sporting events of the employees. I mastered the camera, wrote the headlines, and made up the paper at a local printing shop. I even had the use of a company car and by the end of a year agreed with Mother about college.

Going to college in 1928 was not the complicated and expensive business it became later on. I had a buddy named John Clifford "Fuzzy" Evans, who was one of the best high school football halfbacks in the state. He was attending the University of Illinois, where Red Grange had become famous under the coaching of a little Dutchman named Bob Zuppke. Evans told me he could get me a room at the Sigma Pi house, where he lived, and a job washing dishes for my meals, so I merely got out on the highway with a duffel bag and my sack of golf sticks, bummed to Champaign-Urbana, and registered at twenty-five dollars a semester in the University of Illinois School of Journalism.

The saddest thing for me in those days was that the tension between my parents increased, and in the belief that a short separation might calm things down, my father took what little savings he had and went back to Scotland. My mother was furious. As soon as he departed, she went to court and obtained a divorce on the grounds of desertion. I was amazed and desolate about this, but a few weeks later, when my dad found out what she had done, he dealt with the problem in characteristic fashion. He had no lawyer; he simply went into court himself and said nobody had the right to break up his family without his knowledge. The court annulled the divorce, and, as I prepared to leave for college, he quietly moved back into the house as if nothing had happened. I don't know what my mother thought of this, but she accepted it and I never heard the separation mentioned again all the rest of their long lives together.

At college, I concentrated more on my golf than on my studies, but this was not entirely without advantage. Here I should explain, as only a Scotsman can, that golf is the Lord's punishment for man's sins. It is Scotland's revenge for what it regards as the unfair slights of history. But I was quite comfortable with golf, for it seemed to me to be a continuation of the lessons I had learned at home. It taught me perseverance, it taught me not to cheat—no easy thing for a boy when he's two down and his ball is deep in the woods—and it made me a cub reporter, which in due course made all the difference in everything. I got a job in the university's sports publicity office, enough to pay the rent and tuition, and I washed dishes at the Delta Upsilon fraternity, an accomplishment that came in handy for the ensuing sixty years.

# CHAPTER 4

# University Days:
# Sally Fulton

> They will go two by two 'til the world's end:
> Step by step, and side by side.
> —Alfred de Musset

MY NEW LIFE really began at the University of Illinois, for it was there at the beginning of the 1930s that I met Sally Fulton, the love and companion of my life. I was at that time a skinny little guy, maybe 130 pounds, a bit out of place in those boozy Prohibition days. I didn't particularly like what I saw in the mirror: I wasn't that much taller than Wee Jimmy, my father, and I had green eyes and a nose that was too big for its surroundings. I liked what I saw elsewhere, however; a big armory across the street from our fraternity house where male students played tin soldiers for the ROTC, and in back of that the varsity gym, the soccer fields, the stadium, and best of all, a little golf course.

I looked up the history of the University of Illinois as soon as I arrived and began to understand, maybe for the first time, why my parents had left Scotland, and what was so different about the America of their dreams. The cornerstone of the university had been laid on September 13, 1870, by a friend of Abraham Lincoln named Jonathan B. Turner. Twenty years earlier, Lincoln had urged the federal government to make grants of public lands to the states for the formation of colleges to educate the children of the poor, but it wasn't until 1862 that he was able to sign this into law during the Civil War.

In 1928, when I arrived on the scene, the university was a flourishing institution of imposing Georgian buildings spreading southward into the endless prairie. There were about twelve thousand enrolled in the undergraduate colleges. I couldn't believe it. "How many students are there here, anyway?" I asked my first journalism teacher, Fred Siebert. "About half of them," he replied. Thus began many of the happiest days of my life. I was lost in the mob, but the old dread of feeling out of things, with a different voice and different ways, while still bothering me, was less apparent. I wandered along the crowded broad walk of the central campus under the towering elm trees, all now gone, comfortable in this multitude as the years went by. I even managed to recognize the difference between the Old Ag and the New Ag buildings, and the instructors treated me as if I had every right to belong.

My fraternity house, numbering forty and sounding like eighty, was a refuge. Scotty was tagged as "the cocky kid from Ohio," but I loved its muscular friendship, and benefited from its assumption that all freshmen were dummies. They taught me what to do with the regiment of unfamiliar spoons and forks on the dinner table and how to introduce guests when they came to Sunday lunch. All this was new and high society to me and helped when I had the unusual and intimidating experience of meeting girls.

I went through the usual hazing as a pledge in my fraternity and was expected to perform and make a fool of myself for the enjoyment of the members, but I discovered then, as I had on that first day in grade school, that the old fear of being laughed at hadn't left me. I couldn't explain it and I never got over it. This did not add to my popularity.

Once every week I wrote a letter to my mother and father and posted it on the outside of a big cardboard box that contained my dirty laundry. Back it came the following week with everything clean and darned and with a letter recounting the sparse news from home and admonishing me to behave myself and "mind your lessons."

I fell short on this last point. I was an indifferent student. I had done just enough rudimentary writing and editing before going to Illinois to make the journalism courses easy enough, and since my Spanish teacher was in love with one of my fraternity brothers, she passed me across that language barrier with a wink and a smile.

I read with excitement all about the old editors and pamphleteers who had battled all the scoundrels of politics and led the fight against George III and slavery. I thought Tom Paine was an even greater man in those days than Red Grange, a view that was not widely shared in Illinois, and I read a lot of unlikely things that nourished my dreams of being a newspaper reporter, the only ambition I ever had.

Most of my after-class hours were spent at my work in the sports publicity office or on the university golf course or the soccer field. Competition in soccer was not very stiff in Illinois in those days, and since I had had a ball at my feet in Scotland from the time I could run, I played center forward on the freshman and varsity teams for four years. The publicity job gave me free access to the press box high in Memorial Stadium every football Saturday afternoon, where I watched with envy while famous reporters like Grantland Rice and Westbrook Pegler sent off their accounts of the game by Morse code. My task was to write profiles of the Illinois football players for the consumption of trustful sports editors. I may in the process have violated my mother's strictures ("You're no to tell stories!") but they added in color what they subtracted from the truth. It was there that I learned to be skeptical of press agents, a talent that came in handy when I got to Washington.

One of my greatest joys was walking the campus alone after dark past the big fraternity houses with their joyful shouts and loud music, down to the vast library at Armory and Green streets, and thence past Paul Prehn's dating parlor and the dance halls, where on special occasions young men actually wore tuxedos and the girls floated through my mind in long white dresses.

Dancing, like trigonometry, was one of those mysteries I was never able to fathom, then or now. In a pinch, I could make it around the floor counterclockwise, but the other way around I was in constant danger of guiding my partner into the wall.

Early on, somebody told me music appreciation was a snap course, but for me, sitting in a dark room and listening to music I had never heard before, even on a gramophone, it was not only a snap but also a discovery and a comfort when I was confused or distressed.

I took a course in seventeenth-century literature from Jacob Zeitlin, an admirer of Stuart P. Sherman, who was editor of the New York *Herald Tribune*'s Sunday book review after many years on the Illinois faculty. I retain little from Zeitlin's instruction, but was impressed by his account of Sherman's habits of self-instruction, and memorized one or two of Sherman's rules of conduct:

> Say each day: This day is my opportunity to do something which
> will count for improvement in the lives I touch. This day throw your

weight heartily against the wheel in the mud. This day speak with increased precision and force. This day give a lift or an encouraging word to somebody. There are 365 long days in the year when something might be done. . . . Act so that tomorrow will approve today and not look back with disgust and humiliation.

The "big event" happened one evening in December 1931 of my senior year. A fraternity brother of mine, Freddie Lindall, and I had dates with two girls from the Kappa Alpha Theta house, I with Winnie Haslam, and he with a dream called Sally Fulton, who had dark hair and thoughtful eyes, and a smile that made me feel funny inside.

By the end of the first Coke, I could tell we had the wrong partners. After the melted cheese sandwiches, I had reached the firm conclusion that Sally Fulton was the prettiest and brightest girl on campus, and this was before I even knew she played the piano. By the end of the evening, I had developed an intense dislike for Freddie Lindall.

I had read, of course, about people falling in love, but obviously nobody had ever experienced anything like this. It was not a crush but a crash and it was also a problem. For as "sage" or president of our fraternity, I had insisted on the rule that no member should interfere with another member's girl. Nobody! We had all taken the oath on this, yet here I was cutting in on Lindall's date and taking her out on the sly. We met on campus between classes and "studied" together at the library, but my mind wasn't on the books, and I felt guilty about breaking my word. I began to hate my Scotch conscience, but I finally wrote Sally Fulton a letter in Sycamore, Illinois, saying we couldn't go on. It was the dumbest letter I ever wrote.

After the Christmas holidays, I began to regret this bogus nobility, and prayed that Lindall would either be run over by a streetcar or at least be kicked out of school. I haunted the Theta house, slipping by day after day on the opposite side of the street. I was ready with my little "What a pleasant surprise" speech, but Sally Fulton never appeared. I began to think she was avoiding me or had an escape hatch out the back door, or disaster of disasters, that maybe she was sick.

Then one day while I was scribbling away in the library, she suddenly appeared and sat down beside me. "Your writing's very pretty," she said. "Can you read it?"

I was so excited at that moment that I couldn't read anything. It turned out that she had broken with Lindall. I assumed that he had cut his throat, but I didn't ask.

We took long walks together out into the silent prairie, always remembering the injunction to be back for the strict sorority closing hour. We talked about our families, and discovered an astonishing coincidence, namely that her grandfather James Fulton had grown up in the same small village of Stranraer in Scotland as my mother, and had emigrated from there to Canada and finally to Illinois. I felt I was making progress when Sally invited me to meet her parents in Sycamore, and she introduced me to her brainy friends, who actually seemed to enjoy reading books, and by some sort of magic, she somehow got prettier and smarter with every passing day, a trick she retained in my eyes for the ensuing sixty years.

I was soon startled out of my dreaming, however, by a note from the university bursar saying the bank on which my tuition check was written had closed, like many others in that depression year, and advising me to see the dean of men. The dean of men in those days was one Tommy Arkle Clark, who looked like a saint but had the mind of a cop. He had once kicked Sally's brother Bill out of school for driving the family car on campus against university rules. I told him I felt sure the bank would reopen before my graduation day. He said the university couldn't run on my assumptions. I said I didn't think it was fair to punish me for things beyond my control. He then delivered a brief lecture, the words of which I still remember.

"The University of Illinois is maintained," he said, "by the taxpayers of the state of Illinois, primarily for students who live in Illinois. I understand that the taxpayers do the same in Ohio and have an excellent university in Columbus. Perhaps you could finish your senior year there."

I said I loved the University of Illinois and had strong personal reasons for completing my last few months there, and besides, as captain of the golf team I felt an obligation to do so. He replied that he was more interested in the future of the university than the future of the golf team, and then he rose and showed me to the door.

I didn't even go back to my room but got out on Green Street and hitchhiked to Dayton. I went at once to the *Daily News* building, without going home with the bad news, and explained this disaster to Governor Cox. He immediately wrote out a check for one hundred dollars as a loan, wished me good luck, and to my delight said to come back after graduation and maybe there would be a job for me on the *News* or at his other paper in Springfield.

Here I must remark that there is an odd thing about my quirky memory. The Wall Street crash had taken place in October of 1929, at the beginning of my sophomore year. By 1932, my folks were scraping the bottom, and 12 million people were out of work. Yet not until my talk with Dean Clark did I, in the last year of my college education, have any understanding of what was going on. I have often wondered since then how I could have been so daft. Perhaps it was that all my life I had lived with depression and war in Scotland and so I was not surprised to find adversity in my new country. More than likely, however, though I don't like to admit it, I was so preoccupied with my own concerns that I took no notice of events I could do nothing about.

I talked to Sally about this and found that she was certainly aware of the sufferings of the depression. Her father's law partner had committed suicide after losing his life savings in the crash. Also, Judge Fulton had guaranteed his partner's debts and, as a director of the Sycamore bank that closed, he had to put up twice his own holdings. These debts strapped him all through Sally's years in college and even until his days as chief justice of the Illinois Supreme Court.

In small towns like Sycamore, I then understood, people knew more about the troubles of their neighbors than we did in the cities. Sally remembered her next-door neighbor, an officer of the bank, who had had a serious nervous breakdown, and the plight of the leader of her church choir, who had had all her front teeth removed at the beginning of the depression and then, poor spinster, had no money to replace them until the depression was finally over.

Despite all the human suffering, however, spring arrived as usual in 1932. Sally was working after class at Robinson's Department Store in Champaign, but in the evening we extended our walks and deepened our talks and I think we floated arm in arm above the budding trees, but I could be wrong about that. We even discussed marriage and how long it would be before I would be making fifty dollars a week—our wedding target—and how we would get along for two long years before her graduation.

As a token of our love, she agreed to take my fraternity pin, which was the thing to do if you were serious in those innocent days, and to send it back to me if she ever changed her mind. So I left for Dayton without waiting for the graduation services, inexpressibly happy about Sally but fearful that I might lose her in our long coming separation.

# PART THREE

# THE DEPRESSION THIRTIES

# CHAPTER 5

# *Early Jobs*

Mellon pulled the whistle,
Hoover rang the bell,
Wall Street gave the signal,
And the country went to Hell.
—Anonymous

WHEN I ENTERED the University of Illinois in the autumn of 1928, Herbert Clark Hoover was running for president against Al Smith and the pope and promising the people "a chicken in every pot and two cars in every garage." He was not a conspicuous success. On my graduation day, June 13, 1932, after four years of his benevolent mismanagement, my parents had no chicken, no car (they never did have one), and no garage. The only good news was that Prohibition was on the way out. My father was out of work, the factories in Dayton were operating on half-shift, and the schools were operating only three days a week, no doubt to the delight of the children.

In Washington, General Douglas MacArthur and his principal aide, a young major by the name of Dwight David "Ike" Eisenhower, were trying to put down an army of veterans demanding payment of their military bonus, and when I was finally liberated from the university, over 15 million Americans were unemployed, and there were about 2 million college graduates looking for work, riding the rails, sleeping in flophouses, and existing on handouts. In Kansas City, however, the Republicans nominated President Hoover again, and in Chicago, the Democrats nominated Franklin D. Roosevelt, who promised to bring back booze as a consolation and said, "I pledge you, I pledge myself to a New Deal for the American people."

Adolf Hitler in Germany and Benito Mussolini in Italy and the militarists in Japan were at the same time planning new deals of their own, but the U.S. Army, sixteenth largest in the world, numbered only 132,069, the bankers were going down with the farmers, American industry had broken down, and even United States Steel was operating at only 19 percent capacity. I had no interest in public affairs, however. I noted on my graduation day that the newspapers announced that Babe Ruth had hit two home runs to defeat the Cleveland Indians 13–5, but the rest of the news was beyond my limited concern.

I was luckier than most graduates. Governor Cox kept his promise and sent me to Edgar Morris, the publisher of the Springfield, Ohio, *Daily News,* who gave me a job in the sports department at ten dollars a week. I did a little moonlighting at a hotel, where they gave me a room for doing some publicity for them on the side. Springfield, twenty miles up the pike from Dayton, was in the dumps. Banks and factories were closing and foreclosures on homes and businesses were commonplace. Some citizens even resorted to bartering services for food and supplies.

With the election of President Roosevelt and the passage of the National Recovery Act early in the New Deal, my salary was raised automatically to eighteen dollars a week, and when the sports editor retired, I was appointed in his place, given a two-dollar-a-week bonus, and called to the publisher's office. Mr. Morris said it was an honor for one so young to be made one of the principal editors of the paper and he added that in keeping with this exalted position, he thought I should wear a hat when I came to work in the morning.

I got out seven sports sections a week (two on Saturdays) and wrote a column of commentary every day under what I still regard as the worst column title ever to appear in a daily newspaper: "Rest on This." With my schedule and pay, I couldn't get away to see Sally or even hear her voice on the expensive long distance telephone, but I wrote to her whenever I had a minute. Sometimes silly little notes: "I have a new colored ribbon in my typewriter: I love you in red. I love you in blue."

Most of the time, though, they were sad and serious:

Dearest Sally: This afternoon I walked around Springfield and returned depressed. Everywhere poverty! The stores were almost deserted, the people strangely sad, their future blunted and hopeless. Somehow I felt that for most of them life was unfairly harsh.

Oh Sally, I had not known it was possible for me to miss anyone as I have missed you this past week. Only now am I beginning to realize how alone I would be without you. I have no desire to be with anyone else.

I have recalled the many times when we were together, when, walking by my side, you did not know the love in my heart for you, a love that made me strangely quiet.

But there is much before us now. There will be hearts and minds to discover and experiences to share. And life will be good! If only we can take everything with patience and trust, pleasure and pain and loneliness and doubt, we will enrich our lives and make this obstacle of time and space less formidable. I am sure this night of my love for you.

A few days after this letter, Sally went back to Urbana for her junior year and celebrated her twentieth birthday on September 5, 1932. We then came to a bumpy patch in our separate roads, the result of my stiff-necked Scotch narrowness. I assumed we were practically engaged to be married, which was ridiculous since I had no money, had not yet learned even the rudimentary techniques of newspapering, and had no prospect of breaking out into one of the big-city newspapers.

Meanwhile, Sally, trying to abide by my selfish wishes, was not dating other boys but sitting around the Theta house on weekends, reading and wondering how she had gotten into such a pickle. After about six weeks of this, she wrote to say we had to find another way.

We agreed that she should go out as she pleased. She had taken my fraternity badge but she hadn't taken the veil. We agreed she should keep the badge, but send it back if she changed her mind. If I changed, I would write and ask for it.

All this must seem childish and even comical in these days of free and easy love, but it was deadly serious to me. I was afraid, constantly almost morbidly afraid, that I would lose the one thing that meant more to me than anything else in life.

As usual, I took refuge in work. I studied the New York and Chicago papers. I signed up for a late afternoon literature course at Wittenberg College. I read more than I ever did in Illinois and I pestered the bureau chiefs of the Associated Press in Ohio and the Ohio sports editors in Cleveland and Cincinnati to keep me in mind if they ever had an opening.

I felt more confident after more than a year on Cox's excellent daily paper, maybe because I was in charge of my department with little help on the side. I learned the importance of deadlines, for one thing. When Bert Teeters, the managing editor, called for copy, I began to pay attention. When he shouted "COPY!" I knew I was in trouble. "We're not getting out a weekly paper," he would say, and when he was really sore, "Reston," he'd yell, "what do you think this is, a quarterly?"

I learned to write headlines, an artful challenge in discipline and compression. We all knew the horror of the careless editor on one of the midwestern dailies, who wrote a headline, MAN FALLS OFF BRIDGE, BREAKS BOTH LEGS, and left out the "g" in bridge. In short I discovered that you learned this business the way you learned how to play baseball, not by meditating about it but by practicing it and by ducking at the right time.

By the summer of 1933, I was getting restless to move on, and I got a tip that Ohio State University was looking for a sports publicity director. With the help of Mike Tobin at Illinois, I got the job at forty dollars a week. I moved to Columbus, leaving the hat behind, and worked for L. W. St. John in the athletic department, and then I got another lucky break.

At that time, the Cincinnati team of the National Baseball League was in hock to a Cincinnati bank and looking for a buyer. The principal bidder was Leland Stanford MacPhail, a colorful red-headed character one of whose earlier adventures had been trying to capture the exiled German kaiser in the Netherlands. I had known him in his golfing days in Columbus and one Sunday afternoon he asked me, with the permission of St. John, if I'd like to be traveling secretary and publicity director of the Cincinnati Reds. He would pay me seventy-five dollars a week, he said.

I said I didn't know he had any connection with the Reds. He agreed that was true, but he said the man who should buy the team was Powell Crosley, of the Crosley house appliance and radio company in Cincinnati. Unfortunately, Crosley, while wanting to save the team, didn't see how it could help his business. I said I thought that was easy: if he changed the name of the Reds' playing field from Rhineland Field to Crosley Field, that name would appear on most sports pages in the big cities, and Crosley would get more free advertising than he could afford to buy. At that moment MacPhail decided I was a genius, and Crosley bought the club, with MacPhail as the general manager.

This was an interesting and decisive time in the history of professional baseball. Most of the major league clubs were struggling in the depression. MacPhail was sure they would all go bankrupt unless they attracted a larger following through radio and night baseball. Crosley owned a couple of radio stations in Cincinnati and was not only sympathetic to this idea, but his people found just the right young man to carry it out.

For years Walter "Red" Barber had been coming up from Florida to Crosley's WLW, trying out for a sports announcer's job. He was a skinny, attractive, courteous young man, and he showed up in my office at the ballpark looking for "Scotty Rustun" and announcing that he had been hired to broadcast the games at twenty-five dollars a week. Before long he was better known than MacPhail, and if there has been a better sports announcer in the past fifty years I never heard of him.

MacPhail got more ideas every week than the Reds got hits. In 1934 he introduced the idea of season tickets. That same year, he hired an old Ford tri-motor airplane and for the first time flew a major league team to Chicago for a game with the Cubs. Anything for publicity. There had been little radio coverage immediately before and after the games prior to MacPhail, and he was convinced that radio broadcasts by Barber before, during, and after the games would encourage more interest. He insisted to me every day or so that night baseball was the main hope of the foundering major league teams, and he introduced it first in Cincinnati and later in Brooklyn and in Yankee Stadium.

I had a run-in with Crosley when, not satisfied with the publicity he was getting by giving the Reds' ballpark his name, he built a big Crosley refrigerator on top of the scoreboard, and I denounced this as a silly and greedy bit of promotion. He called me to his office and threatened to fire me, but MacPhail said he would go too unless I stayed and the refrigerator was removed.

The only trouble with MacPhail was that he liked booze almost as much as baseball, and when he was in his cups he was a terror. One night he got into a fight with a couple of detectives in the Sherry Netherland Hotel and made the mistake of calling up the newspapers and reporting that he had been attacked. It was all over the front page the next day, and when Crosley made an issue of it, MacPhail took his talents to the Brooklyn Dodgers, and later to the New York Yankees, where he made a fortune before retiring to his home in Maryland.

I was never any good at baseball but I acquired a fascination for it. I never really understood why it had such an enduring appeal until my son Jim wrote a book (*Collision at Home Plate*) about the conflict between the former president of Yale University and baseball commissioner, Bart Giamatti, and Pete Rose, the star of the Cincinnati Reds, who was drummed out of baseball for gambling. Giamatti saw baseball in terms of the struggle of life itself—as a battle against hostile forces to reach home, as a "quest" for safety through skill and adversity. But I was not thinking in those terms in Cincinnati. In the mornings, I worked out with the team during batting practice, and shagged balls in the outfield. I wrote exuberant publicity handouts on talents most of the players didn't have and listened to their constant alibis about their disasters on the field. I liked these guys. But even for the stars it was a short trip from fame to oblivion. I stayed in Cincinnati for only a year, but I followed the team around the National League, and that got me into the big cities.

In those hairy-chested days before the sports pros wore gold chains around their necks and advertising on their uniforms, the Reds couldn't play baseball very well. But they played it several times a year in Chicago, St. Louis, and best of all, in New York, which was my destination. I took the team, then composed mainly of fading stars from Branch Rickey's baseball empire, to Tampa for spring training, and later in the 1934 regular season I took them on the road around the league.

It was my job to see that they were in good enough shape to get to the park on time—no easy task after their nocturnal adventures—and to check the turnstiles to see that the Cincinnati club got its share of the meager ticket sales. And in the mornings, I haunted the newspaper offices looking for a job—any job, particularly if it was in New York.

I was not alone. At most places I was turned away at the door. There was a plaque in the lobby of *The New York Times* Building saying EVERY DAY THE WORLD MADE NEW, but it wasn't made new for me. I didn't even get upstairs to see anybody at the *Times* all that summer of 1934, but lucky as always, in August I got my first shot at the big time.

The most talented and delightful student at Stivers High School in Dayton when I was there was the brilliant cartoonist Milton Caniff. In New York, he was then doing a daily cartoon called "Dickie Dare," for the Associated Press Feature Service. I went to see him at his apartment in Tudor City and he introduced me to Wilson Hicks, his editor. I went to see Hicks at the AP office on

Madison Avenue the next morning. He said he just happened to have a place on the sports feature page and he told me to report for work the following Monday. I floated out of his office to the elevator, jumped three feet straight up in the air, and when I returned to earth, wrote Sally that American journalism now had a new boy in New York.

# CHAPTER 6

# New York: 1934–37

MY MOTHER DIDN'T think much of all these moves. She thought leaving Springfield for Columbus was going too far from home, that leaving Ohio State University to run after a lot of baseball players was daft ("I hear they drink," she said), and going to a sinful city like New York was downright dangerous. "We brought you up in the ways of the Lord," she kept reminding me, "and now you'll be led into temptation wherever you go." She didn't know how right she was, but my mind was on other things.

I didn't notice it at the time, but everything in New York was not as wonderful as I supposed. With Roosevelt and the New Deal, Washington began to challenge New York as the news capital of the country, but the big city in 1934, with all its glitter, was still a reporters' paradise. I was stunned by the size and noise of everything but encouraged by the fact that many of its most successful scribblers and editors in those days were refugees from the sticks. Stanley Walker out of Lampasas, Texas, was the city editor of the *Herald Tribune*. Harold Ross from Aspen, Colorado, was presiding over *The New Yorker* magazine. Brooks Atkinson from Melrose, Massachusetts, the theater critic of the *Times,* could kill a play with a question mark. And for some mysterious reason the place was overrun by some breezy specimens from Indiana: Roy Howard of the Scripps-Howard chain from Indianapolis; Elmer Davis of the *Times* from Aurora; Ernie Pyle, also of Scripps-Howard, from Dana; Byron Price, assistant head of AP, from Topeka, Indiana; and Kent Cooper, the general manager of AP, from Columbus, Indiana.

Walker published a book called *City Editor* the year I arrived, describing New York's fabulous attractions. "It affords the newspaperman an ever changing spectacle," he claimed. "Its rackets are probably as brutal as those in Marseilles and more devious and varied than those of Chicago. It is deliriously beautiful and as ugly as a mildewed toad. Somehow it cannot be slandered, and anything that may be said about it in praise or abuse is more likely than not to be true. It is a city of yes and no. It has political leaders who can't sign their own names . . . lifeguards who can't swim and subway conductors who lecture before learned societies on early Irish literature." I swallowed all this delicious baloney with the utmost delight.

A young reporter had plenty to dream about in those days. The columnists with their signed editorials were becoming national figures mainly because of syndication. Papers out in the country could buy their thunderbolts in a cheap package along with the comic strips. These opinionated characters were read, if not believed, by millions. Thus Walter Lippmann, Heywood Broun, Westbrook Pegler, David Lawrence, Arthur Krock, and others made a doleful noise in the country and were often led by H. L. Mencken, whose muscular prose and daily insults produced howls of joy and pain.

In 1934, however, most of the New York newspapers were suffering from the depression and less obvious problems. *The World* of Irving S. Cobb, Lippmann, Herbert Bayard Swope, and other such monuments had been mismanaged to death by the Pulitzers in 1931. The *Sun,* still yearning for Herbert Hoover, was slowly sinking. And even the *Herald Tribune*'s brilliant staff and boozy publisher were crying in their beer at Jack Bleeck's pub on Fortieth Street. Adolph Ochs's *Times* on Forty-third Street, however, was picking up speed by throwing seventy reporters into a really big story to twenty for the opposition and the investment was paying off. As one old lady explained: "I read the *Times* because my friends die in the *Times* but never seem to die in the *Herald Tribune.*"

Most reporters those days were making about fifty dollars a week (I was getting forty-five dollars at the AP), and all were in danger of being fired with or without cause. Charles Chapin, the last city editor of *The Evening World,* boasted that he had sacked eighty-one galley slaves in the course of his dictatorship. By all accounts he was a malevolent genius and died in Sing Sing prison for murdering his wife.

Two events added to the tangles of the papers in 1934. The first was the organization of the American Newspaper Guild, and the second was the rising competition for news by radio. In 1932, Ogden and Helen Reid, the owners of the *Herald Tribune,* cut every salary of over $30 a week by 10 percent, and the following spring, while they were renting Otto Kahn's Pink House in Palm Beach for $10,000, they ordered another 10 percent cut across the board.

When publishers could toss reporters on the street and cut wages at will, it was not surprising that Heywood Broun, the most liberal columnist of the day, should call on August 8, 1933, in the *World Telegram* for "A Union of Reporters" with power to bargain over pay and the conditions of work. This did not amuse the owners, who had enough money worries as it was, and it divided the reporters, many of whom, hungry or not, thought joining a union would interfere with their duty to report the news objectively and publish seven days a week, strikes or no strikes.

The challenge of radio news was no joke either. For until the 1930s, the newspapers had been the first messengers of the news. The public depended on them, but when radio got into the news business, announcers could tear the latest outrage off the AP tickers and spread the word instantly to the whole nation. Since it took the newspapers hours to print and distribute the same information, they faced the problem of losing not only circulation but advertising as well.

At first, the newspapers tried to ignore the problem and then to fight it. For a time, they refused to publish the daily listings of the radio programs, arguing that radio stations, like theaters, should buy advertising space to get their notices to the public. They also tried to block the sale of news from the news agencies to the radio owners, but CBS hired Ed Angly, a good pro from the *Herald Tribune,* who began setting up radio news bureaus in the major capitals, and gradually opposition to both the newspaper guild and radio news collapsed, and the newspapers finally had to think about what was called the New Journalism.

Walter Lippmann took the lead in calling for a reappraisal of the way newspaper people should think about their craft. "This New Journalism," he wrote in the *Yale Review,* "is bound, I think, to become less Napoleonic at the top and less bohemian at the bottom, and to take on the character of a liberal profession. It has never been a profession. It has been at times a dignified calling, at others a romantic adventure, and again a servile trade. But a profession it could not begin to be until modern objective journalism was successfully created, and with it the need of men who would consider themselves devoted, as all professions ideally are, to the service of truth alone."

This philosophic proposition was argued for years, and is still not standard procedure, but the papers gradually began to see that it wasn't good enough to go on reporting the who-what-when-and-where of the news, but had to tell the readers *why*. That is to say, they had to consider, and even concentrate on, not merely what had happened, but on the causes of human suffering and violence. They even began to see that maybe radio was not their enemy but their ally: let the radio be first with the news to its larger audience, which would then turn to the papers for explanation of why it had all happened and what could be done about it, especially since the world was then startled and mystified by the rise of Adolf Hitler in Nazi Germany.

All this controversy over unions and radio news and imminent bankruptcy went on over my thick skull in 1934. The only "why" that worried me was why I ran out of scratch at the end of each week. New York scared me then and still does. People didn't look at me and say Hi as they did back home, but somehow looked past me or through me, pushing their way along. I felt sure that if I ever went to hell it would be on the New York subway.

The man who terrified me was not Adolf Hitler, but the monster upstairs at the AP, Kent Cooper. He ordered reporters around at will, and few dared protest. One exception in my time was a brave character named Glenn Babbs, one of Cooper's bloodhounds in the Tokyo bureau, who pleaded for serious personal reasons to be brought back home to New York. Cooper refused not once but several times and ordered him to stick in Japan or quit. Finally, in desperation, Babbs wired back in one of the most famous examples of moneysaving cablese: UPSTICK JOB ASSWARDS. That ended Babbs's career on the AP.

But there were many advantages. Milt Caniff and his wife, Bunny, were unfailingly kind. He didn't draw typical cartoons; every panel was a picture with authentic backgrounds, and this took a lot of time. While he was at his board scratching away, a few other friends and I would read to him. On other free nights, I had time for studying, keeping notes of vivid phrases, or just wandering in the streets and looking at the stores. New York was the biggest free show in the country, and every day seemed a new discovery. This was before the psychiatrists took over and asked you if you had "found yourself." I didn't even know I was lost.

I wrote to Sally, now approaching her graduation day, wondering what to do thereafter.

Dearest Sally: My job is good and has done a great deal for my confidence. It's amazing how quickly the atmosphere here makes one grateful for the happy circumstances of our quieter lives. I took a walk today, for example, through the Lower East Side. The people had come out of their grimy rooms and were sitting patiently in little slices of sunshine. They gave me such sympathy for the folks who are left behind. I'm groping: I mean to say that the man who is not driven to his knees after seeing these poor souls is hard indeed.

Then there's the other side of my job: the association with wonderful, talented, articulate people who have lived exciting lives and fought themselves above the ordinary run of things. Whenever I let myself think on all this in relation to my life as a whole, I miss you very much, Sally. But you are so much an illusion most of the time that I cannot rid myself of little pangs of despair. I do love you, Sally, only please, please let me know your plans. We must get together.

Fortunately, these melancholy thoughts were relieved by a rush of new assignments. I was transferred from the feature service to the city desk, then to the sports department, then to the picture desk, from which the AP was beginning to send photos across the country by telegraph wire. All this got me out of the office at 383 Madison Avenue and into the big clattering city.

For a while, I relieved Eddie Brietz on the boxing beat, and went to Madison Square Garden to cover the fights. This involved sitting at ringside within arm's reach of the ropes, and dictating to a Morse code operator blow-by-blow descriptions of two sweaty pugs beating each other bloody just above my head. This was a test. If you could keep your emotions steady, and report accurately this brutal scene, I concluded you could cover anything but a hanging.

I acquired in those days a love of sports that developed into a lifelong, time-wasting addiction. I hated prizefighting and thought it should have been outlawed with dueling, but doted on everything else with the obvious exception of all-in wrestling. I marveled at the skill and self-control of golfers. It seemed to me that sinking a four-foot, downhill, win-or-lose putt on a fast eighteenth green was infinitely harder than balancing the federal budget. The fathomless duplicity of baseball pitchers; the leaping, twirling precision of basketball ballet; and the cool passing accuracy of quarterbacks defying the murderous charge of malevolent monsters were to me a source of constant wonder and delight.

In my early newspaper days, the professional baseball stars were denied the constitutional protections against slavery and cruel and unusual punishment. They didn't have contract agents and many of them didn't even make a million dollars a year. I wrote the most exuberant nonsense about them and am not a bit ashamed of it, for while they enjoyed a few years of fun and flattery, their off-season lasted for most of a lifetime.

I worked just long enough on the night shift in a factory during college vacations to see the deadening effect of dirty repetitive labor and realize the boon of the forty-hour week when the men could escape at the weekend from this drudgery to the ballpark, and sit in the sun and glory in their heroes, and denounce the judgment and dubious parentage of the umpires. Here was war without tears, even pageantry in the great football arenas, where the bands played and the world seemed younger than it was.

On the city desk, I had the gentler task of going down to New York Harbor on the cutter to meet the great ocean liners and interviewing the arriving big shots on their views of the gathering storm in Europe. It was a choice assignment. For one thing, I got an elaborate free breakfast that lasted me all day. For another, I had a glimpse of Ellis Island and time to be thankful for the day fourteen years earlier when I first had passed through its big immigration hall.

The other reporters on these morning excursions were a rowdy bunch, some of whom took great pleasure in extolling the glories of the Manhattan skyline to the foreign travelers. "And just think, Mr. Prime Minister," one exuberant self-appointed greeter concluded his description, "it's all fireproof!" The prime minister was not impressed. "What a pity!" he said.

This, of course, was long before the so-called communications revolution, even before the introduction of walkie-talkies. The reporters wrote their interviews on flimsy paper and attached them to the legs of homing pigeons they had brought along for the ride. These were sent aloft to their roosts atop the newspaper buildings, and by the time the tugs had edged the big ship into its dock uptown, the news was on the streets.

If it was hard in those depression days for a young man to get a newspaper job in New York, it was next to impossible for a woman. For example, even Adolph Ochs at the *Times,* then in his declining years, was adamantly opposed to women in the newsroom. That was the prevailing antifeminist policy on most newspapers.

Also, Sally's parents had their doubts about Sally job hunting in New York. Mrs. Fulton didn't fancy Sally running off to the wicked city to meet a penniless young man. Finally, however, on Wednes-

day, November 7, 1934, four days after my twenty-fifth birthday,
Sally arrived at the Pennsylvania Station. The mayor didn't order a
parade down Broadway, but I didn't mind. Our long separation was
over at last. She stayed with her brother Bob and his wife, Ruth, in
Hastings-on-Hudson, and I took her that first night to Radio City
and she saw the ocean for the first time in her life. And I felt sure
that all her doubts had been removed, for I had a letter from her as
soon as she returned to Chicago.

> Dear Scotty: The last evening with you in New York was a restless
> one for me. I was longing to be gone once I had decided. I'll never
> forget my feelings as the train pulled away.
> Oh, Scotty, I didn't want to leave you—to see you walk one way
> and I go the other.
> How little I thought before going to New York that those ten days
> would bring such beauty and happiness. I hated to give them up.
> Write to me as often as you find time. Tell me what you're doing, how
> the work goes, and if you're happy. I don't want to remain out here
> a thousand miles away, hanging indefinitely aloof.

We were separated again for almost another year, but finally Sally
landed an editor's job on the *Junior League Magazine,* located, no
less, in the elegant Waldorf-Astoria Hotel on Park Avenue. She
helped celebrate my mother's fifty-ninth birthday on October 9,
1935, and received from her, a few days later, a kindly note: "If I
do say so myself," my mother wrote, "Jimmy has always been a good
boy, and I am praying that your life with him may be very happy
indeed. I also think he has been most fortunate in finding such a dear
girl for his life's partner."

Meanwhile, when I was still twenty-five, the AP gave me my first
nationally syndicated column, called "A New Yorker at Large."
This involved doing six articles a week on all the wonderful nonsense
of New York, interviewing the writers and artists, the actors and
actresses, reviewing the plays and the night spots, riding the city with
the police inspectors, and covering the little human tragedies of the
midnight court.

It is said that all you need to live happily in New York is money,
but that was not my experience. For the theaters and the big fancy
restaurants always have their eyes open for the tourist trade, and
since my column was published in many of the towns and cities
beyond the Hudson, I was a welcome unpaying guest all over town,

with tickets to the shows or the opera and even the run of all the big restaurants.

In addition to this bounty and good fortune, Sally arrived back in New York when the French superliner, the *Normandie,* docked in Manhattan on its maiden voyage, and I took my maiden aboard for the gala ball. She found a room on Irving Street, just off Union Square, I shared an apartment with an AP buddy near Grand Central Station, and we made our plans.

I asked for my old fraternity badge and replaced it with my mother's old-fashioned Scottish engagement ring, and this great event was followed by the happiest announcement I have ever read, before or since:

> *Judge and Mrs. William J. Fulton request the honour of*
> *your presence at the marriage of their daughter, Sarah Jane,*
> *to James Barrett Reston on Tuesday, the 24th of December,*
> *1935, at half after seven o'clock, Larchmont Avenue*
> *Presbyterian Church, Larchmont, New York. Reception*
> *immediately following the ceremony, nine Shadow Lane,*
> *Larchmont, New York.*

Running away from the ceremony, I let my bride fall in the basement of the church. I was running ahead to get the car when I heard her fall and almost fainted with fright. But she, more worried about her granny's wedding dress, assured me she was all right and laughed her way to 9 Shadow Lane.

That was our first house, a little pink gatehouse on a winding lane, furnished in Grand Rapids maple with the last of our savings. The AP, always romantic and generous, gave me Christmas Day off for our honeymoon, with instructions to get my column in on the next morning.

Sally had gone back home to pack just before the wedding and wrote of leaving Sycamore and the Midwest for the last time.

> Dearest: Somehow I seem unable to escape a certain sense of farewell to all things dear to me here. It has been with me all week. Just the whisper of a thought: "Now perhaps, just perhaps, this is the last time I shall ever see this place just so." This curious mixture of happiness and sadness and peace comes over me all at once.
>
> I spent a bright morning alone in the fields and woods not more than four or five miles from the house. And after racing the wind down the creek, I lay for a time under the trees, not so much myself

but more an integral part of the familiar world about me. When you grow up in the simplicity and modesty of a countryside like this, your spirit remains colored by its skies forever, with the cool shadows of the trees, and with the sunlit green of the sloping fields. Therefore, I suppose I shouldn't really regret leaving these surroundings, for I'll carry them with me wherever I go.

These are the truest thoughts I've had these last few days, therefore I write them to you. But I wouldn't have you believe that, in speaking of my friends and life here, I'm discontent in leaving them. My love remains and will always remain the compelling force in my life. We've had through these months natural doubts and discouragements. We've even walked precariously on the brink of misunderstanding at times. That we've won our way through isn't the end, I know. Nevertheless, I'm confident in this love tonight, for I've seen it grow stronger with the threatening winds that have sometimes blown between us.

We made only one mistake about that wedding date. Being married on Christmas Eve meant that for many years on our anniversary we weren't alone talking together about the past and future as we should have been, but were down in the basement putting toys together for the children.

Still, 1935 seemed to me a great year to be married. Hitler occupied the Rhineland, but we scarcely noticed. We read John Steinbeck's books on the trials of the depression, but were not depressed. We got free passes to see Clifford Odets's plays on the coming revolution, and George Gershwin's *Porgy and Bess*. I was making eighty-five dollars a week, but Roosevelt signed the Social Security Act that year, and the guy who made more money in 1935 than anybody else was William Randolph Hearst, the newspaper publisher. So I had my hopes and I had Sally.

It wasn't until later, when I read P. G. Wodehouse's book *Adventures with Sally*, that I realized why she married me. "Chumps always make the best husbands," he wrote. "When you marry, Sally, grab a chump! Tap his forehead first, and if it rings solid, don't hesitate. All the unhappy marriages come from husbands having brains. What good are brains to a man? They only unsettle him."

# Part Four

## PRELUDE TO WAR: LONDON

# CHAPTER 7

# *Sports Reporting on the Brink*

> Go and take your holidays. There will be no war.
> —*Daily Express*

I WAS TRANSFERRED to London in May of 1937. The AP was not counting on my nonexistent knowledge of Europe to warn its subscribers about the dangers of war. My assignment was to cover all the big sporting events: the tennis matches at Wimbledon, the international golf tournaments, the Irish Sweepstakes races at Aintree, and the championship prizefights. I was delighted. The AP would pay the carfare. I would travel and see the Old Country again, and in the winter, when the athletes were in hibernation, I would get a shot at covering foreign affairs.

Alan Gould, the sports editor, gave me my marching orders. I would sail with the U.S. Ryder Cup professional golf team on June 12, he said, and send back some features on the players from the ship. This, however, created a problem. I explained to him that my wife and I were expecting our first child just about that time and added that I was sure he would understand that she couldn't very well be bouncing around the Atlantic, with no place to stay when we arrived. In the kindly manner of news executives in those days, Gould said that was my problem—take it or leave it. Our doctor said Sally had to either go ahead of me or stay behind until after the baby was born. She said she preferred to go first, and off she went on the *Queen Mary* on May 5 with our precious cargo, smiling at my tears.

She coped as usual. She arrived in England when the gardens were in bloom and summer was pausing briefly for the green light. A few days later, she wrote about her first impressions of England, which made me feel a little better.

Dear Scotty: After eight in the evening and still no need for lamps to write you. England is heavenly! It's rather like a land of toys and picture books. The sun was shining gloriously at Southampton when I walked off the boat. The customs officer was no trouble at all. I got into the funniest little train I ever saw. It chuckled over the rails all the way from Southampton to London, and so did I! Never have I seen lovelier pictures nor been so amused by them. I pointed to the left and asked if this was some park we were passing. It was just a field belonging to some farmer. No fences, you see. The fields are all separated by hedges. And NO billboards advertising Gorton's Codfish or telling you to look out the window and watch the Fords go by.

The season is much further advanced here. Everything is beautifully green, the trees heavily burdened with leaves. Fruit orchards in full bloom lined the way. The countryside here in the south rolls gently away to the horizon, and the centuries of cultivation have given it all a polish quite different from the rough unkempt beauty we are used to seeing.

In those long-ago days, lovers wrote letters to one another and I waited eagerly every morning for the mail, and was seldom disappointed. Sally had never been in Europe before or sailed an ocean. She had to find a doctor and a place for us to live, and she wasn't always as sunny and lighthearted as she sounded in that first letter. I kept trying to reassure her in my dumb masculine way that life would be good if only I could arrive before the baby. Then I had a letter from her that I have treasured all my life.

Yes, life is good. But when I came to the end of your letter this morning, I could do nothing but lean back and let the tears come. Not because of unhappiness; they come so easily now, seemingly without reason. I can find no specific fear or pain or relief or joy in my heart.

It is inexplicable. For all feelings, all emotions, all thoughts are in it. The creation of life has brought me nearer to the truth in life than all the years of past experiences, I think. Somehow, it is almost as if I stood upon the very boundary of life and death, seeing into each for the first time. And the longer I look, the clearer the two draw together until they can no longer be set apart. For what is death but the ending of life itself, and therefore it becomes no different thing—no, not even another experience or adventure—but only part of Life, and so to be LIVED.

This is a feeling and thought that only becomes a blur on paper, but nevertheless its truth remains in the heart. And so all other feelings blend together and are integrated there. I feel no happiness without realizing that sadness is also in the smile, and through all this runs my love, which is perhaps the thread that binds these things together, the thread that never breaks or changes in its course.

All else rests on this, depends on this, is caused by this. And because this is so, I sometimes think the world becomes nothing but my love. For all the world's aspects, its circumstances, its beauties—so widely differing from each other—are still related to my love, which is unchanging and secure. There you are, my darling. I have written only what I thought and what my heart expresses—perhaps incomprehensible, but still something of the truth.—Sally

After staying a few days in London, she spent a couple of weeks in Oxford. She visited the Oxford Union when, in one of its mischievous anti-American moods, it was debating the topic: "Resolved, that Christopher Columbus went too far in 1492." Then she returned to London, rented an apartment near Hyde Park Corner, and looked up the fancy Harley Street doctor recommended to us in New York. This gentleman said he would take her "case" for 300 guineas, which we didn't have, but he recommended a new young doctor who might accommodate us.

Accommodating he was. His name was John Peel, a quiet and courteous man. I arrived in London just before the baby. On July 14, Bastille Day, we took a taxi to King's College Hospital in the morning, and Mr. Peel told me to go away and come back around six in the evening. I rode the big red buses all over London most of the afternoon in a state of nervous anxiety and returned to the hospital as directed. "Everything's splendid," the doctor announced, handing me Richard Fulton Reston. He was the first newborn kid I ever saw who needed a haircut, and wasn't nearly as pretty as his mother. We have had many a laugh about that day, partly because John Peel later became the famous Sir John Peel as a reward for delivering the queen's four children.

I cannot say I felt equal to this small stranger in our midst. I naturally assumed that nobody had experienced such joy in the birth of a child before, but I doubted that Hitler was even aware of this great event, and I wondered how our lives would change. What about that "five hundred a year and a room of one's own" recommended by Virginia Woolf? Leah Trelease, Sally's favorite teacher at Illinois, had not explained how she was to get the five hundred or what to do with the baby in the other room. But Sally never mentioned the dilemma, and like most men I never realized how deep it was.

Meanwhile I filed my first big story to New York. It was a disaster. I was sent to cover the Grand National Steeplechase race at Aintree outside Liverpool. It was of interest to millions of suckers at home who were betting more than they could afford on the result, and I had been forewarned by the AP racing editor in New York, "Hoofbeats" Robertson, to "flash" the winner at urgent cable rates.

It all seems a little silly now, but this was my first big chance and I made careful plans. I had a special telephone installed at the top of the grandstand, as close to the finish line as officials allowed. I went to the Western Union office in Liverpool and left precise instructions. I wrote the message to be held for release: FLASH: ——— WINS GRAND NATIONAL—RESTON. I said I would call the operator when the race started, keep the line open, and fill in the name of the winner as soon as it crossed the finish line.

It was a close race, with two horses leading the pack—a big Irish brute called Royal Danielli and an American horse named Battleship. No four-footed animal from the United States had ever won that race, and I was sweating harder than the two survivors as they closed together at the end.

I didn't wait for the official decision but said to the operator in Liverpool: "Ready? Let that message go: Let me repeat it: Flash: Royal Danielli wins, repeat: Royal Danielli wins Grand National." There was a long delay before the official announcement went up, maybe two minutes, which seemed to me two hours. Then the terrible signal: BATTLESHIP, it said. I think I had a heart attack, but I managed to stammer to the operator in Liverpool: "Send another urgent message to AP in New York. Kill Flash. Battleship wins Grand National, repeat Battleship, not repeat not Royal Danielli."

I should explain that the "flash" produces an alarming sound in newspaper offices all along the transcontinental AP wire, ringing bells to bring editors to the tickers. I could imagine the embarrassment and anger in the New York office, but they killed me with silence. I stayed at the track to write the day-lead and the night-lead and then went back to the Angel Hotel in Liverpool convinced that I would be fired before midnight, or at the latest, in the morning.

This was my glorious debut as a foreign correspondent, but I got a suspended sentence and learned a couple of lessons: get it first if you can but first get it right. The other lesson was equally important. My mistake was that I was not directly facing the finish line, but saw it from an angle and therefore saw it wrong. And I learned from this that many things in life depend on the point of view of the observer, that nothing seems quite the same from my viewpoint as it may from someone else's. Chamberlain, for example, did not see the gathering storm in Europe from the same angle as Churchill. Later I could see during the war in London and the politics of Washington that no act, however virtuous, seems quite so virtuous to our enemies or even to our friends as it does to ourselves. "You have to be square with the finish," a man in the press box told me at the racetrack. I never forgot that phrase.

I enjoyed sportswriting. When you cover foreign policy, everything is hidden and you have to wait a lifetime to know how it all comes out, but sports are quite different. They are out in the open. You know the players and feel their pain and happiness. Everything seems so orderly by comparison. There are rules and instant punishment for infractions, and the games have a beginning, a halftime for rest, and an end. And, at the end, you know who has won, except, of course, at Aintree.

Most sports in Britain seemed more gentle, except at the championship soccer matches between England and Scotland, where the Scots, well lubricated by their native firewater, have a habit of tossing their empties at the officials. But the tennis matches at Wimbledon are a social event: a fashion show, a tea party, with ivy on the walls of the grandstand, and geraniums in the window boxes, and ladies in reckless hats in the royal box. Those were the days of Helen Wills and Suzanne Lenglen in her fading glory, and Donald Budge, among the invading American men, all of whom dressed in puritan white long flannel trousers, and accepted close calls from the umpire as if they were royal commands.

I went back to Scotland for the first time in 1938 along with my old sidekick Ralph McGill of the *Atlanta Constitution,* and also Henry McLemore of the United Press, this time to cover the British Amateur Championship and the Walker Cup matches at St. Andrews between the U.S. and British teams. McLemore had never seen a Scottish links course before, and was astonished by the immense spread of the greens. "You mean," said the pro at St. Andrews, "that you have nothing in America like these?" "We do," replied Henry, "but we call them counties."

The Scots took a shine to Charlie Yates, the captain of the American Walker Cup team, partly because of his classic swing and sunny good manners, and also because he came from Atlanta, Bobby Jones's hometown. He won the British Amateur that year at Troon, and then took the American team to St. Andrews, where the British won the Walker Cup for the first time in many years. The Scots were wildly excited. Over twenty-five thousand of them gathered on the eighteenth fairway facing the old clubhouse for the presentation of the cup, and when this was over, somebody shouted for Yates and the vast gallery took up the cry. He got over to the microphone, but he was so overcome with emotion that he couldn't talk. Then he remembered an old Scottish song one of the British players had taught him. So he lifted his arms and began to sing "A Wee Dochin Dorris," and the mob joined him, and then, linking arms and swaying the length of the fairway, they all sang "Auld Lang Syne." It was one of the memorable moments of my sporting days.

I don't know what I expected to find in Scotland after so long an absence. The golfing villages seemed small and sturdy with their stone cottages, especially St. Andrews, where the students wandered among the old gray weathered university buildings in their scarlet capes. I liked their direct ways and could hear the lovely voices of my mother and father on their tongues. But somehow I didn't feel at home, and went back to London vaguely sad and wondering why this should be so.

The political news in London at that time was so bizarre that if I had written the same facts in a novel, it would have been rejected as improbable rubbish: a king running around with a divorced woman from Baltimore and losing his throne in the confusion; a prime minister and foreign minister mixing up their religion with their anticommunist policies; the newspapers telling their readers not to worry; and goofiest of all, a Nazi corporal named Schicklgruber, already in occupation of the Rhineland, shaking his fist at the world.

Before the war, my early routine in London was a happy mixture of covering games in the summer and the Foreign Office the rest of the year. I took the number 15 bus for Fleet Street every morning at Hyde Park Corner, always riding upstairs in the double-decker to watch the crowds and shops on Oxford and Regent streets and the view down Whitehall from Trafalgar Square. I got off at the *Daily Telegraph* and *Daily Express* buildings, where the newspaper sign-boards were usually advertising HITLER'S LATEST OUTRAGE, and the *Daily Express*, convinced that optimism was good for circulation, was carrying above its masthead Lord Beaverbrook's advice to all

readers: GO AND TAKE YOUR HOLIDAYS. THERE WILL BE NO WAR.
He later confessed to the British Press Commission: "I run the paper
purely for the purpose of making propaganda, and with no other
motive."

At the AP office, down an alley from Beaverbrook's black glass
palace on Fleet Street, we knew very little about the divisions within
the British government over Hitler's aggressive and successful diplomatic and military moves on the Continent. Officials regarded American reporters as a nosy bunch, and in those days the AP, serving
papers with divergent political and foreign policy views, did not
encourage "interpretive reporting." Most of the time we merely sent
to New York what was announced in Parliament, and in the British
newspapers, particularly in *The Times* of London, which was a daily
sedative but was known to represent the policies of the Foreign Office
and No. 10 Downing Street.

Some of the papers were complaining about Chamberlain's "policy of appeasement," but the British ambassador in Berlin, Sir Nevile
Henderson, could see silver linings in the darkest Berlin clouds and
was warning Chamberlain that these criticisms out of Fleet Street
were interfering with his mission.

"I have the greatest respect for the power and freedom of that
'chartered libertine' the British Press," he wrote in his memoirs. "I
must, however, reluctantly but in all honesty record that it handi-
capped my attempts in 1937 and 1938 to contribute to the improvement of Anglo-German relations, and thereby to the preservation of
peace."

Chamberlain shared this view, and while he could not influence all
the British papers or the outspoken weekly periodicals, he could
influence *The Times,* then dominated by two editors, Geoffrey Dawson and Robin Barrington Ward, who did more in those critical
prewar years to stain the reputation of that great newspaper than any
other two men in its long and distinguished history.

In May of 1937, Dawson, who by that time was beginning to show
pained surprise at Hitler's increasingly bold adventures, wrote to *The
Times'* Geneva correspondent, E. C. Daniel, "I do my utmost, night
after night, to keep out of the paper anything that might hurt their
[the Germans'] susceptibilities." Dawson and Barrington Ward were
on intimate personal terms with Chamberlain and with Lord Halifax, who took over the Foreign Office after the resignation of Anthony Eden. They didn't cover the news; they smothered it whenever
it conflicted with the official line.

At the height of the Munich crisis in 1938, *The Times,* in a notorious editorial approved by Dawson, suggested that "it might be worthwhile" for the Prague government to consider "making Czechoslovakia a more homogeneous state by the cession of that fringe of alien populations who are contiguous to the nation to which they are united by race." In simpler language, to surrender the Sudetenland and leave Czechoslovakia dependent upon the tender mercies of Adolf Hitler. Lord Halifax said publicly that "the article in no way represents the views of His Majesty's government," but privately he reassured Dawson that it coincided with his own judgment.

Barrington Ward's appeasement was at least understandable. Haunted by the carnage of World War I and having been decorated for bravery with the DSO and the Military Cross, he could not or would not believe Hitler would risk it all again. Ferdie Kuhn of the *Times* called on him one evening and listened to all his hopeful illusions, and then recalled Fairfax's famous rebuke to Oliver Cromwell: "I beseech ye, by the bowels of Christ, consider ye may be mistaken." This same line was hurled at Chamberlain later, but like Barrington Ward, he was tormented by the tragedies of the past.

Lord Beaverbrook at the *Express* with its millions of readers became the most obvious advocate of "the Munich lie." On May 28, 1938, he said in a signed front-page editorial: "Britain will not be involved in war. There will be no major war in Europe this year or next year. The Germans will not seize Czechoslovakia. So go about your business with confidence in the future and fear not." On the day after the Munich surrender, the headline on the first page of the *Daily Express* was a single word, two inches tall: PEACE. (Later Beaverbrook joined the government and helped win the war he said would never come.)

Every evening when I was on the day shift at the AP, I took the bus home and stopped at the Marble Arch to listen to the soapbox orators. Each had his little platform and his little crowd of supporters or hecklers. And each had his certain remedy not only for avoiding war but also for attaining permanent peace. The trouble was that while most of them had the same objective, each proposed a different road to the Promised Land. Some advocated economic reform, others military conquest; all seemed to favor stamping out sin and transforming human nature, but some of them thought this could be done by education or psychoanalysis or religion, though they were clearly in disagreement about what kind of supernatural aid would do the job. The optimists were called the "false dawners."

Aldous Huxley then summed up all this confusion in a book on the difference between ends and means. "About the ideal goal of human effort," he wrote, "there exists in our civilization, and for nearly thirty centuries there has existed, a very general agreement. From Isaiah to Karl Marx the prophets have spoken with one voice. In the Golden Age to which they look forward there will be liberty, peace, justice, and brotherly love. Nation shall no more lift sword against nation; the free development of each will lead to the free development of all; the world shall be full of the knowledge of the Lord, as the waters cover the sea." But as to the means of achieving these goals, Huxley repeated, "Unanimity and certainty give place to utter confusion, to the clash of contradictory opinions, dogmatically held and acted upon with the violence of fanaticism."

I walked home from the Marble Arch to talk it all over with Sally, remembering my father's warning about the clash between good and evil, and thinking for the first time that ideology was not the answer to my own confusion. At least I learned from all this the wisdom of detachment, of avoiding personal association with officials, of avoiding simple answers to complex problems.

# CHAPTER 8

# The Appeasers: 1937–40

I labour for peace, but when I
speak unto them thereof,
they make ready to battle.
—The Book of Common Prayer

IN "THE HAPPY YEARS" of 1935–37, despite the depression and the gloomy news from Europe, it never occurred to Sally and me that we wouldn't somehow make out. We were absurdly happy. I knew where I was going and who was going with me. We didn't have anything, but it was ours. In "the tragic years" of 1937–40, however, we lived in London at the mercy of events beyond our understanding or control. Fleet Street was wallowing in whitewash. Sometimes Europe seemed, in the words of Harold Nicolson, "a foul world of lunatics," and it staggered into what Winston Churchill called "the unnecessary war." That war took the lives of over 70 million people.

The months between Munich and the outbreak of the war were a period of intense personal confusion for me. For the first time I ran into the conflict between personal morality and public policy. I felt surely that it was wrong of Beaverbrook and the editors of *The Times* of London to be instruments of Chamberlain's policy of appeasement, but as the choice between peace and war became increasingly stark, all my old maxims from my mother's kitchen ("Fight for the right," etc.) weren't very helpful. I took some easy potshots at Chamberlain's wobbling, but what did fighting mean for a disarmed Britain, and what was right in "this foul world of lunatics"?

I wandered around talking to the people. It had been fewer than twenty years since the butcheries of Flanders and they were facing a second world war while still mourning the dead of the first. We know now, but did not know then, that Hitler had given orders to his commanders in 1935 to withdraw from the Rhineland if they were opposed by the British and French armies, but nobody called his bluff, and by the time of the Munich crisis in 1938, his margin of military superiority was even greater than it had been in 1935. The British dominions were telling Chamberlain that they would not fight to keep the Nazis from taking the Sudetenland; even Churchill was advising the Czechs privately to submit to Hitler's demands. The general opposition to the war was obvious.

The evidence was not only in the newspapers and in the House of Commons but also in the streets. I watched Chamberlain waving his little paper, the Munich agreement with Hitler, before an enthusiastic crowd on Downing Street and proclaiming "Peace in our time"; and there were pathetic little sugar umbrellas in the shop windows celebrating his popularity, and the pacifists were singing in Trafalgar Square:

> I did not raise my son to be a soldier,
> I brought him up to be my pride and joy.
> Who dares to put a musket on his shoulder
> To kill some other mother's darling boy?

I was bewildered. Chamberlain was clearly between the hammer and the anvil, too strong to ignore the right and too weak to fight, and the antiwar Tories of Nancy Astor's Cliveden set were applauding his every concession. Sally and I were invited one weekend to join these Cliveden warriors at Lady Astor's big mansion on the Thames, and Turner Catledge, the assistant managing editor of *The New York Times,* then at the end of a long trip, joined us. He was as usual the hit of the weekend, particularly with Lady Astor. She was originally from Virginia, one of the lovely Langhorne sisters, and when she heard that Catledge was from Mississippi, she shouted even before she met him, "Where is that southern white trash?" Then she circled around him and finally took his hand, and said, "Shake. I'm southern white trash, too."

She was then in her sixties, the pride of the conservative establishment. It was easy to see, looking at her beautiful house and beyond to the Thames, why she was so conservative, having so much to conserve. She was the first woman to sit in the House of Commons, a strict prohibitionist and deeply, or at least loudly, religious. She sat on the floor after dinner reading from Mary Baker Eddy's Christian Science book *Science and Health* and applauding all the interminable talk and spiteful anti-American jibes of her conservative guests. Even without the stimulant of alcohol (forbidden at least downstairs in that house), her guests tolerated no opposition to their views and denounced Jimmy Doolittle, the famous American flier who was there, for his laments about the inadequate defense of the country. Lady Astor insisted that we stay the whole weekend. "No sense using the sheets for just one night," she said.

Before we left, Lord Astor took us upstairs to the family's private apartment and showed us some letters from George Bernard Shaw about the time he and Lady and Lord Astor had visited Stalin in Moscow. Lady Astor, recalled her husband, had been told to be quiet during the interview, but Stalin made the mistake of asking her if she had anything to say. "Yes," she said, "how much longer are you going to keep shooting people and sending people to Siberia?" According to Lord Astor, Stalin merely smiled and said, "As long as it's in the interest of the state."

Chamberlain's excuse for saving the peace at the expense of the German Czechs was that Britain needed "time to rearm." I thought at first it was a personal cop-out, but after the Battle of Britain, won by an air force greatly augmented between Munich and the blitz, it seemed a more reasonable decision of public policy.

What did not seem reasonable, however, then and even now, was the Chamberlain government's decision to reject an alliance with the Soviet Union and Chamberlain's personal decision to go to war over Poland. His laggard negotiations with Moscow encouraged Stalin to believe that the Allies were willing to give Hitler a free hand in Eastern Europe, and Stalin then responded by giving Hitler a free hand in the west.

Chamberlain had his own conflict between private policy and public morality. He could tolerate the incorporation of the Sudeten- land Germans into the Reich, but when Hitler took over the Czechs as well, he took this as a personal humiliation and gave the Poles an unconditional guarantee he could not possibly fulfill without fighting his way across Germany. In short, he got mad before he got ready.

This was my first experience of the dangers of personal diplomacy.

We were all aware of what happens when a Hitler begins to think he *is* Germany and leads his country into a disastrous war, but Chamberlain was not entirely immune to vanity and self-deception. He really thought for a time that he could influence Hitler by the force of his character and logic. He was convinced at Munich that he had reached a gentleman's agreement with the German dictator. When he returned to Downing Street, proclaiming "peace in our time," all the evidence was that he thought sincerely that he had an understanding, and it was only after the German invasion of Poland that he reached the fairly obvious conclusion that Hitler was no gentleman.

By the time of the Munich crisis, the main hope was an uprising inside Germany against Hitler. It was known in London on the eve of Munich that Hermann Göring and Joseph Goebbels favored a peaceful settlement in Czechoslovakia and that a group of German officers led by Generals Halder and Beck had a plan to overthrow the führer. Fearing war on three fronts, these conspirators informed officials in Westminster—so Ambassador Kennedy told us—that they would arrest Hitler if the British and French took military action to block the invasion of Czechoslovakia. But if Chamberlain knew anything about this, he did not regard it as a practical option.

I heard other detective stories in Fleet Street about individual dreams or schemes to get rid of the Nazi dictator—all of them based on the theory that his death would be followed by a nationalistic government that would come to terms with the Allies.

One of those concerned about Chamberlain's timidity was the British military attaché in Berlin, who thought there was a chance of killing Hitler during a military parade when it passed by the military attaché's drawing-room window on Hitler's fiftieth birthday.

"Easy rifle shot," said Colonel Mason-MacFarland. "I could pick the bastard off from here easy as winking. . . . With that lunatic out of the way, we might be able to get some sense into things." But like so many Fleet Street stories, nothing ever came of it.

President Roosevelt suggested to Chamberlain on January 11, 1938, that all the major nations meet to discuss a general European peace agreement, but Chamberlain showed no interest in it, nor did he act favorably on Moscow's proposal of March 17 for a meeting of the nations to deal with the crisis. Meanwhile, Hitler was giving Poland the same assurances he had made to Czechoslovakia when he was annexing Austria.

Reporters in Fleet Street, especially the Americans, knew little of the negotiations that eventually led to the Nazi-Soviet pact and freed the Germans of the fear of war on two fronts. In fact, it was not until after the war when the State Department released the documents on those negotiations between Ribbentrop and Molotov that we learned that it was the Soviets and not the Nazis who at first proposed that treacherous agreement.

I was asked to write the introduction to those official papers at that time and ended it with these observations: "Nowhere in these documents is there a word of pity for the individual; nowhere is there a suggestion that public opinion is anything but a device to be manipulated to suit the diplomacy of the day; nowhere is there the suggestion on either side that the leaders of the state are accountable to the citizen; nowhere is it suggested that the people in the proposed Soviet and German spheres of influence might not like to be dominated by anybody."

The critical prewar days in London were enlivened by the arrival of Joseph Patrick Kennedy as U.S. ambassador to the Court of St. James's. He did not dispel my confusion. He was greeted in Fleet Street by lurid reports of his adventures on Wall Street, his romance in Hollywood with Gloria Swanson, and what the British reporters called his "peculiar views" on the "German problem." Everything he did made news. He made a point of dressing and acting informally even when he presented his credentials to the king, and he told his first press conference that the American people were more interested in the Boston Braves than in foreign policy.

He was then in his fiftieth year, a recklessly charming, intelligent, handsome man who seldom let his official responsibilities interfere with his personal pleasure. He worked hard and had many other admirable qualities, but judgment wasn't one of them. He was welcomed at the Foreign Office on the mistaken impression that he was a close and influential adviser to Roosevelt, but he wasn't trusted for long.

There was a certain logic to his personal views. He was a sincere nationalist who thought the United States shouldn't be monkeying around in other people's quarrels. He thought wars were bad for business, and what was worse, for *his* business. But he wasn't a hypocrite about it. He didn't go around like other Americans urging the Allies to follow brave policies Washington wouldn't follow itself. He made his opinions quite clear, though he had been sent to London not to peddle his opinions but to represent the quite different pro-British policies of his government.

Meanwhile, he had a good time. He never met a man—or a woman, for that matter—he didn't think he could conquer, but he couldn't keep his mouth shut or his pants on, a combination of weaknesses that no doubt added to his pleasure but detracted from his work. He was, in short, a convinced isolationist, probably closer to the opinions of most Americans at that time than Roosevelt was.

I met him first when he docked at Plymouth to take up his post. He displayed at once his talent for strong opinions and weak judgments. He had brought along a statement for the press of his doubts about the war, but he put it back in his pocket when an official from the embassy protested against its poor timing and bad manners. Once he got to London, however, nobody could deter him from blowing off about the stupidity of trying to fight the Nazis.

His aides at the embassy liked his chummy Irish banter but were appalled by his offensive remarks about what he called "the Jewish conspiracy" behind the world crisis and alarmed by his openness with the press. He hobnobbed with the antiwar Tories of the Cliveden set and he not only agreed with Charles Lindbergh's judgment that the Luftwaffe could lick the air forces of Britain, France, and Russia combined but also handed a memorandum of these Lindbergh opinions to Chamberlain when the prime minister set off to see Hitler at Munich.

Many British officials, of course, were outraged by his outspoken pessimism, but were too dependent on American military aid to make a public issue of it. In private, however, they had plenty to say. When Walter Lippmann, the most influential American journalist of the day, came to London, he attended a dinner at the home of Kenneth Clark, the British art critic, and in the presence of Winston Churchill reported that Kennedy had told him that war was inevitable and the Allies would be defeated. Churchill turned on Lippmann in fury.

"It may be true," he is reported to have said, "may well be true that this country will, at the outset of this coming and to my mind almost inevitable war, be exposed to dire peril and fierce ordeals. It may be true that steel and fire will rain down upon us day and night, scattering death and destruction far and wide. . . . Yet these trials and disasters, I ask you to believe, Mr. Lippmann, will but serve to steel the resolution of the British people and to enhance our will for victory. No, Ambassador Kennedy should not have spoken so; he should not have said that dreadful word.

"Yet supposing, as I do not for one moment suppose, that Mr. Kennedy were correct in this tragic utterance, then I for one would willingly lay down my life in combat rather than, in fear of defeat, surrender to the menaces of these most sinister men. It will then be for you, for the Americans, to preserve and maintain the great heritage of the English-speaking peoples."

That, of course, was precisely what Joe Kennedy feared, that the British would muddle along and the United States would inevitably be drawn into the war. This, he felt sure, would, after unimaginable death and suffering, lead to the defeat of Germany and, what was more important in his mind, to a world economic crisis. In the end, he insisted, the Soviets would strip the wounded on the battlefield and emerge as the dominant power in Europe. He was against Chamberlain's guarantee to Poland and was always complaining about Churchill. "He drinks too much," Kennedy said. "I don't have any confidence in a man who is always sucking on a whisky bottle." This did not, however, interfere with the ambassador's investments as one of the biggest whisky dealers in America.

I wrote a lot of dogmatic nonsense at that time about the "appeasers," often with a sneer between the lines. I saw a lot of Jan Masaryk, the Czech ambassador in London, a delightful character who covered his Slavic pessimism with an appealing sense of humor and later took his life or was murdered in Prague—I never knew which—during the struggle for his country's freedom. I was naturally sympathetic to the Czech cause and offended by the relentless British pressure on the French and the Prague government to submit to Hitler's demands. We know now, however, what we didn't know then—though Kennedy did: how unprepared the British were. Not only were the army and air force far behind their rearmament schedules, but also the radar early warning system of the country and the Civil Defense program were dangerously inadequate, with only sixty fire pumps for the whole of London.

The American press corps in Fleet Street increased with the intensity of the crisis. When heavy-hitters like Vincent "Jimmy" Sheean and H. R. Knickerbocker arrived, we assumed things were getting serious. There were a few knowledgeable "permanent" U.S. reporters, notably Ferdie Kuhn of the *Times,* who had reliable sources of information, and treated me with the utmost kindness. I tried to sit next to him at the Foreign Office briefings in the hope I had nurtured for years that one day I would work for the *Times*. Ed Murrow of CBS, even before the blitz, was something of a celebrity, and seemed to have access even to the prime minister. But most of the rest of us were only vaguely familiar with what was going on and had to rely on the British correspondents, most of whom were helpful, but some of whom, as we later found out, were doing double duty for the British intelligence agencies. It was only later, after the fall of France, when Eric Sevareid and the other American war correspondents arrived in London, that we began to share our information and get a more accurate picture of the impending disaster.

There was, of course, some open opposition to Chamberlain in a few places, even in the small-minded, big-breasted tabloids. Lord Vansittart, the diplomatic adviser at the Foreign Office, was unyielding in his anti-German feelings, and unheeded. He was always saying, "Whenever Germans write a bellicose book or make an inflammatory speech, it's called patriotic, and when I quote it, it's called calumny." The opposition was feeble in the House of Commons. Anthony Eden had resigned as foreign secretary in February of 1938 and Duff Cooper as First Lord of the Admiralty after Munich, and Winston Churchill was not only criticizing Chamberlain but mocking him. London was full of his dinner-party quips. He spoke to his "focus group" about "this great country nosing from door to door like a cow that has lost its calf, when all the time the tiger and the alligator wait for its undoing."

I went to the House of Commons on March 31, when the prime minister announced in Parliament that if Poland were to be attacked, "His Majesty's government would feel themselves bound at once to lend the Polish government all support in their power." The French government associated itself with the commitment. It was the end of the policy of appeasement.

Sometimes it takes a major surgical operation to get an idea into a Scotchman's head, but even I began to realize that this was no sporting event I was covering and that I had better get my family into safer quarters. At first, we moved from Upper Berkeley Street to Temple Fortune Hill up close to Hampstead. Then we took a little timbered cottage at St. Mary's Cray in Kent, which was ideal except for the fact that it was on the bomber flight path to London. Later we moved in with Marvin and Catherine Lowes of the *Reader's Digest* in the village of Penn in Buckinghamshire, and later still Sally moved with our child into safer quarters far from London in Cornwall.

For the first time, I began to stop and wonder what on earth I was doing in this mad corner of the world, chasing golfers and tennis players on the edge of the precipice. When the thirties came to an end, I had just turned thirty. Looking back on the twenty years since my mother and father had left Britain for the United States, I was grateful for many things: my dearest Sally, our new son, our parents still in good health, the recovery from the worst of the economic depression, and the excitement of the most important news story of the century.

And yet I had my doubts: What were the odds on this adventure? Who were these fashionable characters telling us not to worry? Wasn't I reversing my parents' wise decision to leave the torments of the Old World for the promise of the New, and risking the lives and happiness of my young family in the process? Or, now that I was waking up, didn't I have the guts to see it out?

There was, it seemed quite obvious to me, something unrealistic about all this rejoicing over Chamberlain's return from Munich, waving Hitler's little scrap of paper, pointing to the führer's signature, and proclaiming "peace in our time . . . peace with honor" when there was no peace and no honor. There was a sense of thunder in the air, but the little shops showed BUSINESS AS USUAL signs in their windows. Some people brought their children back from the countryside. The theaters opened again, and the stores sold Christmas toys, and while Fleet Street clamored for rearmament, the rearmament was painfully slow.

I was pretty slow myself. I assumed like a lot of other people that "something will turn up" or "somebody will back down," just as Chamberlain had at Munich. *The Times* of London took the diplomatic news so seriously that it actually printed the threats from Berlin under a two-column headline—an ominous innovation—but it also had space to discuss at great length whether Bret Harte had been born in 1836 or 1839, and it printed an indignant letter from one Octavio Lewin about the hardness of the seats at Lord's cricket ground.

Ignoring the facts, Sally and I went off blithely to France for a two-week vacation in mid-August, storing our son Richard in a Hampstead nursery. On our way back, we stayed overnight in a hotel at St.-Omer, and were awakened on the morning of August 22 by the sound of troops clattering past on the cobblestone streets. We hadn't read a newspaper or heard a radio news report for days and drove on happily enough past fields golden with the harvest to Calais, where we boarded the Channel steamer.

We went aft on the steamer and sat on a bench in the sunshine. In a few moments, an Englishman came along and began to talk about "the European situation." Simply to keep the conversation going, I asked him how the Anglo-Russian talks were going. "I should think," he replied, "that they were finished. The Russians have signed a nonaggression pact with Germany."

We went below deck then and discussed this all the way across the Channel. When we arrived at Dover, we ran for the newsstand and a glimpse of an English paper. *The Times* of London confirmed our fears: FULL CABINET TODAY said one headline, and under that, GROWING TENSION. Another, more specific and alarming: GERMAN TROOPS MASSING. When I arrived at the AP office, Bill Brooks said he had been trying to reach me in France to tell me that the nursery had been asking him whether to send Richard to the AP or evacuate him. "What did you tell them?" I asked. "I told them to evacuate him and I guess that's what they did." I think it was then that we finally woke up.

On August 23, I went to the embassy early and saw Ambassador Kennedy. He said he was convinced war was not far off. The conversation turned to the United States' part in all this. Kennedy said that, looking at British policy from our point of view, he hoped Chamberlain would forget about Poland and return to the policy of appeasement.

"I don't see what we've got to gain if Britain goes to war," he said. "I don't care if Germany carves up Poland with British support. I'm for appeasement one hundred percent, and if one thousand percent is more than one hundred percent, I'm for it one thousand percent." Ralph Barnes of the *Herald Tribune* asked him: "Have you been telling this to Mr. Chamberlain?" Kennedy replied, "I've been telling him that every chance I had every day for more than a year."

Kennedy advised us to send our families home, but added, "If you think this isn't serious, I'll tell you another thing, though I don't want this used—right now there are six German submarines in the Atlantic and you can guess why they're there." We guessed this didn't leave us many happy options, but Sally and I decided to stick it out for a while and see what happened.

At the French Embassy, Roland de Margerie, the political secretary, said war would start "any day now." I asked him whether the French army and the British navy and air force were a match for the Germans. He said, "One doesn't know, but you see, Reston, Britain and France cannot, they must not, lose, because if they do it means the end of Britain and France, whereas if the Germans lose, it only means the end of the Nazi party and Nazi principles."

I went to the House of Commons for the special session in the afternoon, and there the war atmosphere was marked and it was not hard to see that this time the British were determined to fight if the Germans marched against the Poles. By late evening, a special Emergency Powers Bill passed by a vote of 475 to 4 and that was just about the odds against peace. Meanwhile, Sally had fetched Richard from the nursery, badly spoiled, and we talked most of the night about what to do but found no answer.

On August 25, however, I was provided with an unexpected answer, thanks to Adolf Hitler. For over two years I had been telling Kuhn of *The New York Times* of my unavailing efforts to join the *Times* staff in New York, and at one point in 1938, when he was short-handed, he asked Jimmy James, the managing editor, for permission to add me to the London staff. James proposed instead that he take Frank Kluckholn, an energetic reporter whose fastball was better than his control, but Kuhn objected and nothing was done until war seemed imminent. Kuhn then cabled that he had to have help in a hurry and proposed my name again, and this time James agreed, and I was told to report for work on Friday, September 1. It was deadline day for the war, but Sally and I were so pleased about joining the *Times* that we thought of little else. But not for long.

On September 3, Ambassador Kennedy received an official notice from the Foreign Office, written in Spencerian script: "His Most Excellent Majesty George the Sixth by the grace of God, of Great Britain, Ireland, and of the British Dominions beyond the Seas, King, Defender of the Faith, Emperor of India, is constrained to announce that a state of war exists with Germany." Winston Churchill was not so "constrained." Chamberlain, he said, had been "given the choice between shame and war. He chose shame and got war!"

# PART FIVE

## WAR

# CHAPTER 9

# War and
# The New York Times

ON THE FIRST night of the war, I wandered through the streets of London and sent my first dispatch to *The New York Times*. I wasn't scared, I was terrified. I had read all the horror stories about the new German bombs that were supposed to pulverize concrete skyscrapers and toss battleships out of the water. I could barely see the outlines of Big Ben and the House of Commons in the blackout. The empty tomb of the Cenotaph, bathed in a dim light, stood in the center of Whitehall like a rebuke from the dead of the First World War. The old noble Mayfair houses, which had survived so much, seemed helpless behind their iron railings and shuttered windows. The railroad stations were full of old folk, invalids, and children being evacuated to the countryside. Big antiaircraft balloons, tethered to the earth by steel cables, were floating in the dark above the empty streets to guard against the dive-bombers, and the newspapers were full of instructions:

Don't let a thread of light escape from the windows; don't toot horns or ring bells or blow whistles or keep pigeons or take photographs or hold certain foreign currencies; don't forget to turn off the gas and fill up the bathtub before you go to bed; and keep the gas masks handy.

As I circled back from Paddington Station, the first shriek of the air raid sirens knocked me into a sheltered doorway and I thought, Here they come. But the government was just trying out its early-warning system to get the people's attention, and after the "all clear" sounded I ran to Printing House Square and turned my shaky fingers to the typewriter.

"The world's largest city folded up tonight just like London, Ohio," I wrote, trying to give it the easy treatment. I kept telling myself, This is a helluva story but don't overdo it. I wasn't told, as at the AP, to "keep it short," so I described everything I saw and a little bit more: the bewildered look of the old men and women being wheeled out of the hospitals; the darkened theaters even around Piccadilly Circus; and the noise from the pubs—the only establishments that seemed to be open for business. I added everything except what I felt. I felt vaguely sick, fearing for my wife and son and for some reason wondering what London would be like without the voices of children.

Only when I had finished did I look around at *The Times'* office. It was in a corner of *The Times* building, down a flight of stairs and through a maze of corridors, and was just what I hoped it would be, comfortably shabby. I was greeted warmly by Frederick Birchall, a former managing editor who had a cheerful face and an obedient white beard, and said to me, "Good story. We help one another around here, sweetheart. Let us know if you need anything." I asked where the news agency tickers were. "We don't have any," he replied. "We think they discourage the reporters from going out and getting the news on their own." I said I understood, but I didn't.

I have a quirky memory, but I remember those first few days of the madness easier than last Tuesday. Everything at first seemed to me remarkably calm considering the threat, but everybody wasn't pleased. Before long George Bernard Shaw was complaining about the closing of the theaters. In preparation for the dreary days to come, he wanted more theaters built and all actors relieved of military service. He called the government's handling of the crisis "a masterstroke of unimaginative stupidity."

I went to the House of Commons for Chamberlain's declaration of war. The chaplain opened the session by saying, "Let us this day pray for wisdom and courage to defend the right." (I assumed he had been speaking to my mother.) The prime minister did not deliver a call to arms but a sad and painfully personal speech. He blamed everything on Hitler and then added, "You can imagine what a bitter blow it is to me. . . . I cannot believe there is anything more or different I could have done. . . . Everything that I have worked for, everything I have believed in has crashed into ruins." One member remarked, "Most unsatisfactory!" After the speech I stopped at Westminster Abbey to say a prayer of my own. There was a little sign in the vestibule of the church: IN THE EVENT OF AN AIR RAID,

PARISHIONERS WILL DESCEND TO THE CRYPTS WITH ALL DUE REVERENT HASTE.

I had a hard struggle with myself that night. I took the train to Bromley to be with Sally, knowing that the declaration of war would take effect at eleven on the following morning. I was tormented by questions and doubts. How could the free nations have loitered into such a calamity? Should Sally and the boy go home? What would Roosevelt do now? What of all my kitchen assurances that the good would prevail in the end? When and what would the end of all this be? Sally and I talked about all this most of the night and decided to stick it out together in London and see what happened. At eleven in the morning Chamberlain announced the official beginning of the war and almost immediately the air raid sirens went off. We put the baby under the stairs, but the warning was a false alarm, set off by a wayward pilot making his way back to London.

Soon after I joined the *Times,* Ferdie Kuhn came to the end of his prior commitment to work overseas and was replaced as chief London correspondent by Raymond Daniell, who for some reason was called Pete. He was very helpful to me. In those days, trying to make a good first impression on the managing editor, I agonized over every paragraph, and though we were five hours ahead of New York by the clock, I was often in danger of missing my deadline. "Think about it as if you were writing a letter to a friend back home," Daniell suggested. I followed this useful advice but could always hear his typewriter clicking along much faster than my own.

The war did not then, or at any time thereafter, follow my expectations. We listened every night to the German broadcasts delivered in BBC English by an English scoundrel named William Joyce and nicknamed "Lord Haw Haw." (The British executed him after the war as a traitor.) He produced nightly threats of spectacular destruction to come, but Hitler held his fire for months of what was called the "phony war." To relieve this ominous silence, the British government decided to send a few bombers over Wilhelmshaven mainly for propaganda purposes and invited Daniell to send a reporter along. I begged for the assignment but as the new boy in the bureau I was passed over in favor of my colleague and friend Bob Post. He was shot down over the North Sea.

This was my first, but by no means my last, experience of the element of luck and random death in war. Even in peacetime, reporters develop ties of friendship, which are stronger than their ideological differences or competitive instincts, and in wartime they are brought closer together by these wasteful horrors. Webb Miller, the leading correspondent for the United Press, missed his step on a train in the London blackout and was killed shortly after we lost Bob Post. Walter Leysmith, an Australian on *The New York Times'* London staff, was killed when a stray German plane, lost in the fog, ditched its bombs and one of them blew up his house. As time went on I forced myself to think on other things.

In my new surroundings I had a better chance to observe the giants of the London news corps. The British correspondents in Fleet Street were a colorful and irreverent lot. They called former Prime Minister Lloyd George "the goat" in reference to his voluptuous tendencies. The American reporters were a fairly cocky lot, but they didn't have the same impudent swagger. Lord Beaverbrook collected some surprising correspondents—from Peter Howard, a brilliant and devout man who later headed Moral Rearmament, to Tom Driberg, a tall talented self-proclaimed homosexual who, unknown to us at the time, was serving double duty as a British intelligence agent. They had, it seemed to me, strange alliances and loyalties outside their newspapers, but they could write and even ask brief and relevant questions, an art still to be developed at home.

The most notorious of this crew was Claud Cockburn, who peddled a publication called *The Week,* full of Communist propaganda and witty mocking attacks on Chamberlain, Halifax, Joe Kennedy, and all members of the Cliveden set. He was a tall, jowly bespectacled eccentric and had an uncle who watered his garden from a hose atop a stepladder in the hope of fooling the flowers into believing that this was natural rain. Cockburn demonstrated that a good sense of humor could often overcome a bad sense of history. He was, without doubt, the most effective Marxist propagandist in London.

These lions wrote serious things in a familiar style, and even in those dark days found time to compose lighthearted satirical verse. A. P. Herbert's jingle in the *Sunday Graphic* on Hitler's fifty-first birthday, for example:

> God moves in a mysterious way;
> The Devil still must have his fun;
> And it is not for us to say
> Why you have lived to 51.
>
> But this new candle on the cake
> Should be the last they light for you;
> God will not make the same mistake;

The Devil soon must have his due.
And recollect, you little fake,
Napoleon died at 52.

Some Fleet Street characters, mocking Hitler's threats of invasion, even recalled the old rhyme from the First World War: "I was playing golf the day the Germans landed / All our men had run away and all our ships were stranded / And the thought of England's shame / Almost put me off my game." Nobody was laughing, however, when Hitler conquered Poland in less than a month and announced his "peace terms" on October 7, 1939. Chamberlain rejected them on October 12, and two days later a surprising and disturbing event shocked his government.

A German submarine somehow managed to penetrate the elaborate defenses of what was regarded as Britain's most secure naval base at Scapa Flow in Scotland, sank the battleship *Royal Oak* at anchor, and escaped. Most of the crew lost their lives by explosion or drowning, and while news of the tragedy soon leaked out, the Admiralty covered its embarrassment by strict censorship. We heard the news at the *Times'* bureau but all our dispatches on the event were killed. We complained about this since the enemy obviously knew all the facts, but we had to admit it would obviously depress the British people, so we let it go as a permissible wartime cover-up.

A few days later, however, much the same thing happened. Another Nazi U-boat got through the barriers in the Firth of Forth and torpedoed the British cruiser *Belfast.* Again it escaped and again the news was censored, though the *Belfast* managed to stagger to safety with most of its crew alive. Daniell called the American members to his room for a skull session and he decided, with our agreement, to get the news out. He tried telephoning it to our correspondents on the Continent and in Ireland without success, so we finally drafted a series of tricky messages and sent them to the *Times* in New York through two different cable companies.

The first message went to an editor in the bull pen with a made-up tale of administrative difficulties with the staff. It promised to send more on this in future cables but said we needed the approval of the managing editor and emphasized that "it's the last word that counts." Sherlock Holmes would have laughed at so obvious a deception, but we proceeded with a few cables in which only the last word was significant: YES, said the first cable, WE'RE SENDING STORY ON SUBMARINE. Then another: PLEASE TELL HARVARD I WANT MY

SON ENTERED. And so on until we got across the fate of the *Belfast.*

Later that night Daniell showed these messages to one member of the staff who hadn't been in on our amateur conspiracy, Jimmy MacDonald. He puzzled over them and finally staggered us by saying, "I get it. The Germans have shelled Belfast!" Daniell got back to New York at once and was reassured that the editors had it right—it was the cruiser *Belfast* and not the city that had been hit. And the *Times* published the story the following morning.

The whole thing was a silly schoolboy exercise, which I approved and have regretted ever since. There was a great hullabaloo about it in the British newspapers. It was a clear violation of our agreement to abide by the rules of wartime censorship. We were all liable to expulsion and even prosecution under the Official Secrets Act, and it was stupid for another reason. A newspaper gathers more news by trust than by tricks, and while in this case the trick succeeded, we lost the confidence of officials on whom we had to rely for future information. We got off easy. Churchill, then in charge of the Admiralty, didn't want any more publicity about the navy's porous defenses and let Daniell go with a warning. During the investigation, I was in a Fleet Street pub one night when a secret intelligence agent approached me, showed me his official identification card, and said, "We know exactly what happened. But it isn't done here. Understand? Never again!" then walked away. I understood.

During the phony war I was able to get out of the office and talk to the people, my favorite subject. Something wonderful happened to them in the crisis. For many, the war was not an unrelieved disaster but an escape from a boring existence. They gave up their rolled umbrellas and their monotonous rides to tedious work. Somehow they seemed younger and felt younger, and certainly they were more considerate of one another. They didn't hoot and sneer at the government as they had before the war, and they found many reasons for hope, most of them ridiculous. Above all, they felt needed.

I went out at night with the Home Guard. This was a makeshift, night shift army of civilian volunteers, many of them old codgers from the First World War, dressed in tin hats and puttees. They guarded bridges and tunnels, watched through the night for enemy parachutists, interrogated anybody with a German accent, and went around beheading street signs and town markers on the theory that the invaders, when they landed, wouldn't know where they were. I loved this nocturnal costume party. They scared the neighbors more than anybody else. After two months of war, the official casualty list read: army nil; air force 79; navy 586; blackout 1,130.

One day I took the number 96 bus from Fleet Street to a conscientious objectors' court at the Fulham Town Hall. On the bench was a serious but kindly man, Judge Hargreaves by name; in the dock one Frank Fairburn, a handsome, straight-eyed young man of twenty-six. "Great Britain is fighting for her life," the judge said, "and you refuse to help. Why is this, Mr. Fairburn? Please tell the court." The lad stammered out a sad story. His eldest brother had fought in the last war, was torpedoed and captured. His father had volunteered in 1914 and had been a cripple ever since. One uncle fought at Gallipoli and came back a stumbling idiot. Still another uncle nursed his war wounds for twenty-one years and finally took his own life.

These things, the young man said, tears now on his cheeks, had haunted him all his life. He was now a Christian Socialist. He recognized no narrow patriotism of class or creed. He quoted the eleventh commandment: "I give unto you another law: thou shalt love one another." The verdict of the court could make no difference to him, he said. He was willing to carry on with his air raid precautions work. "I claim unconditional exemption." The judge consulted his colleagues and then said very quietly, "You shall continue in your present work."

H. G. Wells was not in good health at that time, but the war seemed to revive him and he was calling for a great debate. This, he said, was much more important than the actual warfare. We were plainly drifting toward world catastrophe, he said, yet hardly anybody was talking frankly, modestly, or unreservedly about where we were going. I went to see him at his London house. He was then in his seventy-fifth year, a short, porky, sad old man with a high thin voice and bright blue eyes. He had started his remarkable career in a pessimistic mood, and then, after joining the Fabian Socialists, had written his long and more hopeful outlines of a more orderly world, but during the Second World War, he reverted to his original pessimism. He greeted me quietly from a chair in the corner of his sitting room and appealed for a detached judgment from the United States. "Every intelligent man and woman must get into this debate," he said. "This is especially true of the United States, where you will not be blinded by war. This time the people must make the peace, and the peace is much more important than the war."

He seemed not only sad but also lonely and made me stay awhile because he wanted to talk about newspapers. He had started in Fleet

Street as a free-lancer when he was twenty-seven, and while he had written novels and produced many books, journalism, he said, was his true calling. For, he added, it was only through the daily papers and the weekly periodicals that he could reach mass audiences when they might listen to his thoughts on contemporary problems.

I thought at the time that he was merely being pleasant, but found confirmation of his views on journalism in his autobiography:

"I am a journalist," he wrote. "I refuse to play the artist. If sometimes I am an artist it is a freak of the gods. I am a journalist all the time, and what I write, goes NOW—and will presently die."

Unlike Mr. Wells, George Bernard Shaw wanted to call the war off, and the old Irish jester, as usual, had more fun and outraged more people than anybody else on the island. He agreed that Hitler should not take part in any peace conference "on the grounds of lunacy." He thought Chamberlain had some virtues, but, he said, "He is no match in political argument with Russian and German diplomats." His argument was that Britain could fight just as well after a conference as before. "If we cannot agree," he added, "we must, I suppose, fight it out, but as I am a born coward and dislike extremely all this blackout business and ruinous taxation and all the rest of it, I will still want to know what I'm fighting for."

These infrequent meetings with the people outside the office did more to lift my spirits than anything else, and I usually returned to our opulent hideaway in the Savoy feeling that somehow this spirit of the people would prevail.

Until one day they were confronted with a real disaster. They accepted military conscription without a murmur; they acquiesced in the regulation of industry, labor, and the entire economy by the state; they melted down some of their worst metal monuments of heroes and turned in their pots and pans to be melted and hammered into Spitfires and Hurricanes and accepted food rationing—all without complaint. But one awful day the government announced that tea would be rationed. *Tea!* It was indispensable! Rationing it was intolerable, outrageous, unthinkable! It was, I told myself, only then that they knew the war was serious.

The phony war gave everybody time to think, but few officials took advantage of the opportunity. After two months of comparative inactivity, Anthony Eden said Hitler had "lost the initiative," Churchill said he had "missed his chance," and after seven months, Chamberlain said, "I feel ten times as confident of victory as I did at the beginning. Hitler has missed the bus." Five days later, on April 9, 1940, the Nazis invaded Norway and defeated a larger British force that tried to evict them. In the bitter House of Commons debate that followed, Chamberlain was taunted with cries of "Who missed the bus?" and was replaced as prime minister by Churchill. Sally and I were delighted.

"We await the long-promised invasion," Churchill said. "So do the fishes." After one of his long heroic and defiant speeches, he ended with the promise that the British would beat them into submission, but then added in an aside to one of the radio technicians, "We may have to hit the buggers over the head with beer bottles." He seemed to cast a spell on the people and give them a sense of heroic pride, of seeing themselves as larger than they actually were.

His example made me appreciate the power of words when used at just the right moment by the leader of a government. Roosevelt had something of the same gift, but it made me expect too much of the presidents to come. Even Churchill, however, couldn't console us for long, for the Nazi invasion of Norway ended the phony war and also ended our family's hope that somehow the real war would never come. The Germans broke the weak hinge of the Allied front in the east and swept westward to the Channel; the French were defeated and the British barely managed to escape at Dunkirk without most of their arms.

We didn't feel so brave then. On June 7, with the anti-invasion barricades going up between London and the coast, the U.S. government announced that this might be the last opportunity for Americans to get home until after the war. Emergency shipping was sent from New York to the port of Galway in Ireland, and we picked up our standby reservations for Sally and our boy.

Just before we arrived in Dublin, the American passenger ship *Athenia,* crossing without convoy, was torpedoed and sunk in the Atlantic with heavy losses. The liner *Washington* was sent to replace her and sailed with Sally and Richard on June 12 under the blackest sky I have ever seen. They arrived safely in New York on June 21, and I returned from Ireland in a state of depression. Churchill rejected a peace offer from Hitler, the British newspapers were requested to treat it as an incident of no significance, and General Ismay wrote in his diary: "We were now alone. So far from being alarmed, we were relieved, nay exhilarated. Henceforth everything would be simpler. We were masters of our own fate."

I didn't share this noble nonsense. I felt alone, all right, but not master of anything, including myself. What was I doing here waiting for the slaughter, frightened and ashamed of my fear, amputated without Sally while my own government was standing aside? I felt sure the Germans would then turn on London. I didn't have long to wait.

# CHAPTER 10

......................................................

# The Battle of
# Britain

THE HISTORIANS MARK July 10, 1940, as the start of the Battle
of Britain, for suddenly on that day there were fierce aerial battles
over the Channel and the southern English counties, and the British
spotted German landing craft moving into the ports along the
French and Belgian coasts. Four days later, Bastille Day, Churchill
delivered one of his famous rallying cries, with an aside to the United
States: "We are fighting by ourselves alone, but we are not fighting
for ourselves alone." I went down to the English Channel and lay
in a field at a discreet distance watching the deadly dogfights in the
sky. The little villages with their bright flimsy summer cottages were
shuttered and deserted, as if expecting some monstrous wave to wash
them into the sea, but even Hitler seemed to realize that he had to
control the air before he stormed the beaches. For on July 16 he
threatened invasion but added, "The English air force must be so
reduced morally and physically that it is unable to deliver any significant force against the German crossing."

I toured a few of the British fighter bases and saw no sign of
physical or moral collapse. The pilots, taking turns aloft against the
Luftwaffe, referred to these rallies as their "office hours." These were
the sons and grandsons of the men who had fought in the First World
War and had been mocked by the Germans as "effete literary was-
trels." All they did was save their country.

There was no way we could judge these opening battles, and we
didn't know what was happening on the rest of the island. The
Germans dominated the European coast from Narvik in Norway to
Biarritz in France. Alan Brooke, in charge of the anti-invasion forces

for only two weeks at the start of the battle, had to defend more than two thousand miles of coastline. He had forty-nine squadrons of modern Spitfire and Hurricane fighter planes, but of the seven hundred tanks that had gone to the Continent to help defend France, only twenty-five had returned at Dunkirk. So even he had to guess where the Nazis would land, and the reporters hadn't even a vague idea of what might be happening in the north. We were totally dependent on the announcements of the Ministry of Information, whose reputation for accuracy declined as the menace increased.

The anxiety in London was obvious: trenches in the parks, sandbags around the government buildings, plywood blinding the store windows. Churchill moved into a deep command bunker back of the Admiralty. Lord Halifax found a cushy refuge in the Dorchester Hotel near his favorite church pending his transfer to the British Embassy in Washington. And we took some precautions at the *Times.*

Much has been written about the hardships reporters endured during the blitz, and it was no daisy, but we covered it in comparative safety and comfort. Daniell foresaw that it would be awkward and even dangerous for the reporters to get back and forth from their houses to the office during the bombing, so with the enthusiastic approval of the publisher, who picked up the tab, we all moved into the Savoy Hotel with our office supplies and personal belongings. It stood between the Strand and the Embankment, a little vulnerable to stray bombs along the Thames, but it was a sturdy building, with the deepest shelters and one of the best restaurants in town. Accordingly, we had no cause for complaint, though of course we complained anyway.

Jimmy MacDonald, an irresistibly cheerful Scot, stood guard on the roof during the night raids, despite Daniell's orders to get down into the cellar; David Anderson, a handsome young Canadian, and I did features and manned the all-night desk; and Daniell wrote the main stories and argued with the censors and the Ministry of Information in his spare time. We were all without our families, though Daniell dealt with this deprivation by marrying Tania Long of the *Herald Tribune* and adding her to the staff.

We were a congenial bunch most of the time, and we had the companionship and bogus lighthearted bravery of the other American correspondents. I accused Ed Murrow, the lion of the corps, of inventing Hitler to dramatize his nightly broadcasts, and he condemned the *Times* for hiding in what he called its "fancy bunker in the Savoy." He was already working and smoking his health away, but occasionally on a quiet day I could get him out for a round of golf at the Hampstead Club, where we played around the unexploded bombs marked GROUND UNDER REPAIR. Eric Sevareid, also of CBS, escaped from Paris with his wife, Lois, and their newly born twin sons, Peter and Mike, just before the Nazis occupied that city, and he joined us in London. Murrow, with that urgent catch in his throat, did more for Anglo-American relations during the blitz than any other American, but Sevareid could outwrite us all. We made life-long friends under the pressure of those melancholy days.

We were all unprepared for the terrors of aerial bombardment on largely defenseless cities. Sevareid and others who had been on the Continent at the opening of Hitler's invasion of the Low Countries and France knew something of the bombing of Rotterdam, but most of the rest of us had never heard a bomb fall and were full of horrendous visions of things to come. When it finally started, however, the reaction of the people was surprisingly calm.

We often went out early in the mornings and surveyed the wreckage. It was appalling, especially in the East End near the docks, not because the Luftwaffe was so accurate but precisely because it wasn't. One street of tenements would be totally destroyed, while the next would stand unharmed, and a third would be torn apart, with houses sliced in two and furniture hanging drunkenly out the windows or shattered outside in the street. The bulldozers would already be at work pushing the rubble into vast piles, and always the women would be outside trying as usual to tidy up—sweeping, always sweeping, the rubble of a man-made world.

They reminded me of my mother ("You can get used to anything but hanging"). Something happened to these people when everything was reduced to accidental life and death. Even the people who were not bombed regarded their good fortune as a deliverance. People grumbled, but they did not riot, as many officials had feared.

Even those children who were left in London managed to pitch in. They were terrified of the hideous whoosh and ultimate crash of the bombs, and their screams in the night were almost unbearable, but during the firestorms they played an important part. They huddled with their parents in backyard Anderson shelters—steel-topped dog-houses—and when the little, slow-burning, incendiary sticks landed on the roofs of nearby houses, some nimble little boy or girl would scramble up and toss them into the street.

The government, with its tidy statistics on what areas were hit last night, and the BBC announcers, with their reassuring voices, conveyed only the vaguest intimations of the nightly disasters. It was all clearly beyond my limited powers of description. All I could do was write inadequate accounts each day or so of some human incident in the hope that these vignettes would gradually illuminate the larger tragedy.

I came even to fear the moonlight, for then the bombers could follow the shine of the Thames, and after the raids many people faced the problem of getting around to do the necessary chores of life—getting water or gas after the mains were broken, finding safe food when the lines of supply were interrupted, or just getting to work through the rubble. One man, for example, applied to the Ministry of Labour for permission to show up at his factory at eight o'clock in the morning instead of seven. He needed the extra hour, he said, "to get the baby up to Granny's." Asked why his wife couldn't take care of the baby, he explained she had to be at her aircraft factory at eight, and when asked why Granny couldn't come and fetch the baby, he said, "Granny doesn't get off the night shift until seven."

Covering the raids outside of London, however, was a frustrating experience. Fleet Street was alive with the most frightful rumors. For example, on August 15 we tried to confirm that German agents had landed in the Midlands and the Scottish lowlands. It was said that their parachutes were found along with some other suspicious gear: radio transmitters, detailed maps of the streets in nearby cities, and the names and addresses of prominent British officials. According to the Ministry of Information, the air secretary, Archibald Sinclair, told the cabinet that night that two Nazi parachutists had been captured, but a later investigation found no footprints near all this paraphernalia and the whole scare proved to be just another German trick of psychological warfare.

We did have limited access to the British commanders. I went out one night to British bomber command, headed by Air Marshal Arthur "Bomber" Harris, and had a glimpse of the brutalizing effects of the war. He told me all about how his bombers were obliterating the German factories with their precision raids, and showed me some aerial photographs of a recent successful attack on Düsseldorf. I noted that the workers' houses seemed to have been destroyed along with the factories. "Yes," he said, "they burn beautifully."

The Ministry of Information was a varnish factory that put a shine on everything the Allies were doing and advertised the German atrocities while covering up the hideous human destruction of the

Allied bombers. I wrote to Sally on her twenty-eighth birthday, September 5, 1940: "The censorship is being tightened all the time and the only thing I can say to you is that we are not reporting what is happening over here. . . . There are times when I feel so cut away from everyone I love that I lose all sense of proportion. If the pride in one's work is destroyed by censorship, sometimes it doesn't seem worth the sacrifice. Anyone can grind out the communiqués and rewrite the official handouts, but we ought to be able to tell a little more of the truth of this beastly war without helping the Germans."

Yet even at the height of the anti-German feeling during the blitz, some sense of the common tragedy remained, and one heard stories of human kindness, even by the enemy. For example, I saved a letter published in the *Yorkshire Evening Post* from Mr. and Mrs. J. Gaines of Tong Road, Leeds. Their son was benched in the Royal Infirmary in Worcester, recovering from wounds in one arm and both legs, and he wrote to his mother and father about a wounded German prisoner who was in the same ward, and became his friend. "This German lad," the British soldier wrote, "carried me in his arms one day 70 yards down to the beach, then looked down at me, smiled, put a cigarette in my mouth, lit it, and put his lighter in my pocket. Then he took off his white shirt, tore it into shreds, and dressed my wounds. Having done this, he kissed me, with tears in his eyes, and then walked away to attend to other wounded."

"This was a time," Churchill wrote, "when it was equally good to live or die." I didn't quite share this heroic sentiment, being younger and less courageous than the old warrior, but in the middle of the blitz two personal events took my mind temporarily off the bombing. I had a wonderful letter from Sally saying our second child would be born in the spring. "Under the circumstances," she wrote, "a second child for us may seem unwise to many of our friends and family. To me it seems just right. I am very happy." I was then doing an occasional broadcast for Fred Bate of NBC and was able to talk to Sally on the New York tie-line, but the sound of her voice only made me miss her all the more. When the bombing increased at the end of August, I cabled her: SORRY YOU HAVE TO READ ABOUT THESE RAIDS BUT KEEP YOUR CHIN UP. IT'S TERRIBLE BUT WE'LL MAKE IT. On September 15, the day of the decisive British air victory, I cabled her again: NOW BOTH WORKING AND SLEEPING DEEP SHELTERS. FROM THE MIDDLE OF THIS I TELL YOU MY FAITH COMPLETE. NOTHING CAN OR WILL TOUCH OUR LOVE.

The second event was not so happy. I developed what at first seemed to be an ulcer. This meant that even when the all clear sounded in the middle of the night and all copy was cleared to New York, I couldn't enjoy the convivial nightcap with the rest of the staff, but toasted them with a glass of milk. "That white stuff will get you sooner or later," they told me repeatedly, and they proved to be right. For even the Savoy was cut off from its normal supplies of milk and the ulcer turned into a case of undulant fever, contracted from unpasteurized or polluted milk. At first the London doctors could not figure out what was wrong, for it hung on for weeks, and finally I was advised to get out of London or preferably to go home.

Looking back on those days half a century ago, I still retain even more intensely my hatred of war with all its unexpected consequences. No matter how carefully it is planned, always some unforeseen event, some personal weakness or misjudgment, scatters all the cards on the table. I read a lot during the war in the writings of the Cambridge historian Herbert Butterfield. "The hardest strokes of heaven fall in history," he wrote, "upon those who imagine that they can control things in a sovereign manner . . . playing Providence not only for themselves but for the far future . . . gambling on a lot of risky calculations in which there must never be a single mistake."

The wisdom of this was illustrated during the Battle of Britain. For by September 3, the German attacks on the British radar stations and airfields were succeeding, the available pilot strength of the RAF had been reduced from 1,438 to 840, and at this rate of attrition the British estimated that German air control over the Channel and the southern counties would be assured within three weeks. At that point, however, Hitler, angered over an audacious but strategically unimportant British bombing raid on Berlin, announced on September 4 his decision to wipe out London.

The cost of this order was appalling. After sixty-seven straight nights of bombing, 51,500 people were killed in London alone, and there was so much destruction that it was hard to get through the rubble. We wrote some end-of-the-world stuff about all this and one day, General Raymond Lee, the U.S. military attaché, called the U.S. correspondents to his office. He had a big dictionary on his desk. "I notice," he said, "that some of you are writing that London is 'devastated.' In my dictionary that means 'laid waste, ravaged, demolished.' Please, gentlemen, don't make it worse than it is."

In fact, this savage diversion of the German air power to London saved the radar early-warning stations and rested and supplemented the exhausted British pilots for the climactic air battles to come. By September 6, Hitler had 205 landing barges at Ostend ready for the invasion and Churchill issued Invasion Alert No. 1—"Invasion imminent, probably within 12 hours." I went back again to stand watch at the Channel ports, but the invasion never came. Germany was beaten in the air by the end of the month, and then, in his most disastrous misjudgment of the war and in defiance of his treaty with Stalin, Hitler turned like Napoleon to the invasion of Russia and was on the road to oblivion.

When the pressure on London was relieved, however, I was still staggering around with my undulant fever, increasingly depressed. I sat down one night in fear of death and wrote out my first will, which was crazy for I had nothing to pass along, and I then even wrote a long letter to my three-year-old son to be opened when he was twenty-one. It was full of my hatred of all this fire and slaughter and full, too, of the kitchen Calvinism of my mother and father. I was glad later that he was too young to read it.

Dear Richard:

The other night I sat here in London in the middle of an air raid and made my first will. It was a simple will, drafted quickly and with some embarrassment. To your mother, I left everything I have: a few dollars, a lot of books, and the memories and dreams of a short and happy life. To you, alas, I left nothing. And yet I have thought these last few days that maybe there was something I could leave you, some lesson out of this tragic war, some ideal of life worthy of your consideration.

The first of these is that many of the things we fight for so hard in our ordinary peacetime daily lives are sham. The life and death struggle of war like this emphasizes this point every day. Bombs at least make you think. They blow up all pretense and leave a man naked before his conscience. All petty wars of life, the scramble for money and power, the endless bickering over material things are replaced by a simpler ideal of life in which love and family predominate. I don't pass this on as a great discovery. I am merely reporting to you what has happened to this whole nation under fire. All around us here, the people under great stress have found a greater sense of family. They are more thoughtful and considerate and at the same time they are wonderfully hard and tough. They are fighting for something outside and above themselves. That, I suggest to you, is the first ideal.

The second is that above all things a man must accept his responsibilities. This war came about in the age of irresponsibility. Our own people in the United States did not accept their responsibilities at the end of the first great war of this century; they ran away when a little boost would have spread the ideals of the American Revolution across the whole world. The young men of America did not accept their responsibility under democratic government to prepare themselves for the service of the state but turned that vital task over to the politicians. The successive governments of Britain and France were criminally negligent in the long armistice between the two world wars and the people acquiesced in their irresponsibility. Look anywhere in these two decades and you see the same story—a breakdown in the family, in the church and in the democratic state.

I entreat you, therefore, to accept your responsibilities—first to the dreams of the founders of the United States and the ideals of this country where you were born. I write this because I feel responsibility to fill in the gap of the first few years of your life, to tell you the story of your family's life here, and thus, perhaps, help your understanding of this war. I would not have you think that what happened to our family here in this time was important. Better men are being killed down many streets in London as this is being written, but you'll be the product of this great battle; it will touch your life in the future wherever you go. I make it a personal story because I want you to understand that all these great problems of the world concern you, and that YOU must, with the men of your generation, do your bit in trying to solve them.

These then, are the first two suggestions: live simply and accept your responsibilities. From time to time, I'll try to find the time to write these letters and put them away for you. I shall tell you why we came to England in the first place and what happened to us before and during the war. I do not ask you to accept my conclusions. I merely ask that you consider them, and don't think about what you're going to have, but what you're going to BE!

Shortly after writing this, I flew to Lisbon and sailed from there to Bermuda, taking Bill Shirer's original manuscript of *Berlin Diary* past the censors, and thought along the way of my own good fortune and of the capacity of simple people not only to endure adversity but also to turn away their thoughts from vain regrets. By some will to live stronger than reason, the population of Britain and Western Europe was actually greater after the war than before. I arrived in New York thinking of our own coming child and eager to take Sally in my arms, but I wasn't allowed by the doctors to get her close to my infection. But I looked with happiness on New York Harbor, and on Ellis Island with different eyes. It was not like the day, twenty years before, when I saw it for the first time. Now at last I knew where home was and what it meant, and I was more prepared, I felt, to cover the news ahead.

# Part Six

# WASHINGTON DEBATES THE WAR

# CHAPTER 11

# From Isolation to Pearl Harbor

> If a nation values anything more than freedom,
> it will lose its freedom;
> and the irony of it is that if it is
> comfort or money that it values more,
> it will lose that too.
>
> —W. Somerset Maugham

I WAS NOT prepared for the mood of the United States, however, when I came home from London at thirty-one, grateful to have survived and be reunited with my family, but sick with the undulant fever and anxious about the course of the war. Despite the success of the Royal Air Force, I didn't see how the British, outnumbered and outgunned, could prevail by themselves in a long war against an enemy in control of the European mainland. I had gone to London with sympathy for the Allied cause, but like most immigrants with understanding of the isolationist impulse to stay out of Europe's wars. After the fall of France and the continuing air and naval pressure on Britain, however, I felt sure that military intervention by the United States was the only hope.

I soon discovered that this was not a popular idea in the United States. Arthur Hays Sulzberger, the publisher of the *Times,* welcomed Sally and me at Christmas of 1940—our fifth wedding anniversary—and invited us to dine with him a few nights later. Sally was very pregnant at the time and went out and bought a maternity tent at Macy's for the occasion. At dinner, Tom Lamont, an eminent banker at J. P. Morgan's, questioned me about the war and ridiculed my thought that Britain would lose if the United States and the Soviet Union remained neutral. I blathered along about freedom and comfort until Iphigene Sulzberger, the publisher's wife, rescued me.

She said the United States was avoiding the responsibilities it had blamed Britain and France for evading before the outbreak of the war, and she was particularly critical of Neville Chamberlain. "It's not only that I hated his arrangements with Hitler," she said, "but what he has done to the word 'appeasement.' It used to be a beautiful word. It meant to pacify, to soothe, to try to understand and heal. That's what most women do all their lives, and now he has made the word shameful!" I took a liking to that lady then and there.

Also, I didn't know about my next assignment. I had never seen the inside of the *Times* before or met any of the New York editors. Jimmy James, the managing editor, didn't know what to do with me and suggested maybe I should take over the Boston bureau. I asked him to give me a shot at Washington so that I could continue reporting on the war, but like most things in a managing editor's life, that was a problem. Arthur Krock, the Washington correspondent, had been making room for other reporters whose bureaus had been overrun by the Nazis and complained that he was "just running a damn displaced persons' office," but he relented when the publisher asked him to give me a chance.

Accordingly, I saw Washington for the first time in January of 1941, with its monuments and vast bureaucratic palaces lying in the winter sunshine. Sally and I toured it from Cathedral Hill to Capitol Hill, that is to say from the sacred to the profane, and thought it was the most beautiful city we had ever seen. It seemed so orderly and sanitary after the rubble and stench of bombed-out London. It had magnolia trees and a park following Rock Creek from one end of the District of Columbia to the other, and traffic circles every few blocks, intended, like the Constitution, to keep invaders and other pests from moving too fast.

The contrast with the unity of Britain, however, not only surprised but saddened me. It wasn't that the country and especially the capital were divided over the war—I expected that—but the bitterness of the debate was a shocker. The Republicans were gloomy over losing the 1940 election to Roosevelt for the third straight time and were blaming him for risking war behind their backs. Herbert Hoover was warning him not to make an alliance with the British. The *Chicago*

*Tribune* was saying that he was clearly out "to destroy the Republic," and Charles Lindbergh was particularly venomous.

"The three most important prowar groups," he wrote, "were the British, the Jews, and the Roosevelt administration." And the greatest danger from the Jews, he added, "lies in their large ownership and influence in our motion pictures, our press, our radio, and our government." Meanwhile, Roosevelt was bypassing his own secretary of state, Cordell Hull, as he had bypassed Ambassador Winant in London, and was relying for advice on Harry Hopkins, who was living upstairs in the White House.

Since I could do nothing about all this, I concentrated on getting the family settled and getting acquainted with the work of the *Times*' bureau. The big news for us at the time was the birth of our second son, James Barrett Reston, Jr., a wispy and determined little boy who settled into a furnished house we rented in Georgetown for $50 a month. We hadn't been there long before the rental agent came around and advised us that the owner of the house had died and stipulated in his will that the house and its contents should be offered for sale to the present occupants. The total cost, said the agent in those long-forgotten days, would be $11,000. But we didn't have $11,000 and had been taught that borrowing money was unwise if not downright sinful, so we let it slip.

That was only my first mistake in Washington. The *Times* conducted its business in those days in what had been an old jeweler's office lined with massive safes on the seventh floor of the Albee Building across Fifteenth Street from the Treasury. Like most establishments in the capital, ours was kept going by an intelligent woman, Emmit Holleman of Charleston, South Carolina, known to us appropriately by the affectionate name of Sunshine. We sent our copy to New York by means of the old Morse code tickers that gave off a lovely sound, and part of our staff was still paid in accordance with the length of the stories they managed to wangle into the paper. This did not encourage brevity.

Like my first wrong flash for the AP in the Grand National Steeplechase, my first assignment in Washington was an embarrassment, only worse. I was sent to the Senate press gallery to pinch-hit on somebody's day off, knowing nothing of the procedures or mysteries of that illustrious echo chamber. On that particular day, Colonel Julius Adler, the general manager of *The New York Times,* was nominated to be a general in the United States Army, the ambition of his life. Did I notice this momentous event on the calendar? I did not. Did this news appear in the *Times* the following morning? It did not. Were Arthur Krock and Adler amused? They were not. I called the new general and apologized. He accepted my explanation but added, "It's a good thing you don't work for Colonel McCormick on the *Tribune* in Chicago!"

After recovering from this fumble, I had time to enjoy the capital. It had a big league baseball team that played minor league ball, but it played it there. It had a couple of good restaurants, one for fish and the other for stew, and it made culture hum with a couple of legitimate theaters that were better than we had in Dayton. I had been away for so long that I had almost forgotten the friendliness of the American people—the way they greeted strangers in the street and swung their arms in that comfortable American stride. I marveled at how much easier it was here than in London for reporters to gain access to officials. I covered a few debates on the war. They featured the contradictory lessons of President Washington's isolationist Farewell Address, Woodrow Wilson's internationalist Fourteen Points, the Sermon on the Mount, and the latest stock market reports from Wall Street.

I got the impression that most members thought war was a very bad thing that could be "isolated" beyond our shores or "outlawed" by moral incantation, but certainly not by U.S. military intervention. There were even a few of these right honorable gentlemen who were insisting that we could always "do business with Hitler." All this eventually emboldened me to write a book called *Prelude to Victory*, on the opening page of which I tried to express my feelings as follows:

It is necessary now that we admit the facts: Many of the things we have laughed at, or taken for granted or minimized or despised for years have risen up to plague us. The little man with the Charlie Chaplin moustache who merely wanted living room for the Germans and could not attack us even if he wanted to, is now the master of Europe whose submarines are taking pot-shots at our East Coast.

The little grinning yellow men, the growers of our vegetables, the makers of our cheap toys, the imitators of the West whom we brought into the modern world and could vanquish in three months, are the conquerors of the East.

The people we revered, the immortal French, are stricken down and silent; the people we counted out, the plodding British, are still alive; the great mysterious people of the East, the Chinese, who were good enough to wash our shirts, and the Russians, who were not, are helping save our lives. What is this phantasmagoria? How did this come about? What can we do about it?

This outburst of bad temper pleased Lester Markel, the *Times'* Sunday editor, who encouraged me to do more analytical writing. Arthur Krock, however, was not amused by a new boy in his office blowing off about the big issues of the war, and he was less pleased when the Sunday *Times Book Review* gave the book a big hello. It covered most of one page with a big picture of the author, but it didn't take long for me to discover that not all readers were persuaded by my call to arms. The first letter I received came from Baltimore and ignored my entire sermon. It said: "Dear Reston: I read about your book in the *Times* and I wonder if you'd tell me the name of that long thin cigar you're holding in your hand."

Washington at the beginning of the 1940s was a pleasant place if you lived in the "right" part of town and didn't read or think. There were no security barriers or even checks at the public buildings. It was not only the most isolated of the world's political centers but the most segregated. The Negroes, as they were then called, lived primarily in the eastern part of the District and migrated back and forth to work every day in the offices of the government and the houses of the white folk in the northwest section. It looked like the capital of a great empire and proclaimed its democratic principles on the memorial tablets of its past heroes, but it separated its people like the colonial empires it deplored.

It was different from the Washington of the nineties in many ways. The press corps in the months before Pearl Harbor was composed largely of recruits from the smaller city newspapers, who, like yours truly, scarcely knew the difference between the Baltic states and the Balkans, and they were not alone in their innocence of the warring world.

The mysteries of foreign affairs were conducted in the lovely old Victorian pile at Seventeenth and Pennsylvania Avenue, called, appropriately, the State, War, and Navy Building, where Cordell Hull, a former judge and senator from Tennessee, had the looks and title of secretary of state, but little else. He spent much of his energy on reciprocal trade at a time when there was little world trade, refereed the constant disputes between Assistant Secretaries of State Acheson and Berle, and worried about the superior talents of Under Secretary Sumner Welles.

In those anxious days before television transformed both reporting and politics, officials didn't have to hire a hall to meet the press. The president gathered them around his desk in the Oval Office every few days and in his waggish way told the boldest of them to go stand in the corner if they asked questions he didn't like. Once he pinned a German Iron Cross on John O'Donnell of the New York *Daily News* for objecting to one of the president's customary evasions, but he was an amiable tyrant and the White House reporters clearly liked him and laughed at his jokes, even when they weren't very funny.

At first I was pleased with this easy relationship between the president and the reporters. He held press conferences around his desk, not as often as in his first term—usually every week or so—but after a while I began to wonder about the bantering atmosphere of these clubby gatherings. He acted like a genial schoolmaster joshing with the boys, who seemed flattered to be in his presence and even organized a quartet to serenade him. He suffered from lack of exercise due to his paralyzed legs, and when Charlie Hurd, the *Times'* White House correspondent, noted that he was putting on too much weight, the New York *Daily News,* later one of his most severe critics, raised $10,000 in pennies from schoolchildren to build him a White House swimming pool. Nothing wrong with that, but when any reporter asked a fair but awkward question, Roosevelt would end the discussion by saying: "Remember, no cross-examination!"

This was not as bad as Prime Minister Chamberlain's domination of the news and opinion in *The Times* of London before the war. Roosevelt had his favorites and supplied them, usually through his press secretary or a cabinet member, with exclusive information favorable to himself, but no paper was his obedient spokesman. His press conferences were often likened to the question hour in the British House of Commons, but they were nothing of the sort. The question hour was precisely the sort of cross-examination Roosevelt warned the reporters against.

Another example of this cozy relationship between reporters and officials was Secretary Hull's news conferences. He held one every weekday at noon in his private office with its ceiling fans and latticed swinging doors. When I arrived on the scene, only about twelve of us attended these festivities, and all sat on his three black leather couches and listened to his Tennessee mountain stories and his wayward accounts of the war. We were not allowed to quote him directly, but we were permitted to publish the gist of what he said after it had been cleaned up for respectable consumption.

He was not by nature an unkindly man, but he had learned the tricks of guerrilla politics on Capitol Hill and didn't hesitate to use them against any opponent or colleague who got in his way. He was fond of telling spiteful stories against Under Secretary Welles, a common practice in government disputes, but he continued this feud even after Welles was relieved of his post. I wrote a column at the time regretting the loss of this talented diplomat, and Mr. Hull called me the following day to his office. He said that perhaps I was not well enough informed about "the facts" and offered to remove "this deficiency." He then reached into a drawer of his desk and handed me a thick FBI report alleging homosexual charges against Welles. I asked him if he was prepared to take responsibility as the source of this information, but he said he was not, he was just doing me a favor. I turned the report over to Arthur Krock, but the *Times* didn't print a word of it. I began to understand, however, the depth of competition and personal hostility that existed even at the top of the government.

My new colleagues in the *Times'* bureau tried to explain to me the mysteries of these vendettas. Turner Catledge, the chief political reporter, was especially helpful. He came from Philadelphia, Mississippi, and to the *Times* on the recommendation of Herbert Hoover. He took a tolerant and even amiable view of all politicians, regardless of their shenanigans, on the ground that they were at least more interesting than people in other walks of life and that their blatant hypocrisy made good copy. He collected their lies and dirty tricks and kept the bureau howling with laughter at their devious maneuvers. In due course, I was covering the Senate whenever one of the regulars was off on an out-of-town assignment.

This delighted and surprised me. How did a sports reporter ever get a break like this on the biggest story in the country? I could sit in the press gallery with all the big byline types. I could go to the door of the Senate chamber, and send in a note to Senator So-and so, and to my astonishment this gentleman would actually appear and even answer my questions. Senator Robert Taft of Ohio, a leader of the isolationists, regarded *The New York Times* and all its minions as dreamy internationalists if not secret agents of the wily British, but he came from Hamilton County, Ohio, and I from neighboring Montgomery County, and since I was known to him as a former traveling secretary of the Cincinnati Reds in his hometown, he took me in and tipped me off to the latest laments of Roosevelt's opponents. He even introduced me to Alice Longworth, former President Theodore Roosevelt's daughter, who mocked herself as an "overage destroyer" and invited Sally and me to some of her anti-Roosevelt "hissing parties."

These took place at her old-fashioned house on Massachusetts Avenue near Dupont Circle and were similar to Lady Astor's isolationist gatherings at Cliveden, only with more alcohol and noise. Mrs. L. didn't sit on the floor reading Christian Science literature, but kept a collection of anti-Roosevelt speeches, newspaper clippings, and jokes, which she read out to her guests with boisterous laughter and spiteful comments of her own.

I thought this might change when, at 4:00 A.M. of June 22, 1941, Hitler invaded the Soviet Union, and at 9:00 P.M. of the same day, Churchill told the House of Commons, "Any state that fights Nazism will have our aid. . . . It follows therefore that we shall give whatever help we can to Russia." But when Roosevelt followed Churchill's lead, the isolationists, and many who were not, renewed their campaign against entering the war. They argued not only that U.S. intervention was unwise but that it was now unnecessary.

I called on Senator Taft. He said Stalin was more of a threat to the United States than Hitler. Fifteen other Republicans, including Herbert Hoover and former Governor Alf Landon of Kansas, issued a statement saying that Churchill's announced alliance with Stalin had turned the war into a conflict of "power politics," with no bearing on the future of liberty or democracy. And Harry Truman, in a jibe Stalin never forgot, said he hoped "the Nazis will kill lots of Russians and vice versa," though he didn't want to see Hitler win, he added.

Others, however, thought this was an opportunity to finish the war by forcing Hitler to fight on two fronts, and Roosevelt took a few bolder steps. He had given secret orders to the navy to patrol the Atlantic, where the British were losing 400,000 tons of shipping a month to the German submarines, but on July 7 he ordered the first brigade of U.S. Marines to Iceland "to protect the Western Hemisphere." This was an odd excuse since Iceland was 3,900 miles from New York and only 2,800 miles from Britain, but he took more risks once the Soviets were in the war.

He took some chances I scarcely noticed. Though I was covering the embassies at the time, my mind was focused on the war in the Atlantic and I paid little attention to the critical moves in the Pacific that led eventually to Pearl Harbor. Early in the war, the United States had ended the U.S.-Japanese trade agreement that had been in force since 1911, and at that time, Walter Lippmann wrote that Washington had enough trouble in Europe without infuriating the

Japanese in Asia, but nobody else paid much attention to what Lippmann called a challenge to a great power and a step toward war.

When, however, Roosevelt announced on July 15, 1941, an embargo on the shipment of all scrap iron and gasoline to Japan, a critical move, as it turned out, I went to see Admiral Kichisaburo Nomura at the Japanese Embassy in Washington. He denounced the embargo as an act of war, and said Japan would rather fight than be "strangled." I reported the gist of this conversation to the *Times* and also to officials at the State Department, but both regarded it as just another bit of Japanese propaganda, and I was inclined to agree.

Some U.S. officials were not so casual. In January of 1941, Joseph Grew, the U.S. ambassador in Tokyo, had alerted Secretary Hull to the possibility of a sneak attack on Pearl Harbor, but added reassuringly, though inaccurately, to his diary, "I guess the boys in Hawaii are not precisely asleep." More important, weeks before the attack, Secretary of the Navy Frank Knox predicted in writing to Secretary of War Henry Stimson that "hostilities would be initiated by a surprise attack on Pearl Harbor."

Even after the investigations of the disaster that crippled the U.S. Pacific Fleet and took over two thousand American lives, we never did know whether Roosevelt was informed of these warnings, or even of the intercepted radio messages from Tokyo to the invaders approaching Pearl Harbor. We in the press certainly knew nothing about them. The Japanese ambassador, Nomura, and the special Japanese negotiator, Saburo Kurusu, were pretending to be discussing a peaceful settlement down to the last deadline on December 7.

The assumption in Washington was that the Japanese were planning an attack on the Dutch East Indies, which had cut off their last supply of oil. I went back to see the Japanese ambassador three days before the attack on Pearl Harbor. I took careful notes on that conversation. Admiral Nomura was elaborately calm. I assume he knew that Japanese planes and warships were at that moment moving to their invasion stations, but he said he felt sure war could be avoided, because, he added, if it were not, it would not be the last of wars between our two countries. The loser, he observed, would never accept defeat but would fight again. (I recalled this statement to him in Tokyo after the war. "Yes, I remember," he said, "but I was wrong. There is no spirit of revenge in Japan now.")

On Pearl Harbor morning, Sally and I had just moved into a rented house on Thirty-fourth Street in Georgetown, and after lunch I was assembling a crib for our nine-month-old son, Jim, when the

*Times* called with a bulletin from the Associated Press. It said: "Flash: White House says Japs attack Pearl Harbor." It was timed at 2:22 P.M. I turned on the radio, but Sammy Kaye was crooning on CBS, and NBC was spinning jazz records, so I ran to the office, leaving the crib to Sally, and didn't return until the following morning.

The only reporter who had the inside story at the White House that day was Edward R. Murrow of CBS. He and his wife, Janet, had been invited weeks before to dine with President and Mrs. Roosevelt that fateful Sunday night, and Ed was still around when Roosevelt came up from the Oval Office, exhausted and angry. "Our planes were destroyed on the ground," FDR kept saying, beating on the table, "on the ground, mind you, ON THE GROUND!"

Washington was never the same after Pearl Harbor. It went to war as a great nation should, solemnly but confident in its strength and purpose. By then, its rearmament program was well under way. It was embarrassed by its misjudgment of the Japanese and its failure to intercept the invaders, but it put away the political arguments of the past, summoned the best men and women of both parties, and created in effect a national government.

Despite its fury against the Japanese attack, the Congress accepted Roosevelt's judgment that the first priority was the defeat of Germany, mainly because Hitler, in his worst mistake since invading the Soviet Union, decided after a three-day delay to declare war on the United States. Had he not done so, the anger of the American people against Japan would undoubtedly have forced Roosevelt to give first priority to the war in the Pacific, but he was now free to concentrate on the defeat of Germany, which was what he had wanted to do from the beginning.

Within a few months, a vast military and civilian establishment had taken over Washington, and that put an end to my first experience in the capital. For Elmer Davis, the head of the new Office of War Information, asked the publisher of the *Times* to give me a leave of absence to work with the government's new propaganda effort at the U.S. Embassy in London. Sally and I had planned a long reporting trip in Latin America at the time, but I went alone to London in a much more optimistic mood. For I felt sure that with both the United States and the Soviet Union in the war, the Axis powers would eventually be defeated in both the Atlantic and Pacific. What I did not foresee was that this wartime assignment in London would lead by accident to a turning point in my work at the *Times*.

# PART SEVEN

# TURNING POINTS

# CHAPTER 12

# *The London Embassy*

THE U.S. AMBASSADOR to London when I reported for duty
there in 1942 was John Winant, a big shambling former Republican
governor from New Hampshire, who looked a little like Abe Lincoln
and kept a big portrait of himself in his waiting room so that visitors
wouldn't miss the resemblance. He was popular with the British at
least partly because he wasn't Joe Kennedy. He had studied history
under Woodrow Wilson at Princeton, fought with the Allied Expeditionary Force during the First World War, and backed Roosevelt
against the antiwar America Firsters before Pearl Harbor.

He regarded propaganda as a shabby business and reporters as a
threat to the tranquillity of Grosvenor Square, but accepted me as
one more necessary burden of the war. He was a gentle giant who
did many kindly things by stealth. After work he would occasionally
wander around London in the blackout with a wad of money in his
pocket and slip it to some bewildered air raid victim in the dark. He
had done much the same back in Concord, where he had an arrangement with his milkman to supply milk to the poor families in his
neighborhood.

My brief stay at the embassy was useful to me, if to nobody else,
because I learned on the inside that government is more complicated
than it appears to columnists on the outside. I soon realized that
there were not just two sides to every question, as I supposed, but
maybe ten, all held by "experts" with stubborn conviction. I did
some minor propaganda chores, but this didn't really change my
mind that government propaganda, while necessary in wartime, was
a tricky occupation I could never master or enjoy. "You weren't

meant to enjoy it," Winant told me, "but it's better than carrying a gun."

My experience as a part-time "diplomat" in the London embassy was otherwise not reassuring. It demonstrated how unprepared the United States government was for the battles to come, and what was more surprising, how confused it was about the propaganda war already being waged by Goebbels and the other Nazis. Though the United States knew more about the arts and deceptions of advertising than any other nation, and though Roosevelt himself was a master propagandist, his administration and the Congress were only vaguely aware of this new Office of War Information, and the professionals in the embassy regarded all OWI amateurs with justified suspicion if not downright disdain.

Fortunately for me, the man in charge of the American information and psychological warfare program in London was Wallace Carroll, a former head of the United Press bureau in Fleet Street. We had worked together during the blitz, but in the embassy even he was bewildered by the confusion in Washington about his mission and authority. When Elmer Davis appointed him and took him to see President Roosevelt, the president said to him: "So you're going to London? The minute you get over there, you tell the British they must plug the leaks in their censorship." Carroll explained he was going to work on psychological warfare and would have nothing to do with censorship. But Roosevelt persisted. "That's all right," he said, ending the interview, "but you tell them to tighten up their censorship."

There was a lot of bickering between the OWI people doing open propaganda and the new Office of Strategic Services officials who were in the cloak-and-dagger business, and I was mystified most of the time. I had, of course, observed in Washington the personal feuds that attended and diminished government service, but had assumed that intelligent men and women would get along under the influence of the war. Intelligent they were; cooperative and congenial they were not. Under Davis at OWI were Milton Eisenhower, Ike's brother; Robert Sherwood, the playwright; Gardner Cowles of the Cowles publications; and Archibald MacLeish, the poet. Colonel William Donovan at the OSS was accustomed to command—quick, intelligent, and autocratic. Sherwood, who had been writing speeches for Roosevelt, was vague, unpunctual, and protective of his close personal ties to the president. These two differed about most things, particularly about calling on the Germans for unconditional surren-

der, a policy that had helped wreck the peace treaties after World
War I but suited Donovan's martial instincts.

Carroll assumed, with his usual common sense, that a policy that
cannot be explained to the people is bound to cause trouble for a
democratic government, and he tried, not always with success, to
impose his wise counsel on his squabbling superiors. "Let's put away
the gall and keep the honey handy," he suggested. "Let's strive, as
Lincoln counseled us, to convince the peoples of the world that we
are their sincere friend. . . . Let's remember that money cannot buy
friendship. . . . Let's keep our actions in harmony with our words."
General Eisenhower, who had just taken over the Allied command,
trusted him and listened to this advice.

For example, it was vital, in those days before Ike had the men and
arms to wage war, to reassure the occupied peoples of Western
Europe that the United States, though bombed into the war by
Japan, considered the liberation of Europe to be its first priority. This
meant the preparation of radio broadcasts to go out over the BBC
and other stations, some of them clandestine, that would maintain
the hopes but not exaggerate the expectations of the captive peoples.

Carroll and Ritchie Calder, a Scot who was director of plans of
the British Political Warfare Executive, also had to prepare leaflets
to be dropped by the RAF over Europe, and what was more important, deceive the Germans into believing an invasion of France was
under urgent consideration when Ike was actually planning a critical
strategic move to land Allied forces in Africa. As Carroll later explained in an excellent book called *Persuade or Perish,* if the Germans had learned of this African expedition, they could easily have
aborted it by sending a few divisions through Fascist Spain to Gibraltar and through France to the Mediterranean coast. All sorts of
military feints were employed to keep the Germans pinned down in
the north, and the Carroll propaganda section had a part to play in
this effort to gain time and position.

I knew nothing of this hanky-panky. Carroll never mentioned it
to me until after the war when we shared the direction of the *Times'*
bureau in Washington. I had a simpler task: it was to counter the
insidious Nazi anti-American propaganda drummed into Britain
every night about how the Roosevelt administration was planning to
use British shock troops to do the fighting while it was plotting to
relieve Britain of its economic resources after the war. This poison
did have some effect on British public opinion, but we managed to
deal with it in a fairly simple and inexpensive way. Whenever some

particular anti-American rumor seemed to be gaining an audience, I prepared statements of the actual facts and took them to Anthony Eden's parliamentary secretary at the Foreign Office. He in turn arranged to have a question placed before the House of Commons, and Eden himself answered it and saw that his answer was given appropriate publicity. I doubt that this alone led to the defeat of Hitler, but it was my nickel's worth and made me feel useful.

Meanwhile, I acquired an abiding respect for the Foreign Service officers of the United States, and I still regard them as the most professional and least appreciated body of diplomats in the world. The way they were ignored, treated, and mistreated by most of the presidents and some of the secretaries of state I came to know was, and still is, a political disgrace. I can think of nothing that has contributed more to the misconduct of American foreign affairs than the tendency to appoint inexperienced secretaries of state, bypass the Foreign Service, and try to operate foreign policy out of the White House. Roosevelt dramatized this practice with Secretaries Hull and Stettinius, whose only qualification for the job was that they looked like secretaries of state. The effect of this system was apparent during my days in Grosvenor Square, when Ambassador Winant was treated almost as badly by Roosevelt as Roosevelt had been treated by Joe Kennedy, Winant's predecessor.

The president used Winant as a mail carrier. He allowed him to carry on the routine work of the embassy but much of the time didn't even inform him of his back-channel negotiations with the British government. Whenever there was something important to negotiate in London, he sent over Averell Harriman or Sumner Welles or Harry Hopkins or somebody else to talk to Churchill and Eden.

This not only diminished and humiliated Winant but also became a source of embarrassing gossip in Westminister, so much so that Harriman finally asked the president to either use Winant or replace him. Roosevelt reluctantly agreed to mollify the ambassador and gave him an assignment that by accident made things even worse. At that time, the British were prepared to recognize the incorporation of the Baltic states into the Soviet Union—in short, to reward Moscow for its aggression. Roosevelt was sternly opposed, and instructed Winant to make this clear to the Soviet foreign minister, Molotov, who was then on his way to London. Winant asked for an appointment and was kept waiting until just before midnight of Molotov's last day in London, when he was called to the Soviet Embassy in Palace Green.

He arrived in a state of some excitement with a message from the president and careful instructions on precisely what to say. But not wanting merely to read out Roosevelt's message and in order to emphasize the importance of his mission, he opened with a few unfortunate words of his own. He was going, he told Molotov, "to talk turkey on this issue." Molotov interrupted him. "Turkey? What does Turkey have to do with the Baltic states?" The ambassador tried to explain patiently that "talking turkey" was merely an American expression meaning to talk seriously, but the suspicious Molotov could not or would not understand, and the meeting ended without any useful discussion of the president's message. Winant never really regained Roosevelt's confidence after that, and while he remained at his post until the end of the war, he never took another job. On November 3, 1947, he killed himself with a bullet to the temple at his home in Concord.

I am not suggesting that the blunder with Molotov was the cause, for even now his suicide remains a mystery. It was said he had money troubles, but this didn't quite explain the tragedy. He was only fifty-eight at the time. He must have had opportunities for useful and lucrative work. He had won the confidence of the British Foreign Office, but like many others prominent in wartime, he never adjusted to the more routine activities of peacetime and he drifted into obscurity and despondency.

How to explain these personal puzzles—this I would like to know. Some officials succeeded, no matter what they did; others, tormented or ignored, stumbled into tragedy. It was a topic Sally and I discussed all our lives with only one conclusion—that we were among the lucky ones. Another incident of that stay in London illustrates the point, and gave new directions to my life.

One afternoon in 1942, Arthur Hays Sulzberger, the publisher of the *Times,* came to Grosvenor Square and in a long talk with Ambassador Winant asked some questions about how the British newspapers were handling the German propaganda. I forget now what they were, but Winant called me in for a report. I had seen the publisher only on that one night when I had returned to New York from the blitz two years before, and naturally he didn't recognize me. When this happened again a few days later, however, the ambassador mentioned that I was on a leave of absence from the *Times* and suggested with a ridiculous giggle that the entire Allied war effort would no doubt collapse without my support.

The publisher, slightly embarrassed, asked me to call on him at his hotel and spent an hour talking to me about the war and the effect that it was likely to have on the paper. At the end of this conversation, much to my surprise, he said that if I could do this job for Winant, would I do the same for him when my tour of duty at the embassy was over? He explained that he needed someone to help him with his speeches and particularly someone of my age to make a study of the postwar problems of the *Times*. Things would be different when the next generation took over, he said. I thought this was odd, for he was only at the beginning of his responsibilities as publisher, but life was fragile in a war, he said, and he had to prepare for the future. He didn't have to wait long for my answer, but I didn't take his suggestion seriously until he renewed the offer in a letter after he returned to New York.

London was obviously my lucky town. If I hadn't happened to be around when the war started, I wouldn't have been hired by the *Times* in the first place, and but for this accidental meeting in the embassy, I would never have gotten upstairs in New York. That was just the beginning of many other happy surprises.

# CHAPTER 13

# Detour
# to Moscow

I HADN'T BEEN long in my new job in New York in 1943 when the publisher, who was also a vice president of the American Red Cross, was asked to go to Moscow to check on the delivery of medical supplies to the Red Army, and he took me along to keep a record of the journey. I was surprised and delighted to go. During the Second World War and the Cold War that followed, it was assumed that a reporter on the big papers couldn't earn his spats unless he knew something about the Soviet Union and, even more ridiculous, that he could remedy this deficiency by going to Moscow. There was, of course, some truth to this in theory, but there was little to it in practice, for officials in that grim and suspicious capital regarded reporters as spies of the wicked capitalists. Even so, I was determined to learn whatever I could.

I kept a detailed diary on that first trip—from June 22 until July 12, 1943—but I don't know why, for a diary wasn't really necessary: nobody who saw Moscow when the German army was just beyond the gate was likely ever to forget the hideous destruction of the war, the courage of the soldiers and the women, the zeal but distrust of the officials, or the stunned look of the people in the streets. Moscow was not, like London, waiting for invasion. Here the Germans had advanced across the Soviet land on a front of over two thousand miles, killing or capturing more than 3 million people.

We stayed at Spasso House, the American Embassy, with Ambassador Standley and his two Chinese servants, and drove a couple of days later to the city of Vyazma, which had just been liberated from the Nazis.

This had once been a city of sixty thousand, but in the whole area I saw only two inhabited houses, and these could not truthfully be called habitable. A few wretched people had crawled back into them to get a little protection over their heads. The rest of the houses—not some of them or most of them but all of them—had been blasted into a jumble of roofless, roomless walls and solitary chimneys. Part of the city had undoubtedly been flattened by artillery fire from both sides prior to occupation, but the rest could have been destroyed only by mining each house to prevent its use as shelter from the winter weather. Even the churches had been ruined as places of refuge, but their towers had been spared as guides for artillery fire.

After Vyazma, we continued our journey into the nearby forest, and after bumping along over the tundra, we came suddenly upon a large black hole in the snow. This turned out to be the entrance to an ingenious underground hospital. It was as long as a football field, but was almost invisible, for this vast deep trench had been roofed over with large trees so that it all seemed part of the forest. There we saw hundreds of wounded men attended by immaculately dressed doctors and nurses, who staffed not only the dormitories but modern operating rooms. They gave us a breakfast of cold soft-boiled eggs and vodka, which I don't recommend, and treated us with the utmost courtesy but would not talk about the recent battles, for they had lost over half their men in the Vyazma battle. We returned to Moscow with a better idea of the slaughter of these unreported "incidents" as they were called in the communiqués, but later that evening we had a disturbing glimpse of the Soviet system.

For when we arrived at Spasso House, the Soviet officer in charge of our party explained that some of the wounded would be returning overnight to base hospitals in Moscow, and he asked if we would like to meet them when they arrived. We said we would. "What time would be convenient for you?" he inquired. We said we would be available whenever the hospital train arrived. But he insisted he would meet us at ten in the morning. When we got to the station, we were shocked to find that the train had been standing waiting for us for over four hours. Arthur Sulzberger was furious. "Please unload the train at once," he said. "This is cruel." But the convenience of the state came first—never mind the wounded! Accordingly, not until we had inspected all the hospital rooms in the station would they give the order to evacuate the wounded from the train. Those who could walk were lined up on the platform, a reedy little band struck up a tune, the women put flowers in the hands of the men leading the walking wounded, who hobbled as best they could toward their waiting buses. Arthur Sulzberger looked at me and said, "Don't let this make a Communist out of you!"

You don't gather news in Moscow, you go where you're invited and collect clues or impressions. For example, we had heard that while life was hard for the people at the bottom, officials at the top had their privileges. This we confirmed, for Maxim Litvinov, the Soviet ambassador in Washington at that time, happened to be in Moscow during our visit and invited us to have lunch at Spirido-novka House. This was a large Gothic official mansion built by a czarist merchant named Morozov, with elaborate oriental rugs on the floors and oak-paneled walls covered with tapestries as big as a highway billboard. Despite the war, despite the food rationing, it was clear from the start that we wouldn't go away hungry. I kept score on the proceedings.

First, as always, came the vodka, and there was no escape. The man on your left raises his glass under your nose, you clink and gulp. At the precise moment this depth charge reaches its destination, you feel uneasily that something is happening on your right, and sure enough, Ilya Ehrenburg, the reigning propagandist, is holding up his glass and grinning. *"Za vashe Zdorovye!"* (To your health) he is saying, and zing, that fire is running down your gullet again.

Then comes the meal: mounds of caviar, unsalted butter on light rolls filled with rice; more caviar accompanied, of course, by more vodka; cold Volga fish and trimmings; spring salad; mushrooms and cream; and sturgeon. The main course—breast of turkey, breast of chicken and partridge, green fresh peas, and cauliflower—strawberry ice cream, all served with a choice of white wine, red wine, and sparkling burgundy, followed by coffee and a choice of liqueurs. By that time, the only impression we had was that vodka made the world look funny.

When we recovered from this, we asked to see the official newspaper, *Pravda,* and this was another surprise. They took us through their well-appointed offices. They showed us the composing room, full of German typesetting machines and modern presses. They took special pride in the newspaper's theater, where the employees listened to lectures and were entertained by *Pravda*'s own players. Then the tour ended. "Where," I asked, "is the newsroom?" They didn't seem to understand. "The place," I added, "where the reporters write their stories and the editors work?" There was no newsroom. The articles were written and edited by officials elsewhere.

*Pravda* was not a newspaper in Western terms but a printing factory.
Our hosts were friendly but their explanation was a disappointment.
It was like showing us a paintbrush as an example of Russian art.

We did get into the Kremlin for a brief visit with Foreign Minister
Molotov, and Arthur Sulzberger and Admiral Standley later had a
long talk with him, but Molotov was concerned primarily about
knowing when the Western Allies were going to open a second front
against the Germans, and he seemed little interested in discussing the
organization of a more peaceful world after the war. As our visit was
coming to an end, we tried to sum up our impressions.

Did we know much more about the Soviet Union? Unquestion-
ably, no. Did we have any clear conception of her war effort or future
plans? No. Was the trip, then, worthwhile? Undoubtedly, yes. At
least it gave us a better impression of the difficulties of ending the war
and cooperating with Moscow thereafter. We agreed on the following:

They did not trust us any more than we trusted them. At the depth
of their despair the previous year, when they were crying to the world
for aid, we and the British had made separate proposals to them: the
British had pointed out that a prerequisite of effective delivery of
military supplies around the North Cape to Murmansk was air protection, and asked that the Russians either protect the convoys or
allow the British to place a certain number of air squadrons in
northern Russia, amounting to about five hundred pilots, navigators,
radio operators, and ground repair men. The Soviets told the British
either to put their RAF flyers and staff under Russian supervision
in the Red Army or forget it. The British forgot it. Also, when the
Germans were breaking through the Soviet lines in the Caucasus
Mountains, the United States proposed to send much-needed fighter
support, but again word came back from Moscow that they could not
operate in that theater except under Soviet command.

The Soviets, we concluded, still could not forget that we and the
British and French had occupied part of their country at the end of
the First World War, when they were trying to establish their revolution. They could not forget that Churchill had wanted at that time
to "strangle the Communist baby in its cradle," and had referred to
the Soviet leaders as "a rabble from the gutters and ghettos of Eastern Europe."

Similarly, this suspicious attitude was still working against our
correspondents every time they tried to file anything that had not
appeared in the Soviet press. Cyrus Sulzberger, the publisher's

nephew, who guided us on this visit, had endless evidence of the difficulties he and his colleagues in Moscow were having in trying to gather news and get out any they found. Before leaving, we were invited to a farewell party. This was held in a fancy modern apartment, which had obviously been set apart for the entertainment of visiting journalists. Present in addition to our official shepherds were several Foreign Office types and three beautiful women who paid a great deal of attention to the boss. It was all very proper, but when they got the cameras out to record the hilarity, we decided it was time to go.

Nevertheless, we started home the next day feeling that the Germans could never withstand the pressure of war on two fronts and that it was only a matter of time until the conflict in Europe would be over, and we even retained some hope for the future. Arthur Sulzberger summed up his observations as follows:

They want peace, and they want to reconstruct their country. They will need our help to do both. In peace, however, Russia will be strong militarily but weak economically. She has sacrificed everything she had in the war. Her people were obviously obedient but woefully inefficient, perhaps because vodka seemed about the only provision in plentiful supply.

Sulzberger suggested that the instant hostilities ceased, our Lend-Lease program should be halted and that from then on we should barter with Russia for her needs instead of just giving without conditions. But, he observed, the Soviet Union was just completing its first generation of mass education and one day maybe it would take a different view of the world.

The United States, therefore, he concluded, would be faced with two difficult courses: to collaborate with the Russians on terms that would always be difficult and sometimes repugnant, or to antagonize them and encourage their worst suspicions. Sulzberger wanted to try to cooperate, as he said, "even if it hurts."

Looking back to those days almost half a century before Gorbachev, I think the publisher was not too far off the mark. We left a few days later for Gibraltar and London, where Sulzberger had a long talk with Churchill. "The long agony is slowly coming to an end," the prime minister said.

We returned to Forty-third Street in New York hoping he was right, and I then settled down to learn my new job on the *Times*.

# CHAPTER 14

# The Spy
# on the Fourteenth Floor

AFTER MOSCOW, I approached my new job as assistant to the publisher with some anxiety. The move from the ambassador's office in London to the publisher's office in New York seemed a detour from the main story, the war, but it gave me a better understanding of the paper and a clearer view of what I wanted to do in the future. I knew my way around Manhattan from my former AP days, but I didn't know my way around the *Times*. I didn't have even a vague idea of what an assistant to the publisher was supposed to do, but Arthur Sulzberger was patient and showed me the ropes.

I had always thought of a newspaper office as a noisy untidy place, but his domain on the fourteenth floor was almost forbiddingly clean, and quiet. It had carpets on the floor as thick as mattresses and a men's room with a magnificent view of New York Harbor. There were solemn portraits of deceased editors on the walls and some famous yellowing front pages embalmed under glass, one of them recording the murder of President Lincoln under the headline: AWFUL EVENT! The table in the board of directors' room seemed as long as a bowling alley, and one wall of this sanctuary was covered with pictures of so-called world leaders, including the scowling mug of Mussolini.

I never met Adolph Ochs, the founding father of the modern *Times*. He had died years before I arrived on the scene, but so enduring was his influence that I felt sure he would suddenly appear from some remote hideaway if I raised my voice in these hushed surroundings. His portrait greeted visitors as they stepped off the elevator. A bust of his massive head stood in a corner of the waiting room. Accounts of his struggles and triumphs were in all the book-lined rooms, and statements of his principles and instructions to his inheritors were discreetly displayed along the walls.

When he died on April 8, 1935, he left behind a will, which stated: "I am satisfied that my executors and trustees, without any recommendations or suggestions from me, will exercise their control to perpetuate *The New York Times* as an institution charged with a high public duty, and that they will carry forward and render completely effective my endeavor to maintain *The New York Times* as an independent newspaper, entirely fearless, free of ulterior influence, and unselfishly devoted to the public welfare, without regard to individual advantage or ambition, the claims of party politics, or the voice of religious or personal prejudice or predilection."

Ownership of the paper was passed to his four grandchildren (only after the death of his daughter, Iphigene), but I soon learned that nobody in that family ever thought of themselves as owners but as trustees of the founder's tradition. Certainly not his only child, Iphigene, who married Arthur Hays Sulzberger, or their four children, Marian, Judith, Ruth, and Arthur. They regarded themselves as caretakers in the precise sense that they took care not only to preserve the paper's integrity and financial stability but also to instill in their children this feeling of being temporary custodians of an important public service.

This appealed to every ideal I had acquired from my parents and my wife and remained with me all my life, but I felt a little uncomfortable at the beginning, all dressed up like a junior executive and wondering how I had stumbled into such lofty and opulent quarters. People called me "Mr. Reston," a new experience, and took me out to lunch at fancy places, and many of them had alluring ideas about what the perfect modern newspaper should be and few ideas about the practical ways to attain it.

Some things were fairly obvious. The war had produced new problems for all the major newspapers and particularly for the *Times.* It compelled the broadcast networks to increase and expand their competitive coverage of the news. It established Washington rather than New York as the main source of front-page news. It brought to the fore a new generation of reporters, who were better educated than reporters in my generation, more conversant with the languages of the world, more qualified to deal with the increasingly complicated problems of economic, legal, and military affairs. Equally important, since broadcasting was quicker than the newspapers at getting major news announcements to the people, it forced the newspapers to redefine their mission and pay more attention to explaining the causes and consequences of the nation's new position in the world. The publisher asked me, as he had in London, to make a study of these trends and pass on to him from time to time my observations and suggestions.

Unlike most publishers, Sulzberger was sympathetic to new ideas, but he was also loyal to his editors, who naturally regarded my suggestions as criticisms of their work. After all, the *Times* had become the leading newspaper of the country without any advice from me, and the editors weren't eager to change a system that had succeeded.

In 1943, when I was given this new assignment, the *Times,* like Gaul, was divided into three parts—the news department on the third floor, run by the managing editor, Edwin L. "Jimmy" James, a dumpy little Virginian who dressed like a racetrack gambler and carried a walking stick; the Sunday department on the eighth floor, presided over by Lester Markel, a talented and grumpy martinet from Pulitzer's *World;* and the editorial department on the tenth floor, directed on the one hand and on the other hand by Charles Merz, late of *The New Republic.*

In later days an executive editor was appointed in the hope of coordinating some of the activities of these separate principalities, but in my tour of duty on the publisher's fourteenth floor, the editors devoted most of their time to their separate responsibilities and the rest of their time to criticizing one another. They seldom met to discuss the common problems of the paper, though they did take lunch together in the publisher's dining room on the neutral ground of the eleventh floor. Little business was conducted there, however, for we usually had a prominent visitor to explain some tangle in the news, and the conversation was serious if not solemn. In fact, these visitors found by their plates a folded card illustrated with a drawing of Times Square and containing what amounted to a little prayer or blessing composed by Dr. John N. Finley, the *Times'* designated intellectual:

> O Lord, the Giver of All Good,
> In whose just Hands are all our Times,
> We thank Thee for our daily food
> Gathered (as News) from many Climes.

Bless all of Us around this Board
And All beneath this ample Roof—
What we find fit to print, O Lord,
Is, after all, the Pudding's Proof.

May Those we welcome come again
And those who stay be glad. Amen.

I was one of the glad ones, wondering why I was so lucky. I drafted letters to readers who were denouncing us for inaccuracies and silly opinions, and wrote speeches for the publisher on the glories of the First Amendment. It was my job not only to keep an eye on the *Herald Tribune,* the enemy on Fortieth Street, but also to scrutinize the *Times* each day and send along to the publisher a summary of all triumphs, errors, and absurdities contained therein. When these coincided with his own judgment, the publisher would send them to James, Markel, or Merz, as the case might be, or call them on the phone to ask, in his unfailingly courteous way, for an explanation. The editors were seldom amused by these inquiries and blamed them all on the new "spy" on the fourteenth floor. James was particularly hostile to these little notes, since his skin was a lot thinner than his skull.

No doubt his resentment was, from time to time, justified. No craft, with the possible exception of politics, can compare with a newspaper as a playground for second-guessers. A good argument can usually be made that every headline, story, picture, and editorial in the paper should have been longer or shorter or sharper or displayed higher or lower on the page, but I did not presume to comment on such technicalities. I felt then, as now, that the *Times* should have all the news everybody else had and a lot more and a little sooner, and it was my additional conviction that the publication of clichés was an affront to the English language, punishable by banishment to the midnight watch. We were, I constantly insisted, telling the reader what happened but not why, and worst of all assuming far too often that officials told the truth.

While agreeing with many of my observations, the publisher naturally defended his editors, and when occasionally they protested in writing, he would always send me their rockets with a single word scribbled on top: *Achtung!* Nevertheless, we talked a lot on the side about how the world was changing under the pressures of the war and how we would have to adapt to the new ideas and technologies that were already coming on stream.

For example, he agreed that it wasn't quite true, as the in-house joke had it, that nothing was news until it appeared in the *Times,* and that it wasn't good enough for us to repeat at greater length what had already been distributed by radio and television the night before. The editors conceded that more explanation was necessary as the nation became more involved in world affairs, but feared, with some reason, that this might dilute and even corrupt the news columns with opinion. In a typical *Times* compromise, a few more "explainers" were tolerated and published in the daily, and the principle of change was admitted on condition that it scarcely be noticed.

I learned many things in Arthur Hays Sulzberger's office. Like my parents and Sally, he placed before me by his example an ideal of human decency and responsibility. He agreed that it was the duty of the press to expose corruption, but he was more interested in education than in investigation. He didn't like confrontations with the government and wasn't overly inquisitive about the underground activities of the new intelligence agencies in Washington, but under the prodding of his wife, he campaigned for the teaching of history in the schools and even hired a theater on Forty-fourth Street for free public lectures on contemporary affairs.

He regarded himself as a Democrat, but backed Wendell Willkie for president in 1940 against the judgment of most members of his editorial board, and supported Eisenhower in 1952 and 1956 in opposition to his wife, who favored Stevenson. He helped lead the fight for social security at home and collective security abroad, favored racial equality and denounced McCarthy, and while he was sympathetic to the cause of Israel, he was not a Zionist and took a lot of criticism from other Jews for his moderation. I had to answer a lot of angry Zionists and wrote to one of them that we weren't running the *Jewish Science Monitor,* but the publisher didn't think that was a very courteous reply.

It occurred to me after a while that the higher you go on a big newspaper the less fun you have, and that this applied especially to the publisher at the very top. Publishers are a little like doctors— most of the people who come to see them have a pain, the main difference being that unlike doctors, publishers are usually blamed for causing the pain in the first place.

If the mayor is a crook, a plausible supposition, his first and last line of defense is usually that the publisher plotted his downfall. If the governor is caught behind or on the official sofa with his secretary, and such extracurricular activities leak into the press, the chances are the publisher will be blamed for snooping into his private life. The poor publisher is expected to contribute to every charity, praise every scoundrel, serve on every committee for the salvation of the city, and see to it that every friend's book is favorably reviewed and every acquaintance's daughter gets her wedding picture in the Sunday *Times.*

Arthur Hays Sulzberger dealt with these tribulations as if he not only understood human folly but also was somehow partly responsible for it. His tolerance of bores and sharpies was monumental. He was a kind, merry, and judicious man who treated all people with the same respect and generosity. He wanted the *Times* to speak in moderate tones, and refused to have an editorial page cartoon on the grounds that a cartoon could never say "on the other hand." He thought the way to deal with big things was to pay attention to little things, and he was a nut on punctuality. He was no softie, however. He seldom got taken by the twisters, but somehow could send them away feeling that maybe the *Times* wasn't such a rotten place after all. His only complaint was that, as both the publisher and son-in-law of Adolph Ochs, he couldn't, like other men, go home and denounce the owner as a silly ass.

All this was an important part of my education on the *Times,* but I was increasingly restless in these cushy surroundings. The war was reaching a climax in both the Atlantic and the Pacific, and while I had had my share of the bombing in London, I longed to be closer to the news. Besides, I didn't enjoy criticizing my colleagues, most of them older and more experienced than I. It was easier to spot the weaknesses in the paper than to correct them under the conditions of the war, and I found that I was learning less giving advice on the inside than I had in receiving it on the outside. More than anything else, I missed writing.

Sally and I talked all this over at length. The argument for staying in New York was that I was at the center of the paper, where my chances of promotion would be better than anywhere else. The argument against it was that I wasn't happy in executive work and not very good at it. We discussed going back to London, which would mean breaking up the family again, but Sally, as always, said, "Let's not worry about the future. Go where you think you'll be most useful. I'll take care of the boys." I said I preferred to return to Washington, where the terms of peace were already being discussed with the Allies, and I raised this possibility with the publisher.

He said he understood my feelings and would have a talk with

Arthur Krock, head of the Washington bureau, about it, but this created a problem. Krock wrote to him: "I should welcome Reston back here, of course, but I don't know what I should have for him to do. . . . He resists any routine assignments, the bulk of which we necessarily have, and I can't think of any roving assignment that wouldn't upset the machinery of the bureau." The publisher replied that he was sure I would accept any work assigned to me and told me to go and have a talk with the managing editor about the transfer.

Accordingly, I descended to the third floor, and Jimmy James pretended that the *Times* would never survive the shock of my departure. Normally, when reporters ventured to enter his portal, he assumed they wanted something he was not prepared to give, and he barked at them in self-defense even before knowing what they wanted. But in this case he was so pleased by the thought of getting me off the fourteenth floor that he not only approved the transfer but also asked me if I wouldn't like to take over the London bureau for a few months while Ray Daniell got a much-needed rest. I could take my wife, he added as an incentive.

So back we went again to London, then preparing for the invasion of the Continent. We left our two boys in Dayton with my parents, who thought we were crazy to go back into the bombing. We remained there for several months until Daniell returned. The managing editor suggested that I take over the Moscow bureau, but the thought of going to that grim city without Sally and without any knowledge of Russian didn't seem such a good idea. So I returned to Washington and to Arthur Krock, who took me in with no visible enthusiasm.

# PART EIGHT

# WASHINGTON IN THE FORTIES

# CHAPTER 15

# Arthur Krock:
# Kentucky Gentleman

ARTHUR KROCK RECEIVED me back to the Washington bureau in 1944 with his usual restrained courtesy, but we soon ran into trouble. The publisher had assured me that I would be free to write interpretive articles, but he hadn't cleared it with Krock, who didn't like to be surprised even by publishers. He was then fifty-eight and at the pinnacle of a distinguished career, a proud and sensitive man who looked at the world with wary eyes, usually through a cloud of cigar smoke. He had been in charge of the Washington bureau since Roosevelt's first term and wrote a widely read column on the editorial page three times a week. He had heard of my efforts in New York to give the reporters more freedom to explain and analyze the news, but it was not his favorite subject and he greeted me as though he expected some kind of insurrection. He said we had many things in common but mentioned only one of them: he came from Glasgow in Kentucky and I from Glasgow in Scotland. I didn't know whether this was intended to demonstrate our similarities or our differences. For a while, he revived my old immigrant's dread that somehow I didn't fit or wasn't wanted.

He explained the office routine to me as if I had never seen it before. The bureau, he said, operated under strict jurisdictional lines. Mr. Huston—Krock never called anybody by his or her first name—was the news editor and I would report to him. Mr. Hulen represented the *Times* at the State Department and Mr. Trussell was in charge on Capitol Hill. He added with a mirthless smile that perhaps I could "pick up" some news at the embassies but gave me the impression that I would need a visa to venture elsewhere. Interpretation of the news in Washington, he concluded, would be done in the weekday papers only with his permission.

This seemed a little wintry to me, but was not at all unusual in those more disciplined days. The *Times* had been so suspicious of opinion under Adolph Ochs that he not only opposed bylines for many years, but seriously considered abolishing the editorial page on the ground that editorial crusading might annoy some advertisers and corrupt the objectivity of the news columns. Ochs did entrust the editorial page to Rollo Ogden, a former Presbyterian minister out of Cleveland, but only when Mr. Ogden was sixty-four. Ogden was succeeded briefly by Dr. John Finley, a scholar of the classics and former president of City College, when Finley was seventy-four. It was also remembered in those days that Walter Duranty, the *Times'* Moscow correspondent, had been widely criticized for swallowing Stalin's propaganda, and this did not improve the chances of giving the reporters more leeway.

Krock was the first of the modern columnists on the *Times,* and he had to fight for that independent position against the editor of the editorial page in New York, who felt that a second opinion on the page somehow diminished the authority and dignity of the paper. Krock was regarded, along with the other monuments of the Washington press corps—Walter Lippmann, David Lawrence of *U.S. News & World Report,* and Frank Kent of the *Baltimore Sun*—with the utmost awe and respect, except in the White House, where Roosevelt denounced him regularly as "that Tory Krock-pot." Former Secretary of State Dean Rusk recalled in his memoirs that soon after taking office he had a message from Krock saying that "if I wished to call on them, he would be glad to receive me."

The staff liked their skipper and called him A.K., but not in his presence. His mind, when I arrived, was on what he called Roosevelt's outrageous effort to be elected for a fourth term, while mine was on foreign affairs, and since he didn't believe in staff meetings, I usually saw him only in his passage to and from his office.

He was as regular as a metronome. His driver delivered him to the office at ten in the morning, by which time he had memorized the morning papers. He dealt with his mail and consulted with the news editor until precisely twelve-thirty, when he walked to the Metropolitan Club and had lunch always at the same table and usually in company with the same prominent lawyers and politicians. In the afternoon, he worked the telephones, wrote his column within an hour, scrutinized it word for word before it was put on the ticker, and departed for home a few minutes before six.

This brought him to his favorite part of the day. He was intensely preoccupied in his work at the office, but he shed his forlorn look in the evening. He was much in demand at the embassy dinner tables. He was a delightful companion with an endless collection of stories that improved with age, and he often extracted from these occasions some important nuggets of news. I was never at ease in such gatherings, usually discussing such momentous subjects as how long my dinner partners had been in Washington, and where their children went to school, et cetera, but A.K. loved the glitter and delighted in the gossip.

He didn't run the bureau, he presided over it. He somehow managed to get exclusive interviews with presidents he criticized most of the time. He was the first newspaperman to learn from Secretary of Defense James Forrestal that George Kennan was the author of the famous "long telegram" calling for the containment of the Soviet Union, and he encouraged his reporters to emulate such enterprise. Also, he had some very good legmen. Louis Stark, covering labor, knew every union leader in town and all their political dodges. Charlie Hurd had backdoor access to the White House. Huston, the news editor, was a good man with a surgical pencil and was also admired as a gentleman farmer who grew peonies as big as cabbages in Maryland. The reporters were allowed to analyze the news in the Sunday Review of the Week section, which was run by Lester Markel beyond Krock's domain, but seldom did so the rest of the week.

I thought it was absurd for Krock to oppose interpretation by the reporters in the weekday papers while Markel was insisting that they analyze everything on Sunday. Since other newspapers had no such restrictions and the radio and television networks were tempting our reporters with more money and visibility, I believed that the *Times* would lose many of the best of this new wartime generation of reporters if it didn't give them more freedom and a little more dough. Also, at that time I had been asked by Helen Reid to go over to the *Herald Tribune* to write what I pleased at twice my salary, so I didn't particularly enjoy the prospect of being fenced in.

Mr. Krock felt, with some reason, that his standing would be reduced if the reporters expanded their authority, but he wrote to me a couple of years after this: "My feeling was that if you were restricted in the latitude granted to you by the publisher that you would leave the *Times* and I didn't want that to happen and I don't."

I impose this shoptalk on the reader merely to illustrate not the inevitable clash between old men and young men, but the depth of the conflict between the old *Times* tradition and the new interpretative journalism imposed on the newspapers after radio and television became the first purveyors of the news. No doubt there was an element of self-interest in Mr. Krock's opposition, but mainly it was just one more indication to him that the simpler world of his days in Kentucky was drifting away and being replaced by a more restless, undisciplined, violent, and pushy world of mechanized politics, journalism, and warfare.

His career explained his anxiety. He was always just failing to get the job he wanted or losing it shortly after he got it. He negotiated the sale of the Louisville *Courier Journal* and the Louisville *Times* to Robert W. Bingham and took over the editorial direction of these papers. But when Bingham supported national prohibition and unlimited women's suffrage, which Krock regarded as a threat to the Republic, he resigned and moved to New York as assistant to Ralph Pulitzer, the publisher of *The World.*

There he was Pulitzer's spy and had about as much success second-guessing Walter Lippmann, Frank I. Cobb, Herbert Bayard Swope, and the other luminaries on *The World* as I did under the publisher of the *Times.* He wrote careful and fair-minded observations on the paper for Pulitzer's personal consideration, and later retained the conviction that *The World* would have gone on publishing, if only it had followed his advice. In fact, he kept copies of these memoranda and left them to Princeton University in his will.

He was a proud and in many ways a contentious man. At the *Times,* as at *The World,* he never quite made it to the top, and he nursed a suspicion that he had been passed over as editor of the *Times* because the publisher didn't want Jews in most top editorial positions. Titles and position and social standing were important to him. Accordingly he naturally and warily protected his position in Washington against all intruders.

He was a yearner. He yearned not only for recognition, but also for learning, and read long after midnight acquiring it. He was always seeking the favor of famous people, many of whom were not worthy of his esteem, and the paradox of this was that the character of the man—decent, generous, and thoughtful—was so much better than the pretense.

His writings revealed much more about his longings for the comfortable past and for the noblesse oblige of the well-born families of his beloved Kentucky than they did about his own struggles as a poor boy or his shrewd intelligence of men and affairs in Washington. He was a model of patient command at the presidential nominating conventions and on election night in New York when he wrote the lead stories and decided when to call the final result.

In his column, he stuck to his conservative philosophy and his fear of presidential power, but usually he seemed more interested in the players than in the play. He loved all the roguery of politics. He was close to old Joe Kennedy before the war and expected that Jack Kennedy would continue this friendship in the White House, but Jack's enthusiasm for his father's friends was no greater than his devotion to his father's policies.

A.K. occasionally departed from the Tory line. If his conservative friend and neighbor in Berryville, Virginia, Senator Harry Flood Byrd, was in a political controversy, he would support Harry. And if his liberal friend Senator John Sherman Cooper of Kentucky or Chief Justice Vinson of Kentucky was in trouble, he would support them, too.

In short, he lived a disciplined life of longing, personal loyalty, and regret for a world that was gone. He copied the stylish but complicated prose of the nineteenth-century British historians and essayists, which explained his dignified, subtle, and often mystifying and interminable sentences. But in his private conversation, he was brief, pointed, and witty.

I liked him, in an odd way. He felt he was an outsider and so did I. I admired his early struggles and his hard-won successes, and I was determined to show him that I could make a contribution to his news report if he gave me a chance. Fortunately, this opportunity presented itself quicker than I expected and under circumstances I couldn't have foreseen.

My assignment to pick up whatever I could on the embassy beat proved to be lucky for me, as usual. In 1944, the war was reaching a climax, with Hitler facing invasion from east and west, and the Allies, confident of victory, were beginning to discuss the terms of peace and the organization of the postwar world. After his victory in the presidential election of 1944, President Roosevelt, haunted by President Wilson's failure with the League of Nations in 1920, began planning for a new world peace organization.

His first formal step was to call the major Allies to a conference at Dumbarton Oaks, a lovely old mansion in the Georgetown section of Washington. What was the use of fighting and winning this terrible war, he asked, if the Allies let the world slide again into extreme nationalism and disorder? Mr. Krock told me to concentrate on the conference, and it was disrupted within a week by a controversy in which I was personally involved.

Some years before the war, Iphigene Sulzberger had arranged for a young Chinese student by the name of Joseph Ku to serve as an apprentice on the news staff of the paper. I liked him and tried to give him a hand, but after his training he went back to China and I didn't see him again until, to my surprise, he showed up at Dumbarton Oaks as a member of the Chinese (Nationalist) delegation.

I welcomed him back, discussed the conference with him at great length, and discovered to my delight that he not only knew what the major nations were proposing but also had in his possession the complete texts of the proposals being discussed by the U.S., British, Soviet, and Chinese delegations. I congratulated him on how successful he had become for so young a man and added, in due course, that it would be a pity not to share these wonderful proposals and suggestions with the peoples who had suffered so much. I said I felt sure that the *Times,* as the only paper of record, would be glad to cooperate in such an enterprise and was also the only newspaper that would be willing to devote the space necessary to their careful and complete publication.

Without the slightest delay, he opened up a big briefcase and handed me the whole prize, neatly translated into English. I don't suppose he was authorized to do so, and I didn't ask; but I ran, literally ran, all the way to the office and turned them over to Arthur Krock. He didn't ask me how I got them, so I let him think this was the sort of thing I "picked up" every day or so.

We sat down and planned together what to do with this booty. He looked like a guy who had just won the Kentucky Derby. We decided that it would be cruel to dump the whole load on the *Herald Tribune* all at once, so we gave them the Chinese torture treatment by publishing the U.S. text one day, the Soviet the next, and so on. I don't know what happened about all this at the *Herald Tribune* on Fortieth Street, but there was a big explosion at Dumbarton Oaks.

The first rocket came from Andrei Gromyko, the Soviet delegate, who called on A.K. and charged the *Times* with being involved in a conspiracy to divide the Allies. Krock hadn't come out of Kentucky without learning how to handle politicians. He was elaborately polite. He explained that, like diplomats, reporters merely gathered the news and passed it on to headquarters for disposition. Gromyko said he couldn't accept that explanation, and Krock said that in that event he would inform New York that the Soviet Union disapproved of our actions.

On the following day, Secretary of State Stettinius called on Lord Halifax, the British ambassador, and accused the British delegation of "this outrageous breach of security." Getting no satisfaction there, Stettinius then went to New York and told the publisher that if the *Times* continued to publish these draft proposals, the conference might very well collapse. Arthur Sulzberger said that would be very unfortunate, but he added that if Allied unity was so weak that it couldn't stand publication of the various "suggestions" for peace, we'd better face that fact now rather than later.

I then called on Lord Halifax, a formidable monument, whose notorious distaste for the press was not relieved by the *Times'* daily disclosures. I handed him a letter I had written to Secretary Stettinius stating that the British were not the source of our information. He read it carefully, and then rose. He said he accepted my letter as true, but henceforth could have nothing to do "with a man implicated in this affair." He had not been my favorite statesman since the days of his own implication in the policy of appeasement, and this interview did little to change my mind. The *Times* continued to publish the documents, the conference survived, and I got my first Pulitzer Prize as a reward, though I still think it should have gone to Iphigene Sulzberger, who discovered Joseph Ku in the first place.

Arthur Krock and I never did resolve our differences over who should analyze the news, but for many years thereafter we enjoyed one another's company. Unfortunately, he was sad at the end of his life. He railed against the brutality of the rising generation: what he regarded as its permissiveness, its slovenliness, its discourtesy, its vulgarity. And of course, he was out of sympathy with the liberal Democrats most of his professional life. He liked President Nixon personally and, unlike the *Times,* was pleased to see him come to power, but he was shocked and affronted by the Nixon Watergate scandal and kept complaining in his last year that Mr. Nixon had been unfaithful to the conservative cause.

He was sad for other reasons. When he approached his last deadline between sleep and death, he said to me that it was a man's duty to outlive and care for his wife, and that's what he wanted to do more than anything else, but he knew that he wouldn't make it. Then, always after a serious point, he seemed to feel compelled by some sense of irony or mockery to make a frivolous observation: he wanted, he insisted, to live long enough to go back home for the one hundredth running of the Kentucky Derby, but he didn't quite make that either.

What I prefer to remember about A.K. were his generosity to me at the end and his insistence on printing the truth in the news columns even when it went against his opinions or desires. He was the last of the *Times'* Washington correspondents to be born in the nineteenth century, and he regarded it as a personal misfortune that he took over the bureau just when the Roosevelt revolution changed the world he loved. Among many things I learned from observing him was that the period was the most important key on the typewriter. He didn't use many of them himself, but this was one of our differences we never discussed.

# CHAPTER 16

# Walter Lippmann

DURING THE CONTROVERSY with the government over the Dumbarton Oaks papers, I had a reassuring telephone call from Walter Lippmann. He had heard I was in trouble with the administration for printing these classified documents, but said he hoped the *Times* would not back off. I needed a little support right then and his call began a lifelong friendship. Like many reporters of my generation, I admired Lippmann more than any other writer in our business, even when I didn't agree with him. He was not only the most influential columnist of his day, or any other day I knew anything about, but also he managed to evade most of the problems that tormented all the rest of us. He wasn't a prisoner of the news, he merely used it as a peg for his political philosophy. He didn't interview presidents and secretaries of state as often as they interviewed him. He didn't worry about money or deadlines, but lived elegantly on his capital, and actually got home on time every night for dinner, an incredible achievement.

He was a quiet, studious, self-confident man with large, bright eyes and skeptical views on the wisdom of the people. He was seldom inside a newspaper office after he left *The World* in New York in the thirties, but he used the national newspaper syndicates to reach large audiences when the people were reading about some crisis in the news. He was an educator and he thought the freedom of the press had been guaranteed by the First Amendment because the founders assumed that the papers would not only report the news but also help educate the people about its causes and consequences. He was seldom overjoyed by our performance.

Having no children of his own, he collected young reporters and used our legs as we used his brains. He lived up the street from Sally and me in the house formerly occupied by the dean of the Washington Cathedral, and since he picked up a lot of spot news he didn't use in his column, he passed some of it on to me. Arthur Krock was glad to receive such information, but didn't like the source, for he had envied and detested Lippmann ever since their days together on *The World.*

Lippmann enlarged our vision of what a newspaper could contribute to the life and thought of the nation, and he also gave presidents a larger view of the responsibilities and limitations of American power and a sense of the moral obligations of leadership. "Those in high places," he insisted, "are more than the administrators of government bureaus. They are more than the writers of laws. They are the custodians of the nation's ideals, of its permanent hopes, of the faith that makes a nation out of a mere aggregation of individuals." In short, he thought presidents (and also the press) should talk to the people not about lower taxes and their material desires, but about their responsibility to their country and to their children, and "about all those things that make a people self-respecting, serene, and confident."

When Lippmann was seventy-five, Marquis Childs of the *St. Louis Post-Dispatch* and I got out a little book of tributes from his friends. I wrote that his main contribution was that, more than anyone I knew outside the government, he defined the central issues for decision, but he wasn't satisfied with that. He wanted to be judged by his answers to the complicated political controversies of the age, which was odd because his answers were not always as good as his questions.

In thanks for the book of tributes, he wrote to Childs and me: "When I was a young man leaving college, I asked Graham Wallas [always one of his mentors] to inscribe his book for me, and he wrote in it a line from 'The Vision of Piers Plowman,' which runs: 'I will be truth's pilgrim at the plow for poor men's sake.' As I read this book of yours and Mark's I know that in spite of all my mistakes and follies, my sins and weaknesses, what I have tried to do has not been misunderstood. No man can ask more."

Admittedly, he made mistakes. He was curiously insensitive to the menace of Hitler from 1933 to 1936 and thought the war would not touch America if we kept strictly out of it. He opposed the idea of a united Europe because he feared it would be dominated by Germany. He left college with some dreamy hopes for Fabian socialism, and he was enamored for a time with the idea of world government, but he was especially effective in his constant insistence that the United States should not involve itself in conflicts that were not essential to its interests and beyond its resources.

He misjudged Roosevelt during the 1932 election and couldn't find much difference between him and Herbert Hoover. He hated violence and was inclined to oppose confrontations with the Soviets. He was so upset by George Kennan's policy of containment of Moscow's expansionist strategy in Eastern Europe and the Middle East that he wrote a book condemning it, which he later regretted when Kennan proved to be right.

He did not live the restless unpredictable life of most newspapermen. He knew at the beginning of each year where he would be until the end: in Washington during January for the return of Congress and the State of the Union address; in New York for the theater in February; in Europe in the spring to exchange views with the heads of government; at his camp in Maine for the summer, and so on.

His days in Washington likewise were as regular as the clock. He rose early, read the morning papers, and settled down after breakfast to write, undisturbed by anybody or anything. In those days, his house was covered with ivy and populated by some noisy mockingbirds. He didn't flush them out but had his study and chimney padded to silence their chatter. He watched television occasionally but kept his set in a hall cupboard with the sweeper and thought both should be pulled out only when required.

To the rest of us who wrote in the equivalent of a boiler factory, all this seemed odd if not slightly monkish, but we admired his ability to use his work as a means to his private life and not vice versa. He wrote in longhand. When he finished a column, he then read it into a tape recorder to get the rhythm right, and had it typed. He would finish correcting it by noon in time for a messenger to pick it up precisely at twelve-thirty. He would then have lunch with some knowledgeable official, walk his poodles and rest in the afternoon, and wind up the day dining at home or at some embassy, where he was usually the center of attention.

He seldom departed from this orderly routine. John Morton Blum, the Woodward professor of history at Yale, who edited his letters, recalls that in 1961 Lippmann had a date with Nikita Khrushchev in the Kremlin, and refused to change the date at Khrushchev's request. The Soviet leader adjusted his plans to accommodate Lippmann's.

Order was the watchword not only of his private life but also of his political and social philosophy. He wrote a great deal about the abuses and diseases of democracy. He disapproved the untidiness of the American election process, and the noisy squalor of the Congress. He distrusted the judgment of the people. ("The public can produce only muddle when it meddles.") He believed in a strong executive government advised by the intellectual elites. Dean Acheson thought his answers were usually clearer than the truth, and Roosevelt admired his elegant writing but not his judgment. "I wish sometimes that he could come more into contact with the little fellow all over the country and see less of the big rich brother," FDR said.

One of the many things that intrigued me about him was that he didn't always live by the principles he recommended with such zeal and clarity. He was always lecturing me on the virtues of detachment—of avoiding personal involvement with influential officials or politicians. "Cronyism is the curse of journalism," he would say. But actually, he was more involved with them than any other major commentator I knew. When he got out of Harvard, he worked briefly with the socialist mayor of Schenectady. He was in President Theodore Roosevelt's political circle; he was an assistant secretary of war during the First World War; he wrote General Pershing's Aid to the Allies speech in 1940; he went to the Versailles peace conference in 1919 as an adviser to Colonel House and President Wilson; he showed up in London during the first Roosevelt term and helped rewrite U.S. policy at the failed world economic and monetary conference. And even during his last days in Washington, he was working privately with President Johnson and even drafting speeches for him in the vain hope of getting him out of the Vietnam War.

There were actually two Lippmanns: the intellectual prophetic Lippmann, who lived with the mockingbirds in the shadow of the cathedral—the writer of *A Preface to Morals* and *The Good Society*—and the everyday Lippmann, who always seemed surprised when his prophecies came true and interrupted his private life. He foresaw, long before many of the most perceptive minds in the country, the revolutionary effects of modern machinery, mass production, and the growth of the cities. The crush and noise of an increasingly urbanized nation, he predicted, would shatter the serenity of family life, as the competition of the nations with new weapons of destruction was threatening the security of the world. But when he fled from Washington after quarreling with Johnson, he thought he could find peace and quiet in Florence close to his old friend Bernard Berenson, only to discover to his dismay that they had motorcycles in Italy and that these infernal machines made noise.

Accordingly, he left there for Fontainebleau, only to find much the same racket, and departed from there and bought a villa in the south of France, only to discover that France had run out of servants and that the changing world he had predicted forty years before was now an intolerable reality.

His wanderings, he wrote, convinced him there was no escape from the torments of the world. "In vain does a man imagine that he can go anywhere these days and shut himself away from the clamor of the front page. Even when the newspaper does not come, he is trying to imagine what is in the newspaper he has not seen. The best one can do, I find, is to fret quietly for a few weeks instead of openly in public print."

It grieved him that the ancient solidities of religious faith were in decline, and he wrote about this with great passion and pessimism, especially after Hitler had conquered all of Western Europe. He did not like the new secular society of the West; he hated the tendency to blame all America's troubles on its enemies; he thought our salvation lay within ourselves and could not be achieved by looking elsewhere.

"Our civilization can be maintained and restored," he wrote in 1940, "only by remembering and rediscovering the truths, and by reestablishing the virtuous habits on which it was founded. There is no use looking into the blank future for some new and fancy revelation of what man needs in order to live.

"The revelation has been made. By it man conquered the jungle about him and the barbarian within him. The elemental principles of work and sacrifice and duty—and the transcendent criteria of truth, justice, and righteousness—and the grace of love and charity are the things which have made men free. . . . Only in this profound, this stern, and this tested wisdom shall we find once more the light and the courage we need."

I was deeply impressed by this philosophy when Sally and I came to Washington in 1941, and I talked a lot to him, particularly about his reference to righteousness as a guide to personal and political life, but seldom with satisfaction to either of us. We agreed that religion had been the moral foundation of the young American republic, and that in this century the country had increasingly departed from its religious moorings. Could it remain steady amidst all its new responsibilities and torments as a secular state? I asked him.

He agreed that the nation had suffered from the loss of its "forgotten foundation," and particularly that its leaders no longer served in their private lives and public actions as models for the respect and conduct of the people. But he was almost scornful of Judaism, the religion of his youth. He agreed, as he wrote in *A Preface to Morals,* that those who rejected orthodox religion found "a vacancy in their lives," that they missed the conviction that there was "an order in the universe that justified their lives because they were part of it." Nevertheless, he felt that modern man could find a testament of faith outside orthodox religion.

He believed in a new moral foundation of humanism, that there could be an intellectual basis for morality, and that when people found that they no longer believed seriously and deeply that they were governed from heaven, there was "an anarchy in their souls until by conscious effort they find ways of governing themselves." I had lived too long under the influence of my parents' faith, and remained too skeptical of man's ability to govern himself, to go along with this philosophy, and I thought that even if he was right his habit of denouncing his own religion as "a piece of blatant hypocrisy" was insensitive and even cruel.

"If I think religion makes people try to be more decent and considerate, why condemn it?" I asked him. He liked to write about this, but he didn't like to talk about it. I sat with him several times during his dying days in New York and ventured to ask him once if he had changed his mind, but he said he had not.

He was never a defender of the status quo. He believed we were living in a revolutionary age, which required leadership, purpose, and order. "A modern nation," he insisted, could not be built by "Georgia crackers, poverty-stricken Negroes, the homeless and helpless of the great cities. They make a governing class essential." He was an elitist who believed in government by the elites, but he knew nothing about the lives of the poor. What he was seeking, he said, was "the substitution of conscious intent for unconscious striving."

It was this elitist posture that irritated his critics, who took pleasure in attacking him personally when they couldn't deal effectively with his arguments. Many of them thought he was brilliant but callous. He made many friends, but also many enemies, for example, Dean Acheson, who thought Lippmann theorized too much about "the Western traditions of civility" and "the good society" without bothering to consider the practical obstacles to these admirable objectives. He was bitterly resented by his fellow Jews for supporting a quota for Jews at Harvard and for writing so little about the horrors of the Holocaust. He was never a Zionist, for he feared that an independent Jewish state in a hostile atmosphere would create the disorder he hated.

I always found him appealingly sensitive to the feelings of other people in his own privileged circle, though sometimes his verbal cruelties were unintentionally wounding. For example, though he wrote with great nobility about fidelity to the family, he showed little affection as an adult for his own parents, describing his mother as "a little too ambitious and worthy," and his father as a successful businessman "without much color or force." Also, he ran off with Helen Armstrong, the wife of Hamilton Armstrong, the editor of *Foreign Affairs* and one of his best friends. She was a good wife to Lippmann, fierce in her opinions, and vindictive to his critics. She had an unhappy end. During his long and final illness, she could not bear the isolated vigils at his bedside, and called Sally and me one evening saying she had to come back to Washington to get away and see her friends. This she did and was stricken on the way back to New York and died without seeing Lippmann again.

Nevertheless, to the end of his eighty-five years he demonstrated the capacity of the daily newspaper to provide large audiences for philosophical analysis of the news. Though he was aware of the sorrows of the world, and for a time despaired for the future of democracy, he never really lost his hope that it would one day prevail, and it was one of my regrets, sixteen years after his death, that he did not live to see the great year of 1989, when the last of the empires collapsed in Eastern Europe and many of his dreams of freedom and liberty came true.

# CHAPTER 17

# Dean Gooderham Acheson

OF THE FIFTEEN secretaries of state I covered, Dean Gooderham Acheson was, I believe, the best of the lot, and he would not have regarded this as an unwarranted or even as a very generous compliment, for he had a limited regard for those who preceded and followed him in these fifty years, with the possible exception of General George C. Marshall. He was smarter than most of his colleagues in the Truman cabinet, but not smart enough to hide it. He looked more like a British foreign secretary than any British foreign secretary I ever saw. He was a little shorter than the Washington monument: erect, elegant, dogmatic, and ironically witty. Accordingly, as one of his associates remarked, "Dean was not the sort of man you'd hand your hat to by mistake."

In a quieter time, he would probably have been bored, but during the clash of armies and the collapse of empires he was constantly in collision, his favorite element. He respected the professionals in his department, and had the confidence of his president, an unusual combination; the foreign ambassadors in Washington, accustomed to the meanderings of the likes of Cordell Hull, Edward R. Stettinius, and Jimmy Byrnes, responded to his intelligence with unaccustomed relief.

I saw him from time to time in his morning walks to work with Justice Felix Frankfurter. They were a photographer's delight, the best Mutt and Jeff parade in town, and occasionally I was summoned to his office to listen to his favorite lecture on the invincible stupidity of the press. He could intimidate a room full of reporters with a twitch of his mustache, but as a good lawyer, he was responsive to brief intelligent questions and derisive of the opposite. In short, I liked the guy and occasionally wondered why.

He was the strategist for peace in the Truman administration, and spent a long apprenticeship there before reaching the top. Some remarkable men spend a lifetime in Washington reaching for a job they never get. Others get it and wish they hadn't, but Dean Acheson was different. He longed to be solicitor general but never got it. Roosevelt wanted to make a judge of him, and he wouldn't take it. He started as under secretary of the treasury and wasn't successful at it, but as secretary of state he was clearly the right man in the right job at the right time.

He didn't have an easy task. In fact, he was attacked more viciously than any other secretary of state in the entire Cold War period, but he was proud of his enemies, including, of course, Senator Joseph McCarthy of Wisconsin and Senator William E. Jenner, Republican of Indiana. He regarded McCarthy as "essentially a lazy, small-town bully" who would have had little influence without the support of Senator Robert A. Taft of Ohio and other conservative Republican leaders. Unlike Secretary of State Dulles, who avoided open conflict with McCarthy, however, Acheson made no concessions to what he called "the attacks of the primitives," explaining that he found it difficult to conceal his "contempt for the contemptible." Though the Soviet leaders regarded him as their most effective opponent, Acheson was accused of everything from insolence to treason.

His central ideas were simple enough. Unlike his successors, he thought a secretary of state should stay on the job in Washington instead of flying around the world to other capitals. He didn't believe that peace could be maintained by good intentions and a bad military organization. "Charm never made a rooster," he was always saying. His trust in the brotherhood of man, or even the sisterhood, was somewhat limited. He preferred peace to war and argument to absurdity. He helped get the United States into the United Nations but didn't think much of that organization. He was derisive of both the new isolationists and the one-world internationalists. When many others in Washington thought an alliance of the free nations was unthinkable, he insisted it was indispensable. He bet on power and collective security, and more than any other man he suggested the policies that dominated the nation's foreign policy in the generation after the Second World War.

In fact, if you're looking for the decisive point in the politics of the twentieth century—the emergence of the United States from isolation to the protection of Western civilization—the place and time are Washington in the late forties and early fifties, and Acheson, in my view, was the central figure in the drama. He had little interest in the struggling countries of the Third World, but he did more for U.S. participation in the reconstruction and defense of Europe than any other official. The newspapers called the European recovery program "the Marshall Plan" and the decision to defend Greece and Turkey "the Truman doctrine," but they had the wrong labels. Acheson was really the principal architect of these policies, with considerable help from Assistant Secretary of State Will Clayton, George Kennan, and Ambassador Chip Bohlen, and by a combination of intelligence, persistence, and calculated anticommunism, he also persuaded and frightened the Senate into ratifying the North Atlantic Treaty Organization.

He had a number of qualities that were not widely distributed in Washington. He could think and say clearly what he thought. Even more surprising, he could stick to the main point. He liked to define his policy objectives before making decisions on the theory that there should be some connection between what he was saying and where he was going. He hated what he called "ad hoc-ery"—mindless actions unrelated to one another. He was a superb committee chairman, patient or tyrannical by turn. He was intolerant of windbags, and above all he knew what he wanted, an astonishing achievement in government circles.

For example, he favored Truman's decision to send aid to Greece and Turkey, but not to send more billions to China when the Nationalists, in his judgment, were defeated. When he was told that this was "inconsistent" with Truman's doctrine of opposing communism anywhere in the world, he demonstrated his gift of argument and his willingness to put his head through the canvas.

"The United States, in my judgment," he told the pro-Nationalists in the Senate Foreign Relations Committee, "acts in regard to a foreign nation strictly in regard to American interests or those wider interests which affect it. And if it is to American interest or those wider interests which affect it to do one thing in one country and another thing in another country, then *that* is the consistency upon which I propose to advise the president. And I am not in the slightest bit worried because somebody can say, 'Well, you said so and so about Greece, why isn't all this true about China?' I will be polite. I will be patient, and I will try to explain why Greece is not China, but my heart will not be in the battle."

Acheson attributed his habit of clear definition to the day when as a young lawyer he was presenting an interminable and incoherent argument before the Supreme Court, and Mr. Justice McReynolds leaned over the bench and said to him, "Counselor, what is this case all about?" Acheson took this as a command for clarity and brevity and he obeyed it from then on. He worked all the fat out of a problem until he got down to the bone, and then stuck to it. This was, he often suggested to me, not a bad idea for reporters, a tip I tried to remember, not always with success.

He came to Washington out of Yale and Harvard Law School and got a job through Frankfurter as clerk to Mr. Justice Brandeis at the end of the First World War. He and his wife, Alice, lived down the street from Sinclair Lewis. His first important job was as under secretary of the treasury, where he differed with Roosevelt over monetary policy and resigned. His only consolation about this was that in later years, while he didn't even get a reply to his letter of resignation, Roosevelt praised him as a man who knew how to resign with "style."

The word was significant. Everything about Acheson had a kind of personal grandeur. His appearance, his writing, his speech, his wit, his manners, and especially his astonishing mustache, which was a triumph of policy planning. As the son of a Connecticut bishop, he inherited a liberal nature, but he disliked speculative argument and dreamy idealism. By his training in the law, he learned to overcome obstacles by careful research and definition. He had a gift for "lopping off the heads of tall poppies," and his sharp dissents drew blood, often to his regret. "Let's get the question straight," he would say, looking at his questioners with an air of gentle pity.

He was too decorative and too candid to be popular with the back-slappers on Capitol Hill, but his intelligence, precision, and wit impressed the Allied diplomats during that critical passage from war to peace. In those days, the major nations were sending their best diplomats to Washington, among them Oliver Franks of Britain, Mike Pearson of Canada, and Henri Bonnet of France. Lord Franks, as he was in the eighties, recalls an incident that illustrates Acheson's decisiveness and his influence on Truman.

In December of 1950, Mr. Truman, who had ordered the atomic bombing of Hiroshima and Nagasaki, made a casual remark indicating that he wouldn't hesitate to do it again under circumstances he didn't bother to define. Prime Minister Attlee of Britain was alarmed and immediately arranged a meeting with the president in Washington. They met alone in the private quarters of the White House, and

Truman not only reassured Attlee but also agreed that the United States would not use the atomic bomb again without the approval of the British government. In addition, they wrote out a communiqué to this effect in private.

Acheson was appalled. No president, he was sure, could imagine what military problems would arise in the future or allow another nation to veto the use of the atomic bomb, nor would Congress approve any such arrangement. Lord Franks recalls what Acheson did when Mr. Truman announced the British veto in the Oval Office: "At this point, I saw Dean having the equivalent of convulsions. Within two minutes, there were five of us in the president's office: the president, the prime minister, Bob Lovett, Dean Acheson, and I. Dean began to do what he called 'unachieving' the agreement. It was really the most remarkable exhibition—quite short, absolutely devastating, serious, impassioned—and it was utterly convincing. (He had merely eliminated the veto and substituted a promise to 'consult' the British.) And when he had finished, nobody had anything to say.

"So," Franks concluded, "the denouement of that was that there were no chairs somehow in the president's office. We had to pull out a sliding panel of his desk, and I had to kneel down beside it to write out a revised communiqué in the light of what had been reachieved. And while I was doing this, the president suddenly turned to me and said, 'How often do you think a British ambassador has knelt before the American president?' "

In his lighter moments, Acheson liked to propose with mock seriousness simple solutions to complicated problems. For example, I found in my notes an account of a luncheon conversation with him dated January 10, 1970. He was complaining that President Nixon and Secretary of State William Rogers were lost in the confusions and ambiguities of the Israeli-Arab conflict, but he remarked, almost blithely, that "the solution is really very simple.

"We have trouble with the Arabs," he said, "because they have power. Their power comes not from their intelligence but from their oil. Therefore, we must make their oil irrelevant. This can be done," he added in the glow of a second martini, "in two ways: first, we must stop producing electrical power with fossil fuels and produce it entirely with atomic energy. And second, we must eliminate the internal combustion engine and substitute electric cars for transportation."

This reminded me of the story Chip Bohlen used to tell when he was the U.S. ambassador to the Soviet Union: A grasshopper had trouble getting through the winter and asked a cockroach how to manage it. "Very simple," said the cockroach. "At the sign of the first frost, you find a nice warm bakery, make a place for yourself in a cozy bed of flour in back of a radiator, and turn yourself into a cockroach."

"But how do I do that?" asked the grasshopper.

"Look," replied the cockroach, "I'm merely giving you policy guidance."

Acheson had a way of picking out the significant sounds from the background noise. Even on Capitol Hill, where exaggeration is a disease, he practiced the art of understatement. When he was denounced by some of his critics who proposed to cut off his salary and impeach him, he responded by saying that "in that event, my position could become unenviable."

It was Acheson who, in a more serious mood, advised Roosevelt how to get the overage destroyers to the British before Pearl Harbor, and who wrote out the strategy for defeating Wendell Willkie in the 1940 presidential election. At Roosevelt's request, he produced a memorandum for Harry Hopkins, and as usual it was studded with questions. "Is this a time to trust the party which has let us drift to the very brink of disaster with assurances that recovery is just around the corner?" he asked.

He made speeches with a clear definition of his objectives. "We must make ourselves so strong that we shall not be caught defenseless or dangerously exposed in any even possible eventuality. The future is unpredictable. Only one thing—the unexpected—can reasonably be anticipated. . . . I waste no time arguing the metaphysics of defensive as against offensive weapons. Nothing seems to me more foolish than a policy designed to assure that if we must fight, the fighting shall be upon our own territory. In a situation as confused and dangerous as this . . . you can be wrong only once. If I may quote Justice Holmes: 'The judgment of nature upon error is death.' "

Noting all this, Roosevelt drafted him into the State Department just before Pearl Harbor, and he spent the war years haunted by the power and menace of Hitler and the appeasement policy of Chamberlain. The absence of American will and power, he believed, had encouraged the Nazis, and only the power and leadership of the United States, he insisted, would restrain the Communists.

As the U.S. prosecutor in the angry debates with the Soviets, he tried for a while to apply reason to political differences, but his sense of humor occasionally overcame his sense of history. When Andrei Vishinsky prolonged an argument over whose item on the agenda should go first, Acheson proposed the experiment of having the "cart and the horse" work in tandem. And when Vishinsky tried to get him to agree to a deal whereby all foreign troops would go home, leaving the U.S. Army three thousand miles away and the Soviets just over the river, Acheson reverted to scorn: "Now I say in all conscience that argument is not worthy of the Council of Foreign Ministers. It is just as full of propaganda as a dog is full of fleas. In fact, I say it's all fleas and no dog." He did not, however, expect to win all arguments with the Soviets. When he lost or had to cut a deal, he would sometimes say the result was "just right." And when he was asked what that meant, he would laugh and say, "If it had been any better, I wouldn't have got it, and if it had been any worse I couldn't have swallowed it."

He was less restrained in his tactics. He thought that Hitler and Stalin had similar objectives—to weaken the democracies and dominate the politics of the world. He emphasized this point knowing that anticommunism was the best, maybe the only, argument that would persuade the Congress to build an effective defense of the free world. But he never forgot that the Nazis had to be defeated in war, while the Soviets, in a world of atomic weapons, had to be deterred from resorting to a nuclear war nobody could win. He wanted to stretch American power far from home. "I think it clear that with a nation, as with a boxer," he said, "one of the greatest assurances of safety is to add reach to power."

This brought him into direct conflict with George Kennan, who agreed with him that the containment of Soviet power and expansion was essential, but thought this was primarily a political and not a military problem. Kennan, first as ambassador to the Soviet Union and later head of the State Department's policy-planning staff, thought it was a mistake to confuse the Russians with the Nazis. He believed the Truman doctrine was excessively grandiose and military. He opposed the advance of MacArthur's armies beyond the 38th parallel in Korea. He thought the development of the hydrogen bomb was a mistake, and he thought Acheson's support of the French in Indochina was both unnecessary and stupid. After this, Kennan was soon practicing freedom of speech at Princeton.

I admired these two men more perhaps than any other officials in Washington and regretted their disagreements. I thought Kennan put too little emphasis on military power and Acheson too much, but

Acheson had power and Kennan didn't. When the Chinese warned Truman that they would intervene in Korea if MacArthur's armies approached their borders, Acheson thought they were bluffing and was wrong, and he was less reliable as an adviser when he was out of office than when he was in. It took him a long time to lose faith in the conquest of Vietnam, but his belated switch helped turn President Johnson around. His advice to President Kennedy on Khrushchev's threat to Berlin was almost recklessly belligerent, and his judgment on the Bay of Pigs disaster was almost as bad as Kennedy's. On the big questions for which he had responsibility, however, no secretary of state in my time earned so much gratitude or got so little.

He was a complicated character. He liked reporters—of his own choosing—but hated the press. He was always wagging his head sorrowfully at my persistent questions. Once, after I had printed several stories that were true but embarrassing to him, he instructed his colleagues in the department not to see me or answer my calls. He said I was going around picking up one fact here and another there, and "Pretty soon that Scotchman," he predicted, "will make off with the State Department's safe." He constantly insisted that the newspapers couldn't even get names straight, and just for fun I offered one day during the postwar Senate debates to put an end to the confusion about the authorship of the Truman and Marshall plans by attributing them to him. He did not deny that this would be more accurate but was not amused by my mischievous suggestion, for in those days his intelligence was matched only by his unpopularity, and his guess was that anything with his name on it would probably be defeated.

To assure passage of the security legislation, he selected every word, memorized every clause, and anticipated every possible objection. He was also a master of minor deceptions. He didn't merely consult Senator Vandenberg, the chairman of the Senate Foreign Relations Committee, he courted and educated him, and what was more to the senator's liking, flattered him into compliance. He was less successful with another chairman of that committee, Senator Tom Connally of Texas, who was always complaining that "Acheson worries too much about all them two-bit countries."

He was so sure of the importance of the Marshall Plan and the NATO alliance that occasionally he even reached out for the cooperation of the press, not his favorite pastime. He couldn't very well denounce what he regarded as the impenetrable stupidity of the congressional opposition or complain publicly about its devious practices, but he wasn't above providing a few of us with evidence of their absurdities in the hope that we would expose the limitations of his detractors. Also, when he sent up a trial balloon for the Marshall Plan in a speech at Cleveland, Mississippi, he saw to it that Leonard Miall of the British Broadcasting Corporation and one or two other Fleet Street reporters were advised in advance about his dramatic proposal. He did not tip me off, however, because he was afraid that his remarks, if prominently reported at home, would provoke opposition in Congress. The result was that *The New York Times* ran only a few paragraphs deep inside the paper.

No reporter, however, ever betrayed his trust more than once. His insistence on the privacy of his conversations was total, and his punishment for infractions was instant and enduring banishment. I was, from time to time, on his blacklist and then the word would go out from his seventh-floor office not that I had broken the rules of confidentiality, but that I was "getting too nosy." On such occasions, when I called his principal aides, they were invariably and mysteriously "in conference" or "out to lunch."

His capacity for tolerating legislative bores whose votes he needed was inexhaustible, at least in public, but in private his verbal cruelties were often indiscreet and even offensive. For example, once when President Johnson called him in for advice during the worst days of the Vietnam War, he told the president, "The cross you have to bear is a lousy Senate Foreign Relations Committee chairman. You have a dilettante fool [J. William Fulbright of Arkansas] at the head of that committee." Later he came to believe that Fulbright's judgment on Vietnam as "an unwinnable war" was right, but as on many other occasions, he forgot the offending remark though the object of his wounding jibes did not.

He was not foolproof. His failure to heed China's warning that it would enter the Korean War if the United States approached the Chinese border was a major blunder. He shared Roosevelt's opposition to the continuation of French colonial rule over Indochina after World War II, but when France insisted on it as a price for joining the European Defense Community or NATO, he called it blackmail but went along with it, and he approved the first U.S. aid to Vietnam. This was understandable, but it started the slide that ended in disaster long after he was out of office.

Occasionally, his stylish ways led him into trouble. When Alger Hiss, a State Department colleague accused of Communist sympathies, was convicted of perjury, the reporters asked for Acheson's reaction. "I should like to make it clear to you," he said, "that whatever the outcome of any appeal which Mr. Hiss or his lawyer may take in this case, I do not intend to turn my back on Alger Hiss." That was the next day's headline, but it wasn't all he said, and for once he didn't make his meaning clear. He went on to say that each person could decide for himself about Hiss, but his personal views of the matter were quite firm. They had, he said, been stated on the Mount of Olives "and if you're interested in seeing them you will find them in the twenty-fifth chapter of the Gospel according to St. Matthew." But you had to look them up and study them from the thirty-fourth verse to the forty-sixth to understand that he was not really questioning the judgment of the court but merely saying in a roundabout way that when a friend is in trouble, you don't turn your back on him. The *Times* allowed me to print all thirteen verses and he thanked me for it, but the whole controversy could have been avoided if he hadn't been so fancy and had merely said, "I never kick a colleague when he's down."

To relieve his frustrations in office, Acheson grew dahlias and took up cabinetmaking at his farm in Sandy Spring, Maryland, where he built a workshop for himself and a studio for his lovely wife, Alice, a talented painter. Sally and I went to dinner with them once, and Alice showed us a handsome new table he had brought into the hall of his Georgetown house. Mrs. Acheson explained: "He likes to make these things. When he completes one, it either stands or falls. It's not like a foreign policy; he doesn't have to wait twenty-five years to see how the thing comes out."

When he left the State Department, I called on him one day at his old law firm of Covington and Burling and made the mistake of asking him how he liked being back in his old office. "I hate it," he said. "I sit here getting more money for more people who don't need it or deserve it. After State, I hate it." I urged him to write his memoirs as an escape, especially since he could look back on an interesting life. Acheson said that others had made the same point and he did go on and produce several wise and graceful books of reflections on politics and diplomacy, one of which, *Present at the Creation,* won the Pulitzer Prize.

But there was a problem. When he came to Washington as clerk to Mr. Justice Brandeis, he was invited along with the other clerks to an occasional tea at the home of Mr. Justice Holmes, who reflected casually for the adoring clerks on the mysteries of the law and the follies of lawyers. Acheson was so impressed by the wisdom of this venerable monument that he would go right home and put the old man's remarks in his private notebooks.

Until one day his wife said she thought this was a violation of the judge's privacy. Acheson apparently did not take kindly to this act of bravery and love, but his wife insisted that he put the question to Holmes, who handed down a peremptory judgment: no privacy for his talks . . . no more talks. Acheson went home and burned his notebooks. This incident made such an impression on him that he kept no personal record of his stewardship in the government, didn't even take away copies of his official papers, and thus had few notes to guide his writing in retirement.

He had been lucky in his enemies—McCarthy, Nixon, and MacArthur, among others—and had been savagely criticized for being "soft" on communism when he was in office and criticized again when he was out, for being excessively tough on Communists in Cuba, Vietnam, Korea, and Berlin. He did not, however, as I expected and as so many other officials had done, settle old scores in his memoirs. Instead, he concentrated on his pleasant memories and on the colleagues he admired the most. He did not fail to express his admiration for President Truman, but he skipped his distaste for President Kennedy, and he followed this rule in writing about his early life. For example, he wrote about his days at Yale, when he was happy, but not about his prep school days at Groton, when he was not.

For a while, he even took to writing fiction. My wife wrote to him once in praise of his stories. He sent back a handwritten note as follows: "They were written," he said, "by a close relative of the same name who showed great and early promise, but who unhappily took to drink. For many years he tried to write serious books but could never stay really sober to the end. Recently, I have encouraged him to write fiction and gave him some leads. Your note delights me into the belief that the poor but gifted chap may finally have found his métier."

This, of course, was a spoof, for unlike President Johnson, Acheson led a moderate life to the end. But like many others who miss the hurly-burly of power, he felt amputated when separated in retirement from the satisfactions and even the agonies of official life. "It was like the end of a love affair," he said.

In Lord Keynes's words, "Acheson was skeptical of most things except those that chiefly matter, affection and reason." He looked back on the most dangerous and decisive days of the Cold War, on the ghosts of Hitler and Chamberlain, and on the trust and affection of Truman with modest satisfaction. "Our efforts for the most part left conditions better than we found them," he said in what must be the most understated epitaph of recent history.

When he put electric lights in his old farm house in Sandy Spring, he gave Sally and me all his old kerosene lanterns for our little cabin at Fiery Run. "I have tried, without success," he told me, "to light your way. Maybe these will help." He also left me his favorite quotation from Joseph Conrad: "What one lives for may be uncertain; how one lives is not. Man should live nobly though he does not see any practical reason for it, simply because in the mysterious, inexplicable mixture of beauty and ugliness, virtue and baseness in which he finds himself, he must want to be on the side of the virtuous and the beautiful."

# CHAPTER 18

·········································································

# *Vandenberg:*
# *An Unlikely Tale*

WITHOUT THE HELP of Senator Arthur Vandenberg of Michigan, even Acheson with all his skill might have lost the battle of Capitol Hill during the first critical phase of the Cold War at the end of the forties. Senator Vandenberg knew the power of isolationism—he had helped invent it—but he gave Truman and Acheson the formula for destroying it. The only way to get Congress to face up to the Russians, Vandenberg said every time I saw him, was "to scare hell out of the American people." It was a successful but costly formula, for while it did scare hell out of the American people, it also frightened and infuriated the Soviets.

I was often either predicting things that never happened in Washington or being astonished by things that did. If I informed the readers of the *Times* that Secretary of State What's-his-name was the one shining star in Foggy Bottom, within a month at most, the right honorable gentleman would inevitably make some bonehead move that delighted nobody but our enemies. Fortunately it also happened occasionally that remarkable and even historic events occurred as a result of unexpected deeds by improbable heroes. Vandenberg was to me the prize example.

I met him soon after I arrived in Washington in 1941, and I thought he was a pompous windbag. He was a big, loud, vain, and self-important man, who could strut sitting down. He never seemed in doubt about anything—a trait I assumed he had acquired as an editorial writer on the Grand Rapids *Herald*. But later I learned better, and thus he helped me to curb my Calvinist tendency to pass quick judgments on politicians. Many limited men, I later learned, achieved good things, and many good men did bad things.

Vandenberg spent most of his twenty-three years in the Senate proclaiming the glories of nationalism and his last few years denouncing its dangers. In short, he was that rare character—a public man who could change his mind—and he switched precisely when the war was coming to an end and a battered and divided world was wondering whether the United States would organize the peace this time or retreat.

If isolation had been the intent of the country, Vandenberg was clearly the man to replay the destructive role of Senator Henry Cabot Lodge after the First World War, and to repeat the tragedy of the League of Nations. He had been one of the leading isolationists in the Senate since his first election in 1928. He had led the fight against Roosevelt's policy of aiding the Allies, even after the fall of France. When the Lend-Lease Act was passed, he wrote in his diary, "I had the feeling that I was witnessing the suicide of the Republic. . . . If America cracks up, you can put your finger on this precise moment as the time when the crime was committed."

But when the Japanese bombed Pearl Harbor, he began to review his old assumptions and convictions, at first slowly and tentatively, until, as the end of the war approached, he finally turned right around and led his party to support the United Nations, to aid Greece and Turkey, and to support the North Atlantic Treaty Organization.

How did this conversion come about? Partly through the influence of his nephew, Hoyt Vandenberg, who later became Chief of Staff of the United States Air Force, and who insisted in many long talks with the senator that modern aircraft could vault our ocean moats and destroy the illusion of a secure and isolated America. John Foster Dulles, later secretary of state, also insisted to Vandenberg that both world wars had started because the Germans assumed the United States would remain neutral. But even at the beginning of 1945, the senator was still unsure how the United States could make clear in advance that it would intervene in any future war that threatened the peace of the world.

Thus, in the first days of that year, he began preparing what was later called "the speech heard round the world." He didn't see it in any such grandiose terms when he started to write it. He was alarmed, and with good cause, by Stalin's efforts to establish a ring of Communist states on the western and southern borders of the Soviet Union. He felt that the Soviet dictator was thinking only of a crippled postwar Europe dominated by the USSR, and that Roosevelt and Churchill, who were about to meet him at Yalta, were not opposing his aggressive diplomacy, particularly in Poland. Accordingly, Vandenberg, who had a lot of Polish supporters in Michigan, was determined to speak out before the Yalta Conference.

By accident I happened to be roaming the halls of the Senate Office Building one day early in January of 1945 and bumped into him. He asked me to come to his office, and he handed me the first draft of this speech. It was a sharp criticism of Stalin, and also of Roosevelt for not asserting America's interests in the postwar political and geographic settlements. It was tough, but it was accurate and fair. He asked me what I thought of it.

I said it was good as far as it went, but it was only half a speech. I added that it dealt with Stalin's outrageous actions, but didn't analyze why he was acting this way or what should be done about it.

We chewed this over for a while, and finally at his request I said the obvious thing: that Russia had been invaded first by Napoleon, and then almost overwhelmed by Hitler, and Stalin was determined to protect his country from the revival of German power in the future. Also, Stalin probably assumed the United States would retreat into isolation again when the war was over, and leave the Soviet Union with power to dominate the weakened Western Allies.

The only possible but probably unlikely remedy for this, I suggested, was to propose a postwar treaty of alliance by which the United States, Britain, France, and the Soviet Union would agree to oppose any future German aggression that would threaten the peace of the world. He seemed interested, but I went away thinking no more about it and was as surprised as everybody else when he delivered the speech on January 10, including precisely this unprecedented proposal.

The speech was an immediate sensation, and he later said he was astonished by its success. The *Chicago Tribune* called him "Senator Judas" when it wasn't denouncing him as "Benedict Arnold," but otherwise he was praised not only by some of the leaders of his own party, but by the internationalists and the opposition Democrats, and the editors and columnists who had condemned him throughout most of his political career.

Roosevelt didn't lead this chorus at first, but the senator was on the cover of *Time* magazine and the other weeklies, and he gave me much more credit than I deserved, saying in a news conference that I had put the idea of the treaty into his mind. In fact, he had talked it over with Dulles and others before rewriting the speech, and the irony of it was that my analysis of the problem proved to be wrong.

For when the administration finally got around to accepting the treaty proposal, the Soviets not only rejected it but also condemned it as a trick by the United States to intervene in the postwar affairs of Europe.

This did not surprise Vandenberg or divert him from his new role as founder and leader of the bipartisan—or as he called it, nonpartisan—foreign policy in the Senate. Roosevelt appointed him to the founding conference on the United Nations in San Francisco, where Vandenberg held court in a big fancy suite in the Fairmont Hotel for many of the leaders of the world. When Roosevelt died in April of 1945, President Truman sent Vandenberg to the first conference on the postwar peace settlements in London, where it was obvious that Moscow did not want to see the reconstruction of a democratic Europe, and this revived all the senator's anti-Soviet feelings. So when the British decided they could no longer protect Greece and Turkey from a Communist insurrection, he backed the Truman doctrine of blocking Communist expansion anywhere in the world.

It was not really the speech that converted him but the popular public reaction to the speech at home and abroad. He rode around the country warning one and all that the Russians were coming, and in the Senate he helped Truman by identifying all isolationist arguments before the issue came to the floor for debate.

He lived at that time in the Wardman Park Hotel, where Secretary of State Stettinius and his successors, Dean Acheson and General George Catlett Marshall, called on him regularly in the evening to make sure he understood and agreed with their plans. They accepted any innocuous amendment he suggested and told him they wished they had been bright enough to think of his point. He was delighted. Despite all his early prominence as a partisan and factional politician, nothing like this had ever happened to him before. He kept up an avalanche of correspondence, and it gave him immense pleasure to receive letters from Churchill and other leaders, who encouraged him in the belief that he was one of the leading statesmen of the world.

His written statements were masterpieces of confusion. He couldn't spell, but he could split more infinitives than a college freshman, and he seldom missed an opportunity to do so. He never used one word if three or four would do. He had an old battered portable typewriter, which he kept on his lap and pounded on for emphasis, capitalizing his main points and scattering superfluous exclamation marks and underlinings all over the page. Pity the poor copyreaders and biographers who had to decipher and give continuity to his mystifying clarifications and make sense out of his diaries, which flowed in torrents, often without dates, and then would go blank for weeks.

I came to admire Vandenberg's energy and tenacity. I lived up the street from him on Woodley Road and took advantage of his invitation to drop in any time, not entirely for unselfish reasons. For while he meant to be discreet, he was so excited about his new flood of official information and so eager to talk about it that I thought it only fair to relieve him of some of his burden. This did not amuse the State Department when his indiscretions appeared in the *Times,* but the last thing it wanted to do was get in dutch with its new ally in the Senate.

At no time did I ever hear Vandenberg suggest that he had been wrong in his isolationist views or his enduring conviction that Roosevelt had jimmied the country into the war. He hadn't changed his opinions about what was best for the country, he insisted. He kept saying it was the world that had changed, with the rise of the Soviets and the invention of atom bombs, and long after his famous speech that did so much to end the long era of isolation, he still retained his suspicion that the sneaky Democrats were up to some sort of monkey business behind his back.

For example, I heard about the Marshall Plan for the reconstruction of Europe weeks before General Marshall proposed it in a commencement speech at Harvard. I wrote a story about it, which led the front page of a Sunday *Times,* saying the administration was planning a five-year aid program that would cost around $17 or $18 billion. Vandenberg woke me up before seven the next morning to suggest, not for the first time, that I must be out of my mind. The Senate, he roared, would never swallow anything like that, and he would never support "any such goddamned foolishness." Later, he led the fight for its successful passage and never failed to take credit for its success.

He was reelected to the Senate in 1946 on the basis of his newly acquired prominence, without making a single campaign speech in Michigan, and also despite the fact that Roosevelt tried to beat him—an act Vandenberg never forgave. He was urged to seek the Republican nomination for president in 1948, but even at the height of his popularity, it never occurred to me that he was of presidential stature. I did, however, make the foolish mistake, not of endorsing him but of "stating the case" for him in *Life* magazine. The *Times* properly rebuked me for taking sides in the campaign. Besides, he was taking digitalis for a heart ailment at that time and his health declined steadily until he died at home in Grand Rapids on April 18, 1951.

In those last painful years, he thought a lot about his own conversion and even of writing a life of Saint Paul, the famous convert to Christianity. "Perhaps," his son wrote, "one of the reasons was that he found in the story of Paul an inspiration that sustained him in the trying days of his own conversion from isolation to a belief in collective safeguards for the maintenance of peace." The senator's last letter, dated March 7, 1951, was to President Truman, whom he addressed for the first time by his given name.

Dear Harry: I am deeply touched by your telegram of March 6. I know it is inspired by a long-time personal friendship which you and I enjoy. Your message is good for my morale. . . . I have abiding faith in the future of our good old U.S.A.

# CHAPTER 19

# *The*
# *Outsiders*

EVERY PRESIDENT IN trouble—the only kind we had—was surrounded by battalions of inside advisers, but like a man facing a serious operation, he usually felt the need of a second opinion, and often sought it from some disinterested mind on the outside. There were actually two kinds of presidents and two types of "outsiders." Some presidents couldn't stand advisers who were better informed than they were, and brought to the White House and the cabinet a few cronies who told them what they wanted to hear. But most of them weren't comfortable without the judgment of some old outsider, even when it hurt. I mention here in particular four of this latter type—John J. McCloy, who graduated from outsider to insider as assistant secretary of war and U.S. high commissioner to Germany; Jean Monnet, a Frenchman who influenced every president from Roosevelt to Kennedy; Associate Justice Felix Frankfurter, who had advice for everybody, including *The New York Times,* whether or not his advice was requested; and Clark Clifford, a shrewd political friend of Truman from Missouri.

They had several qualities in common. They didn't want anything, an unusual trait in Washington. Except for Clifford, they were all little guys with more than the normal supply of both physical energy and brains. They were all self-confident and optimistic even during the alarming deadlines of the Second World War and the Cold War, and no story of this remarkable period would be complete without a glimpse at their character and achievements.

## JOHN J. McCLOY

Jack McCloy was sort of a magnet for people in trouble. He was trusted in both the White House and the Congress, an unusual achievement in our suspicious capital. He was a plain, spunky, cheerful man who listened to people, really listened, and who never saw a problem he didn't think he could solve. He came to Washington early in the Second World War as an assistant to Secretary of War Stimson. He attracted Roosevelt because he was one of a group of men who helped form the Council on Foreign Relations in New York City to combat isolationism after World War I. He had made an international reputation as a lawyer in a famous case against the German government for plotting the Black Tom munitions explosions in Hoboken, New Jersey, during the First World War. Stimson used him first in counterespionage, and later as his liaison with foreign governments. It was Stimson's view that nobody in the cabinet ever handled a critical problem in the days after Pearl Harbor without "having a word with McCloy."

Sally introduced me to the McCloys. Early in the Second World War, they moved into a house across the street from us in Georgetown at the corner of Volta Place and Thirty-third Street, and on their first night, Ellen McCloy, having to produce one of her husband's sudden dinner parties, found she had no roasting pan and borrowed one from Sally. That started a long family friendship. Their son Johnny was about the same age as our eldest son, Richard, and Ellen always drove them to St. Albans school together on cold wintry mornings, counseling these two youngsters in the backseat to put their hands under her fur collar to keep them warm. Thereafter, whenever I had occasion to thank McCloy for some bit of information, he often replied with a smile, "Thanks, too, for the roasting pan."

I liked him for various reasons. He had a sense of humor, for one thing. He was blamed for the absurdities of that five-ring circus called the Pentagon. It was for a time nicknamed "McCloy's Folly," and he delighted in telling the story of the Western Union boy who got lost there trying to deliver a telegram and in the confusion was appointed a colonel in the air force. More important, he had the good lawyer's gift of studying not only the problems of his client, but also the problems of his adversaries. He had the good fortune to be born poor and later to live most of his life among the rich, understanding both. He lost his father when he was six and was raised by a strong mother in Pennsylvania. She ran a hairdressing parlor, saw him through Amherst College, and even moved to Cambridge, Massachusetts, and looked after him there when he went to Harvard Law School.

The main thing I learned from McCloy was that the important thing in Washington was not only what decisions were made but also how they were made. Did the president decide on his own? If not, who advised him? Did he hear all sides of the issue before acting? Who was in the room at the time and who wasn't in the room who should have been there? "Everybody talks about the decision-making process," he told me one day, "but often there's no process and usually something or somebody is left out."

His favorite example was the decision to release the atom bomb on Hiroshima and Nagasaki at the close of World War II. Jean Monnet, whose story comes later, had told me McCloy was upset about how this decision was reached, and since I always went to see officials who were "upset," I called on him for an explanation, but he wouldn't talk to me about it at the time.

He was not the sort of official who participated in decisions and then blew off about how much better things would have been if his rejected advice had been taken. I badgered him about this, arguing that we'd never get an effective decision-making process if secrecy and modesty covered up the mistakes of the past. At least, I insisted, he should tell the story of the bomb in his memoirs. He began writing them in his eighties, and promised me an advance copy, but he was looking after his beloved and ailing wife, Ellen, at the end and never finished them. His son Johnny and daughter Ellen, however, kept his promise and gave me the relevant part of his unfinished manuscript about the bomb. It is the main source of the following account of that event.

McCloy was not against using the bomb. He thought it should, if necessary, be used but only as a last resort and not before offering to amend the U.S. demand for unconditional surrender by promising to allow the Japanese emperor to remain as a constitutional monarch. He also favored dropping it first on an uninhabited area in the hope, if not the belief, that sparing the symbol of the emperor and demonstrating the terrifying power of the bomb without killing tens of thousands of innocent civilians would produce the surrender he favored.

He agreed with President Truman and with Stimson, whom he greatly admired, that the objective of the United States must be the earliest possible end of the war with the fewest possible casualties.

He showed me one day in 1945 a summary of the military problem: the United States had lost more men than it could count in its battles against the Japanese in the Pacific islands. Though the Japanese losses were much greater, their fighting was fiercer the closer it came to their home islands. On those islands of Kyushu and Honshu at the beginning of the summer of 1945, they had military forces numbering approximately 2 million men, and another 3 million in Korea, Manchuria, China, Formosa, the Philippines, French Indochina, Thailand, and Burma. On the basis of intelligence estimates by the War Department General Staff, Secretary Stimson told President Truman that invasion of the main Japanese islands might cost the lives of over a million Americans. McCloy did not quibble with this alarming prospect, but insisted that every alternative should be carefully discussed before the invasion date, set for November 1, 1945, on the southern island of Kyushu.

The first thing that impressed me about McCloy's unpublished memoir (see Appendix) was the part accident plays in historic decisions. Roosevelt had expressed doubts about whether the atom bomb should be used at all in the war, but he died just before the bomb was perfected. President Truman knew nothing about the bomb when he replaced Roosevelt, and apparently didn't share Roosevelt's moral doubts about its use. And, by coincidence, the long process of assuring that the bomb would actually work came to an end just when the decision had to be made about how to bring the war to a close. Also at that time, Truman had decided to replace Edward R. Stettinius as secretary of state, so nobody from the State Department attended the decisive meeting, not Under Secretary Joseph Grew, a former U.S. ambassador in Tokyo, who probably knew more about the Japanese power structure and psychology than anybody in Washington, or Dean Acheson, the assistant secretary of state, who had never even heard about the bomb until he read in the newspapers about its destruction of Hiroshima.

The decision to invade Kyushu and use the bomb was taken at the White House on June 18, 1945, just before the president left for the Potsdam Conference with Stalin and Churchill. It was also an accident that McCloy attended that meeting. Secretary of War Stimson had a long talk with McCloy about the bomb and the planned invasion the day before the June 18 meeting, but felt ill and asked McCloy to take his place. As it turned out, Stimson did attend and, despite McCloy's contrary advice, agreed with the other service chiefs and the Joint Chiefs of Staff on the plans for the invasion.

"As we were packing up to leave," McCloy recalled in his unpublished memoir, "the president noticed me and he said, 'McCloy, you didn't express yourself, and nobody gets out of this room without standing up and being counted. Do you think I have any reasonable alternative to the decision that has just been made?' I looked at Stimson and he said I should feel entirely free to express my views. So I said, 'I think you have an alternative that ought to be fully explored and that, really, we ought to have our heads examined if we do not seek some other method by which we can terminate this war successfully other than by another conventional attack and landing.' . . .

"I said [McCloy's memoir continued] that a political solution at this stage would not only be honorable but also highly desirable. . . . President Truman asked that I spell out what I meant. I said I would have him send [from Potsdam] a strong communication to the emperor describing our overwhelming military superiority and stating that we would demand a full surrender but one that would recognize Japan's right to continue to exist as a nation after ridding itself of the elements that had brought such destruction to the country; that this might include the continuation of the mikado but only on the basis of a constitutional monarch; access to necessary raw materials outside Japan but not such control over them as they had been planning. Then I said that if after such an offer no surrender was forthcoming, we should notify the Japanese of our possession of a weapon of revolutionary proportions and so devastating in its effect that it could destroy a city at one blow; that we would be compelled to employ it if they did not surrender. I said I was prepared to use the term *atom bomb* but realized that there was such an air of secrecy about it that we could use other words to describe its effect but they had to be graphic enough to be more compelling than the threat of Hitler's secret weapons had been."

After hearing this, the president instructed McCloy to take it up with Jimmy Byrnes, then serving as assistant to the president (he was not at the June 18 meeting), but Byrnes thought this would indicate American weakness. The upshot was that the communication sent to Japan from Potsdam a few days later demanded surrender but mentioned neither the emperor nor the bomb. McCloy went to Potsdam, and while he was not in the room with Truman, Stalin, and Churchill, he reports that when the president told Stalin about the bomb, Stalin simply said, "Well, that's fine. Let's use it. What's the next item on the agenda?" (After hearing about the bomb, however,

Stalin decided to invade Manchuria sooner than originally planned, though by that time Truman was not eager for Soviet participation in the war.)

McCloy made clear in his memoir that he did not question the good faith or intentions of those who favored using the bomb, but he concluded that surrender was attainable without using it, and he was particularly critical of the absence of the State Department when the decision was made. "At the June 18 meeting," he wrote, "it should not have been left to the assistant secretary of war to bring up the possibility of a political settlement. The secretary of state should have been present. . . . And the White House should take care to see that the ultimate decision maker—the president—is presented with a full consideration of all the plausible alternatives and options. This is what I was told he [Truman] asked for and what I believe he did not get."

At the end of the European war, McCloy talked General Jacob Devers out of bombing the famous walled city of Rothenberg in Germany, and after the war he was influential as U.S. high commissioner in drafting a democratic German constitution. During the missile crisis of 1963, when the Soviet Union tried to send nuclear missiles to Cuba, President Kennedy called him back from Europe, and McCloy and the Soviet deputy foreign minister, Vasily Kuznetsov, helped negotiate the withdrawal of those missiles during a long backyard conversation at McCloy's house in Connecticut. McCloy didn't serve all those years without criticism. He played a major role in the decision after Pearl Harbor to incarcerate the Japanese in California, including many born in the United States, though he did so on the instructions of Secretary Stimson.

President Carter was about the only president in my days in Washington who did not have a word with McCloy whenever there was trouble abroad, and President Reagan honored him with a ceremony in the Rose Garden of the White House on McCloy's ninetieth birthday. But by then, as he told Sally and me at Iphigene Sulzberger's, he was sorry the old foreign policy establishment was gone, and that his advice about how to reach foreign policy decisions had still not become common practice in Washington.

## JEAN MONNET

Jean Monnet was not only an adviser to presidents from Roosevelt to Kennedy but a student of human nature and a philosopher of diplomacy, and, like McCloy, he lived into his nineties. He did more for the unification of Europe than all the noisy politicians of his day. He was always quoting his friend Dwight Morrow as saying, "There are two kinds of people in politics: those who want to *be somebody,* and those who want to *do something.*" (He thought this also applied to journalists.) He did things—only a few carefully selected things— by being a connecting rod between people, by being obscure, patient, and obstinate, and never taking credit for what he did.

I met him first during the early days of the last world war in London, when he was head of the Anglo-French Coordinating Committee, and a lot of "be-somebodys" like Prime Minister Chamberlain, General de Gaulle, and Ambassador Kennedy were going their separate ways. "More progress is made by cooperation than by competition," Monnet was saying. "We will win this war and maintain the peace only when the political parties in the United States and the Allies learn that lesson."

He was born in 1888 into a family of Cognac vintners, and he worked for almost seventy years on the problems of the Western Allies. In both world wars he struggled with their differences. Through his efforts in favor of the Lend-Lease program and the Marshall Plan, he helped to save Britain and speed the liberation and recovery of Western Europe. He was a key figure in the early days of the League of Nations, and a financial adviser to China, Austria, and Poland. He even managed to soften the differences between General de Gaulle and President Roosevelt during the Second World War, an astonishing achievement.

He lacked all the attributes usually associated with politicians. He was almost invisible in the Allied meetings—a roly-poly rosy-cheeked little man, bald as a peeled onion. He lived simply at Houjarray outside Paris in an old farmhouse with a vast thatched roof that came down to the first-story windows like a hat over a man's eyes. He was not a very good public speaker, but he listened in four languages and won the trust of all the squabbling Allied leaders because he was precise, informed, and detached, and he never spoke ill of people or tried to displace them.

He got on with Roosevelt because they agreed there could be no Allied victory without Allied unity of command, and he established a warm relationship with President Kennedy because they shared the hopes of a unified alliance in the future. When Kennedy died, Monnet wrote: "Institutions are more important than men . . . but some men have the power to transform and enrich what institutions pass on to succeeding generations. Kennedy was one such man . . . but the bearers of hope are never of an age to die."

This was typically Monnet. I liked him because he could cry, as he did when Roosevelt died, but he did not allow his emotions to get in the way of his work. Near the end of his mother's life, he wrote to her every day, as he did to his wife, Silvia, when they were apart, but he had few close personal friends, and he kept his deepest personal feelings to himself.

He distrusted perfectionists, abstractions, and vapid idealism. He never grieved over the past but accepted life as a series of obstacles that he was sure could be overcome. Former Under Secretary of State George Ball, one of his many admirers, recalls that he was always saying with a shrug: "What has happened has happened, but it doesn't affect anything fundamental. The important thing is not for us to be deflected, not to lose momentum. We must find a way to go forward."

His advice was never very complicated. He was alarmed by the early German victories in the First World War and put them down to the fact that the German forces on land, sea, and air had a unified command, while the British and French commands were separate. That was his first imperative—joint Allied command in planning and action—and that was his theme again after the United States entered the war in 1941 after Pearl Harbor. Alone, we were amputated; together we were whole and could do anything.

Air power would be decisive in the Second World War as naval power had been decisive in the first, he insisted. He urged Roosevelt to think not in terms of building thousands of planes, but hundreds of thousands. He never doubted that the Allies would win the war even if Britain fell and Churchill had to move the British government to Canada. The only time I ever heard him express anxiety was after he had read an intercepted message indicating that the Germans were ahead in the invention of an atom bomb. (As a matter of fact, a review of the German secret files after the war proved that they were far behind the United States in that race for the decisive weapon.)

When Monnet died at the age of ninety-two, he was celebrated as the father of a united Europe, but he never talked in such grandiose terms. He knew the power of nationalism, and particularly the historic enmity of the Germans and the French, so he approached the problem, as usual, in practical terms. If Germany and France could merge their coal and steel industries, he felt, they would not only increase production in the short run but in the long run be forced to cooperate politically. This was the beginning of the European Coal and Steel Community, which eventually led to the Common Market.

Clarity and continuity were achieved by concentration on practical but limited objectives, he believed. He had a few things to say, and he kept saying them and saying them earnestly and sometimes tediously. "Oh, Jean," his wife, Silvia, said when my wife and I were visiting them one day at Houjarray, "even when we want to talk about the children you come back to the future of Europe." Monnet replied, "Yes, I want the children to have a decent Europe to come back to."

He was always writing notes to himself, but he was no writer. He didn't have a college degree. He didn't read a great deal; in fact, when he went to China as a young man, his father discouraged him from taking books on the ground that he could learn more by talking to and observing people. Yet before he acted or spoke at critical moments, he would jot down the main points on a notepad to make sure that what he said was precise and in keeping with his objective. All his papers were destroyed by the Germans when they occupied France, and his wife, for some mysterious reason, burned all his letters after he died, but he did define his beliefs in his memoirs, which were written with the help of his colleague André Fontaine. Thus he insisted on the following:

"1. It is a privilege to be born into our civilization. 2. Are we to confine these privileges within the national barriers and laws that protect us? 3. Or are we going to try to extend them to others? 4. At their origin at birth, people are the same. Later, drawn into a framework of rules, everyone wants to preserve the privileges he has acquired. The national framework supports this fleeting vision. We are unaware of the extraordinary privilege we enjoy. We must extend it to others. How can this be done? Only by freedom on the one hand and collective effort on the other, so as gradually to enable the underdeveloped countries to share in our privileges."

He talked about these things constantly in private, as if always trying to keep on course. "I liked to sit around the fire and talk about our underlying motives," he said. "I found that if those motives became obscure to others or to myself, we lost our way. We had to work to keep them alive, like the flames in the hearth we stared at as we tried to see our way through the problems."

His sense of history was better developed than his sense of humor. He was determined to do what he could to end the division of Germany and quell the anti-German feelings in Paris after the war. Some Frenchmen were saying in those days, "We like Germany so much that we're glad there are two of them." Monnet didn't think that was very funny.

He didn't live to see Mikhail Gorbachev's reforms in the Soviet Union, but he wouldn't have been surprised. "We won't change Russia," he once told me, "but the computers will." He never forgot the potential power of China. "Wait till China wakes up," he kept saying. "Then the Russians will realize that they are really part of Europe."

When the Nazis entered Paris in 1940, he convinced Churchill with some difficulty that this disaster required a dramatic declaration of the unification of Britain and France—not only with a unified command but also with one Parliament and common citizenship, committed to fight the war to a successful conclusion and cooperate in the reconstruction of Europe. This was uncharacteristic because he usually avoided dramatic political proposals, and even discouraged talk about a United States of Europe. But the conquest of France by the Nazis convinced him that some startling move must be made.

"We cannot live through these things separately," he wrote, "and we cannot tell our peoples that they must go on fighting for fighting's sake. The British and the French must be convinced that they share the same duty. Only then will they understand why the struggle must be pursued in Africa or in Britain and why there will be no defeat so long as both peoples together are not conquered. . . . The only catastrophe is to give in to oneself." In the end, this proposal of marriage was announced, but it never led to the stirring vision of "one parliament, one cabinet, one flag" that he suggested.

It was from him, on long walks through the woods in Houjarray and Washington, that I came to believe that you can defend a nation in this modern world only by defending its civilization. He had more maxims than McGuffey's *Reader*. "It is only when we climb that we see the new horizons," he would say. Or, "When you see a difficulty, never think that the people responsible are busy solving it. See to it yourself." He talked to people to nourish their hopes, lift their imagination, and inspire them not only to think but to act.

He hated shoddiness, triviality, vulgarity, and brutality. He was always walking early in the morning wearing a sweater under his jacket in the warmest weather, and reflecting on the next practical step, always confident that, as cooperation had led to progress in the village, and moved then from the village to the region, later from the region to the nation, so the nations would move in ever wider circles of cooperation.

Like Alexis de Tocqueville, he watched with constant admiration the great adventure of the American federal system, always pointing out that our states had not lost their identities by adopting a national constitution. Europe, he thought, would, very slowly, mesh its industries if not its politics if you gave it time to mature like the brandy in his father's warehouse.

He did not believe, even in the depths of the war, that all good rested on the Allied side and all wickedness on the side of our adversaries: "Let's face it: We in the West were not blameless." He knew how to fight the Allied differences while preserving their unity. "Some people refuse to undertake anything if they have no guarantee that change will work out as they planned," he would say. "Such people condemn themselves to immobility. Today no one can say what form Europe will assume tomorrow, for the changes born of change are unpredictable. But the sovereign nations of the past can no longer solve the problems of the present. We must push the obstacles before us; there is no going back."

This was his unvarying testament. Clear thinking and kindly feeling, humility, honesty, and above all, practicality. I call all this back now, for I realize only at the end of my life that the influences of one's youth, for good or evil, make all the difference, and it makes me appreciate my good fortune in the example of a great man like Monnet.

Accordingly, I remember him with admiration and affection, for he proved even in a cynical age that good men don't finish last, and that it wasn't essential to be noticed or have a great position to do good work and even achieve great things.

The French government tried to honor his memory by removing his remains from his village grave and burying them in the Panthéon in Paris. The intention was noble, but I cannot imagine that Monnet, always obscure, always modest, would have approved.

## FELIX FRANKFURTER

Justice Felix Frankfurter was a friend of both McCloy and Monnet. Most judges of the Supreme Court inhabited the higher and quieter regions of Washington in my days, avoiding the contamination of politics and the press, but Judge Frankfurter wasn't one of them. He not only was a political adviser to FDR and particularly to Secretary of State Acheson, but also wallowed in journalism and even had an accidental and unintended influence on my work in the Washington bureau of the *Times*. He disproved all my preconceptions of the judicial temperament. He was not aloof and he was not judicious. He never talked outside about the work of the Court, but he talked about everything else and was particularly interested in in the follies of reporters.

I never learned much about the advice he gave to Roosevelt, but I do know that he was instrumental in recruiting some of the most creative authors of the early New Deal legislation. He also introduced FDR to John Maynard Keynes, the British economist, who helped Roosevelt ease the burdens of the depression, and he brought Niels Bohr to the White House with information about the possibility of producing an atomic bomb.

He was close to both McCloy and Monnet and worked with them and others on rearming the nation and finding ways to assist the Allies in the critical days before Pearl Harbor. He knew how to interpret the laws, and how to get around them when the Congress was insisting on isolation and neutrality, and he was constantly telling me what he would write if he worked for *The New York Times*.

It was his view that his purchase of the *Times* in the morning entitled him to pass judgment on all its political crimes and grammatical misdemeanors, and when some particular outrage in the paper annoyed him, his driver, Tom Beasley, would appear at our door on Woodley Road and say, "The judge wants a word with you." He would seldom come in, but his "word," delivered in the backseat of his car, usually turned out to be a torrent of amiable abuse. For example, he kept insisting that our criticisms of the Court's decisions might be improved if we took time to read them. I remember with gratitude that he devoted very little time to listening, for usually I was stunned by the vigor of his argument and baffled by the problem of keeping up with the speed and volume of his thought.

I suppose that occasionally he got a good night's sleep or, when he was the guest of honor, left a party before anyone else, but I cannot prove this from personal experience, for he was always rattling along when I ran out of gas and headed home. As his friend Isaiah Berlin observed, "He talked copiously, with an overflowing gaiety and spontaneity. . . . He was a merciless persecutor of pretentiousness and humbug, but had an uncommon capacity for melting reserve, breaking through inhibitions, and generally emancipating those with whom he came in contact."

After his teaching days at Harvard, he seemed to miss the companionship of the young and was always giving me advice, most of it shrewd and original. Reporters lived only for the day, he kept telling me, there was no continuity to our lives. Therefore, he felt, I should be working on a long book, which probably I would never finish, but finishing it wouldn't matter. What mattered, he insisted, was that I should be thinking about yesterday and tomorrow as well as today, for as I grew older it was important to have some sort of connecting line where I could hang my fleeting thoughts.

He talked a great deal about how his clerks in the Court kept him in touch with the rising generation. Many of the torments of Washington, he observed, could be traced to old politicians and editors— he didn't mention judges—who "lived in a world that was gone." I asked him one morning if it was true that he permitted the dean of the Harvard Law School to choose his clerks primarily on their academic record, and that he accepted them sight unseen. He said this was true, that Professors Henry Hart and Albert Sacks selected them not only on their grades but on their fondness for argument. I expressed surprise.

That would never work in the newspaper business, I said, for while academic excellence was welcomed and even admired in newspaper offices, many of our best reporters could run faster than they could think. He was not impressed by this heresy. Every writer on public affairs, he insisted, should have somebody around the office who knew his weaknesses and could challenge his judgments before these were inflicted on a long-suffering public. Accordingly, since I had a tendency to preach and repeat myself, I adopted his suggestion when I began writing a column, and applied his clerk system to my office.

Each year, with the permission of the *Times,* I looked around for some smart and confident young college graduate who helped me find that missing fact or quote, questioned my sermons, eliminated my repetitions, and reminded me when I had promised to do something or be somewhere. They were not my clerks but my partners, and while they were hired for only a year, it pleases me to realize that many of them, companions for a year and friends for a lifetime, went on to distinguished careers on the *Times* and elsewhere.

The judge helped me in other ways. "Posterity may or may not take our word for it," Archibald MacLeish once wrote, "but Felix

Frankfurter had more influence on more lives than any man of his generation." I learned from him to be careful about predicting what a judge would do after he was appointed for life to a place on the Supreme Court, or any other court. When Frankfurter himself was nominated, he was condemned as a liberal who would impose Roosevelt's philosophy on his opinions, but he turned out to be less liberal than his opponents predicted. Also, he was meticulous in his choice of written if not spoken language. For him, as for the Bible, "the beginning was the word," and he was constantly saying that a man should choose his words as carefully as he chose a wife.

You had to know his own wife, Marian, a lovely, witty, and wise woman, to appreciate the force of this point, and to understand, too, the importance he placed on family life. Andrew Kaufman, one of his clerks, recalls an incident that illustrates this particular aspect of his character.

"A particularly heated discussion between a law clerk and the justice ended early one evening with the justice charging the law clerk with intellectual arrogance," Kaufman reports. "The law clerk departed for home, and the justice telephoned the law clerk's wife immediately to tell her that he had been hard on her husband in the heat of discussion and hoped he had not given unintended offense. His advice: 'Meet your husband at the door with a dry martini in hand.' The only thing missing was the recipe for the drink. 'We can supply it—heated discussion mixed with concern, humor, and confidence in the wife's ability to put everything right.' That was the recipe for Felix Frankfurter's cocktail."

What I learned from this and tried never to forget was that private life and professional life could seldom be separated, and when later on, one of my colleagues was in a slump at the office, many times the reason was that his mind was on some misfortune or misunderstanding at home.

One of the saddest experiences for reporters in Washington is to watch the decline of once strong and wise officials. We last longer than most senators or presidents, probably because we don't have to stand for reelection, so we're still around when they are defeated and, deprived of influence, drift into sickness and death. Fortunately, this wasn't true of Frankfurter. He seemed relentlessly youthful until the end of his seventies, when he was suddenly stricken, and even then I could not believe he would not soon recover.

He never returned to the Court after that illness but moved out of his old house on Dumbarton Avenue and his book-lined library with his little carpet chair into a comfortable apartment on Massachusetts Avenue, where both he and his wife spent their last days in wheelchairs. He retained his love of reading and music to the end, and once when the Vienna Boys Choir came to Washington from the place of his birth, I asked their sponsor, Patrick Hayes, if they couldn't visit the judge and sing to him. This they did to his great pleasure. Before he died, he asked Dean Acheson to look over his "estate" and advise him how to distribute it, but after a lifetime of teaching and serving on the Court, there was nothing left to distribute.

### CLARK CLIFFORD

No list of "outsiders" would be complete without mentioning the role of Clark Clifford, whose memoir, *Counsel to the President,* tells us more about the influence of these periodic advisers than any other book on Washington during the Cold War period. I didn't know him well, but every good reporter in Washington from the days of President Truman to the administration of President Bush knew that Clifford was often summoned to the White House for advice during times of crisis.

It would be wrong to identify him with McCloy, Monnet, or Frankfurter, for he played a different part. He began under Truman during the Second World War as a White House insider with the modest title of assistant naval attaché, and ended as secretary of defense under Lyndon Johnson. All told, he held official positions for only six years, but for forty-five years he practiced law in Washington and practiced politics on the side, usually on behalf of Democratic presidents. I never had the impression that he allowed his easy access to the White House to interfere with the success of his legal practice.

President Truman, surprised by the hostility of the Soviets in 1945, asked Clifford in the summer of 1946 to give him a "second opinion" on the problem. With the help of George Elsey, his assistant, Clifford gave him a 100,000-page opinion in September of 1946. He went well beyond the warnings of George Kennan, describing the Soviet menace in the most alarming terms, and concluding: "The important point is that the United States must be prepared to wage atomic and biological warfare if necessary. The mere fact of preparedness may be the only powerful deterrent to Soviet aggressive action, and in this sense the only sure guaranty of peace." Some observers praised Clifford for persuading Truman to take the necessary military measures; others thought the Clifford memorandum contributed to the militarization of American policy for the rest of Clifford's public service. Truman ordered all copies of the memo destroyed, and, according to Clifford, Truman said: "If it leaked, it would blow the lid off the White House."

Clifford looked more like a president than any of the occupants of that office during my time. He was tall, attractive, increasingly courtly in his latter days, with silvery hair, a quiet confidential voice, and strong liberal convictions in favor of activist Democratic administrations. His career in government began and ended in violent controversy.

In May 1948, President Truman decided that the United States should recognize the state of Israel as soon as the British gave up their trusteeship over Palestine, but he had a problem. His secretary of state, George Marshall, whom he regarded as "the greatest living American," was against immediate recognition. So were Dean Acheson; Under Secretary of State Robert Lovett; George F. Kennan and Charles E. Bohlen, the Soviet experts; Secretary of Defense James V. Forrestal; Loy Henderson, assistant secretary of state for Near Eastern affairs; and Dean Rusk, then director of State's Office of United Nations Affairs.

President Truman, cognizant of this formidable opposition, and particularly fearful that General Marshall might resign over the recognition of Israel, gave Clifford the task of avoiding this embarrassment. I was supposed to be covering this story at the time, but never knew about the uncharacteristic vehemence of Marshall's objections until Clifford published his memoirs in 1991.

In a critical meeting in the White House on May 12, 1948, presided over by President Truman, Clifford made Truman's argument for recognition, with his own persuasive, quiet eloquence. He concluded it by saying: "I fully understand and agree that vital national interests are involved. In an area as unstable as the Middle East, where there is not now and never has been any tradition of democratic government, it is important for the long-range security of our country, and indeed the world, that a nation committed to the democratic system be established there, one on which we can rely. The new Jewish state can be such a place. We should strengthen it in its infancy by prompt recognition."

General Marshall responded: "Mr. President, I thought this meeting was called to consider an important and complicated problem in foreign policy. I don't even know why Clifford is here. He is a domestic adviser and this is a foreign policy matter."

"Well, General," President Truman said, "he is here because I

asked him to be here." But Marshall was not satisfied. He made clear
in his official account of this meeting that he thought Truman and
Clifford were engaged in a "transparent dodge" to win votes in the
presidential election of 1948, and finally, according to Clifford, said
to the president, "If you follow Clifford's advice, and if I were to vote
in the election, I would vote against you."

Clifford described this in his memoirs as "the most remarkable
threat I ever heard anyone make directly to a President. . . . Everyone
in the room was stunned. Here was the indispensable symbol of
continuity whom President Truman revered and needed, making a
threat that, if it became public, could virtually seal the dissolution
of the Truman Administration, and send the Western Alliance, then
in the process of creation, into disarray before it had been fully
structured." But it was not made public at the time, and by the most
patient negotiations, Clifford managed to avoid Marshall's resignation, though not his wrath. In fact, Marshall never spoke to Clifford
again or, according to the general's official biographer, even mentioned his name.

Thus, Clifford had a harder role than McCloy, Monnet, or Frankfurter. He was not only advising but operating and negotiating within
the government. It was often said of him that he thought of presidents not only as his clients but as his friends, and that he carried
out the presidents' wishes regardless of his own, but Clifford disproved this charge in the most dramatic way at the end of his long
career, when he used both his skills and his friendship to persuade
a reluctant President Johnson that he had to get out of Vietnam even
if this meant abandoning Johnson's determination not to be "the first
President to lose a war."

# CHAPTER 20

# The Night Churchill
# Came to Dinner

AS THE FORTIES came to an end, I had one last glimpse of
Churchill when he came to the *Times* for dinner and reflected on
Yalta, Stalin, Roosevelt, and the atom bomb. The date was March
28, 1949, when he was seventy-five, after his first term as prime
minister and before his second. I kept careful notes on the occasion.

He looked considerably more rounded fore and aft than when I
had seen him about a year and a half earlier. There was a curious
sort of grayness to his flesh, which gave me a start when he entered
the eleventh-floor dining room. I saw him take a quick look at the
scowling photograph of Mussolini in the gallery of big shots on the
wall, but he made no comment. He asked for a glass of tomato juice,
which I thought was newsworthy, but he corrected this impression
when the brandy was passed around, and he complained that everybody kept him talking so much that he didn't have time to drink.

I thought the old man snorted and lisped more than usual, but this
may have been induced by sobriety. He referred pleasantly but inaccurately to one of his forebears who had been "proprietor" of *The
New York Times,* though this gentleman, Mr. Jerome, had held only
15 percent of the stock from 1858 until 1868. He congratulated the
*Times* on its preference for "great themes" and suggested that we
would increase our influence by concentrating on thoughtful readers,
and decreasing our circulation by about a million. Since we didn't
have anything like a million readers, this proposal was received with
an envious sigh. After dinner, he said he would answer our questions
and did so in the following terms:

On the Russians and the bomb: If we ever found out that the

Russians were really manufacturing the atom bomb with any rapidity, he would put serious pressure on them and force a showdown. He added that one of the things he would do preliminary to forcing a showdown would be to send aircraft over the major cities of the Soviet Union, dropping leaflets in order to put pressure on the Soviet government to reach a general settlement. Since this seemed vaguely alarming, he was asked to elaborate and he then said, "You must take the occasion to let them know that if they exceed certain limits it is your intention to use the bomb without hesitation—if indeed that is your intention." It was an odd statement, for later he said with some pride that the British, like nature, never draw a sharp line but always smudge it.

On Yalta: It was not fair to judge the decisions of chiefs of state at a conference held in the midst of war by the political questions that arise after the end of the war. What was in his mind and President Roosevelt's mind at Yalta, he said, was the speediest way to stop the effusion of blood and to avoid the expenditure of young men's lives. Their thoughts were on the young wives and their children and their parents. This led to concessions that were made to bring Russia into the war against Japan.

"You must remember also," he added, "that at the time of Yalta, there had been no atomic explosion in the Mexican [New Mexican] desert. We had asked the scientists, and they could not assure us that there would be anything beyond a pop. I might say that if we had known what was to happen at Hiroshima, the words we would have spoken would have been quite different."

On Pearl Harbor: I asked him if Britain could have carried on the war if the Japanese had not attacked the United States at Pearl Harbor. He said he had always thought that was a very stupid thing for the Japanese to do. If the United States had not come in, the British would have gone on anyway; of course, he added, they would have had to write off everything east of Suez, but they could still defend the British Isles, they could still defend Egypt, and they could still have bombed the Germans.

On Roosevelt: If Japan had not struck at Pearl Harbor, Roosevelt would have drawn a line in the Pacific as he did in the Atlantic. FDR had told him at the Atlantic Charter conference: "We may not declare war, but we will wage it."

What was reassuring was that the old Churchillian wit survived. He asked whether the resources of the *Times* could "be extended" to get him a little mustard for his filet mignon. When he looked out on the advertising bright lights and saw one reading KINSEY BLENDED WHISKEY, he smiled and said, "A soothing thought." When he was asked the best way to write, he said, "In bed," though he added that he didn't write most of his speeches but dictated them. He was generous to the Germans. "When my foe is beaten my hatred dies," he said. But he called the Soviets "criminals," and said they puzzled him. "Why do they bolt the doors to their paradise?" he asked. "Saint Peter usually stands inside the door and welcomes people in, but in Russia he stands outside the door and dares them to enter or leave."

As he left at a few minutes past eleven, a little shuffly and a little bent, Dr. Howard Rusk, the *Times*' favorite doctor, remarked, "Jesus, prop him up." I thought his political days were over, but he became prime minister again in the fifties. The only thing I missed was his cigar. Usually he used it like a baton, but the doctors must have made him choose between the brandy and the weed. In retrospect, I preferred to read him rather than remember him as he declined, but I don't think I'll ever forget the old man that night.

I should add here that there were few political leaders of the world who didn't participate in these private meetings at the publisher's table, many of them talking with reckless candor, but in fifty years I cannot remember a single occasion on which the *Times* ever violated their trust.

# PART NINE

## THE FIFTIES

# CHAPTER 21

# America
# at Midcentury

AFTER FIFTY YEARS of wars and other insanities, I figured the world would rest for a while, but the first half of the century ended with a bang. In August of 1949, the Soviet Union exploded its first experimental atomic bomb, ending the U.S. monopoly about two years earlier than Washington expected. Earlier that year I had attended the signing of the North Atlantic Treaty and assumed, wrongly as it turned out, that this might make the Communist nations a little more cautious, but on June 25, 1950, the North Korean Communists invaded South Korea, and the first military crisis of the Cold War began.

President Truman, then beginning his last two years in office, and declining in the popularity polls, sent his troops into the battle, ordered a naval blockade of the Korean peninsula, and turned General Douglas MacArthur loose on North Korea. On two occasions, once personally, MacArthur reassured Truman that there was no reason to fear Soviet or Chinese intervention. I reported at the time that on October 3, 1950, Communist China had warned Truman through the Indian ambassador in Peking, K. M. Panikkar, that it would enter the war if American troops crossed the 38th parallel and approached the Yalu border of China, but this warning was ignored, and MacArthur, surprised by a hidden Chinese army of over 400,000, was forced to retreat.

It is difficult now, at the end of the century, to realize the dangers of that period. Washington was in the grip of the McCarthyist hysteria. MacArthur was in contact with the "win the war" enthusiasts in the Congress, and was not only bombing the North Korean port of Rashin close to Vladivostok, but was blaming his retreat on Truman's refusal to permit the bombing of Manchuria beyond the Yalu. There was no doubt in my mind then, or thereafter, that if Truman had agreed with MacArthur and bombed beyond the Yalu, not only China but the Soviet Union, then allied to the Chinese, would have retaliated and risked a third world war.

Truman, of course, was denounced for "losing North Korea," which he never had, and for promising during the Greek-Turkish crisis to support any country under Communist attack. Secretary of State Acheson was condemned for failing to include South Korea in his list of protected nations, and a hunt was on for scapegoats and spies in the State Department.

I was still covering the diplomatic beat in Washington at that time, and it was obvious that the administration was even more divided than the people about how to deal with the Communist menace. Moscow's military domination of Eastern Europe had been ominous enough, but now the Communist threat seemed to be assuming worldwide proportions. Truman responded to this by instructing Secretary of State Acheson and Secretary of Defense Louis Johnson to appoint a committee of diplomatic and military experts to analyze the problem and make their recommendations to his National Security Council.

Thus began a debate that divided and tormented officials of the government for years. There was general agreement that Communist expansion had to be opposed, but some officials thought this was primarily a military problem while others, though conceding the need for stronger conventional forces, thought it was primarily a political problem. In fact, this latter group, headed by George Kennan, a former U.S. ambassador to Moscow and author of the policy of containing Soviet ambitions, argued that a U.S. military buildup would only increase Moscow's paranoic fears of another invasion from the West and lead to a dangerous arms race.

In opposition to this, other officials, led by Paul Nitze, who succeeded Kennan as head of the State Department's policy-planning staff on the first day of the fifties, argued that the Soviet government was clearly embarked on a policy of world conquest and would be stopped, not by political compromise, but only by fear of military defeat. I knew Paul Nitze well; he was another neighbor on Woodley Road in Washington. In fact, we lived next door to each other for twenty-nine years, with a convenient hole in the fence for easy communication, and while I tried to be both a good neighbor and a good reporter, I learned something of Nitze's approach to the Soviet problem.

He was a gloomy warrior and a superb negotiator, almost too "hard-charging" for even his close friend at State, Secretary Acheson. He had studied, almost memorized, Spengler's *Decline of the West* at Harvard, and he was haunted by its pessimistic analysis. He began his public career as a member of the strategic bombing survey after the Second World War, and while Kennan was studying Russian psychology in Moscow, he was studying the effects of modern bombing, not only in Germany but also on the ground after the war in Japan at Hiroshima and Nagasaki.

He was the staff director and principal author of the Acheson-Johnson reappraisal study at the beginning of the fifties, and produced the final document for the National Security Council, identified as NSC-68. It reflected Nitze's personal view that the Nazi and Communist forms of government were similar and equally dangerous. It was his conviction that since Moscow had the capacity to wage nuclear war, it probably, with its ideology and ambition, would do so when the balance of power was in its favor. NSC-68 did not, as is often charged, predict a major U.S.-Soviet war in the year 1954, but it said that year would be the time of "maximum danger" if the United States did not start rearming at once. He thought that the defense budget should be raised from $13 billion to $40 billion a year for the first five years of the fifties, but Acheson thought these figures would scare the Congress, and they were excluded from the NSC report.

I knew nothing about the details of NSC-68. It was kept secret in 1950, including from Congress. Even President Truman apparently had doubts about it, and sat on it for a while, but when the North Koreans invaded South Korea, he accepted it as government policy. He wasn't interested in the philosophic speculation about Moscow's intentions or its capacity to wage war. "We're at war," he said, and later fired MacArthur to demonstrate who was in charge.

It seemed wrong to me then, and still seems so, that the executive branch could adopt such a policy without discussing it with the congressional leaders in advance, but that was not unusual. I thought Kennan was much nearer to the truth about Soviet intentions than Nitze was, and I felt then, as I did about Truman's decision to drop the atom bomb on Hiroshima and Nagasaki, that the diplomatic course was inadequately explored before the military strategy was accepted.

The policy of trusting the Germans and the Japanese after the war had turned these former enemies into allies, but I saw nothing in the record to justify a similar policy of reconciliation with the Soviet leaders. They had refused to join the Marshall Plan for the reconstruction of Europe. They wanted an impoverished Europe, which they hoped they could help Communize. They had rejected the U.S. government's proposals for the international control of nuclear energy. They had broken their Yalta and Potsdam guarantees of free elections in Eastern Europe and were waging proxy wars of national subjugation in defiance of their treaty commitments to the United Nations.

Even so, I didn't share Nitze's conviction that the Soviets were somehow like the Nazis, or that they would risk a nuclear war with the United States. They were, it seemed to me, far more cautious and incompetent than the Nazis. They had come to power during the confusion of World War I, and stood to lose their power and their new empire as well in a nuclear war. Besides, having suffered over 20 million deaths in World War II, it seemed to me they would know the difference between life and death. Nitze always won this argument by saying to me, "Why take the chance? If I'm wrong, all we lose is money, but if you're wrong, we could lose everything!"

When Eisenhower won the election of 1952, he dealt with the Kennan-Nitze controversy very simply: he got rid of both of them. And if he read NSC-68 I never heard of it. Anyway, Ike led the Republicans back to power after twenty years, negotiated a truce in Korea, and embarked on a crusade to make friends with everybody.

I saw a different America at midcentury. The population of the country had been increasing by over a million a year in the thirties and forties and was estimated by the Census Bureau at 150 to 155 million at the end of 1953. Accordingly, there were problems at home as well as abroad, and I thought and wrote at the time that the most important story in America was what was happening to America. It was not only having to find a million new jobs a year to keep pace with the rising population, but also in 1951 more women came into the work force than ever before—even more than during World War II. Wages, prices, inflation, and taxes were all rising, and so were the divorce rates and the crime rates—all this and tension between the races as well.

There was much speculation at home and abroad about how the return of the Republicans would affect U.S. policy. Many observers assumed a popular military leader would give priority to building up the power of the armed forces. Moscow expected intensification of the Cold War. But the new president wasn't in a hurry and he wasn't in a provocative mood. He thought this midcentury changing of the guard was a time for reflection, and unlike Truman and, later, Kennedy, Johnson, and Bush, who started their presidencies by getting into wars, Ike demonstrated a remarkable gift for staying out of them, despite the combative instincts of his secretary of state, John Foster Dulles.

# CHAPTER 22

# Eisenhower:
# The Republican Revival

EISENHOWER MADE HIS purpose clear soon after he brought the Republicans back to the White House after a twenty-year absence. "We have to unify the country," he said, "as we unified the Allies during the war. Only with a bipartisan foreign policy can we try to make peace with the Russians." This was the central theme of Eisenhower's administration but not necessarily the objective of many other Republican leaders.

I learned early in Washington that it was a bum idea to have heroes or even intimate friends in government, but Ike put a strain on that ideal. He had a smile that lit up like a Broadway sign. The intellectuals mocked him, and the Republican extremists denounced him, but everybody else liked him and he tolerated people he didn't like, including, unfortunately, Richard Nixon.

I had met Ike when he took over the Allied command near the end of the war in London, where he was extremely popular. The British had originally favored General Marshall as the Allied commander, but Ike soon won their trust. He was direct and modest, and went around London like a new boy in town, saying, "My name's Eisenhower." He made clear from the start that this was not merely an American military operation but a unified "Allied crusade." When one of his aides described General Montgomery as a "British son of a bitch," Ike replied, "He may be a son of a bitch, but not a *British* son of a bitch."

He was the tenth general to become president, but except for Zachary Taylor, he was the first to reach the White House with so little political or civilian experience. Andrew Jackson had been a senator and a judge; William Henry Harrison had been governor of Indiana, and Benjamin Harrison had been a senator from the Hoosier state; Franklin Pierce had served in both houses of Congress, as had James Garfield; Ulysses Grant had been in Andrew Johnson's cabinet; and Rutherford Hayes had been both a congressman and a governor.

Eisenhower spent twenty-seven years as a comparatively obscure army officer, then six as a world-renowned commanding general, and only two in civilian life as president of Columbia University. When he returned from the wars and replaced Nicholas Murray Butler at Columbia in 1948, he was the first to admit that he had no training for the job. "I hope," he told *The New York Times,* "to talk with various officials while I'm here and possibly get some advance inkling of what a college president is up against. I know nothing about it." He astonished the Columbia faculty by saying he had wondered about taking this position since he had also been offered the presidency of the Boy Scouts of America. Later he discovered why Columbia had chosen him. "You know what?" he remarked to a friend. "The damned place is broke!"

From the day he completed a triumphant tour of the Allied capitals and reported for duty as Chief of Staff of the Army in 1945, however, both political parties were talking of nominating him for president, and the reporters began looking behind his military braid. We all took a shine to him, but couldn't tell what he thought about most political issues of the day. He made bundles of speeches without dropping a clue on a single domestic issue. He played a lot of poker, bridge, and golf, and devoured pulp western stories, but nobody knew whether he was a Republican or a Democrat. And if he knew himself in 1945, he wasn't telling.

He was, however, always available and always agreeable. He put on that hayseed "just a farm boy from Kansas" act, but otherwise seemed free of pretense or ambition. I tried to smoke him out on the presidency on various occasions, but got nowhere. He insisted that he had all the glory any soldier needed—"more than I ever expected," he said—and was looking forward to retirement at Gettysburg. Besides, he was convinced that President Truman would seek reelection in 1952 and would probably win. This was not a prospect he enjoyed, for he thought both Truman and Roosevelt had bloated and misused presidential power. But when Truman announced that he would not run in 1952, the general was overwhelmed by Republican leaders who insisted that he was the only candidate who could restore their party to the White House after almost a quarter of a century in opposition.

Eisenhower is now such a dominant figure in Republican history that it's hard to realize what a battle he had to win the nomination. I followed him all over the country when he was fighting against Senator Taft for the nomination. At that time, Taft was the sentimental favorite of the delegates, but Ike was convinced that "Taft's isolationism would wreck the victorious Allied coalition, if Taft ever reached the White House." He was the favorite of the eastern Republicans—the Deweys and the Dulles brothers, the Cabots and the Lodges—but Taft was the favorite of the Republican "regulars" who blamed Dewey and the moderates for losing the elections of 1944 and 1948.

It was a nasty convention; it listened reverently to Herbert Hoover, and even stomped and hollered for Joe McCarthy. I was watching the proceedings on television with General Eisenhower in his room at the Blackstone Hotel, when Senator Dirksen of Illinois was blaming Governor Dewey of New York for taking the Republicans down to defeat in 1948, and implying that Eisenhower would do the same. It was a blatant effort to stampede the convention for Taft. Ike was furious, but he cooled off when the Taft deserters outnumbered the Taft supporters.

Typically, one of Ike's first acts after the nomination was to sign an agreement with Taft on the principles of the campaign. Adlai Stevenson, his opponent, called this Ike-Taft deal "the surrender of Morningside Heights," and added that "Taft lost the nomination but won the nominee." However, while Stevenson got most of the laughs, Eisenhower got most of the votes.

On the stump in the 1952 campaign, Ike sounded like a preacher on the old Chautauqua circuit. He repeated every Sunday-school maxim from "God is Love" to "Suffer the little children," but this didn't keep him from denouncing his opponents and condemning them for policies he himself had approved under Truman. He supported the NATO alliance and some unidentified New Deal social reforms, but said he thought they cost too much. He took a bold stand, however, for "peace and prosperity" and he left no doubt that he was against "wickedness in government." This seemed to please multitudes of hero-worshipers, who came out to see him more than to hear what he had to say.

He infuriated his campaign managers, including his brother Milton, by refusing to attack McCarthy in the senator's home state of

Wisconsin for calling General Marshall a traitor. Ike had approved a speech denouncing McCarthy for this slur, but was talked out of it on the ground that he had defended Marshall elsewhere, and attacking McCarthy in Wisconsin would hurt the Republican candidates in that state. When Ike deleted the defense of Marshall, he was roundly criticized, and the Scripps-Howard papers, irritated by Ike's soothing generalities, complained that he was "running like a dry creek." Thereafter, while never forgetting the virtues of vagueness, Eisenhower became a little more specific. He promised if elected to go to Korea and bring that war to an end, and from then on there was no doubt about the election, if there ever had been.

He was as optimistic about the outcome of his bid for the presidency as he had been about the invasion of Europe. He annoyed his campaign managers with his affable confidence and his addiction to golf, even when his friends were advising him to work harder and play less. He was a brassy golfer. "Let there be no wailing from any quarter when I sink this one," he would roar as he stepped up to an impossible downhill side-hill putt. If he couldn't outplay you, he'd outnegotiate you on the first tee. Finally, he was the kind of golfer whose worst shots carom off trees, stones, or other hard objects onto the green, and whose putts strike invisible bumps and drop into the cup.

It was easy in those far-off days to mistake Ike's casual ways for indolence. He never pulled his rank or swanked around. He had served under General MacArthur long enough to detest that officer's majestic posturing. He wore no medals. He was gabby as a barber, but he trusted his subordinates, encouraged their opposition, and inspired trust and loyalty in the process. In London, he wouldn't let the reporters say their dispatches came from Eisenhower's headquarters or quote his garrulous ramblings, but his friendly compromising way was in many ways misleading. For he didn't hesitate to differ even with Churchill on invasion strategy, and to his later regret he insisted on permitting the advance of Soviet power deep into Western Europe; but it was undoubtedly wrong to think, as many of us did at the time, that his military training did not prepare him for high political office.

When he was Supreme Commander of NATO, before returning to Columbia, he was dealing constantly with the economic and political concerns of a dozen nations, and while he was never quite able to speak in coherent sentences, he wrote remarkably well, and was often the principal author of many of General MacArthur's soaring orations. He hadn't made his way up through the ranks of the military without learning how to lead men while giving them the impression that they were leading him.

Before he could change his party's ideas, however, he had to change his own. He came to the White House with some fixed ideas he later regretted and modified or abandoned. For example, he switched the CIA from an intelligence-gathering and -analyzing instrument to an operating arm of the military services. He used it to topple the governments of Guatemala and Iran, and even at the end of his second term urged President Kennedy to proceed with the CIA's Cuban adventure that led to the disaster at the Bay of Pigs. And he made other mistakes.

He couldn't quite make up his mind about the atom bomb. At first he called it "that awful thing" and wished it had never been invented. He opposed its use against the Japanese, not only because he thought the Japanese were on the point of surrender when it was used against Hiroshima and Nagasaki, but also because he thought it would create a mood of fear and instability in the world. Later, however, he talked as if it were merely another more powerful and cheaper military weapon that could and inevitably would be used in future wars, and he went to considerable lengths to remove the taboo against it. In fact, he personally approved in October of 1953 the Basic National Security Policy document, which stated: "In the event of hostilities, the United States will consider nuclear weapons to be as available for use as other munitions."

He didn't like John Foster Dulles's doctrine of "massive retaliation" but he tolerated this threat "to retaliate instantly, by means and at places of our own choosing." To be effective a policy had to be credible, and it wasn't credible that the United States, if losing a war in Korea or Vietnam, would use atomic weapons on China or the Soviet Union. But he didn't mind the bluff—talked carelessly but acted cautiously—always insisting on the consent of the Congress and the Allies for atomic action, which he knew he wouldn't get. Arthur Schlesinger, Jr., the historian, criticized Ike's careless talk about the bomb but gave him credit for saving the Republic from his advisers.

He made his position clear on "preventive atomic war" in answer to a question I posed to him at a press conference in 1954. "A preventive war, to my mind, is an impossibility today," he said. "How could you have one if one of its features would be several cities lying in ruins, several cities where many, many thousands of people would be dead and injured and mangled, the transportation systems destroyed, sanitation, implements, and systems all gone? That isn't preventive war: that is war. I don't believe there is such a thing, and frankly I wouldn't even listen to anyone seriously that came in and talked about such a thing."

He wasn't above giving the impression that he might use the bomb, however, and once moved atomic weapons and their planes to Okinawa to encourage a truce in the Korean War. But at the end of his second term, he was saying that after an atomic war, we wouldn't have enough bulldozers to scrape the bodies off the streets.

He was helped in his public dealings by choosing Jim Hagerty, a former reporter on *The New York Times,* as his press secretary. Ike seldom made a decision without checking with Hagerty, who told him what the reaction would be in the next day's newspapers. Hagerty regarded Eisenhower's personality as a national asset and convinced him that a presidential press conference was not a problem, but an opportunity to set the agenda for discussion in his own terms. "You can dominate the news and the debate or leave it to your opposition," Hagerty told him. Ike held more such conferences and saw more reporters on the side than any other president until George Bush came along.

The downside of this was that in addition to his mischievous charms, he had a temper and a tendency to talk too much. When Churchill, alarmed by all this gabble of using atomic weapons, urged him at Bermuda in December of 1953 to combine the policy of strength with "the hand of friendship," John Colville, Churchill's secretary, recalled that the president replied with a short, very violent statement in the coarsest terms, describing Russia as "a woman of the streets in a new dress, but the same whore underneath." He liked to blow off, but usually parked his temper in the White House safe, and in calmer moments was deeply troubled by the horror and waste of war.

When Stalin died, for example, he sent the usual message of condolence to Moscow and then called Emmet Hughes, one of his favorite speech-writers, to the Oval Office. Hughes's account of that meeting provides an interesting insight of Eisenhower's more sensitive feelings:

"Look, I'm tired," the president said, "and I think everyone is tired of just plain indictments of the Soviet regime. I think it would be wrong—in fact, asinine—for me to get up before the world now to make another of those indictments. Instead, just two things mat-

ter: What have we got to offer the world? What are we ready to do
to improve the chances of peace?

"Here is what I'd like to say: Let us talk straight—no double-talk,
no sophisticated political formulas, no slick propaganda devices.
Let's spell it out, whatever we really offer . . . withdrawal of troops
here or there on both sides . . . United Nations–supervised free
elections in another place . . . free and uncensored air time for us to
talk to the Russian people and for their leaders to talk to us . . . and
concretely, all that we would hope to do for the economic well-being
of other countries. . . . Here is what we propose. If you—the Soviet
Union—can improve on it, we want to hear it. This is what I want
to say."

In this conciliatory spirit, Eisenhower addressed the American
Society of Newspaper Editors on April 16, 1953, in a speech that was
widely praised thereafter for helping end the war in Korea. The
president made no such claims, however. Dulles had opposed the
speech and suggested instead that the president send a vague warning
to China through Nehru in India that the United States would use
tactical atomic weapons unless the Chinese stopped the fighting. Ike
played it both ways, with the public conciliatory speech and the
private threat, and said nothing when Dulles insisted that it was his
warning that had ended the Korean War.

My wife and I were in Japan with our son Jim at that time and
I went to Panmunjom for the signing of the truce. Nobody was really
satisfied with the compromise—it left Korea a divided country—and
yet it did achieve something. It stopped the killing after thirty-seven
months of war and almost 2 million dead, 54,000 of them from the
United States. It proved that the balance of power was not, as Roosevelt had insisted, an outworn and useless theory, and for the first time
in history an international organization, backed by the United States,
had proved equal to the aggressors.

It wasn't really until Eisenhower's presidential papers were made
available that we began to understand how careful he was in action,
how patient in trying to unify his party, and how shrewd he was in
saying no to his old buddies in the Pentagon. He didn't believe
in splashy theories. He didn't think effective military intervention in
Korea proved, for example, that it would work in Vietnam. When
Vice President Nixon, Admiral Radford, the Chairman of the Joint
Chiefs of Staff, and Dulles all flirted with rescuing the trapped
French garrison at Dien Bien Phu in Vietnam, Ike said he wouldn't
intervene without the approval of Congress and that he wouldn't put

a single American foot soldier in that elephant grass ten thousand miles from home. Having made this clear, he then went out to the Burning Tree Club in Maryland and worked on his slice.

He wasn't always so careful, however, in questioning the judgment of his subordinates, and he sometimes trusted them more than they deserved. Prodded by Dulles in 1958, he dispatched 9,000 U.S. marines to Lebanon, backed by 70 Sixth Fleet warships and 420 fighter planes, to deal with one of the many internal uprisings in Lebanon. Dulles told the Congress that unless the United States intervened, the free world would not only lose the Middle East and three fourths of the world's oil reserves with it, but would also lose Africa and noncommunist Asia as well. The Congress approved this "Eisenhower Doctrine" on the ground that it was necessary to "save American lives" and block the spread of communism, but it merely embarrassed Ike when he was asked four months later by a new Lebanese government to bring his marines back home. More important, he ran into trouble with the Soviets in the last year of his presidency when nobody thought to call off the U-2 spy planes flying over Soviet territory before Ike's summit meeting with Khrushchev in Paris. I went along for that meeting and at no other time saw him in a more troubled state of mind.

The U-2 fiasco, caused by Ike's absentmindedness and poor staff work, ruined his disarmament conference with Khrushchev, who acted as if the Soviet Union never engaged in espionage. He mocked Eisenhower's spying and lying for their "clumsiness." The president stuck around Paris for a couple of days to prove that he hadn't been responsible for breaking up the conference, but he couldn't hide his depression, even from the press.

It was with this same inattention to details that he allowed others to force one of the most brilliant scientists of the age—J. Robert Oppenheimer—out of government service (see later in this volume) in a miscarriage of justice that Ike never seemed to regret, even in retirement. This was not typical of his behavior.

He wouldn't go along with the isolationists who wanted to avoid the problems of the world, or the Cold War warriors who wanted to meddle in problems all over the world. He often talked a lot of nonsense and tolerated a lot of brutality in the South before using the troops to keep the school doors open to blacks, but he made Earl Warren chief justice of the United States (and later regretted it) and he backed things if they worked and changed them if they didn't.

All this he managed by being faithful to the constitutional rights of Congress, by being agreeable to people he didn't agree with, by denouncing the Soviets one day and overlooking their outrages the next, and just by being an amiable practical human being, with a baffling way of expressing or concealing his thought.

One of the amusing paradoxes about him was that he was always condemning the government for doing for the people many things they could do for themselves, but he relied for fifty years on the personal services of the government, and when he retired he discovered that he couldn't do many of the simplest chores of life.

As Stephen E. Ambrose notes in his biography *Eisenhower the President*, when Ike finally left the White House on January 21, 1961, he had never been in a public barbershop, rarely carried any money in his pocket, didn't know how to make his own travel arrangements, could not adjust a television set, or use a dial telephone. On the night he left office he tried to telephone his son John, and then, according to Ambrose, he "picked up the receiver, heard only a buzzing sound at the other end, shouted for the operator, clicked the receiver a dozen times, and finally bellowed for his Secret Service agent, Richard Flohr, 'Come show me how to work this goddamned thing!' "

He conquered the Nazis and for a while, he even conquered the Republican party. He didn't, however, make provision for its future, and the right-wingers never forgave him for that. But the historians gave him credit for handling the really big issues of his time, and ranked him higher than we did in the story of the presidency.

# CHAPTER 23

# *Washington Bureau Chief*

ARTHUR KROCK TURNED over the Washington bureau of the *Times* to me during the Eisenhower administration, in 1953, and I held that job for eleven years through the tragic Kennedy and Johnson Vietnam days. Mr. Krock said this switch occurred to him one day when his pencil rolled under his desk, and he was so tired that he wondered whether he had enough energy left to retrieve it, but there was probably another reason. At that time, Herbert Elliston, the editor of the editorial page at *The Washington Post*, being in ill health, decided to retire, and Philip Graham, the publisher of the *Post*, asked me to take his place.

When A.K. heard about this, he called me into his office and, without even checking with New York, offered to give me his job if I would stay on the *Times*. I was surprised and touched by this, remembering our difficulties in the past, and when I accepted, he stood up and shook my hand, and that same night before going home, he left a little handwritten note in my mailbox: "I have known many of the reporters of my time who were called great. I have worked against some of them, and unworthily directed the services of others, but in my opinion, none has been your superior." I felt then that he had finally accepted me and I vowed to work harder than ever before to justify this unexpected move.

I spent a few weeks getting acquainted with the leaders of the new Eisenhower administration, and then went off with Sally and our son Jim on a long freighter trip to Japan, Korea, and Vietnam to get a perspective on the increasingly complicated news in the Pacific.

There was considerable anxiety in Asia at the start of the fifties over Washington's future policies in the Pacific, particularly after MacArthur's military reverses in North Korea. Would the United States, so long preoccupied with the problems in Europe, pay as much attention to the threat of Communist expansion around the rim of China and the Soviet Union? I went first to Formosa and interviewed Generalissimo Chiang Kai-shek and other leaders of Nationalist China.

For an hour and a half at his official residence above Taipei, Chiang argued that "the time is ripe to drive the Communists out of Asia." I asked how that was to be done. He said that there were certain moments in history when great things could be done and this was one of them. The Communists had not yet consolidated their control over mainland China, he said. The leaders in Moscow were divided. Later the dangers would be greater.

He was not proposing that the United States make war on China— that would be "stupid," he remarked—but if Washington gave a clear political guarantee of support to Formosa, South Korea, Vietnam, and Thailand, that would impress the Communists. And, he added, if Washington provided the military aid he had requested, he would be able to land his troops in China "within six months." He was not against a military truce in Korea, he said, but it was essential that the United States remain there and strengthen the military forces of the Korean president, Syngman Rhee.

I then flew to Seoul and interviewed Rhee at his camouflaged villa above the South Korean capital. He lectured me for over an hour about what the United States must do and must not do. He was absolutely opposed to a truce with the North Korean Communists. It was inconceivable to him, he said, that the United States would not keep fighting until all of Korea was free and under the control of his government. Anything else would be "appeasement."

"It is not popularity but survival that we are seeking," he said. "The division of Korea is the death of Korea. It is great ideals we are fighting for. These things are far mightier than armies, and we shall fight for them even if everybody else abandons them."

He mocked the idea of a negotiated truce. The United States, he said, was not going to quibble or try to gain some little period of peace by "temporary tricks." It was not interested merely in having peace and quiet, and football games and more time for television. "The people of the United States know they have to fight communism or be left without allies."

This, of course, was precisely the theme President Kennedy heard at the beginning of the sixties, on the critical importance of fighting in Vietnam, and President Nixon heard again in the seventies, and President Reagan heard in the eighties about the Communist threat in Nicaragua.

Always it was the same story: it was the "duty" of the United States to solve other people's problems and rid the world of communism. I returned to Washington fearing trouble ahead and moved into Arthur Krock's office in the summer of 1953.

I had never had any such responsibilities before, but I had been around for a while and thought I knew where they hid the news. Also, I kept in mind the managerial philosophy of Casey Stengel, the wily skipper of the New York Yankees. When he was asked the secret of his success, Stengel said he was always a better manager when he had Joe DiMaggio or Mickey Mantle in center field. With the Stengel rule and the promise of Turner Catledge, the managing editor, that I could add to my staff, I hired a few heavy hitters and set up sort of a mutual aid society under which everybody was not only invited to read his own story in the paper but also encouraged to read everybody else's.

The head of the Washington bureau of *The New York Times* starts with certain advantages in that city of open secrets. The influence of the *Times* rests on the fact that it is read by people who have influence—the leaders of government and diplomacy, business tycoons, and other deep thinkers in the universities. In short, many of the *Times'* readers are the who's-who types who make and follow the news and refer to the *Times'* index. They also know that we handle the news with care and will probably write their obituaries. This opens a lot of doors.

Also, while my generation wanted to go to New York, many of the best young reporters of the post–New Deal era preferred to work in Washington, where it was easier to hit the front page and cheaper to raise a family. So a bureau chief on the prowl in the fifties didn't have to appoint a search committee.

Running a news bureau in Washington is first of all a job of gathering, decontaminating, and transmitting the day-to-day proclamations of the federal government. This requires the intelligence, energy, and skepticism of experienced men and women who don't mind getting home an hour or so after dinner. We play hide-and-seek with officials on the side, but reporters and officials are not always, like cats and dogs, natural enemies. They just get that way by constant contact with one another.

In all his years as chief of the *Times'* Washington bureau, Arthur Krock had only two meetings of his whole staff: the day he took the job and the day he gave it up. He was one of those inclined to the belief that nothing happened unless the *Times* printed it, and he was invariably tolerant of reporters he liked, regardless of their talents. One of his favorites, for example, was Lewis Wood, who covered the Supreme Court with a paste pot and a pair of scissors.

Lew was a cheery and handsome Southern gentleman who lived up on Waterside Drive near Rock Creek Park with his wife and a cat called Jasper. He had often heard that "a cat could look at a king," so one day when the British sovereign came to Washington, Lew took Jasper on his arm, walked down to Constitution Avenue, and when the king passed by, held up Jasper for a good look and then walked home again.

His paste-and-scissors technique was known in the bureau as "the Lew Wood treatment." It consisted of a first paragraph, written by himself, recording the decision of the court, followed by a long scissored quotation from the majority opinion; then a few more words by Lew on the minority opinion, followed by another long paste-up from the author of the dissent.

I didn't think much of this technique, so I made a few changes.

We had a staff meeting almost every working day on the theory that the sum of our brains and legs was necessary to outthink and outnumber the *Herald Tribune.* We operated out of a whole floor in an office building overlooking Farragut Square a few blocks from the White House. In those precomputer days, the reporters were not separated in rooms or cubicles. They sat at their desks in one long room, and in the late afternoon, approaching deadline, there was a lively din of clicking typewriters, and shouts of "copy," and telephone conversations that could be heard by one and all. It was not the sort of place for quiet meditation, but there was an urgent sense of time and common work.

The field commander or news editor of this daily battle was Wallace Carroll, assisted by Bob Whitney and John Finney. Carroll could have edited Lincoln's Gettysburg Address and improved it. He brought from Milwaukee a studied respect for the English language, and from the UPI and his wartime intelligence activities the instincts of an amateur spy. He was a student of foreign affairs. He knew many of the top foreign service officers in the State Department. He was liked and trusted by the reporters, for he was unfailingly kind. He took an interest not only in their work, but also in their families and their ambitions, and wrote funny, mocking verses in his spare time.

There was a touch of Lewis Carroll in Wally Carroll. One day when there was some kind of disturbance in the Persian Gulf, the Imam of Oman came to Washington, and Jack Raymond turned in a story about this misty character, without troubling to identify him. Within three minutes, Carroll sent Raymond the following:

> Who . . . is the Imam of Oman?
> Is he a yes-man or a no-man?
> Is he a pro-or-anti-status-quo man?
> Might we call him the noblest like the Ro-man,
> Or as abominable as the Snow Man?
> Quickly, this our readers need to know, man!

Carroll collected unusual bylines in the *Times,* not always to the delight of the editors in New York. He wrote a note one day to Turner Catledge: "Now that you have a reporter named Sylvan Fox, you must quickly find another one named Urban Wolf. This will support the *Times'* reputation for objectivity, and what a lovely double byline it would make: by Sylvan Fox and Urban Wolf . . . and while you're about it, please do something about Isadore Barmash. That's not even a good rhetorical question."

His sense of history was as keen as his sense of humor. As heretofore mentioned, I worked with him in the U.S. London Embassy during the war, and later brought him to Washington when Allen Dulles was director of the Central Intelligence Agency. When Dulles retired, Wally wrote an analysis of his work, which occupied half a page of the *Times.* In those days, the head of the paper's bull pen in New York, Ted Bernstein, circulated every fortnight a useful critique called "Winners and Sinners," one of which dealt with the differences between "as" and "like." This hit everybody's desk just before Carroll's blockbuster on Dulles went to New York. When Wally read his story the next morning, every "as" had been changed to "like" and every "like" had been changed to "as," all of them wrong. I seldom saw him angry, but even in retirement he was still sputtering at Nat Gerstenzang, the offending copyreader.

Maybe there was a better editor than Carroll in Washington during our days, but if so I never met him. He could be tough. He made Dave Halberstam, one of our resident wonder-workers, rewrite his first story for the paper five times. Carroll was a good man with a pencil and had a way of getting his reporters to write leads that combined the professional with the personal. He and Allen Drury, who was brought aboard from the *Evening Star,* combined on a lead paragraph still remembered: "Arthur Miller revealed to a congressional committee today a past filled with Communist connections and a future filled with Marilyn Monroe."

Drury left us for a successful career as a novelist, but we had some other stars. I spotted Russell Baker writing iambic pentameter in London for the *Baltimore Sun* and invited him sight unseen to come around if he ever got jumpy. He became in turn our White House, State Department, and congressional reporter and designated poet, and has by some magic managed to make us smile at human folly ever since. Tom Wicker, who knew every trick in the county courthouse business, came up from North Carolina as roving political correspondent, and on the day before Tony Lewis won the Pulitzer Prize at the *Washington News,* he joined us as legal correspondent. The *News* died shortly thereafter, but that may have been a coincidence.

Tony didn't give the Court the Lew Wood treatment. He set a standard that won the praise of even so vigilant a critic of the press as Mr. Justice Felix Frankfurter. At that time, the Court on Mondays would sometimes hand down as many as a dozen or more decisions. Even on the *Times* we couldn't give a lot of space to all of them, and decided to summarize a few in our own words. When I asked Judge Frankfurter what he thought of this idea, he denounced it as a cheeky presumption. Nevertheless, Tony Lewis quietly and carefully produced the summaries and the *Times* printed all of them. The next morning Justice Frankfurter called me at home. "I can't believe what that young man achieved," he said. "There aren't two justices of the Court who have such a grasp on these cases." I never asked him the name of the judge.

Tony Lewis wasn't the first to demonstrate the need for specialists in an increasingly complicated world, but he set a standard never equaled until Linda Greenhouse covered the Court. In those days, we also had on the *Times* two men with the same name, though spelled slightly differently—"Atomic Bill" Laurence, who worked out of New York and was so named because he was the only reporter entrusted with the advance information before the first atomic raid on Hiroshima, and "Non-Atomic" or "Wild Bill" Lawrence, who was equally explosive and liked politicians, almost too much.

There were about twenty of us all together, including Peck Trussell, who covered Congress and had an eye for social trends. "Great changes are taking place," he announced at one of our morning meetings. "When I was young, men were partial to paramours; now that they're older they seem more interested in power mowers."

We didn't always agree, of course. I thought we paid too little attention to the destructive activities of the political cheapjacks. I also believed that politicians' nocturnal adventures sometimes influenced the public's business. But Carroll wasn't particularly interested in keeping up with the amorous high jinks or drinking habits of senators, and Baker thought that the fewer trivialities he kept up with, the more time he'd have left to watch Eisenhower or read Henry James. Carroll was really the presiding skipper of our report, and perhaps as a result of his government experience, he read the foreign news with great care and believed he could anticipate the government's decisions.

Accordingly, we specialized in amateur speculation. By imagining that we were running the State Department, we would guess that the secretary of state would have to react to the latest outrage of the Soviet government, so we would call up officials at State on the assumption that they had already reacted. We were often wrong, but it was remarkable how many times our guesses were right and how often we got ahead of the competition by this device.

Most days we worked away amiably enough in accordance with a few general assumptions: we not only wanted "all the news that's fit to print" but we wanted it before anybody else and preferably before it happened. Nothing pleased us more than the thought of waking up the *Herald Tribune* bureau at midnight with howls of protest from their home office about some story we had and they didn't. We weren't so amused when this process was reversed, and we were careful not to be sorry tomorrow for what we had printed today. We didn't think all officials disregarded the truth all the time, but we didn't think either that they lied to us by accident. And when they tried to bully our reporters, a favorite official pastime, I reminded them that we had been around before they arrived, and would probably still be in Washington when they were gone.

On the whole, we favored early copy rather than late copy and understatement rather than overstatement. Carroll especially hated breathless, or as he called them, "Christ how the wind blew" stories. We had a rule against ever saying anything that happened in Washington was "unprecedented," and we were against saying something was approved "universally" when most people in the universe had never heard of it. I believed in what came to be known as "the dumb-boy technique." This was based on the theory that pretense was the downfall of many reporters, and that ignorance was not always fatal but could actually be useful, for the more questions we asked the more information we'd be likely to gather. I also believed, and still do, that the best way to get ahead of the news in Washington is to look for it not at the center but at the fringes, where anonymous officials usually tell the big shots what's coming up. This didn't always work, but it was better than sitting around waiting for hand-outs.

Some good reporters wore tuxedos in those days and scraped some useful crumbs off embassy dinner tables, but in my experience, this added more to their weight than to their knowledge. News had become increasingly complicated by the fifties and this put a strain on the old notion that a good reporter could cover anything from the balance of payments to a hanging. Louis Stark and Abe Raskin were specializing on labor relations and Walter Sullivan on science in the *Times* before my time. But when the State Department moved into Foggy Bottom, and the armed services and the CIA moved across the Potomac to Virginia—a separation that didn't improve the conduct of American foreign policy—we became a bureau of specialists on everything from the missiles and the budget to the social activities of the president's wife.

The last year of any president's term in office is usually a hard time for everybody in Washington, and this was particularly true of President Truman's final days at the beginning of the fifties, just before I became bureau chief. His popularity in the polls had dropped into the 20s—a fact that minimized his ability to handle McCarthy. The Republicans, out of office for so long, were demonstrating that not only power but also the absence of power corrupts, and many of them, including Dulles, thought Governor Tom Dewey had lost the 1948 presidential election by failing to exploit the Communist issue.

It was not exactly a heroic period. The fifties were different from the creative forties and the turbulent sixties. The young were far more interested in personal security than in public purposes. The sociologists were condemning the selfishness of the "silent generation," which in turn was blaming the politicians, the press, and the Communists for all their frustrations.

Covering all this from Congress to the Pentagon, and everything in between, was obviously impossible, but we had fun trying. We

Lording it over my sister,
Joanna, in Scotland, 1911.

My father atop Dumbarton Rock, Scotland.

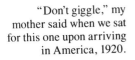

"Don't giggle," my
mother said when we sat
for this one upon arriving
in America, 1920.

A fake follow-through when I was
captain of the University of Illinois
golf team in 1932; we won the Big Ten
championship that year.

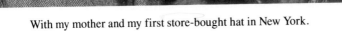

With my mother and my first store-bought hat in New York.

Sally in her mother's wedding dress, when we were married on Christmas Eve, 1935, in Larchmont, New York. This was the dress she was wearing when I let her fall in the basement of the Presbyterian church while we were running away from the ceremony.

Sally's parents, Laura Busey and William John Fulton, in Urbana, Illinois, before their marriage.

With Sally, at the University
of Illinois, 1932.

Sally, with Jim, left, and
Richard on the front stoop of
our house in Washington,
1941, before Tom was born.

With Sally in correspondents'
uniforms on the Thames embankment,
London, 1943.

With my eldest son,
Richard, returning
from Europe, 1947.

This was taken at
Sally's parents' house
in Sycamore, Illinois,
when we returned
from London, where
Richard obviously
left one of his front
teeth. Jim is in
the middle.

With my favorite Speaker of the House of Representatives, Sam Rayburn, in his Capitol Hill office, otherwise known as the "Board of Education." He let his staff handle all the mail, but, he said, "I want to see all the letters from voters written in pencil on lined paper."

In a state of suspended animation at the *Times* Washington bureau, 1947. (*The New York Times*)

Secretary of State Dean
Acheson, trying to be
patient with a nosy
visitor.

With Sally and our
three sons in the
Woodley Road
house, Washington,
1950. Dick is next
to his mother, Jim
and Tom are on
the floor with
our cocker spaniel,
Blackie.

Arthur Krock, the *Times* Washington bureau chief from 1933 to 1953, just before he invited me to be his successor. (Bruce G. Hoertel/*The New York Times*)

In my scoop-artist days, I saw a lot of Senator Arthur Vandenberg of Michigan on Capitol Hill, when he switched from politician to statesman.

In the *Times* office after appointment as bureau chief.

Asking President Eisenhower
a question at a press
conference in the Indian
Treaty Room of the old State
Department building.

The right Hon. Secretary of State John Foster Dulles, probably complaining about my latest comments on his doctrine of "massive retaliation." (*The New York Times*)

Working the phone, Washington, 1960.

Lyndon Johnson, at his ranch in Texas during the first month of his presidency, telling me, over his shoulder, how "humble" he felt in "this new job."

President Johnson's idea of "gentle persuasion." Sometimes I had the uncomfortable feeling that he might bite.

With Sally, searching for the
Great Wall in China.

Interviewing Foreign Minister Chou En-lai of China in Peking, 1971.

At a five-hour dinner with Chou En-lai in the Forbidden City, 1971, when, to his horror, I tried to eat the lotus leaves.

With President Pompidou of France and President Nixon, who, in an absentminded moment, invited me to dinner at the White House.

Listening in the White House to Jimmy Carter, the best ex-president we ever had.

With George Bush in the White House when he was vice president.

Celebrating the end of *Deadline*. (George Tames/*The New York Times*)

At home, Washington, 1990.

Checking the manuscript of *Deadline* in my den at Kalorama Square, Washington, overlooked by my friends the presidents. (George Tames, *The New York Times*)

"Leave 'em laughing" was our goal and here they are, left to right, sons Jim, Tom, and Richard at Fiery Run, 1990.

discovered that many ambassadors in their fancy embassies up and around Massachusetts Avenue were actually lonely most of the time and seemed glad to swap rumors with us when we dropped by. Some of them got drop-copies of diplomatic cables on the latest thunderclaps in the news, and confided in us when in a trusting mood. Occasionally, they even knew what was going on at the CIA, one of the underdeveloped areas of the journalistic world.

In our bureau we made a big deal of presidential press conferences. There were two problems on such occasions: the first was to decide what were the really important questions we wanted to put to the president, and the second was how to get recognized so we could ask them. Accordingly, we drafted our questions carefully. We made a point of keeping them brief, which has since become a lost art, and we sent six or seven reporters in the hope that one of them would catch the president's eye. Since many of these conferences took place near deadline, when it was hard to find a taxi, we even hired a limousine and drafted our summaries en route back to the office. The *Times* expense-account man thought this was an outrageous extravagance, but he knew more about meeting a payroll than meeting a deadline.

Relations between the Washington bureau and the editors in New York had been uneasy from time to time after Roosevelt turned the capital into the main news source of the world, but Turner Catledge, the managing editor, knew and assumed that we knew, or should know, more about what was happening in the capital than he did in New York. "As long as you beat hell out of the *Herald Tribune* every day or so," he said, "I'll be happy."

This was not so easy. The head of the *Herald Tribune*'s Washington bureau in those days was Bert Andrews, a hell-raiser from San Diego, who wouldn't commit murder for a good story but would certainly consider it. Richard Nixon regarded him not only as a source of favorable publicity but also as an adviser, and gave him credit for Nixon's campaign to prove that Alger Hiss of the State Department was procommunist and a perjurer to boot.

Andrews won the Pulitzer Prize for exposing unfair procommunist charges against several State Department officials—a 4,600-word story he took from Carl Levin, one of his own reporters—and then turned around and joined Nixon's anticommunist crusade, boasting that one day he would "make Nixon president." We didn't admire Bert's tactics, but we had to deal with his successes. By the time Nixon did reach the White House, Bert had been dead for fifteen years, "a burnt-out case at the age of 52," as Richard Kluger observed in his excellent history of the *Herald Tribune.*

We rather enjoyed this scoop business in the Washington bureau. We had a good offense, and an excellent defensive arrangement with several editors out in the country who subscribed to the *Herald Tribune*'s and other syndicated news services. They tipped us off whenever Joe Alsop, Walter Lippmann, or Drew Pearson filed some exclusive bit of information. These tips enabled us to check and avoid embarrassment by making the main run of the *Times* the same morning they appeared elsewhere.

Also, we printed texts of unreadable speeches, and covered trifling events other papers ignored. Still, we believed that if we gave all the varied constituencies of the New York community more news of their homelands and other special interests, we would attract enough readers to interest the advertisers. This, inevitably, produced the heaviest newspaper ever dumped on a long-suffering public, the Sunday edition of which is said to destroy around seventy thousand trees. I never counted them, but the *Times* prospered while skinnier and brighter papers expired.

I had the bad luck to take over the Washington bureau just when the Central Intelligence Agency was expanding its activities under Allen Dulles, whose brother, John Foster Dulles, was then secretary of state. It was something new in the peacetime American experience. After the devastation of Hiroshima and Nagasaki, it was gradually realized that nuclear war threatened the survival of the organized world, but war went on with conventional weapons and increasingly by subversive means. There was general agreement that this war by stealth was necessary, since the Soviets, like the Nazis, were expanding their authority by subversion and proxy wars, but it created more problems for a democratic government and a free press than anything else in all my fifty years on the job.

There had, of course, always been tension between the president and the Congress over sharing authority for the conduct of foreign affairs. The Constitution was not designed for a U.S. government leading a worldwide coalition of nations. Presidents Wilson and Roosevelt blamed this for their failure to take early and effective action at the start of the two world wars, but this subversive warfare, often carried on without the knowledge of the Congress, let alone the press, was a new and difficult problem.

It had been the policy of the *Times* to trust the government in delicate issues involving national security, but in 1954, when the CIA was planning the overthrow of the Arbenz government in Guatemala, Allen Dulles told his friend and Princeton classmate General Julius Adler, the general manager of the *Times,* that he had reason to believe that Sydney Gruson, who had been covering the events in Guatemala, was an "unreliable correspondent." Adler reported this to Sulzberger and Turner Catledge who asked for evidence, and took Gruson off the story when Dulles promised to provide it. Meanwhile, the Arbenz government was overthrown, but Dulles never produced any evidence of unreliability on the part of Gruson, who went on to become the principal assistant to the publisher at the end of a long and distinguished career.

Emboldened by its success in the Gruson affair, the CIA expanded its efforts to interfere with the normal reporting activities of the *Times.* It tried, occasionally with success, to recruit *Times* reporters overseas to serve as secret informers, and it tried to pass on to our reporters false information, often of an alarming nature, without taking responsibility as the source.

For example, the CIA tried to influence the *Times* when Dr. Otto John, the head of West Germany's counterintelligence, defected to the Soviet Union. John had been working closely with Allen Dulles, who put out the story that John had been kidnapped and forced across the Iron Curtain. Dulles peddled this deception to Joseph and Stewart Alsop and others in Washington, and at that time I intervened with a long memo to Sulzberger and the editors in New York.

I said that we were probably right not to publish what we knew about CIA agents being captured and CIA planes being shot down over East Germany and the Soviet Union, but these calculated leaks of "disinformation" were going too far. I asked our bosses in New York "whether the *Times* wishes to make its columns available for the publication of unattributed speculative articles, which we would not normally publish but which might be very useful to the government. I am against this, but it is obviously a question beyond my authority to decide." Sulzberger decided that if the government wanted us to print something, we would do so if they took responsibility for it, but, he added, if they would not allow us to attribute it to them, "then we must impose our own judgment as to whether or not it is true and use the story only if we believe it is true." Thereafter, all reporters and editors on the paper were clear about *Times* policy, but this did not stop the CIA from continuing to recruit *Times* reporters, despite our repeated efforts to get assurance that they would not do so.

From the Bay of Pigs fiasco under President Kennedy all the way through the Vietnam War under Johnson and Nixon and the Iran-Contra scandals under Reagan, the CIA did more to break down confidence in the government's statements than anything else. And this problem was made worse by the fact that during the Reagan administration, the head of the CIA authorized secret and illegal activities that even the president said he knew nothing about.

Nevertheless, I look back on those bureau-chief days with some pride. No doubt Washington will go on producing its share of good reporters, but I'm not about to predict that they will do any better than our gang did in reporting the mysteries of how the United States avoided a third world war and led the Alliance to the liberation of Europe, first from the Nazis and later from the Communists.

I took time out from my work in Washington to get another look at Moscow after fourteen years, for in 1956, Nikita Khrushchev had startled the 20th Communist Party Congress by denouncing Stalin's brutalities, and I asked to interview him. Besides, for the first time since the end of the war, the Soviet government invited tourists in 1957 to drive into the capital "on our magnificent new roads." One road went to Moscow from Brest Litovsk in the west through Smolensk and Vyazma, and the other from Moscow south through Kharkov and Simferopol to Yalta on the Black Sea. So Sally and I bought a fancy new car with a metal top that retracted into the back trunk, deposited our son Jim at St. Albans school in Washington for the summer, dropped son Tom off with a family of seven kids to learn French in Bourges, and appointed our eldest son, Dick, then taking his junior year at Edinburgh University, as our official bodyguard and driver.

I wanted to follow Hitler's invasion route to Moscow and at least see something of those vast plains and try to imagine the terrible battles that took so many millions of lives during the war. We drove first through Czechoslovakia and Poland and were well received across the Soviet border at the Brest railroad station, which sported a big sign stating: FOR PEACE IN THE WHOLE WORLD. A pleasant woman named Raya Kulashova had been sent from Moscow to act as our interpreter, and she had plenty to do, for the new black and gold Ford was a sensation, and the cops kept pressing a button on the dashboard to move the top into the trunk, and we were surrounded by young men and women asking: How much does such a car cost? Could a working man afford to buy one? How fast will it go? And the children, always a reassuring sight after a war, had never seen anything like our shining monster and kept touching the American flag on the bumper and shouting with delight, *"Amerikanski! Amerikanski!"*

The roads, however, were not magnificent. The farmers had put their grain on the hard surface to be flailed by the few passing cars. There were only five "benzine" stations in the six hundred miles from Brest to Moscow, but all was well, for they gave us a copy of the official "rules of the road," which stated: 1. While being at the wheel, you should always be capable to drive the car. 2. When necessary, the car should be stopped to avoid an accident. 3. Blowing horn in the city of Moscow is prohibited.

I had promised Arthur Hays Sulzberger that I would give him a report of the changes in Moscow since 1943, so after we had looked around, I wrote him as follows:

> I send you greetings from our old stomping grounds. Spasso House is just the same, though they tell me the plumbing now works, and our Chinese valet has vanished. For all I know, he may be Mao Tse-tung. I can find not the slightest evidence that they have benefited from all the advice we gave them. They are still insisting that we were wrong about everything and that only they have the answers to human misery and desire.
>
> I detect only one advance of any great importance. They are no longer serving cold soft-boiled eggs with the vodka. Otherwise, the vodka still scorches the gullet and, if you keep your legs straight, tickles your toes. Sally and I went to the British Embassy for lunch. Trevelyan is now the ambassador and his minister is a nice character named Brimlow, who served as Archie Clark Kerr's counselor when we were here in 1943. He recalled the night Stalin and Eden came to the embassy for dinner, and Archie, after a hard evening with the firewater, rose after midnight to make the farewell toast, and fell, sled-length onto the table, scattering the glasses to the walls. Stalin, according to Trevelyan, helped him to his feet, whereupon Archie straightened up and finished his toast. This is still regarded here as one of the greatest accomplishments since Stalingrad. More later.

You have to have patience in Moscow, whether you're waiting for Khrushchev or waiting for an elevator in your hotel, and you don't just get an interview, you negotiate it. After waiting for over three weeks, I was told by Mr. Federenko at the Foreign Office to prepare a series of questions "immediately" and show up at Central Committee headquarters on October 7 at 3:00 P.M. for Khrushchev's answers. When I arrived with Bill Jorden, the *Times'* Moscow correspondent, Khrushchev greeted us as if we were old friends, but there was a problem. He turned the answers over to Viktor Sukhodrev, his interpreter, who started reading out the usual propaganda, so I asked to question each reply and Khrushchev not only agreed but finally spent three hours and twenty minutes with us, as if he had nothing else to do. In fact, he talked so much that the *Times* had to publish his replies in three separate editions of the paper.

He was, in turn, provocative and positive. He proposed bringing all pilotless missiles under international control as part of an agreement with Washington. He talked, as usual, about the importance of peaceful coexistence between the two major nuclear nations, and kept insisting that Secretary of State John Foster Dulles was a barrier to understanding. The Soviet Union didn't want war with the United States, he said, but it would survive even such a calamity. He was confident about the future, he said.

I asked him why, if he was so confident in the Soviet system, it was necessary, forty years after the Russian Revolution, to insist that reporters and novelists, artists, and even musicians should have to follow the party line. Why not a little competitive coexistence for ideas in the next forty years? He smiled and picked up a little plastic letter opener and began drumming on the table. There was competition among ideas in the Soviet Union, he said, and there would be much more in the next forty years. Then, suddenly, he asked me how old I was. I said I was forty-eight. Then, he added, if I was going to fight communism I should know more about it, but at forty-eight I should live to see the day when what he was predicting—coexistence—would be realized. He hoped, he said, that he had not offended me, and I said he had not.

It was clear in this talk, as in his previous condemnation of Stalin's barbarities, that he was defending the Soviet system but searching for ways to modify it both at home and abroad. He was constantly insisting that the Soviet Union must be treated as an equal in its negotiations with the United States, but was aware that the world was changing and that the great powers had to change with it. "What sort of Communist society is it that has no sausage?" he kept asking. I have often thought since then that he at least helped prepare the way for Mikhail Gorbachev's reforms in the eighties, but despite his infectious smile, he was crude and cruel, and even reckless in his threats to force the Allies out of Berlin and place nuclear weapons in Cuba. When these adventures failed, he was finally banished into a little dacha in the countryside, and even his memoirs were denounced as a fake.

Over the years I have wondered if these interviews with Soviet leaders were really useful. They gave us disturbing glimpses of the official Soviet mind, and occasionally provided hints of possible compromises, but most of the time they were used by the Soviet government as instruments of provocation and intimidation. For example, I went back to Moscow in December of 1965 to interview Khrushchev's successor, Premier Aleksei Kosygin, who was supposed to be a moderate and even reflective man. Instead, he was almost as harsh as Stalin. He accused the United States of whipping up a military psychosis in the world and compelling the Soviet Union to raise its military budget.

"You are keeping the dangers of war before the eyes of the European people," he said, "and the European peoples will never forgive you for not letting them live out their lives peacefully." When I denounced this as a "monstrous distortion," he merely turned to a tirade against President Johnson's policy of arming the West Germans and fighting in Vietnam. "I cannot agree," he observed, "that you have the right to kill defenseless people. You have more than a hundred thousand troops in Vietnam and you are sending another hundred thousand. You'll see what this leads you to. . . . Everywhere you are seeking to intervene and to extend the war."

In all the trips I made to Moscow, I cannot remember a single calm objective conversation with a single Soviet official. In the Gorbachev days, when the Soviets were talking about more open policies, I tried to persuade them to open up their archives so that at least historians could get a better understanding of the Cold War, but they refused, maybe because many of the Soviet records of that unhappy period no longer exist. But I'm getting ahead of my story. I returned to Washington with a better understanding of just how cold the Cold War was to be.

# CHAPTER 24

# McCarthy and

# *the* Times

NO JOURNALISTIC MEMOIR of my days in Washington would be complete without an attempt to explain, however painful, the role of the press during Senator Joseph McCarthy's anticommunist crusade in the late forties and fifties. If his malevolent influence had died with him in May of 1959, he would probably have been forgotten like many other two-bit demagogues of the past, but even near the end of the century, traces of "McCarthyism" hang on like an old infection.

In the name of anticommunism, he tried to strike down the freedom of the mind, which, above everything else, provides our greatest advantage over the Communist regimes. He had a remorseless, penetrating voice, a villainous face, and a treacherous mind. He didn't fool the press and the people by stealth; his techniques were as obvious as a punch in the nose. But for almost ten years he intimidated the Senate, weakened the president's conduct of foreign affairs, dominated the news, and proved that McCarthyism was a powerful political technique. Even in the nineties it is still the last refuge of our political scoundrels, and has been embalmed in our dictionaries as "indiscriminate, often unfounded accusations, sensationalism, inquisitorial investigative methods, ostensibly in the suppression of communism."

Fear of the rising and expanding power of the Communists in the Soviet Union and China at that time was no doubt the source of his influence. President Truman, McCarthy asserted, had "lost" China—as if Harry had ever had it. Stalin, in defiance of his promises to President Roosevelt, had built a new empire in Eastern Europe as the old British and French empires were collapsing. General MacArthur's armies had suffered over 100,000 casualties and had been run out of North Korea by the Chinese, and the people at home were looking for scapegoats.

They had understandable reasons for anxiety. Moscow had broken Washington's monopoly on the atom bomb and occupied the northern outer islands of Japan. The Chinese Communists were threatening the Chinese Nationalists on the island of Formosa, and the American people had not forgotten Roosevelt's warning to "Remember Pearl Harbor." It was also popular in those days to say that the Communists were just like the Nazis, out to conquer the world.

So McCarthy had plenty of inflammatory stuff at his disposal. He was up for reelection in 1952 and was looking for an issue. He didn't mind what that issue was, just so long as it was dramatic enough to get him publicity. He had some friends in the press, notably Willard Edwards of the *Chicago Tribune,* who dug up some old discounted claims that there were nearly three hundred "security risks" in the State Department, and on Lincoln's Birthday 1950, of all times, McCarthy went to Wheeling, West Virginia, and presented these old chestnuts as a "great discovery" of Communist subversion. This was denounced as a "witch-hunt" by some papers, but in fairness that was a wrong name, for McCarthy wasn't looking for mythical witches but flesh-and-blood Communists, such as those who had recently infiltrated the Canadian government, and the British scientists who had defected to Moscow.

By the fifties I didn't look to the Senate for moral guidance, but it never occurred to me that a senator of the United States could charge hundreds of State Department officials with treasonable activities and get away with it—certainly not without producing the evidence he always said he had but never produced. He not only thought the Russians were coming but also believed they were already twisting U.S. policy in their favor. He was desperately bold and cunning. He knew that big lies produced big headlines. He also knew that most newspapers would print almost any outrageous charge a United States senator made in public, provided he put his name to it, and he counted on the fact that newspapers didn't like to print denials of charges from anonymous sources.

I digress here to explain how these newspaper practices originated. In this big diverse country, most papers could not afford to send reporters to Washington. So in the past century they banded together to form the Associated Press, a cooperative association that established bureaus in Washington and all other news centers, shared each other's local news, and shared expenses.

Since these papers were of different political persuasions, it followed that news agency stories for such diverse clients had to be as factual as the multiplication table, and the sources of all dispatches should be carefully identified except under the most unusual circumstances. Thus, most news going to the papers and to the radio and television stations was comparatively free of analysis or even explanation. It was a sound enough theory and took into account everything but the arts of political deception. For example, putting quotation marks around McCarthy's false charges did not relieve us of complicity in McCarthy's campaign.

Many newspapers condemned him on their editorial pages but gave him plenty of space on the front pages, which had more effect on public opinion. He denounced those who failed to do so as being soft on communism or worse. Also the papers were more partisan in those days, and many of them not only shared his fear of Communist subversion, but also favored his attacks on the Democrats, who had controlled the White House since 1933. His charges may not have made sense, but they made headlines and they sold a lot of papers.

McCarthy knew how to take advantage of this "cult of objectivity." He made the front pages by announcing his discovery one day and embellishing it a few days later, and each time he still hit the front pages. All this began when MacArthur was calling privately on Washington for atomic weapons to avoid disaster in Korea, and Peking and Moscow, then sworn to an eternal alliance, had everybody talking about falling dominoes abroad and Communist spies at home.

I had assumed that the administration and the Senate would challenge McCarthy—which they finally did—but at first Eisenhower hesitated to take him on. He has since been condemned for letting McCarthy cause so much damage for so long, but Ike had his own way of dealing with personal enemies. He came to the White House believing that Roosevelt and Truman had accumulated too much power in the executive branch, and he didn't want to attack members of his own party in the Senate. He was convinced from the start—and eventually proved to be right—that McCarthy would destroy himself in the end. "I won't get in the gutter with that guy," Ike said. But the trouble with this technique of judicious leaving-alone was that McCarthy destroyed a lot of other people before Eisenhower finally had enough. Besides, the president was disturbed by evidence of Communist espionage in Canada after the war, and was afraid it might be repeated in the United States.

McCarthy wasn't all talk. He also proved that he had a lot of popular support. In the senatorial election of 1952, he ran a vicious campaign against Millard Tydings, the Democratic candidate from Maryland, printing a fake photo of Tydings shaking hands with Earl Browder, the leader of the American Communist party. Tydings lost by forty thousand votes. This increased McCarthy's power of black-mail, which had been rising ever since President Truman had fired General MacArthur in 1951 for insubordination in Korea.

From Korea, the *Times* reported in great detail MacArthur's side of the story, and in Washington we compiled a careful record of the Truman-MacArthur differences and the political consequences of his dismissal. But elsewhere in the country, McCarthy's defense of the general was popular—69 percent for MacArthur in the Gallup Poll. In some cities, the American flag was flown upside down. In others, Truman was burned in effigy. McCarthy told a Milwaukee audience that Truman was a "son of a bitch" surrounded by men "drunk on bourbon and Benedictine." Speaker Joe Martin of Massachusetts presided over a Republican caucus that he said discussed the im-peachment of Truman, and the president was booed at Griffith Sta-dium—the first time a president had been subjected to such indignity since Hoover during the depression.

This was my first test as an editor and I didn't handle it well. I decided that we should assign a reporter to cover McCarthy day by day and keep a careful record on him, being sure to report anything he said that was new but to avoid repeating his undocumented charges. I chose the best congressional reporter we had, but was stunned one day when McCarthy got up in the Senate and attacked the *Times* for its coverage of his activities. "But what can you expect," he said, "for the reporter they have covering me used to be a member of the Young Communist League!" There was no evidence of bias in the reporter's work, but he admitted that the charge was true.

I wrote to Catledge, the *Times'* managing editor, as follows: "I don't think our reporter was fair to the paper or to me or to his other colleagues in the bureau. If I had responsibility for other sections of the *Times,* where no political material was handled, I would not feel that this record had destroyed his usefulness to the paper. To fire him outright would seem to me too drastic, and an unnecessary cruelty not only to him but to his wife and three children. But I am clear that he has forfeited the confidence of this bureau and cannot continue to do the kind of work expected of him here." Catledge agreed and ordered the reporter back to New York, where he did excellent work until he retired.

We continued following McCarthy, however, wherever he went, and one night he got into a brawl that started his decline. After a party at the Sulgrave Club near Dupont Circle in Washington, Richard Nixon found him in the men's room beating up Drew Pearson, a prominent newspaper columnist and one of his critics. "This one's for you, Dick," McCarthy said and belted the bloody and half-conscious Pearson in the mouth. When Nixon finally got him out of the club, McCarthy couldn't remember where he had parked his car, and they wandered around for over half an hour before they found it. The story was all over the capital the next morning, but McCarthy kept going for years, until Ed Murrow of CBS finally exposed his character on television, and the Senate censured and got rid of him.

Not, however, before he mounted another campaign against the Democrats, charging that Roosevelt had sold out to Stalin at Yalta, Truman had lost Korea, and that Eisenhower and Dulles were still carrying on a policy of appeasement. Somehow he had gotten hold of parts of the official record of the Yalta Conference and was using these to prove that his charges were based on unquestioned facts. I went to Dulles and argued that only by printing the entire text of the Yalta Conference could these rumors be put into proper perspective. He gave me the entire Yalta file and the *Times* printed it in the longest dispatch ever published in the paper.

I mention this to illustrate that the press is not always the adversary but sometimes is the ally of government officials. Eisenhower and Dulles would not make an open break with a member of their own party, but they often turned to the press to release information they didn't want to publish on their own authority.

They could not, however, prevent the Senate from continuing its charges against the press, and Senator James Eastland of Mississippi joined the McCarthy crusade and launched another attack on *The New York Times* in 1955. This produced intense debate among the executives of the paper, especially over what was to be done about an employee who invoked the Fifth Amendment against self-incrimination and refused to testify. Arthur Hays Sulzberger fired the first reporter who did so. "It is my opinion," he wrote, "that as a member of *The New York Times* staff, it was your duty to answer the questions put to you by the committee, and that your refusal to do so has ended your usefulness as a reporter." The publisher felt that even though the reporter had the same right as any other citizen to take the Fifth, he could not retain the confidence of the *Times'* readers if he did so. Later and with great reluctance, Sulzberger felt that such a blanket rule was unjustified and that each case had to be decided on its own merits.

When the Eastland committee's investigation dragged on for months without producing a single case of Communist influence in the reporting of the paper, the *Times* stated its position in the following terms:

> We cannot speak unequivocally for the long future. But we can have faith. And our faith is strong that long after Senator Eastland and his present subcommittee are forgotten, long after segregation has lost its final battle in the South, long after all that was known as McCarthyism is a dim unwelcome memory, long after the last congressional committee has learned that it cannot tamper successfully with a free press, *The New York Times* will be speaking for the men who make it, and only for the men who make it, and speaking, without fear or favor, the truth as it sees it.

Despite these fine words, everybody, with the exception of Ed Murrow, came out of the McCarthy period feeling vaguely guilty— the president, who had even refused to defend General Marshall against McCarthy's shameful charges; Secretary of State Dulles, who had not stood up for some of his best foreign service officers; the Senate, which was late in censuring the senator; and the press, which served up and dramatized his lies. Many editors made a lot of speeches about the problem of printing or suppressing undocumented charges, but never really solved it. And the final irony of the whole disgraceful affair was that, when McCarthy finally drank himself to death, his body was displayed in the place of honor in the Senate, and he was given a hero's memorial service, where he was described as a patriot destroyed by political and journalistic trickery!

At the beginning of McCarthy's campaign, I treated it as political theater, then reported his gradual decline, and tried to get out the facts he was suppressing. But it wasn't until 1954, when I had the greater freedom of writing a column, that I was able, along with many other colleagues in the press, to take a stiffer line. In the process, however, I learned for the first time as the *Times'* bureau chief that getting out a complete, accurate, and fair account of the news was no easy task. Even with a superb staff, we were, I'm sorry to say, intimidated much of the time by the popularity of McCarthy's lies and his charges that his opponents were "soft on communism."

# CHAPTER 25

# The
# Oppenheimer Case

WE REMEMBER SENATOR McCarthy long after his death, but tend to forget the public officials whose careers were destroyed during his campaign of intimidation—for example, Dr. J. Robert Oppenheimer. The Oppenheimer case sounds like one of Arthur Conan Doyle's tales of mystery and intrigue, but even his old sleuth Sherlock Holmes could scarcely have imagined the tragedy of the man who, more than anyone else, invented the atom bomb and was then dismissed by the U.S. government in 1954 as a potential security risk. By accident, I played a part in that famous case and report the details here for the first time to indicate the role newspapers play sometimes in public policy and what happens when officials become prey to their worst suspicions.

I met Oppenheimer by chance one morning in January 1954 on the Eastern Airlines flight en route from Washington to New York. He was at that time a famous but remote and mysterious figure, thin and slightly stooped, with short gray hair and startling blue eyes. At forty-one, he was the most honored nuclear physicist in the world, consultant to the Atomic Energy Commission and the Defense Department, and head of the Institute for Advanced Studies in Princeton, New Jersey.

If there hadn't been a vacant seat beside him on the plane, I would have no story to tell, but there was, so I introduced myself and sat down. He was not visibly overjoyed by this chance encounter, but reporters are used to that. We talked vaguely about President Eisenhower's first months in the White House. I never mentioned anything about Oppenheimer's work, and yet he seemed unaccountably nervous in my presence and obviously under some strain. Acting on this alone, I began asking questions when I returned to the capital and found out more than I expected.

In November 1953, William L. Borden, who shortly before this date had been secretary of the Joint Committee of Congress on Atomic Energy, wrote a letter to J. Edgar Hoover, the head of the Federal Bureau of Investigation, which concluded:

> 1. Between 1929 and mid-1942, more probably than not, J. Robert Oppenheimer was a sufficiently hardened Communist that he either volunteered espionage information to the Soviets or complied with a request for such information. . . . 2. More probably than not, he has been functioning as an espionage agent; and 3. More probably than not, he has since acted under a Soviet directive in influencing United States military, atomic energy, intelligence, and diplomatic policy.

In support of this, Borden asserted in his letter that Oppenheimer had in the past made substantial monthly contributions to the Communist party; that his wife and brother were Communists; that he had "at least one Communist mistress"; that he had no close friends except Communists; that he had recruited Communists or pro-Communists into the atomic energy establishment; that he had "worked tirelessly, from January 31, 1950, onward, to retard the United States hydrogen bomb program"; and that he had repeatedly given false testimony about his friends and activities to the government.

Sensational as they were, these charges cannot have been a surprise to the director of the FBI. Oppenheimer's bizarre habits and his past associations with Communists had all been admitted by him to be true years before Borden's letter. What was new was the assertion that more probably than not he was a spy passing secret military information to Moscow. Even though Oppenheimer was never restored to his old position, he was acquitted unanimously of ever having passed official information to the Soviet Union. In fact, when Eisenhower heard that most of these charges had been made before and asked Admiral Strauss, head of the Atomic Energy Commission, why Oppenheimer had been kept on in these sensitive posts for years, Strauss replied, "Because we couldn't have built the atom bomb without him."

Nevertheless, on November 30, 1953, J. Edgar Hoover circulated copies of the Borden letter to the relevant agencies of the government and to the office of the president. On December 3, 1953, President

Eisenhower discussed it with Strauss, Charles E. Wilson, secretary of defense, and Arthur S. Flemming, director of defense mobilization. After that meeting, the president issued a private order that "a blank wall be placed between Dr. Oppenheimer and any secret data," and that a secret investigation be made of the Borden charges.

I heard about this merely by snooping around and asking, "What's wrong with Oppenheimer these days?" I tried to see Oppenheimer, but he was in Britain delivering the Reith lectures and getting an honorary degree from Oxford, and I was referred to his New York lawyer, Lloyd K. Garrison. He confirmed that a list of government charges had been given to Oppenheimer, that his Q clearance to receive secret information had been suspended, and that a date had been set for the official investigation.

Garrison asked me not to publish the facts of the charges and the "blank wall" order of the president. For, he said, if I published such sensational news before Oppenheimer had time to prepare his answer, he would never be able to catch up with the negative public reaction. I said I understood his concern, but added that the decision to publish was not for me but for the *Times* to decide. I asked him, however, for a commitment that if we withheld publication until Oppenheimer could prepare his answers, the *Times* would have first and exclusive rights to publish both. He indicated that this could be arranged but not before he had cleared it with Oppenheimer.

The *Times* agreed to the arrangement, as I felt sure the responsible editors would, and I should add this: in fifty years on *The New York Times,* I was involved in quite a few cases in which the immediate competitive interests of the paper conflicted with the honor of an individual, and on not a single occasion in my personal experience did the *Times* put its competitive interests first.

Weeks passed after Oppenheimer approved our publication plan, and I got increasingly nervous, for we knew that J. Edgar Hoover was in close touch with Senator McCarthy, and I was told that the senator planned to charge the government with harboring an "atomic energy spy" in a speech he was scheduled to make in Texas. I reported this to Garrison, but he insisted that we withhold publication a little longer. On the day of the opening of the Oppenheimer hearings, however, Garrison was convinced that he could risk a McCarthy leak no longer and assured me that the *Times* alone would break the news.

When the story led the front page of the *Times,* President Eisenhower was furious. "This fellow Oppenheimer is sure acting like a

Communist," he told his press secretary, Jim Hagerty. "He is using all the rules that they use to try to get public sentiment in their corner." Gordon Gray, the chairman of the board of inquiry, had warned Oppenheimer and his counsel that everything was to be confidential, and while Garrison told him in advance that he had authorized me to publish the charges and answers, Gray regarded this as additional evidence of Oppenheimer's bad judgment and deviousness.

Oppenheimer told me later that he knew he would irritate the members of the Gray board by going public without their approval, but, he added, he didn't "trust" Strauss. This surprised me, for Admiral Strauss had chosen Oppenheimer to head the Institute for Advanced Studies, and had given Oppenheimer a chance to resign privately and avoid the investigation. This had angered Oppenheimer, who sent him a letter, saying: "Under the circumstances, this course of action would mean that I accept and concur in the view that I am not fit to serve the government that I have served now for some twelve years. This I cannot do."

I later understood Oppenheimer's anxiety, however, for I visited Strauss at his farm in Virginia and gained a clear impression that he had persuaded Eisenhower to order the proceedings and wanted Oppenheimer out of the government. He justified trapping Oppenheimer into vague or inaccurate answers by withholding from him transcripts of documents in possession of the Gray board's counsel, Roger Robb. This was justified, he said, to test Oppenheimer's truthfulness, though all it did was to test his fallible memory.

Oppenheimer was, of course, hurt by his former close Communist associations, and particularly by visiting Haakon Chevalier, a former associate on the French faculty at the University of California. Chevalier was known to have tried to get secret U.S. documents for the Soviet Union, and when Oppenheimer spent a few days with him in Paris, I was told, and published, that the members of the board of inquiry thought he had risked being "forced at gunpoint into a plane and taken behind the Iron Curtain." When I asked Oppenheimer about this, he said it was a fantasy but he had no more assurance on this point than did the board of inquiry.

He was also hurt by his prior opposition to the invention of the hydrogen bomb. This was strongly supported by Edward Teller, who was generally credited with solving its mysteries, by Strauss, and by Gray, the chairman of the investigation committee. Gray agreed in principle that a man should not be punished for expressing his honest opinions, but he felt that it was "beyond dispute" that the United States should develop "the strongest possible offensive weapons." Teller agreed and told the board that Oppenheimer's "confused and complicated actions" left him (Teller) with a feeling that "I would feel personally more secure if public matters were left in other hands." Eisenhower apparently felt the same way, but he did not consult with some of his closest advisers, among them John J. McCloy, Vannevar Bush, and James Conant, the former president of Harvard, but relied mainly on the advice of Strauss, even on the hydrogen bomb question. This was odd, for Ike himself had originally expressed grave doubts about developing this so-called ultimate weapon.

Once the whole story of Oppenheimer's background and Communist associations became the center of controversy, public sentiment was against him. He was a loner and an eccentric. In the letter he authorized me to publish about his private life, he said, "I read very widely, but mostly classics, novels, plays, and poetry. . . . I studied and read Sanskrit [he spoke eight languages]. I was not interested in and did not read about economics or politics. I was almost wholly divorced from the contemporary scene in this country. I never read a newspaper or a current magazine like *Time* or *Harper's*. I had no radio, no telephone. . . . I was deeply interested in my science but I had no understanding of the relations of man to his society."

He did become intensely interested in the struggle against fascism in the Spanish Civil War, and also in helping the scientists and other refugees in Hitler's Germany. He contributed generously to their causes, subscribed to procommunist publications, and kept in touch with old friends from his teaching days in Europe, but he always denied that he had ever passed secret information to the Communists, and the board agreed.

This case troubled me for years. I often wondered whether my scoop had prejudiced the board of inquiry against Oppenheimer and thus had implicated me in his tragedy. Indeed, just before writing this book, I went to New York and called on Mr. Garrison, now elderly but gentle and courteous as always. I told him of my anxiety and he told me to forget it. The cards were stacked against Oppenheimer before the inquiry ever started, he felt, and if the charges had come out first, through McCarthy or anybody else, without Oppenheimer's letter of defense, things would, if possible, have been even worse.

I had no personal feelings about Oppenheimer. I had used him to get an important story and he had used me for his defense. The more I thought about the case, however, the more I felt I had missed its deeper significance. Many things were on trial other than Oppenheimer. The security system, which assumed guilt and undertook to probe Oppenheimer's "soul," was on trial. The members of the board and the AEC were on trial, for while McCarthy had helped create the climate of fear and suspicion, it was assumed that these highly intelligent men would not be influenced unduly by the emotions of the time.

What was also on trial was the ability of the government to handle eccentric geniuses. If Oppenheimer had been just another bright physicist with traditional ways of thinking and acting, the chances are he would never have invented the atom bomb, but he was an oddball who lived in a cocoon and apparently enjoyed the company of other oddballs. McGeorge Bundy, in his excellent study of the atom bomb, *Danger and Survival,* pointed to Oppenheimer's combination of "charm and arrogance, intelligence and blindness, awareness and insensitivity." And one of Oppenheimer's defenders on the Atomic Energy Commission, after staying up all night writing an appeal for acquittal, wondered, "Why am I doing this? I don't even like the guy."

Two vague thoughts bothered me about all this. First, if Oppenheimer were as unreliable and even as unpatriotic as some of his detractors believed, might he not, if abandoned, go over to the other side with all his special knowledge of nuclear physics? General Groves of the AEC also wondered about this. And second, didn't the future economic as well as military security of the country rest at least in part with these inventive scientific minds?

In the end, however, and not only in the case of Oppenheimer, most controversies involving the threat of Communist power and doctrine tended to be won in Washington by those who feared the most and assumed the worst. No doubt this worst-case mentality helped rebuild the military defenses of the nation, but it also limited objective discussion of the Communist problem.

Oppenheimer died early and unhappily but he was not bitter. He said he looked on his experience as a natural disaster, as if he had been caught in a train wreck or an earthquake. I thought there were many other reasons, including McCarthy, but many more intelligent men, including Eisenhower, Strauss, and Oppenheimer himself, contributed to the tragedy.

# CHAPTER 26

# John Foster Dulles

No annihilation without representation.
—Allied reaction to Dulles's doctrine
of massive retaliation

JOHN FOSTER DULLES was a nonstop talker who was not averse
to publicity and thought he could use the *Times* to his advantage.
I saw more of him than any other secretary of state from the forties
to the nineties, but I still write about him with divided feelings. He
was widely regarded, particularly by other foreign secretaries, as an
inflexible moralist who combined religion and diplomacy to the detriment of both, but I'm not sure that this sassy judgment was quite
fair. Like all secretaries of state, Dulles had to reconcile the demands
of foreign policy with the harsh realities of domestic policies.

This was particularly difficult for a Presbyterian minister's son
representing a Republican party that was wavering between isolationism and imperialism, but I thought he sacrificed policy to politics
more than necessary. He talked like a preacher and thought the
Soviets were beyond redemption, but his private advice to Eisenhower was more cautious than his sermons, and his official correspondence, now available, indicates that his threats of "massive
retaliation" and his practice of "brinkmanship," while risky, were
mostly calculated bluff.

Even when he was in office, I was struck by this difference between his private conversation and his public pronouncements. In public, he came across as a muscular Christian, with the Bible in one hand and the atom bomb in the other: rigorous, self-righteous, and crafty. In private, while seldom in doubt, he could be generous, thoughtful, and even amusing, with odd habits of twirling his key ring or stirring his whisky with his finger. He had a remarkable talent for getting rid of many of the most qualified men in the State Department when he thought they disagreed with him or embarrassed him politically—two examples, George Kennan and Paul Nitze, the heads of the policy-planning staff—but he was sensitive to the pride of the Congress and the Allies, promoted a bipartisan foreign policy and the integration of Europe, and was undoubtedly one of the most influential secretaries of state in the postwar period.

He regarded himself, with good reason, as the best-qualified man in the United States to replace Dean Acheson as secretary of state. He was the grandson of John Watson Foster, secretary of state under President Benjamin Harrison, and served as his grandfather's secretary at the second peace conference at The Hague. Thus he began his diplomatic career when he was nineteen and still an undergraduate at Princeton. His uncle, Robert Lansing, was secretary of state under President Woodrow Wilson, and with this family background, Dulles represented the United States at the peace conferences after both the first and second world wars. His appointment as secretary of state in 1953, therefore, seemed to him inevitable and did nothing to discourage his conviction that he was better trained to be secretary of state than any American of the century. Also, he was appointed to the U.S. Senate in 1949 and defeated in 1950, and he excelled for many years in the practice of international law, where he mastered the arts of negotiation, manipulation, and even deception.

Eisenhower respected this record. Ike treated members of the cabinet as his theater commanders—same as in the army—and he gave them wide authority in their separate fields. Thus, Dulles was his theater commander at the State Department, and George Humphrey his theater commander at the Treasury. It took Ike a while to realize that George Humphrey's penchant for cutting the budget reduced the power of the armed forces on which Dulles's militaristic approach to foreign policy depended, but when they differed he tended to agree with both of them and then do as he pleased. Ike refused to go along with Dulles's recommendation that the United States intervene in the Vietnam War, but most of the time he followed Dulles's advice.

I first met Dulles during the 1944 presidential election campaign when Governor Thomas E. Dewey, the Republican nominee, sent him to Washington to arrange some way to keep politics from wrecking the United Nations as it had wrecked the League of Nations in the 1920 election. Dulles strongly supported this objective and was successful at it. In fact, I always thought he made a greater contribution to the nation's foreign policy before he became secretary of state than after, for he not only helped bring the parties together under Truman but also backed Secretary of State Byrnes in the first critical confrontation with the Soviets over the peace treaties in 1946.

On that occasion, at Church House in London, Molotov tried to expel the French and the Chinese from the negotiations and bully Byrnes into accepting Soviet domination of Eastern Europe. I was with Byrnes at Claridge's hotel when he asked Dulles to support him in rejecting the Soviet demands, and Dulles not only agreed to do so but also went home and convinced the other leaders of the Republican party that the postwar settlement of the war would be fatally flawed unless they went along. This was one time when his taste for the politics of melodrama really succeeded.

Outside of Eisenhower and Vandenberg, I felt Dulles did more than any other Republican to end the isolationist tradition, but he put a strain on my political and even my religious convictions. For at first he thought any compromise with the Communists was downright sinful, and negotiated anticommunist alliances in the Middle East and Southeast Asia that contributed ultimately to the disaster in Vietnam. In contrast, however, he once proposed to Eisenhower the possibility of making "a spectacular effort to relax world tensions and execute mutual withdrawals of Red Army forces and United States forces abroad." The result of this, he explained, would be a "broad zone of restricted armament in Europe, with Soviets withdrawn from Eastern Europe and the United States from Europe" (Dulles memorandum, September 6, 1953). This extraordinary proposal was surprising, for it would have achieved Moscow's main objective of putting U.S. power three thousand miles from the Rhine. It did not win Ike's approval.

Dulles was the only man I ever knew who actually devoted a good part of his mature life to running for the office of secretary of state, and of course he was sure he had it in the 1948 presidential election, when everybody, except Harry Truman, thought Dewey would win. When Dulles was finally appointed by Eisenhower in 1953, he was not impeded by undue modesty. In fact, he originally wanted to have his office in the White House, where he thought his influence on

President Eisenhower would be greater, but Ike didn't think that was a very good idea, so Dulles settled for Foggy Bottom.

Once there, he saw no need to share his responsibilities. He once pointed out to me that forty-five agencies of the government in addition to the Department of State had a hand in the conduct of foreign policy, and he devoted much time to keeping them out of it. He was also suspicious of what he called "breezy intellectuals." In 1953, handling the Soviet Union was his main problem, but almost the first thing he did was to get rid of George Kennan, the most knowledgeable Soviet expert in the country, who had been kicked out of his post as U.S. ambassador in Moscow for comparing Stalin's Russia to Hitler's Germany.

Though Kennan was the star of the Foreign Service with twenty-five years of experience behind him, Dulles called him in and told him he didn't have a job for him. He did, however, ask Kennan to tell him what he thought of U.S.-Soviet relations, and when Kennan did so with his usual candor and clarity, Dulles remarked, "That's very interesting. You know, you interest me when you talk about these matters. Very few people do. I hope you'll come in from time to time and let us have your comments on what's going on."

When Kennan got home that night, he said to his wife it was as though he (Kennan) had said to her: "You know, I'm divorcing you as of today, and you're to leave my bed and board at once. But I love the way you cook scrambled eggs, and I wonder if you'd mind fixing me up a batch of them right now, before you go."

Before he became secretary of state, Dulles had studied the causes of the two world wars. He was convinced that they would never have happened if the United States had made clear to Germany in advance that it would intervene, as it ultimately did. I saw him frequently at his timbered house in Cleveland Park, and invariably he kept insisting that peace depended on U.S. participation, and he helped persuade Vandenberg that this should be the basis of our policy.

He had another reason for encouraging a private line of communication with the *Times.* He didn't want to attack McCarthy, a powerful member of his own party, but he knew a great deal about McCarthy's lies and drunkenness, and had a cunning way of telling me all about them without asking me to do anything about it or putting it off the record.

More important, when he and Eisenhower decided in 1953 that they had to put pressure on Communist China to force a negotiated settlement of the Korean War, without resorting to an ultimatum,

Dulles allowed me to know not only that they were considering the use of atomic weapons in an expanded war, but also that specific actions had been taken to move nuclear weapons and the appropriate bombers to bases close to China's mainland. This same information was also passed through diplomatic channels in such a way that the Chinese leaders would take them seriously, and both Ike and Dulles later concluded that these indirect threats were finally responsible for the Korean truce.

I was uneasy at first about this confidential liaison. Most of the time, he informed me of his views on important events but did not allow me to quote him. It was a form of compulsory plagiarism, and I feared that he might try to use the *Times* to distribute inaccurate and unattributed information. Accordingly, I sought and received permission from the responsible editors in New York to continue this arrangement. But at no time did I ever have reason to believe that he was using or implicating the *Times* in a diplomatic fraud.

I did, however, presume to tell him I thought his so-called loyalty program in the State Department, run by a friend of Joe McCarthy, was a cruel disgrace that violated his own moral principles. He replied that he had been haunted all his life by Woodrow Wilson's failure to assure congressional support of the League of Nations and he was determined to hold the votes of senators, regardless of what he thought of them. He also reminded me that Dean Acheson, whom he respected, had almost been forced out of office precisely because he would not pretend to agree with senators for whom he had contempt. It was on this ground, but not on this ground alone, that I respected Acheson more than his successor.

I got the impression that Dulles regarded the atom bombing of Hiroshima and Nagasaki as an unnecessary slaughter of helpless civilians, but later he felt that perhaps that terrible event was a restraining influence on the Soviet leaders, and he boasted about his willingness to go to the brink of war in order to intimidate the Communists. No doubt there was something to this, but since he could not know how Moscow would react to his threats, it was risky business and troubled the Allies, who didn't want another war on their territory and insisted on a policy of "no annihilation without representation."

Dulles described his policy of massive retaliation in an address before the Council on Foreign Relations in New York on January 12, 1954. "The basic decision [of the Eisenhower administration]," he said, was to "depend primarily upon a great capacity to retaliate, instantly, by means and at places of our own choosing." Dean Acheson, no fan of Dulles, was appalled. He said that a threat, to be effective, had to be credible, and that Dulles was saying the United States wouldn't meet Soviet or Soviet-inspired aggression at the point of the attack but maybe at some other point, even in the Soviet Union.

This, Acheson insisted, was not credible, was not even rational, and would divert the United States from other necessary and neglected means of meeting limited wars, and destroy the unity of the Western alliance. "To keep the opponent guessing," Acheson emphasized, "may be useful in some fields but not in this one. For if he [the enemy] wrongly guesses that we are going to hit him, the likelihood is that we shall be hit ourselves. One of the most dangerous ways to keep our opponents guessing is to keep ourselves guessing."

I was interested in this controversy from another and more personal angle and talked at length with Dulles about it. He was a prominent leader of the Federal Council of Churches of Christ in America, and was constantly mourning the decline of religion and summoning the people to return to the virtues of fair dealing and kindly feeling. I asked him once how he could defend the sanctity of every human life on the one hand and the doctrine of massive retaliation, even nuclear retaliation, on the other. He was visibly uncomfortable with this question. It was necessary, he said evasively, to "keep the enemy off balance." The morality of nations was not the same as the morality of individuals, he said, and while this was true enough, he insisted that he was leading a moral crusade against an immoral enemy. One of the less theological aspects of his policy of massive retaliation was that this bluff didn't prevent Soviet-supported aggressions in Korea and Vietnam, or help the anticommunist forces in East Germany, Poland, and Hungary when they defied their masters in the Kremlin.

He liked these philosophic wanderings with a fellow Presbyterian, but like most people, he preferred praise to criticism. He was irritated when accused of letting McCarthy rifle the files of the State Department, particularly when I pointed this out in the *Times,* which was circulated among his friends in New York and read by officials in the capitals and embassies of the world, and he accused me and the *Times* of carrying on a vendetta against him and the Eisenhower administration.

He said he felt, and he thought the president felt, that we had been unfair in our reporting of the administration's foreign policy. He could have gone to Arthur Sulzberger about this, he said, but he decided to talk to me since I was head of the Washington bureau (also, he implied, the principal offender). In recent months, he thought we had been trying to elect the Democrats, that we were out to get him, and he wanted to assure us that we would fail in this. Therefore, he concluded, since the administration would be in office for four more years, he hoped that we could reach some more satisfactory understanding than in the past.

I said that before I responded to his charges I wanted to be sure that he was referring to news stories and not to analytical Q head pieces. He replied that he was talking about everything. With this out of the way, I reminded him that the *Times* had supported Eisenhower in both the 1952 and 1956 elections, and said I rejected his charges in toto. No doubt, I added, the *Times* in Washington, and I personally, had written a great number of background or analytical pieces, all of them clearly labeled not as news but as analysis, in which he and his policies had been sharply criticized. I said we had done so because his policies and his personal diplomacy were often the subject of the sharpest possible criticism even among many of the best-informed and most experienced colleagues in his own administration. This was, in my judgment, part of what was going on here and therefore a legitimate and necessary part of our report to the *Times.* To characterize this, however, as a campaign to get him, and further to suggest that this was done with a political motivation to help the Democrats, was, I said, wholly false.

He responded to this by saying that he thought we were taking entirely too much of our information from the Washington embassies. He said ambassadors had nothing else to do but try to influence public opinion. I said we went to them because most of the people in his department who were available to us weren't informed, and those who were informed weren't available. This was the only serious confrontation I had with Dulles in all his years in office, and he showed no resentment thereafter.

By this time, I had come to moderate my own early excessively moralistic approach to foreign policy, but the Dulles habit of dividing the world into the good and the bad was still apparent long after he was gone. President Reagan was still condemning the leaders of the Soviet Union in the eighties as immoral men presiding over an evil empire. This proved to be popular politics but bad diplomacy not only in the fifties but also in the eighties.

Dulles's philosophy also confronted me with a professional and personal dilemma I was never really able to fathom: how to choose when expediency and morality were in conflict. It was, I came to believe, no good to look for saints in the midst of the endless and dangerous complexities that confront presidents and secretaries of state in the atomic age. At the same time, it was hard to avoid the conclusion that many of the disastrous decisions taken in the past were traceable to ignorance, presumption, vanity, fear, and other personal shortcomings. Accordingly, I was always fascinated by the contradictions in Dulles's character.

For example, it did not bother him that the United States was selling vast quantities of modern arms to impoverished nations that couldn't even feed their people, and in lesser ways his actions sometimes violated his moral soliloquies. Also, he was not immune to the tricks of politics. Two small incidents illustrate the point. During his campaign for election to the Senate in 1950, Dulles, who had never forgiven his son for leaving the Protestant faith to be a Roman Catholic priest, suddenly trotted him out on the campaign trail to impress the voters of the Catholic faith. He had seldom seen his son after what Dulles regarded as a heresy and a personal affront in leaving his father's church, and I couldn't help feeling that this political reunion was an act of blatant hypocrisy.

On another occasion during that campaign, I was standing in the snow at the foot of the stairs leading to his front door in New York. He came out with his wife, who slipped on the steps and fell several steps to the sidewalk. Fortunately, she was not badly hurt, but Dulles hesitated. His look was unmistakable. He was clearly more irritated with her than concerned for her safety. Somehow this incident stuck in my mind like his treatment of George Kennan, and was revived when after firing Kennan he appointed Scott McLeod, an ally of Joe McCarthy, as his administrative assistant with access to all personnel files and orders to impose what he called "positive loyalty" on the State Department and the Foreign Service.

"Be fair, hang it!" he would say in irritation when I ventured to say that he was mixing up his moral foreign policy with vote-catching. "The State Department is not a school of moral philosophy. I probably dislike the obstructionists even more than you do, but we need their votes or at least their neutrality or we won't have any foreign policy at all."

There was, however, a limit to Dulles's appeasement of the militant conservatives, and he demonstrated all his talents for creative manipulation when Senator McCarthy and his supporters tried to force Eisenhower to repudiate the agreements signed by President Roosevelt and Stalin at Yalta in 1945. This led to a most serious conflict over the control of the nation's foreign policy during Eisenhower's first term.

McCarthy had obtained limited access to these secret Yalta agreements, and was using them selectively to prove that Roosevelt had sold out to Stalin, who was ignoring the Yalta promise of free elections in Eastern Europe. McCarthy not only wanted the president to repudiate the agreements but to agree to a constitutional amendment that would forbid future presidents to sign any such agreements. Here Dulles intervened.

He pointed out that if the United States could repudiate one part of the Yalta agreements, Stalin could repudiate the Yalta commitment of U.S. rights in Berlin and Vienna. Also, that Yalta had assured the Soviet Union's support in the final phase of the war in Japan and that McCarthy's talk of liberating Eastern Europe was unrealistic, since the Red Army occupied all the Eastern European states.

Dulles considered releasing the secret Yalta agreements, but the British refused. Hearing of this, I suggested that he allow *The New York Times* to print the text of all the agreements—amounting to over 380,000 words. This, I said, would prevent McCarthy's selective use of the agreements for his own devious purposes. Dulles did not commit himself, but this led to the most interesting government-newspaper negotiations in my experience, the details of which are printed for the first time in the following chapter.

# CHAPTER 27

# *Yalta and*
# *the* Times

THE RELEASE OF the secret Yalta agreements to the *Times* supports an old newspaper joke in Washington that "the government is the only vessel that leaks from the top." Actually, it seldom happens. Usually, when you test it, you get the fishy eye, but occasionally, to your astonishment, you get what you want. The story of the Yalta leak is as follows:

On Sunday afternoon, March 13, 1953, I had a telephone call from Sidney Hyman, the young historian who wrote *The American President* and helped Robert Sherwood write *Roosevelt and Hopkins*. In doing this second book, Hyman was permitted to go through the private Yalta papers, or at least a considerable portion of them. He was disturbed about what he found in the papers, particularly an exchange of views between President Roosevelt and King Ibn Sa'ūd of Saudi Arabia.

My understanding of this conversation is that the president said he had stopped to see the king because he was worried about the position of the Jews in Palestine. Ibn Sa'ūd is understood to have replied that he was not worried about the Jews in Palestine but "the Jews in New York."

This led to a discussion in which Roosevelt was said to have used some contemptuous language about the "kikes in New York." It was an offhand remark, but many Republicans found out about it and hoped, by quoting the Yalta papers selectively, to weaken the Democratic party's influence on the Jews in the large and northern cities, which have traditionally been Democratic strongholds. Hyman's point in calling me was to say that he heard the Yalta papers might be released and that he understood Prime Minister Churchill was opposed to their publication.

I made several telephone calls and confirmed there was active discussion between London and Washington on the subject, but they were not on the point of publishing them because they might harm U.S. relations with other countries, particularly France and Germany, who were then discussing the rearmament of West Germany. I wrote this story that same afternoon.

I had little hope of getting hold of the papers, but the following noon the State Department's spokesman, Henry Suydam, held a press conference, which indicated to me that there was some funny political business afoot. Suydam confirmed the story that they were not going to "put out" the papers because, he said, publication would not be in the interest of national security.

He added, however, the obviously contradictory point that the department was going to send twenty-four copies of some of the documents to top legislative leaders on Capitol Hill—the speaker, the vice president, the chairmen of the various major committees concerned with foreign relations, and so on. The deduction everybody here made about this was that the State Department was trying to placate the Republican senators who wanted the papers put out for political reasons but was trying to avoid the responsibility for publication by sending a great number of edited copies to the Hill, knowing that in this case, as in others in the past, the information would "leak out." At that point we really went after the full document.

As soon as the Suydam announcement was put on the press association tickers, I got into a cab and went straight to the Senate and saw the chairman of the Senate Foreign Relations Committee, Senator Walter F. George of Georgia. I told him what had happened. He had not heard of it. He agreed that the motivation could only be political and that something had to be done either to prevent the excerpts from being sent to the Hill or to see that the entire document be published. His fear was that bits and pieces of the document would keep leaking out for weeks if they (the documents) were put into the hands of twenty-four different persons and that this would poison the whole atmosphere just at a time when unity was extremely important in the face of the Far Eastern and European crises. He noted, for example, that under the rules of his committee, any document sent on a confidential basis to him would be available to all ninety-six senators and that under these conditions the information was sure to leak out.

Consequently, he stated publicly that full publication of the document was preferable to calculated political leaks, but he refused to accept the documents himself. I recorded this in the second story on the Yalta papers.

On Tuesday morning, at nine o'clock, I called Secretary of State Dulles's office and said that I would like to see the secretary personally for five minutes. I said it was extremely important, that I had had a talk with Senator George that was not private and that I thought he would want to know about. I was told that this would be passed on to the secretary. Mr. Dulles had scheduled a press conference at eleven o'clock, and I attended.

After the conference, the assistant secretary of state for public affairs, Carl McCardle, who was sitting with Mr. Dulles during the conference, motioned me to go up to the secretary's office. I went up in the private elevator with McCardle, and the secretary was standing at his desk when I went in.

I told him I had been upset by the possibility that excerpts of the documents would be sent to the Hill and would get into the hands of people who merely wished to make a political football of them. I said I thought they were too important for that, and that I had talked to Senator George and he agreed.

The secretary remarked that he didn't think the documents proved what some of his Republican colleagues had indicated they proved, that some of the inflammatory offhand remarks, such as Roosevelt's reference to the kikes in New York, had been cut out. I reminded the secretary that I had discussed with him over the years the uses of the "calculated leak," and I said that if there ever was a case for the so-called calculated leak I thought this was it.

I made the following points: First, if the secretary of state released the documents himself he would be accused by the British of releasing documents against the wishes of the other participants at Yalta, and thus make it difficult to have frank and private conversations with them in the future. Second, if he merely sent them to the Hill, where they leaked out, he would be blamed again because nobody would think he was naïve enough to believe that the senators and congressmen would abide by his "confidential" restriction. And third, since he was now more or less committed to let a large number of congressmen and senators see the documents, the only issue was whether the documents would be published in full or be put out piecemeal by politicians who wished to make political capital out of them. In these circumstances, I said, I thought it would be better to let the *Times* publish them on its own responsibility. This, I thought, would be the simplest course all around.

He seemed interested in this. He asked whether the *Times* would publish them in full. I said I was not authorized to say that the *Times* would, but my belief was that it would and I would certainly find out at once. He then replied that he was not in charge of the calculated leak department; this, he said, with a smile and a nod to McCardle, who was in the room, "is Carl's business."

In accordance with the old rule that when you've made a sale, stop talking, I got up and left. I went at once to McCardle's office and we had a long talk about our relations in the past, which were not satisfactory to either of us, and in which he gave me the background of the negotiations between the British and the secretary of state on releasing the document.

When this meeting was over I called the New York office and told them what the situation was and asked whether they would be prepared to carry the papers in full. At that time our estimate was that they were 383,000 words long, and that it would take something in the neighborhood of fifty pages of the *Times* to do it. How we could possibly manage this I didn't know, but in any event a decision was made in New York to publish, and I at once called McCardle and advised him of this point.

I kept pressing McCardle after lunch for an answer, and he said he felt sure everything would be all right. Just to button this up I called Catledge and suggested that he call McCardle and thank him for his cooperation. I urged Catledge to discuss the thing very briefly with him on the assumption that agreement had been made. This Catledge did. I then waited around the office for McCardle's call, but nothing happened until 7:45 P.M. At that time somebody in McCardle's office called me and told me he had gone home, and asked me to call him there. I assumed that everything had fallen through and went home feeling slightly harassed and dispirited.

Sally and I had arranged to go that evening to the St. Albans school glee club performance at the Washington Cathedral, and I was preparing to do that when the telephone rang. It was McCardle. He said, "Can you drive out to my place?" I said of course I could, and he gave me directions how to get there. He lived out by the late Justice Jackson's house in Langley, Virginia. When I got there he was sitting in his living room eating supper off a tray.

We discussed the papers, and he held one string on them: he said the communication between Washington and London was not yet complete, and, of course, he could not anticipate what might happen in the course of these negotiations. If something came up, however, he would feel obliged not to publish. I said that I would advise New York about this.

I told him that I felt sure *The New York Times* would not wish to proceed with publication if this meant getting caught in a controversy between the United States and the British governments, and besides, if this issue arose of a serious difference, he had my word, which the *Times* would sustain, that nothing would be published. Thereupon I left his house at 10:15 P.M. and drove as fast as I could down along the canal and over the freeway to the office.

There was one other restriction on the use of these documents, which must be understood because it caused us enormous complications for the next eighteen hours. This was that if the security officers or anybody else should demand that McCardle return his numbered copy (it was number two), I would be obliged to return it within fifteen minutes.

Thus when I got back to the office with these two books, which were as big as Washington telephone books, totaling 834 pages, the problem was how they could be transmitted to New York. We couldn't send them there because of the time limit, and we couldn't break them apart because of the necessity of returning them whole, if necessary, and in a hurry.

Also, it was obviously impossible to hand the books to one telegraph operator and expect him to transmit them for publication the next night (a good teleprinter puncher will do three thousand words an hour, so that if one man punched steadily for twenty-one hours we would have been able to transmit only sixty-three thousand words by our deadline the following evening).

There was another complication. We had in those long-ago days a fast duplicating machine in the office, called a Thermo-Fax. If a typewritten or printed page was placed flat on an illuminated screen and covered by a chemically treated sheet of pinkish paper, it would duplicate on the treated paper when an air-cushioned rubber mat was brought down over it and a strong light turned on underneath. The trouble with this was that the books were so big that we could not get them into the machine. Therefore, we had to devise a makeshift mat and hold the book steadily on the edge of the machine. It took us about an hour and a half to solve this problem by making a cardboard mat and putting heavy books down on top of the treated paper. At first we were spoiling nine out of ten sheets, but by five in the morning we were duplicating them at the rate of one a minute.

Meanwhile, I called New York and explained these various problems. Jack Goulette and Walter Burton were the late telegraphers that night. I asked them to wait, overtime, and they agreed to do so. We started filing around midnight so that Catledge, Bernstein, and Jordan, who were in New York, could begin to see the substance of the material and make their judgments on the basis of that, rather than on theories of what the documents contained. I called Western Union, too, and asked them for additional operators, but they could give us only two. We then called in our day crew, and by five o'clock in the morning we had six wires open to New York.

As soon as we started moving this copy, Bill Lawrence called in and offered to come down. Bob Whitney was on the desk, and he worked with Sal Nerboso, the librarian, and Al Shuster on the duplicating process.

By two-thirty in the morning, however, it was obvious that even after we had solved the duplicating problem we were not going to be able to move the copy fast enough. Consequently, I called George Tames, the best photographer we ever had, and asked him to take the second volume, set it up on a stand, and photograph two pages at a time. This he did all night long, and by six o'clock he had completed the second book.

We then woke up Bess Furman and asked her to take the seven o'clock plane to New York with the film, but both the Washington and New York airports were under fog, and she had to catch the eight o'clock train to New York, arriving at the office at twelve-thirty. At five o'clock I asked Felix Belair, Elie Abel, and Allen Drury to come in, and they took over the copyreading at six-thirty.

Just when the copy was rolling well, I had a call from McCardle's office and feared the worst. It was not McCardle—it was his assistant, who said, "Mr. McCardle *must* have lunch with you." I said, "Fine, have him meet me at the 1925 F Street Club at twelve-thirty."

When he arrived there he was in a stew. He reported the following, which was the one thing I had not expected. He said that yesterday afternoon Arthur Krock, trying to be helpful, had called Bob McIlvaine, an assistant in McCardle's office, and asked him if we could have the documents. McIlvaine said he didn't think so, but if he could do anything he would call Arthur Krock back. After that telephone call McIlvaine went in to McCardle and criticized the

*Times* for trying to get the documents and made it quite clear to McCardle he thought it would be most improper to let the documents get out. McCardle, being up to his ears in negotiations to do just that, indicated that he thought there was something to be said for letting them get out but made no other comment.

However, McCardle reported, Mr. Krock called McIlvaine back this morning at eleven o'clock and said to him, "Never mind about those documents, everything is all right." As soon as this was said, of course, McIlvaine knew we had the documents and went into a staff meeting and announced this in McCardle's presence. There was quite a to-do back and forth, and naturally McCardle was embarrassed.

He then said it was absolutely essential that the documents be held up for another day. He said he was going to Ottawa with the secretary of state the following morning, and that once he was out of town everything would be all right. I said that I didn't think this could be done, but I understood his problem and I would explain it to New York.

I warned him, however, that the transmission of so many words over six different wires into our office was almost certain to be known, and since we had many syndicate clients there, I would transmit his request to the *Times* but I could promise nothing.

I went straight back to office and reported the facts to Turner Catledge and told him that as I saw the situation it was as follows: McCardle at the last moment had raised a whole new objection, which was purely personal. There was no principle involved that I could see. Furthermore, McCardle had told me that the difficulty with the British, which was one thing that could have blocked publication, had been settled by an agreement on Mr. Dulles's part to eliminate one or two points the British wanted taken out. These had to do with rather acid remarks by Churchill about the French. The other point that had worried Eden, his difference with Churchill over Byelorussia and the Ukraine coming into the UN, disappeared at the last moment when it was found that former Secretary of State Edward Stettinius had actually reported this business in his book several years before. I told Catledge at that time that I was perfectly willing to call McCardle at once and tell him waiting was out of the question, and after discussing it at some length we decided this should be done.

McCardle was very upset. I told him that the situation was now extremely hazardous because of the syndicate clients knowing about the documents, indeed that my information was that copies of the document had already gone to the Hill and would, of course, be either given over to the other papers or leaked out, and that we thought it best to proceed. He did not accept this explanation, and kept pressing for a day's delay. However, we kept transmitting the copy and waiting for developments.

They came faster than we expected, and under peculiar and in some ways amusing circumstances. As a result of an arrangement against which I had protested ever since I had worked as Arthur Sulzberger's assistant, *The New York Times* had an odd deal with the *Chicago Tribune*. The *Tribune* had a syndicate of its own and paid much more attention to its syndicate than we did. Under this arrangement, which had been made by Mr. Ochs many years ago, the *Chicago Tribune* transmitted all *Times* Syndicate copy over *Chicago Tribune* wires, west of the Mississippi. It even represented the *Times* in the sale of the *Times* Syndicate in this area and in Canada. More relevant to the immediate story was the fact that the *Chicago Tribune* office in *The New York Times* building was located in *The New York Times'* communications room so that the copy would be immediately available over these *Chicago Tribune* wires.

When the *Tribune* staff came to work on Wednesday morning, the communications room, which is usually dark and quiet at that time, was, of course, humming with activity, and it was not difficult at all for the *Tribune* people to find out exactly what was up.

They informed Chicago at once. John Maxwell, the managing editor of the *Chicago Tribune,* telephoned Turner Catledge and made a proposition about sharing the text, the cost of transmission, and everything else. Catledge, of course, refused. Maxwell then notified the *Chicago Tribune* office in Washington and they got in touch at once with Illinois Senator Everett M. Dirksen. Dirksen got in touch with the Republican leader of the Senate, William F. Knowland and another Republican member, Senator Styles Bridges of New Hampshire, both of whom had been at the forefront of the campaign to get the Yalta documents out.

This was late Wednesday morning, and it so happened that Mr. Dulles had lunch on the Hill that day with Knowland and Bridges. They made an impassioned plea to him to release the documents for general publication, and after a telephone call to London in which he got British acquiescence—though not approval—he did agree to a 9:00 P.M. release. Ordinarily, we would have been disappointed, but the papers were so important and so controversial, so certain to raise a great international controversy over the propriety of publishing, that we were actually relieved by this decision.

By that time we had already transmitted over 300,000 words to New York; all our mechanical arrangements had been completed; the promotion department had arranged for advertisements in various cities, including Washington, about publication of the text; and the copy kept flowing in until 8:20 P.M., when it was finally cleared.

Thus, *The New York Times* was the first paper on the street with the text, and the only other was the *Chicago Tribune,* which did a most resourceful job of photographing the pages in the official documents and doing a special section by the photographic plate method without setting any type. However, this did not get out in Chicago until very late on the following morning, and only reached a small portion of the *Tribune*'s circulation.

Incidentally, though there were many people at the *Times* who thought the *Tribune* had been dishonorable in taking advantage of their physical presence in the *Times*' communications room, I felt that this was our own fault for letting them be there in the first place. Nor did I blame them for putting pressure on the senators.

The only thing I did think unfair was that the *Chicago Tribune* of the following morning came out condemning the State Department for leaking the information to "one favored eastern newspaper," blowing its own trumpet about how wise and fast it was, and covering about a quarter of its front page with *New York Times* dispatches, printed word for word, without any attribution to *The New York Times.*

The result of the whole thing, however, was that the *Times* got the main credit for publishing the text anyway, and while the State Department's release was widely criticized around the world, there was still general agreement on the main point: the choice before the *Times* was not whether to print the text or not to print the text, but whether the text was to be printed or leaked out piecemeal by the politicians. Even those who disagreed with publishing were in agreement that publication of the text was useful, and we regarded it, even at the end of the fifties, as a pretty good job of reporting.

# CHAPTER 28

# Family Affairs

> Politics will undoubtedly bedevil us all till the day we die,
> but it would be a crime against nature for any generation
> to take the world crisis so solemnly that it put off those
> things for which we were presumably designed in the
> first place: I mean the opportunity to do good work, to
> fall in love, to enjoy friends, to read, to hit a ball, and
> bounce the baby.
>
> —Alistair Cooke

I TRIED TO keep Cooke's advice in mind during all these exciting days, without notable success. He was an old buddy of mine. We discovered America together shortly after Christopher Columbus, and while I didn't always follow his lead, I admired his ability to reconcile his personal and professional interests. He spent one half of his life at the BBC and the other half on the first tee, but even during the midcentury pause of the Eisenhower fifties, I wasn't so wise. I not only didn't bounce the baby, but, I'm ashamed to say, I wasn't even home for the birth of our second son. I was off much of the time climbing the ladder at the *Times,* or chasing politicians or diplomats at some important conference, the importance of which now escapes me. This didn't make things fair or easy on the family.

In Washington, the chances of a newspaper reporter winning the Pulitzer Prize and being elected Father of the Year at the same time are not very good. It is theoretically possible, like balancing the federal budget, but the practical demands of keeping up with the conduct and misconduct of both children and officials are beyond most mortals, and the divorce statistics seem to suggest that newspaper reporting was meant for bachelors and spinsters.

When I was in my early twenties, I had no children; when I was in my thirties and forties, I had children but little time for them; and when, in my fifties and sixties, I had time for them, they were gone.

Like most families, we had to deal with the accidents of young children, for we almost lost our youngest son at birth, and our middle son, Jim, gave us a couple of scares. On the first occasion, he was at his Granny Fulton's house in Sycamore, suffering from measles and a high temperature, and while protesting his medicine, bit and swallowed part of a thin tumbler as well. It was, I think, his first declaration of independence. I don't remember where I was, but we got together in Washington, and in accordance with the old rule of adversity—"this too shall pass"—screened the evidence and waited for deliverance.

He survived this experiment, but the second was more serious. When he was about seven or eight, we were living in Georgetown across the street from a playground, where I was determined that he should develop into a second baseman as handy as his Illinois grandfather. One day when he was shagging fly balls, a big neighborhood kid hit one out of the park, and Jim chased it onto Q Street right in front of a big passenger bus. He never knew what hit him. He ended up unconscious under the rear end. The driver couldn't see him and started backing up. He would have crushed the boy with the big back wheels if a passerby hadn't screamed at him to stop.

In time Jim recovered, looking like a battered pug and limping sideways with a twisted back, grateful to his brother Dick, who was first and last at his side in the Georgetown hospital. One good thing, however, came out of that scary event. We decided to get these kids out of town and into the country beyond the bus lines—more about this later.

After our Georgetown days, we lived for over thirty years in Cleveland Park on Woodley Road, which for some reason, as mentioned, attracted some other newspaper folk. Walter Lippmann resided up the street in the former Washington Cathedral dean's house. John Chancellor and Tom Brokaw of NBC were our next-door neighbors at different times. Dan Schorr of public broadcasting and Elizabeth Drew of *The New Yorker* lived in the next block, and my old boss of London days, Ferdie Kuhn, and his wife, Delia, had a big house just down the alley.

My days on Woodley Road began early. During my apprentice-ship at Gallagher's Drugstore in Dayton, I had learned the tricks of short-order cooking, and I took command of the kitchen at breakfast time. By the time I got home after work, the boys were usually in bed, so my best chance of seeing them was flapjack time in the morning. It was also in this house that I entered the world of publishing with my first newspaper.

It was called *Reston's Weekly,* printed in the basement on an old mimeograph machine, and it had an outside subscription list of twelve at ten cents a copy. It recorded all the achievements, visitations, and misdemeanors of the children and their noisy friends in our alley, all written with the solemnity of history. I have before me, for example, Volume 3, Number 10, dated December 24, 1955, which contains the following items:

"Tom Reston, 9, of Woodley Road, has been selected as the new eraser-beater in Miss Koobendorfer's fourth grade class at John Eaton school. . . . The cook who couldn't cook has flown the coop. . . . The editor [Jim] is back in school and his sore back is mending. . . . The basement has been CLEANED! . . . Mr. and Mrs. James Reston celebrated their 20th wedding anniversary. Interviewed by the staff of *Reston's Weekly,* he said the secret of a happy marriage is an 'obedient wife.' Mrs. Reston, who knows better, said, 'Boo!' "

One other event of more-than-passing interest made the columns of *Reston's Weekly* during the administration of President Eisenhower and Vice President Nixon. Across the street from our house stood the estate of Joseph Davies, a former U.S. ambassador to Moscow. It had a noble house called Tregaron, surrounded by a little golf course on about ten acres of rolling hills. When Davies died, there was much discussion about what would happen to this elegant spread in the middle of Washington. I discovered that the Soviet Union was trying to buy it as its own embassy, and also, I was told, as a Communist enclave for other Communist embassies. I thought this was undoubtedly the worst idea ever proposed since L'Enfant laid out the capital city. I went to see Speaker Rayburn about it.

I said this was the first time I had ever appeared as a lobbyist before him, but surely this scheme or whatever it was should be stopped. He agreed. I said he could stop it by agreeing to a different idea, then under discussion, namely that Tregaron should be purchased by the nation as an official residence for the vice president.

"And Richard Nixon would occupy it?" he asked. When I said, "Yes," he said, "No." "That man," observed the speaker, "is the meanest man and has the meanest face of any man who ever sat in the House of Representatives. I will do nothing for him." I don't know what the old growler did about it, but Tregaron didn't go either to the Russians or to Nixon.

Sally and I tried in those increasingly secular days to rescue for our children something of the religious faith of our own parents. I say "something," for we were not thinking of the strictures of the old Scottish Kirk with its intolerance and insistence on conformity. But we did believe in many of the things often associated with the Christian religion, not the crust of self-righteousness, but consideration for others, self-discipline, and common courtesy. It was with this in mind that we bought that house on Woodley Road close by the cathedral and sent our boys to school there, believing in its gravitational pull, and hoping that at least its music and poetry would stay with them in later life. In this, I believe, we were not wholly unsuccessful.

By the 1950s, much to my surprise, our three boys had survived all the accidents and follies of childhood, thanks primarily to the love and vigilant eye of their mother. Not that I didn't love them, but I was away somewhere saving the world much of the time and often wondered when I returned about these skinny strangers in the house. Sometime during the Eisenhower administration, I think it was, the eldest of the three, "Richard the Lion-Hearted," was ready for college, and we naturally assumed that nobody, meaning nobody, had ever before faced such a formidable decision.

We made a big exercise out of it. I read him interminably from the catalogs all about the glories of various colleges, and invariably got the same reaction: "*Zzzzz.*" (That's a direct quote.) I told him, without excessive objectivity, all about the University of Illinois and the pretty girl in the red coat. "I know, I know," he said. He was a determined and inventive young man. Once when he was in Jackson grade school the teacher asked how many Catholics in the class wanted to be excused for Ash Wednesday. Up went his hand and out he went into the sunshine, undeterred by his Presbyterian conscience. When he was taking his exams at St. Albans school, the assistant principal (whose name, no kidding, was Mr. True) found him fiddling around and looking out the window. "Aren't you interested in this exam?" Mr. True asked. "Sometimes I am and sometimes I'm not," he replied.

So, ready or not, we took him all over the country, looking at the big culture factories, and at the little coed colleges in Ohio, and at the Ivy League, and this cost us so much money that Sally and I, to recoup our expenses, wrote an article together for *The Saturday Evening Post* entitled "How NOT to Send Your Kid to College."

We suggested that helping your eldest son pick a college was one of the great educational experiences of life—for the parents. Next to trying to pick his bride, it was, we thought, the best way to learn that your authority, if not entirely gone, was slipping fast. Age seventeen, we said, was the time when you stop being critical of your eldest son and he starts being critical of you. He was always a new experience. Just when you got used to him at five, he suddenly turned into something different at eight. When you thought you had figured out the mysteries of age nine, all at once he was an adolescent, and of course, we concluded, nobody had ever fathomed *that.*

Our first stop at the University of Illinois was not successful. It had indeed spread out into the cornfields. The student body had doubled since our time and I noticed at once that the girls weren't nearly as pretty as they used to be. Dick was interested in the stadium, and I took him to varsity football practice. This was a mistake, for while he had swivel in his hips and was cocaptain of the St. Albans football team, he weighed only 155 pounds, and when he saw these Big Ten monsters at play, I knew that Illinois was out.

We then approached Harvard with what we regarded as appropriate reverence, and there a very nice man in the admissions department explained the difference between "the newer universities" and the old. It was true he said, that the large state institutions had no doubt "democratized" education, but they had also "reduced the undergraduate degree to the level of a vaccination certificate." Whereas, he continued, "the Ivy League colleges cling to the somewhat mystical notion that a candidate for the eight-hundred-year-old baccalaureate degree shall be, among other things, a person of marked intellectual promise."

"Uh-huh," murmured Dick.

"The Ivy colleges hold further," this Mr. Robinson insisted, "that the candidate shall be a person capable of achieving a rigorous kind of excellence, not limited to mind, manners, or even muscles, but penetrating into the very marrow and matrix of life itself."

I could tell that this "mystical notion" had not penetrated into the marrow and matrix of Richard Fulton Reston's mind, but we had better luck with Robert Frost's definition of the problem. "Education," said the old poet, "is hanging around the right places and the right people until you get an idea." About a thousand dollars' worth of carfare later, Dick announced that he intended to hang around the University of North Carolina because Pete Killinger, the other St. Albans cocaptain, was going there. Dick spent his junior year at Edinburgh University, picking up a little Scottish moral philosophy, and ended up at the University of Wisconsin, where he met and married Jody O'Brien, who has been educating him ever since.

Sally and I concluded our *Saturday Evening Post* article with the following advice:

1. Don't grieve over your eldest son going to college. Console yourself with the thought that you're not losing a son but gaining a bathroom.
2. See that he goes far away to college. This makes you appreciate him, and maybe vice versa.
3. Suggest as deftly as you can, that co-educational colleges have one advantage which should be apparent to him. Remember what Edgar Wallace says: "A high-brow is a man who has found something more interesting than women."

By the time our second son was liberated from high school, we followed this advice. He was my namesake but fortunately he had his mother's smile and style. He was the one who was hit by the bus, the lucky one, then and thereafter. He just checked into the University of North Carolina, and later taught in the English department there for a while. He spent his junior year at University College, Oxford, where he fell in love with soccer and the English language. I tried to persuade him, as I had persuaded his elder brother, that newspaper reporting was a lifetime educational process, but he rejected all suggestions that he join the *Times* and chose instead the reckless adventure of writing books.

Son number three, "Doubting Thomas," decided in due course to go to Harvard, and when he was admitted, I had a letter from the freshman dean, a man with the unlikely name of F. Skiddy von Stade, asking me to tell him about "the background, interests, and special needs of your son." I replied: "Tom Reston is small in the sense that some tactical nuclear weapons are small, and after eighteen years of experience with him, I understand President Johnson's insistence that such weapons should be kept under strict presidential control. He is a thoughtful, independent, pugnacious, and original lad, with a gift for friendship and a healthy skepticism toward fathers and freshman deans. Also, in my prejudiced view, he has a knack for speaking and writing.

"His mother and I, keeping in mind the normal tyranny of elder brothers, have tried to see that he excelled in something they didn't have, so we sent him into a French family when he was quite young and into a Paris newspaper as a copyboy when he was a little older, and he now speaks good Parisian French. He is not a brilliant student except in the things that take his fancy, but he will, I think, do well at Harvard, provided he doesn't try to attend every lecture, join every club, demand the editorship of *The Crimson,* and write editorials denouncing the whole trend of Harvard education.

"He has been working on a country weekly this summer in Virginia and living by himself in our log cabin. Last summer, he worked in the Canadian woods. At St. Albans school, he was the liberal leader of the political club, chief cheerleader, editor of the editorial page of the school paper, and self-appointed critic of the Episcopal church. This may give you some idea of the combustible material we are transferring from our supervision to yours, and I give you fair warning that ever since he was a page at the 1956 Democratic convention, he has been addicted to politics."

Those were the days when a Harvard student could choose any course he liked, and Thomas Busey Reston majored in Revolution. Accordingly, there were few uprisings, rebellions, or demonstrations in the world he didn't study or approve, but fortunately he viewed the turmoil of his time from a prudent distance.

I don't know what else all three of them learned, but they learned to come home, and even now that they are in middle age, there is scarcely a week when one of them, to our delight, doesn't come running up the stairs with a happy shout.

Ever since we had that quiet little house at St. Mary's Cray outside London during the war, we longed for a hideaway in the country. One of the vexations of Washington reporting is that you never catch up. It is both irresistible and inexhaustible. You spend so much of your time with the depressing conflicts of politics that you long for an escape hatch. We found ours in a log cabin at Fiery Run near the village of Hume in Fauquier County, Virginia.

It hides in a little valley looking up across the foothills to the long line of the Blue Ridge Mountains on the west and Rattlesnake Mountain to the east. Sally discovered the place, to get the kids out of town. It was a wreck, with no roof, water, or electricity, but it had ten acres and Fiery Run, which is one of the headwaters of the Rappahannock. It also had the remains of an old mill and miller's house, and it cost us, during those far-off days of the last world war, the staggering sum of $3,400. (We have since paid off the mortgage.)

We taught our boys to work there, clearing the wilderness; they courted their girls there; Jim and Denise Leary, and Tom and Vicky Kiechel were married there and now our grandchildren are hearing the stories of its past. According to local legend, it was part of the free state of Virginia—so named because General Washington is supposed to have persuaded the German Hessians to desert the British during the American War of Independence by promising them free land there and their own laws as long as they lived. It stands, too, alongside Fairfield Farm, which was the storehouse of General Lee's supplies during the Civil War, so it reminded us that other generations had had some problems, too.

This property was listed by the Virginia Landmarks Commission as the Fiery Run Miller's House. It was built around 1820 and operated as a corn mill until 1946, with an "overshot" waterwheel fed by a millrace from Fiery Run. It was at one time, according to the commission, owned by a man named Sims, the father-in-law of Jesse James, a famous or infamous robber who lived up the road and was killed by another neighbor by the name of Robert Ford. Apparently Sims did not take kindly to the murder of Jesse James, and followed Ford to Kansas, vowing revenge. The commission reports that "although it was never proved that Sims got his revenge, Ford was found dead on Sims' front lawn in Kansas." Incidentally, the log cabin we restored was at one time used as a blacksmith's shop, but originally was occupied by slaves. After struggling to get this cabin into order for years, Sally remarked that she was merely carrying on the old slave tradition.

We learned in the process what country neighborliness meant. As a certified mechanical incompetent, I couldn't fix the things that were always breaking down, but the neighbors invariably answered my cries for help. We found that the issues that so agitated us in Washington didn't worry Henry and Mamie Baxley or Fred and Sarah Wayland across the road, or Mrs. Wright at the village store. When we were struggling along without any running water, Fred had our deed amended to give us a spring down the lane. "It's not bold," he said, "but it's true." Mr. Tinsley, the plumber from Marshall, Virginia, came by in emergencies with his tools and his little grandson, and always found time to visit and distribute his pearls of philosophy. One day when I complimented him on the little boy at his side, he said, "Yes, when they're little they step on your toes, and when they're big they step on your heart."

After struggling along with airplane toilets and no electricity for a few years, we found another log cabin up on the ridge and had a neighbor haul it down and build it up next to our own, complete with a roof, a bathroom, and electric lights. It still didn't rate a spread in *Better Homes and Gardens,* but we thought it was beautiful and it was ours.

My father loved the place. The sheep on the hills reminded him of Scotland. He would sit on the porch in the evening, humming his hymns and marveling at the shapes of the clouds as the sun loitered down over the ridge. Once when our son Jim was isolated after a threat of polio at a summer camp, the old man stayed there with the boy for weeks, following Fiery Run to its source and putting in a vegetable garden, which he advised me to maintain after he left. This I attempted with no visible success.

I wasn't bad at turnips and other root vegetables, and the rabbits seemed to like my lettuce, but my tomatoes and apples always contracted spotted fever and grew no larger than walnuts. One of the puzzles of our back-to-the-land experiment was that the rain always seemed to fall on the grass but never on the garden. In the pasture and in the yard around the cabin, the grass went wild in the spring, and if I didn't tame it in April it was up to my knees by the beginning of the summer.

We tried to deal with this problem by putting a few steers on the pasture and sheep on the lawn, but the wild dogs got into the sheep and the steers got out onto the road when we were away, and while I finally solved the grass problem with a tractor, just when we got the place all neat and clean, it was time to go back to town.

I was not, however, a total failure with the land. One year, the state of Virginia, which is always straightening out roads, if nothing else, decided that the old iron bridge over Fiery Run by the miller's house was becoming a menace to the public safety and had to be replaced by a cement platform that was not so creaky but not so pretty either. It was the judgment of the commonwealth that the old bridge had to be dismantled, plus all the honeysuckle vines and bird's nests that had accumulated on its iron shoulders for years. This, of course, would cost the state time and money, so I entered into negotiations with the officials in Richmond, and though the state's budget was in deficit at the time, they sold us the bridge for one dollar.

Not only that, but they deeded over to us the little curve of state-owned land between the two bridges to be added to our ten acres in perpetuity, and while they insisted on an additional payment of ten dollars to defray the costs of postage and telephone calls, I still regard this as the greatest diplomatic triumph of the weak over the strong since the Louisiana Purchase.

I loved to go to Fiery Run and would shout up the stairs at Woodley Road on Saturday mornings, "Let's get this show on the road." Until one morning Sally said, "Look. I can either get ready to go to the country or I can go to the country, but I can't do both!" The only thing I regretted about the cabin was that the federal government, probably by malicious intent, always seemed to plan some thumping news announcement as soon as we crept out of Washington, so that, just as I sat down to watch for the orioles on their way to Baltimore, I'd have to return to the capital.

Once in a while, like most natural things, Fiery Run would get tired of its accustomed channel, and after a few gulley-washers, would make a mad rush for the sea, breaking its banks and tossing trees into the pasture. Most of the time, however, all was calm, and the Virginia spring with its dogwood and redbud ablaze on the silent mountain slopes was as beautiful as any prospect I ever saw.

Every year Nature seemed to have a surprise for us. One year the dogwood would be resting from its spectacular exertions of the year before, but the wildflowers would be showing off and the violets and trillium would be running for office.

One thing that never failed us was the dandelion. Year after year these brassy weeds held a convention in the middle of our lawn. At first I tried to dig them out, but this just fertilized them and doubled the next year's crop. I was in despair about this until I read in G. K. Chesterton's autobiography that he thought the main lesson of his long life was not to take simple natural things for granted but to regard them with gratitude. He used the dandelion as a symbol.

"The pessimists of my boyhood," he wrote, "when confronted with the dandelion, said with Swinburne, 'I am weary of all hours / blown buds and barren flowers / desires and dreams and powers / and everything but sleep.' " And at this, Chesterton added, "I cursed them and kicked at them . . . and at the strange and staggering heresy that every human being has a *right* to dandelions and need feel no wonder at them at all. . . . The aim of life," he concluded, "is appreciation."

Chesterton would not have liked the demanding me-generation that came after him. He took his philosophy from the old penny catechism that the two sins against hope are presumption and despair. So thereafter I didn't fight my dandelions but fertilized them, and when they went to seed with their misty white clocks, I blew them away to the delight of my grandchildren.

Meanwhile, I learned something about writing a column at Fiery Run. For when I was there, I wrote about simple human things, about families and schools, and the triumph of the Republic over old fears and problems, and somehow these got more reaction from the readers of the *Times* than most of my solemn epistles on the passing political tangles in Washington.

I now see Fiery Run and walk on the hills in silent joy, like my father, and visit my neighbor's sheep barn when the lambs arrive in the spring. All this brought me closer to my family and my search for faith. The thump of the waves on Martha's Vineyard, much as I liked it, sounded like the beating of my heart and made me restless, but the solid hills of Virginia seem to me eternal and peaceful, and I plan to spend a lot of time there in the next couple hundred years.

# Part Ten

# INTRODUCTION TO POLITICS

# CHAPTER 29

# *From Illusion to Disillusion*

> Hatred, cruelty, hypocrisy, and graft
> belong to no single Party;
> stupidity to no single regime,
> error to no single system.
> —Paul Valéry,
> *History and Politics*

---

I DIGRESS HERE to say a few candid and critical words about American politics, the weakest link, as I believe, in our political system. It seems to me that our foreign and domestic policies all have improved during these past fifty years, but that our politics have declined below the level of common sense or even decency. Maybe I was excessively optimistic in the forties and am excessively critical in the nineties, but the older I get the more I feel our politics are unworthy of a great country.

When I was introduced to political reporting in the presidential campaigns of the forties, the candidates peddled their wares from the rear end of a railroad train. In those whistle-stopping days, I was then in my thirties, full of dreams and moonbeams, and I regarded all the clatter and excitement as a prodigious adventure. The spectacle of the Republicans hurling verbal rocks at the Democrats, and the Democrats slinging mud at the Republicans, was great fun, and it got me around the country. Later on, when the candidates took to the air, the higher and faster we flew the less we knew, but in the

forties the campaign trains poked into the downtown freight yards
of the growing cities and the sidings of the little towns where we
could see and hear more of the people.

At every stop the local politicians came aboard with their problems of the farmers or their fears of unemployment when the war was
over and "the boys come home." We didn't have much time to listen
to the speeches and get our copy to the telegraph office before the
train started off again, but after that scramble, we had a press car full
of noisy companions, and in the long rides between stops and drinks
we could even question the candidates when they were talking more
freely about their hopes and fears.

I began then for the first time to understand why, in a large
continental country, political power was shared with the state governments that knew more about regional issues, and what the press
did to provide a link between the candidates and the people. The
more I saw of the federal system in action the more I admired it, but
the more I saw of what was called "the great game of politics," the
less I liked it.

I tagged along after the Roosevelt bandwagon in 1944 and bumped
into political reality for the first time. The reporters were saying the
president didn't look well, and I reported this when I got back to the
office. Turner Catledge, the captain of our political team, called on
him privately at the White House and came back saying he was
shocked by the president's appearance and by his rambling conversation. Catledge wrote in vivid and disturbing terms about this incident
later in his memoirs, but not at the time.

It was assumed then, and is still widely accepted in the nineties,
that the president, like all other citizens, was entitled to doctor-
patient privacy, so we took the word of Steve Early, the White House
press secretary, and Admiral McIntire, the White House physician,
that the president was no doubt tired from his exertions in the
depression and the war, but was otherwise in sound health.

One man who knew better was Dr. Howard G. Bruenn, a cardiolo-
gist in the Navy Medical Corps, who examined the president four
months before Roosevelt announced that he would seek a fourth
term. Dr. Bruenn found that the president's heart was enlarged, and
that he was suffering from cardiac failure in the left ventricle, and
from hypersensitive heart disease, but this was concealed until
Roosevelt died a few months after his election. As in the case of
President Woodrow Wilson, the excuse for covering up the facts was
that the president was needed at the end of the war. The story is

familiar, but not the lesson, for even fifty years later, the health and stability of presidential candidates is still inadequately examined before they are nominated and elected.

In the 1948 campaign, there was nothing wrong with Harry Truman's health and stability; we could see that, but that's about all we saw, and we misjudged Harry. We saw him through the eyes of the pollsters, rather than through the eyes of the people in the freight yards. After Roosevelt and the other wartime giants, he seemed just another little guy who had stumbled into the presidency with no visible qualifications for the job. On the back platform of a train, however, he was "Give-'em-Hell-Harry" to all the other little guys, and then he'd come back to the press car with his little black notebook and show us his calculations of just how many states he would win in November, and how wrong we were to count him out. His predictions were not far off the mark. I was so ashamed of our record in that election that I wrote a letter of apology to my own paper, and the *Times* was so embarrassed that it actually printed it.

"Before we in the newspaper business spend all our time and energy analyzing Governor Dewey's failure in the election, maybe we ought to analyze our own failure," I said. "For that failure was almost as spectacular as the President's victory, and the quicker we admit it the better off we'll be. . . . In a way our failure was not unlike Mr. Dewey's. We relied too much on techniques of reporting that are no longer foolproof; just as he was too isolated with other politicians, so we were too isolated with other reporters; and we were far too impressed by the tidy statistics of the polls. . . .

"The great intangible of this election was the enduring influence of the Roosevelt era on the thinking of the nation. It was less dramatic than the antics of Messrs. Wallace and Thurmond, but in the long run it was more important and we didn't give enough weight to it. Consequently we were wrong, not only on the election, but what's worse, on the whole political direction of our time."

And yet I often looked back on that election with a kind of secret pride that we didn't know how it was going to come out; I felt that it was right somehow that we were wrong; that this great act of decision by millions of people was intensely private, and that we were properly punished by presuming to guess how the people would vote.

Presidential campaigns were different after that. They picked up speed but lost altitude. They improved technically but declined morally. With the spread of television across the nation, the power of the political parties decreased and the influence of the political manipulators increased. With the movement of the blacks out of the South and of more affluent factory workers and more numerous "service" employees into the suburbs, the traditional alignments of the two-party system were upset; the issues became less parochial and more international, and the campaigns became trivial and even nasty.

In the forties, the reach of a candidate depended largely on the power of his lungs, but thereafter he didn't have to shout and wave his arms but could tell lies quietly and be heard from coast to coast. How he looked became as important as, and sometimes even more so than, what he said. Accordingly, even the local political bosses we interviewed at the airports were guessing almost as much as the reporters about what the voters were thinking in the rest of the country.

In fact, after Eisenhower's two victories in the fifties, the campaigns were dominated not by the old political bosses but by the new political "consultants," who applied the techniques of television advertising and wartime propaganda to the "game." The candidates were packaged like cornflakes—big package, half full—and delivered speeches to carefully selected flag-waving partisan audiences. Also, in the sixties new militant factions of a pushy new generation challenged the power of the two dominant parties with their demonstrations in the streets and on the campuses in favor of blacks, women's rights, and religious preferences. These vied with other splinter groups opposing regional wars and industrial pollution. This was called "the new politics" or in the fancier terms of the campus militants, "participatory democracy."

What was new was that "the great game of politics," like baseball, was played increasingly on artificial turf. Trickery, charges of intemperance, infidelity, and even mental instability could now be spread not merely to local audiences, but to vast television watchers nationwide. Money to buy expensive time on the networks was increasingly solicited from special interest groups in business, labor unions, and others that expected favors from the candidates in return. This was at a time of great tension during the Cold War, when vast expenditures for military arms produced an alliance between the government and the big industries. It was also at a time when powerful single-issue organizations, thinking about their special interests rather than the national interest, played an increasingly important role with their campaigns for and against the right to carry guns, for and against abortion, and for and against the exploitation of the nation's resources of oil and timber.

What was also new was that it was increasingly difficult to tell where the speeches of the presidential candidates came from. The candidates no longer spoke extemporaneously from local platforms, but read speeches off hidden TelePrompTers written by unknown speech-writers in accordance with the latest polls on what the people wanted to hear. They even deceived themselves by rigging their own polls. The story was told in the 1952 elections, for example, of Senator William Benton of Connecticut, who would walk down the street with an aide asking passersby how they intended to vote. One man told Benton he wouldn't vote for him even if Joe Stalin was the only other name on the ballot, but Benton was not deterred by the facts. "Put that man down as undecided," he told his aide. All this political hokum produced an atmosphere of mistrust toward not only the politicians who were making the news but also the newspapers that were printing it.

The presidential campaign of 1968 was actually fought out in the streets over the mounting casualties in the Vietnam War, and I was almost as wrong about that contest between Richard Nixon and Hubert Humphrey as I had been about the Truman-Dewey election twenty years earlier. Humphrey was a gallant, merry, garrulous man. ("Oh, Hubert," his wife once told him, "you don't have to be interminable to be immortal.") He was one of the most appealing and popular senators and vice presidents of his time, and since Nixon was the opposite, I was sure Humphrey would win. But he quarreled with President Johnson over the Vietnam War, and lost to Nixon, who got only 43.4 percent of the popular vote. Humphrey, always unlucky, was then stricken by cancer and faded away until there was little left of him but his smile.

This was a time of profound political and even spiritual bewilderment over the Vietnam War—just after the murders of Martin Luther King and Robert Kennedy—and Humphrey was nominated in the most rancorous convention of the century, with the Chicago cops fighting antiwar demonstrators outside the hall, and the National Guard protecting the delegates inside. I always thought he lost the election because he did not express his true feelings of opposition to the war and was more loyal to President Johnson than Johnson was to him. Accordingly, he opened the White House door to Nixon and began the slide of the Democratic party, which has continued through most of the last quarter of the century.

Maybe I didn't like political reporting because I wasn't very good at it. I was no doubt wrong in expecting that national interests would prevail over local interests at the polls; and wrong again in expecting that presidents would set a high standard of truth and personal behavior and pick the most qualified vice presidential candidates available. But I still think it was not wrong to expose the deceptions of the so-called new politics.

What troubled me in particular was the capacity of politics to corrupt even the best of men, who were not originally deceitful, and didn't want to be deceitful, but were knowingly and cunningly deceitful under the compulsion of ambition. George Bush's victorious campaign of 1988 was only one example. He was by family training and ambition an honorable man, intelligent, generous, and proud of the noble tradition of Skull and Bones at Yale, but in that campaign he was all bones and no skull, unfaithful to his natural character.

He often denied, in order to survive, the convictions that had brought him into politics in the first place. He talked constantly about morality and the need for cooperation between the parties, but sent an army of half a million to the Middle East without advance consultation with the Congress, and thus helped create the conditions that led to war with Iraq.

The newspapers didn't appreciate the good qualities of Presidents Ford and Carter until after they left the White House. The press was, I thought, too hard on President Ford, who held things together after the disaster of Nixon, and too easy on President Bush when he invaded Panama and went to war in Iraq. Corruption was not exactly condoned—much of it was not only exposed but condemned by the newspapers—but a lot of it was accepted with an everybody-does-it shrug.

This triumph of expediency over principle, of winning at any cost, not only hurt the political losers but made governing more difficult for the winners. Many capable men and women simply refused to get into the scramble for campaign money and votes, and many others preferred retirement from the Congress to a life of endless money-raising and haggling over policies everybody wanted and few were willing to pay for.

It wasn't until the sixties that I learned what I could have learned in college by reading *The Education of Henry Adams:* that even in the days of Lincoln, the struggle for political power was not an exercise in moral philosophy.

By the eighties, however, I learned from Ronald Reagan that

personality was more decisive in presidential campaigns than policy or even intelligence. Accordingly, I looked on the financing and conduct of politics in America, and the appointment of unqualified politicians to powerful cabinet positions, as a corrupting outrage, and it seemed to me that the people were surprisingly indifferent to its failures.

# CHAPTER 30

# *Do the People Know Best?*

I often wonder whether we do not rest our hopes too
much upon constitutions, upon laws, and upon courts.
These are false hopes; believe me, these are false hopes.
Liberty lies in the hearts of men and women; when it dies
there, no constitution, no law, no court can save it.
                                        —Justice Learned Hand

ONE OF THE first unwritten rules I learned in Washington was that
everything was criticized except the people. Every politician and
newspaperman knew that questioning the wisdom of the multitude
was a sappy way to pick up votes or circulation. Accordingly, when
I first arrived in the capital, I swallowed every cliché from "the
people know best" to "the voice of the people is the voice of God."
I denounced Mencken for saying, "Democracy is incomparably idi-
otic, and hence incomparably amusing," but as the years passed, I
began to suspect that maybe there was a twinkle of truth at the
bottom of the old grouch's barrel. Also, this subversive doubt was
encouraged by the growing and widespread tolerance of deception
and corruption, and by the popular illusion that our system of government was so good that half the people didn't have to vote, and
my doubts were not removed by the indifference of so many voters
to many of the absurdities of Reagan's absentminded and scandal-
ridden administration.

Maybe I was rebounding from excessive idealism to excessive

skepticism, but starting in the sixties I couldn't help feeling that in the performance or avoidance of their democratic responsibilities, the people elected and reelected some outrageous dubs, passed snappy judgments on complicated issues they knew little or nothing about, and developed a gluttonous tolerance for political baloney.

Worse than that, they increasingly demanded more and more government services they weren't willing to pay for and then blamed the government for not cutting their taxes and balancing the budget. Most presidents encouraged the people in this folly. At the beginning of the nineties, for example, President Bush went out in the country during a budget crisis and blamed everything on the government he was supposed to be running. "How nice it is," he said in Omaha, "to be out where the *real* people are, outside of Washington, D.C." He added in Glen Ellyn, Illinois, "I know Americans are fed up with much of the political debate coming out of Washington. It's the same old inside-the-Beltway hogwash." I thought this cheap flattery, coming from a president who had spent most of his mature life in Washington, was a disgrace, but it was cheered as a well-deserved tribute to the people.

My mistake all along was in not paying enough attention to the founders of the Republic. It was precisely because the delegates to the Constitutional Convention distrusted the people to pass judgment on such issues as the budget that they denounced what one of them called "mobocracy" and chose their own form of "representative government." The people, they thought, could choose among candidates selected by political leaders who knew something about their character and intelligence, and kick them out if they failed; but the people couldn't be expected to tell the difference between good and bad candidates by looking at them or decide complicated issues of foreign and domestic policy that often baffled even the experts.

With the development of television, however, the latter-day presidents, when opposed by Congress, increasingly appealed to the people to decide even such mysteries as the defense of outer space and the selection of intricate weapons systems. If presidents couldn't persuade the Congress, they thought that maybe they could fool the people, and the record abounds in evidence that they often could and did. For the old idea that "what you see is what you get" often proved in political television to be "what you see is precisely what you don't get."

I thought for a while that the founders were onto something when they thought the people might learn to trust a responsible press, but even when the newspapers corrected many of their careless ways, they ranked little higher than the politicians.

The public reaction to so much information was not reassuring. The media were denounced for delivering bad news, as if they had made it all up, and when the people had to choose between the statements of the politicians and the reports of the press, they usually sided with the politicians who promised them the most. Not always, of course, but from Harding to Reagan, I came to realize, the evidence didn't invariably prove that the people know best.

They often seemed stunned by the weight and complexity of each day's events, and preoccupied with a thousand diversions. The more people there were, the less they seemed to think the individual vote counted. So they tended to regard themselves as spectators rather than players in what Frank Kent of the *Baltimore Sun* called "the great game of politics."

It was the only game I knew anything about where incompetents were put into key places and kept there year after year no matter how many errors they committed. The result was that the United States had the worst voting record in the free world, and those who did vote often seemed to make up their minds mainly on the basis of the personalities, slogans, and sexual appeal of the candidates. I didn't want to be a grouch on this subject. But I didn't think this was a wholly satisfactory way to elect a Commander in Chief who has control over atomic weapons, and a lot to say about the defense of peace and freedom in the world.

It may be that I started out with some unjustified and romantic illusions about all this, fifty years ago. I felt confident that the public discourse would improve: the cream would rise to the top; political leaders who could speak and write and tell the truth would encourage a spirit of toleration in the country. With equal assurance, I believed that the increasingly rapid distribution of news was bound to produce a more enlightened electorate and a stronger sense of citizenship, and while some progress has undoubtedly been made along these lines, the results have certainly not measured up to my innocent dreams.

In 1932, my senior year in college, I acquired what became a lifelong admiration for Walter Lippmann, who at that time was deploring the decay of decency in American political life. The drastic changes brought about by science and machinery and the modern city, by democracy and by popular education, he thought, had struck with cumulative force against the traditional morality, the social conventions, and the ideals of our people.

"That a period of profound spiritual bewilderment had to ensue was inevitable," Lippmann wrote during the week of my college graduation in 1932. "But this bewilderment has been greatly aggravated in the United States by what I believe may truthfully be called the moral apathy of those in high places. At the beginning of the decade [the twenties], the national government was attacked by brutal and conspicuous corruption. No clear word was spoken by those in high places. On the contrary, they sat silent, hoping that the people would forget. . . .

"During this same decade," Lippmann added, "those in high places have steadily preached to the people that it was their ideal to be acquisitive, to seek feverishly to become richer and richer. But if you teach a people for ten years that the character of its government is not greatly important, that political success is for those who equivocate and evade, that things are what matter . . . then you must not be astonished at the confusion in Washington. . . . You cannot set up false gods to confuse the people and not pay the penalty."

The same thing, word for word, could have been said of the decade of the eighties, sixty years after Lippmann's warning. There was conspicuous corruption, not only in the executive branch but in the Congress, not only among the money changers in Wall Street but among the money grubbers and even some preachers on Main Street. And there was "moral apathy" among high officials who defended or ignored the corruption, deceived the Congress, glorified officials who were running their own personal foreign policies, advocated personal acquisitiveness and even greed, insisted that government was the cause and not the cure of the nation's problems, mocked the liberal tradition of the nation, and despite widespread publicity on these scandals, were reelected by the people.

It would probably be wrong to say that there was more corruption in the eighties than in the twenties. Maybe it was merely exposed and publicized more by the press, but the people seemed to tolerate it more. Also, it was muffled by the hypocrisy of officials who proclaimed moral values while violating them, and in the eighties they had more powerful instruments for deception.

The balance of power shifted during the communications revolution in favor of the politicians who made and manipulated the news. Their pollsters told them what the people wanted to hear and what they didn't want to hear. Their photographers and makeup artists coached them in the most favorable camera angles. Their researchers showed them how to doctor the facts. They had speech-writers and even gag-writers who produced the best speeches money can buy, and these were read out by the candidates from invisible screens. Finally, their campaign managers and tour directors mapped out their itineraries, picked their sympathetic audiences and flag-waving backgrounds, and arranged for them to avoid, whenever possible, the nosy questions of the press.

All this originally came under the heading of "public relations," which is the art of giving the public that part of the truth that sells the "new and improved" candidate and suppresses the rest, and this science of political huckstering spread beyond the presidential campaigns to most other phases of government. For example, the budget for public relations activities in the federal government amounted to over $1 billion a year in the eighties, and the cost of campaigning multiplied each year, most of it for slick television ads designed to demonstrate that "the other candidate" was a threat to the peace and security of the Republic.

The television magnates didn't seem to mind all this political vaudeville so long as they got good action pictures for the tube, and the newspaper reporters didn't figure out how to deal with it. Most of the time the scribblers were herded away from the candidates and made to look like disorderly and discourteous jumping jacks shouting questions that were usually answered with a wave and a smile.

The politicians persisted in these practices because they succeeded on election day, but the cost was great. First, these calculated misrepresentations led to public indifference, cynicism, and mistrust, which debase orderly democratic government. Second, they encouraged the belief in other walks of life that success goes to those who fiddle with the facts, make promises they cannot possibly fulfill, and accuse opponents of nefarious schemes with no basis in fact.

Nixon was a tragic example. He was overwhelmed by events and tried to cover up the facts by misleading and outright false official statements. I wrote during the worst of this scandal, "There is scarcely a noble principle in the Constitution that he [Nixon] hasn't defended in theory or defied in practice." I regard it, however, as an honor that he added my name thereafter to his official "enemies list" of those who were causing him the most trouble.

In short, while it's true that "I saw a new heaven and a new earth," it was not quite true that "the old heaven and the old earth were passed away." At the beginning of the nineties, or so it seems to me, the people are living better and behaving worse. The hangover of wartime propaganda disrupted and stained the great post–World War II chapters of American history. But the people eventually discovered in Korea, Vietnam, and even Cuba that the promises of the politicians were easier to make than to redeem, and in these crises, the people, to their credit, did finally come to their senses.

One consoling thing about all this was that, while it elevated some inferior characters to the presidency and some gangster techniques to the "game," the system of checks and balances under the Constitution limited the damage. The Founding Fathers at the Philadelphia convention proved to be a canny and skeptical bunch. They didn't assume future presidents would be saints or that the members of the Congress would be incorruptible, so they arranged for them to watch one another. Finally, they didn't even trust the people, but assumed that even when a majority supported some outrage—slavery or war, isolation or segregation, for example—it shouldn't be assumed that the people know best.

Having gotten all this off my chest, I am aware of the contradiction in these pages. On the one hand I praise, and stick by, the remarkable achievements of the nation in these past fifty years, and on the other I criticize the system that helped bring them about. My answer to this is that we are so rich and strong that we survive our blunders. We won the Second World War but had to be bombed into it. The systems of fascism, socialism, and communism were so much worse than our flawed system that we got away with it. In the process, we saved democracy, but it is not a self-operating mechanism, and I still hold that the people are not infallible and that the only way to preserve democracy is to raise hell about its shortcomings.

# CHAPTER 31

# Stevenson: My Favorite Loser

Man is a strange animal; he doesn't like to read the
handwriting on the wall until his back is up against it.
—Adlai E. Stevenson

ALL REPORTERS IN Washington have their favorite political losers, and mine was Adlai Stevenson of Illinois. He always seemed to
be getting what he didn't want and losing what he wanted. He
wanted to remain as governor of Illinois in the fifties but was pres-
sured into two presidential elections he knew he would lose. He
wanted to be secretary of state under both Kennedy and Johnson, but
they wanted him on tap and not on top. He was as unlucky in love
as he was in politics. He lost the marriage he wanted to save and
didn't know what to put into its place. He took all these disappointments with a rueful smile and at the end told my friend Eric Sevareid
that all he wanted to do was "sit in the shade and watch the dancers,"
but he died on a sidewalk in London of a massive heart attack.

I guess I liked him because he was a gallant and honorable
dreamer, always coming to bat at the wrong time and predicting he
would strike out. His remark as above, about how man "doesn't like
to read the handwriting on the wall until his back is up against it"
was a fairly good description of Adlai himself. His parents had an
unhappy marriage, and then when he was not quite thirteen, he had
a terrible accident, killing a playmate while tinkering with a gun.
When he was elected governor of Illinois, he wrote, "I need help,

understanding, and encouragement and I have none." Even his successes surprised and disappointed him. When he was nominated for the presidency in 1952, he was full of self-doubt. "I have asked the merciful Father to let this cup pass from me," he said in his acceptance speech, and was denounced for this comparison to Christ's prayer at Gethsemane.

Such mournful requiems didn't make him popular, and this didn't help or bother him. He had a reckless habit of telling the truth, even when he knew it would lose him votes. He hated pretense and even wrote his own speeches, the best since Woodrow Wilson's. They were designed to make people think rather than act, but were often marked by blistering facts most voters didn't want to hear. His acceptance speech in 1952 was remembered long after his defeats:

"The ordeal of the twentieth century—the bloodiest and most turbulent of the Christian age," he said, "is far from over. Sacrifice, patience, understanding, and implacable purpose may be our lot for years to come. Let's face it—let's talk sense to the American people. Let's tell them the truth, that there are no gains without pains. . . . Better we lose the election than mislead the people and better we lose the election than misgovern the people."

This passage has haunted me ever since, for most presidential candidates from the sixties to the nineties succeeded by doing the opposite. Stevenson wasn't a good politician because he was always saying the right thing at the wrong time, or laughing at the wrong places. Once in the 1952 campaign, he offered the Republicans a deal: "If you'll stop telling lies about us we'll stop telling the truth about you!" But he was up against the hopeless task of making the voters laugh at anything but a wisecrack, and he was overwhelmed by Eisenhower's fame and personality.

I confess to a certain partiality. He came from Lincoln country in Illinois, where my wife's father, William J. Fulton, then chief justice of the Illinois Supreme Court, swore him in as governor of Illinois. He was a lonely man and used to walk over to the Supreme Court in Springfield with his dog, Artie, and take supper with the judges just for company. I saw a good deal of him in the governor's mansion during the 1952 campaign, rattling around in that lovely old house, and telling stories about the Chicago political characters or his days in Washington.

"How," I kept asking him, "could a man like you who had a chance to stay in the newspaper business be dumb enough to get into politics?" Because, he replied, "politicians are so funny." He enjoyed his days early in the war when he served in the Navy Department, supervising the shipment of U.S. arms to the Soviet Union. Inevitably, he'd tell his favorite story about the day a Soviet official complained to him that we were behind schedule in delivering our military supplies to Moscow. Adlai agreed that we were behind but insisted that was because the Soviets were behind in giving us a schedule of their needs. "I have not come here," the Russian remarked, "to talk about my behind but about your behind."

I followed him from those disappointing campaign days of 1952 and 1956 until his death at sixty-five. In my mind, he was never quite able to adjust to the idea that he was a permanent resident of this brutal world, but somehow saw himself as a tourist constantly baffled by the antics of the natives. He served in a period of haphazard groping, an incorruptible man, always courteous, and always dreaming of a more decent world he never expected to see.

I was in Sycamore, Illinois, at Sally's parents' house on Christmas of 1951 and asked to see him but he was busy and said he would call me next time he was in Washington. Next time happened to be the night President Truman summoned him to the White House and asked him to seek the presidential nomination, adding that he would back him if he did. After a testy conversation with Truman, he told the irritated president he would consider it, and a little after midnight, keeping his promise, he called me and I put my pants on over my pajamas and went to see him. He was bunking at the Roger Smith Hotel, a two-bit joint on Pennsylvania Avenue, where he always hired a room because he was tighter than a Pullman window.

He had a clear idea that night of his political future. He sat on the edge of his bed and said he was grateful for Truman's support, but was opposed to running. Truman had told him, "Adlai, if a knucklehead like me can be president and not do too badly, think what a really educated smart guy like you could do in the job." Stevenson said he had "made a hash" of his conversation with the president but was still opposed to running. I said I didn't think he had a choice—when your number comes up in a democracy you have to go, especially if the president asks you. This didn't make sense, he said. The Republicans would nominate General Eisenhower, the hero of the Normandy invasion. Ike would win, and, he added, he should win. For the Democrats had held the White House for twenty years and it was time for a change. This would finally break the Republican isolationist tradition, he said, adding that the NATO alliance would never work unless the Republicans joined it. Besides, he said, "I like being governor of Illinois. Nobody needs to try to save the Republic from Ike Eisenhower, and couldn't if they tried."

On that date in January, Eisenhower had not even said he was available, but when Senator Taft of Ohio began campaigning, Stevenson finally decided to give it a try, with the result that he was soundly defeated as he predicted. The people didn't just "like Ike," he said. "It was a love affair." When he lost in a landslide, he said he felt like the little boy who stubbed his toe in the dark: "He was too old to cry but it hurt too much to laugh."

I admired this ability Stevenson had to see things as they were, even when he didn't like what he saw or heard. Once during the 1952 campaign, a woman approached him after a rally and, referring to his divorce, asked him how he could hold the country together when he couldn't even hold his family together. He remarked to me later it was one of the hardest questions he had to answer, and he never did answer it so far as I know.

He was a good listener and was fond of saying, "What this country needs is a hearing aid." Many people said he couldn't make up his mind, but often this charge came from critics who had no mind to make up. He was, of course, full of doubts, mainly because he wasn't capable of pretending that he had simple answers to complicated problems. This led him from time to time into distressing soliloquies on the tangles and ambiguity of life, which the voters didn't want to hear, but he refused to indulge in lazy optimism or sentimental twaddle.

It may be that I was overly impressed by his gift of public speech, for Churchill had taught us during the war that words are sometimes more powerful than bullets, and can unify a nation. But if Stevenson had the words in 1952, Eisenhower had the melody the nation wanted to hear, and he looked like a champion. For one thing, he greeted the crowds with both arms stretched above his head in the V-for-victory sign, while Adlai raised only one hand to his ear as if he were waving a handkerchief. When I told him this sissy wave would cost him a million votes, he said, "I know, but I've got bursitis and can't get my arms any higher."

He originally married Ellen Borden, an intelligent beauty from Chicago, who devoted most of her time to the adornment of her person and the rest to the neglect of her duties. She never forgave him for outshining her in the public eye. My wife and I called on her during the Democratic nominating convention in Chicago in 1952, where she imagined that Stevenson's success was a threat to her life.

We were startled when she suddenly opened her purse and drew out a handgun, which she said she always carried for protection. "Adlai should never be president," she said. "Never!" Near the end of her life, she complained that she couldn't even afford to buy food, but when her family sent her money, she spent it on flowers. Eventually, she was declared incompetent by the courts.

I should say here that I agreed with her as far as 1952 was concerned. Despite my respect for Stevenson's character and abilities, I voted against him that year precisely for the reasons he gave that night at the Roger Smith Hotel. The Republicans had been out of power for so long that the habit of opposition had entered their bones, and it was clear that they would never really understand the problems of the changing postwar world until they had to deal with them in the White House.

In Eisenhower, they had the perfect candidate. He had spent most of his military career abroad and was assumed to know more about the world than he actually did. From his boyhood days in Abilene, Kansas, he had had an easy, friendly small-town manner, and he looked like a president. He was never able to get the subject and predicate of an English sentence in proper order, but he punctuated his speeches with a wonderfully expressive face and he had a genius for getting people to compromise.

As mentioned earlier, Ike wasn't sure he really wanted to be president; he said he would have retired gratefully to his farm in Gettysburg, Pennsylvania, if he had known the Democrats would nominate an "intelligent, decent man like Stevenson," but he didn't want his party to nominate Senator Taft because, as he blurted out one day in a Denver press conference, "Taft's just a damned isolationist." The pressure on him, however, was so great that for a time Ike even entertained the preposterous notion that both parties would nominate and elect him by acclamation. As it turned out, he had a harder time winning the nomination from Taft and the Republican ultraconservatives than he did in winning the election from Stevenson. "How," asked the governor of Illinois, "could anyone defeat a man called 'Ike' with a name like Adlai?"

This self-mockery was only one of Stevenson's endearing qualities. He was the darling of the intellectuals, but he wasn't all that intellectual himself. He had a sound grasp of American and world history, but he didn't really read books; he gutted them and squirreled away every good story or historical analogy he could find, to use on the platform.

Most candidates since then have made the best speeches other people wrote, but Stevenson not only wrote his own, he rewrote them, fiddled with them until the very last moment, driving his staff and the reporters to howls of despair and contributing to the false impression that he didn't know what to think until he heard what he had to say. He was not a quibbler but a perfectionist, who worked for twenty years to make his speeches sound easy, but somehow they usually sounded too hard or visionary to the voters.

In the 1956 campaign, for example, he proposed a ban on the testing of all nuclear weapons in the atmosphere and under the sea. Eisenhower dismissed it as a "theatrical gesture" but signed a test ban treaty with the Soviets shortly after he was reelected. Stevenson also anticipated the national political debate on health care and public school integration. He urged Eisenhower to explore a proposal by Nikita Khrushchev when the Soviet general secretary suggested total disarmament, but again Eisenhower dismissed this as meaningless political propaganda. Stevenson was always getting the support of unpopular people. Khrushchev sent him a message in 1958 through the Soviet ambassador in Washington, Mikhail A. Menshikov, asking if the Soviets could do anything to help him if he sought the presidency for a third time. He rejected this, of course, and told me at the time, "I've got enough troubles without help from them." He did make a halfhearted effort to challenge John F. Kennedy at the Democratic convention, to the annoyance of Kennedy, who then rejected him as secretary of state on the ground that he was too controversial. Stevenson described this as "poppycock."

Johnson treated him shabbily. On the day of President Kennedy's funeral, Johnson called Stevenson to the White House, and according to Arthur Schlesinger, Jr., who saw Stevenson after the meeting, Johnson told him, "You'll be my man on foreign relations. You kept your word to me that you would stay out of the campaign of 1960, and that's why I'm sitting here instead of you, and you know more about foreign affairs than anyone in the party." Stevenson believed this at first, but actually his relations with Johnson were worse than his strained dealings with Kennedy.

I will always remember his kindness. When he sought the presidency in 1956, my youngest son, Tom, then ten years old, ran errands at Stevenson headquarters, and Adlai took a shine to this adoring supporter. Tom was inconsolably unhappy when Stevenson lost again. I found him in his room surrounded by Stevenson banners and told him it was time to get rid of this stuff now that the election was over. The following day, I discovered him in an attic room, still surrounded by Stevenson campaign banners, writing on a yellow pad his imagined acceptance speech. "Fellow Americans, fellow Democrats," the boy had written, "I accept your nomination." Barry Bingham told Stevenson about this and Adlai sent Sally and me a note.

"There's one Democrat who will be READY. Tell Tom I love him; that I apologize; that in 1952 I didn't want to be ready; in 1956 I didn't have time to get ready, and in 1980 I'll be cheering for him—here or there."

He always seemed to see his public life as something outside himself, often referring to himself in the third person. I rode down Michigan Boulevard in Chicago one day with him at the wheel. When we stopped for a traffic light, another car pulled up alongside us and the driver recognized him and said, "Hi, Adlai." I asked as the light changed if he knew the man. "Oh no," he replied, "he wasn't talking to me, he was talking to Adlai."

This was the way he ran for the presidency—as a spectator, as if somebody else were doing it. Maybe, as the Scots say, his "miss was his mercy." Maybe, as he said, he wasn't meant to succeed.

Ironically, during the week of Stevenson's funeral in 1965, President Johnson ordered another 100,000 Americans to Vietnam. At the funeral, the Reverend Frank Sayre, Woodrow Wilson's grandson, remarked at a memorial service for Stevenson at the Washington Cathedral, "He had the courage to fail."

I didn't think, however, that he was a failure and neither did Eric Sevareid, who wrote at the time: "Governor Stevenson died of exhaustion; he just wore himself out. Of course, the gathering frustration [over Vietnam] was part of this, but he did not die of a broken heart. If others regarded him as a 'tragic' figure, I don't think he thought of himself that way. Let others call his life a failure; I think it was a wonderful success. When he was fifty years old, almost nobody but his private friends knew his rare quality; when he died fifteen years later, a million people cried."

# PART ELEVEN

# THE UNHAPPY SIXTIES

# CHAPTER 32

# The Worst of Times

IN MEMORY, MOST decades seem a little more reasonable to me, or at least more understandable, than they did at the time, but the sixties are an exception. They were marked by unpopular wars, particularly Vietnam, brutal assassinations—President Kennedy, Robert Kennedy, Martin Luther King, Jr.—wobbly leadership, anti-war and racial demonstrations in the streets, and fatalistic talk about a third world war. In addition, it was a time of difficult professional decisions for me, and of death in our family and among our friends.

I thought and wrote at the time that the anxiety of the country was excessive and uncharacteristic. It was not the result of military or economic weakness. The United States had come out of World War II as the most powerful nation on earth. Even after the demobilization of millions of GI's, it had the most modern and formidable air and naval forces in the world. Unlike the other Allied nations, its major cities and industries had not been battered, and its gross national product equaled that of all other industrial nations combined, but it had lost the trust that had unified the government and the people after Pearl Harbor. In sum, it was strong militarily and economically, but divided politically and weak psychologically. It had never been so rich or powerful, but it had never felt so vulnerable.

Eisenhower, the oldest president until that time, left the White House on a snowy afternoon in January of 1961, cheery as always, and Jack Kennedy, the youngest man ever elected to the presidency, came in proclaiming the arrival of a new generation that would "pay any price, bear any burden" to assure the success of liberty in the world. But by the end of the decade this new generation was denouncing the burden of Vietnam and tossing deans out of second-story windows.

This was not the America Eisenhower saw when he returned from his victories after the Second World War. Its population had increased by more than a million a year since 1945, and by the mid-sixties was over 190 million. Over 30 million of them lived in little communities like Ike's Abilene, Kansas, and 23 million lived on the farm. All this, however, was changed by the sixties. There had been a vast internal migration of the people, first from south to north, then from north to south, and from east to west. In the sixties, the people in the suburbs equaled the number living in the cities; workers in the service industries greatly increased, including many more women and blacks; and by the sixties, organized labor had declined to 22.2 percent.

There was another major change. Eisenhower had spent the last year of his second term in a worldwide peace crusade, flying from one continent to another appealing to all leaders, especially those of the Soviet Union, for "peaceful coexistence," but Kennedy came in talking about "the challenging revolutionary sixties," and was soon embroiled in alarming confrontations with the Communists in Cuba, Vietnam, and Berlin.

I was confused and divided in my own mind most of the time during the sixties, but at least I learned how easy it was for a great nation to stumble into war and how difficult to admit the mistake and get out. In the process, I not only learned how important but also how hard it was for the press to be aware of the debates going on inside the government *before* decisions were taken to risk a war. The slide into Vietnam was so deceptively slow, and explained with such heroic purposes, that we scarcely noticed it until the body bags came home and the antiwar and racial riots erupted in the universities and in the streets.

There had, of course, been Red scares and other threats of foreign influences in the past: fear of German-Americans during the First World War; fear of Japanese-Americans, who were rounded up and fenced in after Pearl Harbor; much earlier, fear of anarchists after the assassination of President McKinley in 1901; fear of massive immigration and dilution of the old religions; and fear of the liberated slaves. From the days of the Know-Nothings in the last century to the rise of the Ku Klux Klan after the First World War, this suspicion of foreigners and foreign ideas as a threat to native ideals was a recurring part of the American story, but it was never so widespread as the fear of Communist power, ideology, and treachery in the sixties.

The explanation, of course, was that the Soviet Union had the atom bomb in production by the start of the sixties, and, in defiance of its promises at Yalta and its treaty commitment to the United Nations Charter, had built an empire by force in Eastern Europe, refused to join the Marshall Plan for the reconstruction of Europe, supported Communist insurrections in Africa, Asia, and Latin America, and rejected Washington's proposals for constant aerial inspection of both countries and for the international control of atomic energy.

Franklin Roosevelt had counseled the people to "Remember Pearl Harbor" at the beginning of the forties, and successive governments didn't let them forget it. The Joint Chiefs of Staff warned of "a new type of Pearl Harbor attack of infinitely greater magnitude than that of 1941." Kennedy had scarcely found his way around the White House before he was urging every family to build air raid shelters and learn how to deal with the effects of nuclear radiation.

He didn't imagine that the government was riddled with Communist sympathizers, but Dean Rusk, his secretary of state, among many others, was concerned about the continuing atmosphere of fear and suspicion in the capital. "I viewed domestic surveillance and bugging in particular as a real danger to American society," Rusk said later in his memoirs. "I felt strongly about this, strongly enough that when I was in a meeting in the cabinet room with President Kennedy, J. Edgar Hoover [the head of the FBI] and four or five others . . . I turned to Kennedy in Hoover's presence and said, 'If I ever catch anyone in our government bugging me, I will resign and make a public issue of it.' "

No doubt precautions for civil defense and the protection of official secrets were justified by the alarming policies of the Soviet government and its agents, but it wasn't easy to protect the people without scaring them. Accordingly, many people not only remembered Pearl Harbor, but couldn't keep it in proportion.

By the sixties McCarthy had gone to his justified reward, but the clash continued between the optimists and the pessimists inside the government, on how to deal with the Communist threat. Officials of unquestioned intelligence and integrity were in general agreement about the facts of Soviet power and intransigence, but they differed about how to handle it. The pessimists felt that Moscow's means to wage atomic war and its objective of world domination had to be considered together. They thought that since the Communists had the power to wage war, it had to be assumed that, like the Nazis, they would use it.

The optimists, in contrast, thought it was a mistake to assume that the Communist leaders were the same sort of mad and reckless men as Hitler and the Nazis. They agreed that the Soviet Union would undoubtedly try to blackmail weaker nations to achieve its political objectives, but didn't think it would risk a third world war after its terrible losses in the first two. In short, the pessimists thought the problem was primarily military, while the optimists thought it was dangerous to emphasize the military aspects without also emphasizing the possibility of a political compromise.

This understandable debate, however, did not proceed in a calm and serious atmosphere. Keeping things in proportion had never been a common practice in the United States. Its literature, its advertising, its politics, its press, and even its private conversation didn't favor understatement but exaggeration, and encouraged public excitement. The loudest voices got the biggest headlines, which in turn encouraged the greatest fears.

Kennedy started the sixties by talking about the need for more military power and political negotiations, but when Moscow tried to force the Allies out of Berlin in 1961 and put nuclear missiles in Cuba in 1962, the military side of the argument prevailed. Better safe than sorry won the debate.

It cannot be easy at the end of the century to remember the emotions of that time. There was a lot of loose talk about inevitable war—this time with nuclear weapons. The government broadcast instructions on radio and television about what to do in the event of an atomic attack. Emergency evacuation headquarters were set up for the government departments, one of them for the State Department in the Blue Ridge Mountains near our cabin in Virginia. And a solitary military plane was kept in the air twenty-four hours a day every day of the year, in the hope that somehow the president and his cabinet would be able to escape if the capital were bombed.

Meanwhile the Soviets were acting on their own nightmare suspicions. They, too, were assuming that since the United States had the capacity to wage war, it might do so. Many Americans talked about "destroying communism," Moscow noted; after all, they argued, it was the Americans who had entered Russia after World War I and tried to overthrow their revolution, and it was the Americans, not the Russians, who had used the atomic bomb in unlimited warfare. Thus, both sides were dominated during much of the sixties by their worst anxieties.

I was so busy covering all this that, like most people, I took no precautions, spending much of my time as head of the Washington bureau reporting the angry political exchanges. When President Kennedy was murdered in 1963, it was at first suspected that this was part of a Communist conspiracy, and when his brother Robert and the Reverend Martin Luther King, Jr., were assassinated in 1968, there was a feeling of anarchy in the air.

Thus, in the latter half of the sixties, the East-West conflict produced an atmosphere of tension and alarm. It was seen by many not merely as a contest between independent national states for power, position, and prestige—though it was that, too—but as a conflict over the meaning of life and the place of individual freedom in the world. Like the religious wars of the Middle Ages, it was widely regarded as a clash of philosophies that could not be resolved by compromising with the "heretics."

This was the mood of mutual suspicion on both sides. I understood Moscow's fear of invasion from the West; after Napoleon and Hitler, how could it have been otherwise? But I had few doubts about which side started the Cold War. It was not, after all, the Western Allies who made a deal with Hitler in 1939, or rearmed after the Second World War, or took over other countries by force when the war was over. On the contrary, the Allies made no hostile moves toward the Soviet Union, but reduced their military forces, invited the Soviets to join the Marshall Plan for the reconstruction of Europe, offered to join with the Soviet Union for the international control of atomic energy, and suggested an open-skies program for mutual surveillance of all suspicious military movements.

Accordingly, when the Soviet Union broke the promises of non-intervention made at Yalta and Potsdam, violated its commitments under the United Nations Charter, mounted proxy wars in Korea and Vietnam, and tried to squeeze the Allies out of Berlin and place nuclear missiles in Cuba, it was scarcely surprising that the United States decided to act boldly this time and not timidly, as it had with the rise of Hitler.

The Hitler nightmare probably did more to determine U.S. policy in those years than anything else. Until Stalin died at the beginning of the fifties, talk of another Hitler was no doubt justified, but in the sixties, every dictator was seen in terms of Hitler, and every attempt at compromise was denounced as "appeasement." Mao Tse-tung in Peking and Ho Chi Minh in Hanoi were compared to the Nazi tyrant, and even after the end of the Cold War, Saddam Hussein in Iraq was compared to Hitler when he invaded Kuwait, and was soon confronted by over 500,000 American troops on Iraq's Saudi Arabian border.

Accordingly, I looked back at the sixties with anxiety and regret, wondering, despite all the obvious changes at home and abroad, whether we had learned the lessons of the two German wars too well and confused areas that were clearly vital to the nation's security with areas that were not vital. I was relieved by Kennedy's victory over Nixon and felt sure he would bring new energy and imagination to Washington, but he did not make a good beginning.

# CHAPTER 33

# The Kennedys:
# Triumph and Tragedy

I ALWAYS SEEMED to run into the Kennedys when they were in trouble, probably because trouble was the story of their lives. I saw the founding father in his controversial London embassy days, Jack in his battles from the Bay of Pigs to Dallas, Bobby whenever he didn't like my critical comments about President Kennedy, and Teddy in Martha's Vineyard a few hours after he plunged off the bridge at Chappaquiddick. They were always, I thought, getting more credit than they deserved and more sorrow than they could bear, climbing into jobs before they were ready and falling just when they were succeeding. It was really unfair to draw conclusions about them, for they never had time to conclude anything, but they paid for their triumphs and established a legend that outlived their history.

My first instinct was to compare President Kennedy to his father. He had all the old man's personal charm and many of his wayward habits, but unlike his father, he knew the world was round, and he was loyal to his party and to his allies. He was a little too clever and fancy for my taste, but he was intelligent, half Irish and half Harvard, irresistibly witty, and like all the Kennedys, recklessly handsome. He delighted in the absurd. He mocked everything, including himself and his success, and, unlike most presidents, who talk more than they listen, he was a relentless questioner, especially after swallowing the disastrous advice of his experts at the Bay of Pigs. The Washington reporters enjoyed his jokes, and still remember the opening of his speech to the Gridiron Club in 1960. At that time, some politicians were saying that Kennedy's father might even "buy" the election.

Jack began his remarks by saying he had a telegram from his father: DON'T BUY A SINGLE VOTE MORE THAN NECESSARY. I'LL BE DAMNED IF I'M GOING TO PAY FOR A LANDSLIDE.

I have many vivid memories of Jack Kennedy, three in particular. The first was of the wild night at the *Times* when we elected him prematurely and then stopped the presses; the second was the day I saw him alone in Vienna after his first stormy summit meeting with Nikita Khrushchev, the general secretary of the Soviet Union; and the third was the day he ordered the blockade of the Soviet missiles off Cuba. The election-night incident almost gave me a heart attack; the second still seems to me to mark a critical decision in the Vietnam War; and the third seems more important with every passing year.

It was, by tradition on the *Times,* the duty of the Washington correspondent to write the main news account on presidential election nights. Arthur Krock had done so with the utmost calm and confidence but with little pleasure, through four elections of Roosevelt and one of Truman. I took his chair outside the bull pen in the New York City room on November 8, 1960. It was not a scene for quiet meditation, and I was neither calm nor confident. The managing editor, Turner Catledge, an old hand at these parties, was in charge. The newsroom, stretching a full city block from Forty-third to Forty-fourth Street, wasn't quite as crowded as Times Square, but almost.

We were ready by the time the polls closed in New York for everything except what happened. All the so-called B-matter had been set in type; that is to say, editorials had been written in advance to celebrate the victory of either Kennedy or Nixon; we had biographies of both, and of their parents and wives and children, accounts of their childish sayings, school records—ten whole pages of everything but their love affairs—all waiting for the single fact of who won.

In addition, I was surrounded by charts of the states with their electoral votes, and batteries of telephones open to our correspondents in the big states and the dubious states, with trucks blocking both Forty-third and Forty-fourth streets to carry the news to the paper stands, the railroad stations, and the airports. The first edition, at 9:31, was easy. I informed the waiting multitudes at great length that "voting was heavy," that "early returns" were following "normal patterns," and that some little towns in Maine had voted for Nixon by a small margin, while others in Vermont seemed to be favoring Kennedy. I heard the circulation manager remark that we wouldn't break any circulation records with startling, historic stuff like that.

By midnight quite a few papers were announcing that Kennedy had won, but we were still hypnotized on the *Times* by that grinning picture of Harry Truman holding up the front page of the *Chicago Tribune* announcing that Governor Dewey had won the election of 1948. Our charts showed Kennedy two electoral votes short of the winning 269, so we still held back. The headline of the second edition, which rolled at 12:36 A.M., said KENNEDY HOLDS WIDE LEAD. At 1:03, however, Austin Wehrwein, the *Times* Chicago correspondent, called to say that Illinois was in the bag for Kennedy and a few minutes later, Larry Davies, our man in San Francisco, assured us that California was "safe" for Kennedy, so Catledge came over to me and said, "Let's go." So out came the big type for the late city final at 3:18—KENNEDY ELECTED—with front-page pictures of Kennedy and Johnson, the editorial proclaiming Kennedy's youth and other virtues—page after page of background boilerplate, all sounding as if we had been sure all along.

All we needed was Nixon's concession, but it didn't come and it didn't come, though we had 485,000 papers on the streets saying it was all over. Before long Wehrwein was calling back saying he was not so sure about Illinois and Davies was saying, sorry, California was running dead even. That's when I felt sure of the heart attack. Orvil Dryfoos, Catledge, and I retreated into Catledge's office, and at 4:47 Catledge stopped the presses. All ten pages were made over; Charlie Merz, the editorial page editor, withdrew his congratulations of Kennedy, and it wasn't until 7:17 A.M. that the extra edition came out with the banner: KENNEDY IS APPARENT VICTOR; LEAD CUT IN TWO KEY STATES.

I staggered home to Sally and told her it was the worst night since my wrong flash at the Grand National Steeplechase in England, but she said no great damage was done. I wasn't so sure. All the old immigrant doubts and fears I had long since forgotten returned for a few days, but when I got back to Washington, Kennedy laughed at me. "If you were scared at the *Times,* you should have seen me," he said.

I didn't get on with him during his first days in the White House. When he decided to televise his press conferences, I annoyed him by writing that it was "the goofiest idea since the hula hoop," and when I protested that he stop playing favorites with reporters in the White House, he sent back word that Charlie Bartlett of the *Chattanooga*

*Times* and Ben Bradlee of *Newsweek* were old friends and he'd damn well see them whenever he liked.

He assumed I was sore because I was excluded from these private bull sessions, but I never thought there was much mileage in confidential relationships between reporters and presidents. It was common practice in the last century, when big-city editors dined with presidents and even wrote speeches for them, but usually they gave more than they got. If presidents agreed that you could print what they said, fine, but most of the time in my experience, they told reporters little in these back-room parleys, and put it off the record.

Kennedy was so used to getting what he wanted when he came to the White House that he thought he could ignore the old rules that had governed White House reporting. For example, he would occasionally announce his travel plans and then order his pilot to peel off for some other destination, not always on government business, leaving the reporters in the press plane to guess where he was.

I told Pierre Salinger, his press secretary, that I was not interested in the president's personal monkey business, but as head of the Washington bureau, I was responsible for covering his public activities and didn't see how I could explain it if somebody took a potshot at him one night after he had ditched the reporters. I got no assurance that even the Secret Service would tell us where he was, but a little while after this dispute about his ditching the reporters I had an experience with him that may be worth more than an asterisk.

In the spring of 1961, Nikita Khrushchev began increasing pressure on the United States to sign a peace treaty that would give Communist East Germany control over access to Berlin. Kennedy was preoccupied early that year with the consequences of his disastrous intervention at the Bay of Pigs, but though he disliked summit meetings, he agreed to meet Khrushchev early in June in Vienna.

Maybe because of our row over his snookering the press, he promised to see me as soon as the Khrushchev conference was over, and by arrangement with Salinger, I was instructed to slip into the American Embassy in the Austrian capital and wait until the president arrived. I remember that Saturday morning very well. He arrived at the embassy over an hour late, shaken and angry, having been delayed by an unexpected extra meeting with the Soviet leader. He was wearing a hat—unusual for him—and he pushed it down over his forehead, sat down on a couch beside me, and sighed. I said it must have been a rough session. Much rougher than he had expected, he said.

Khrushchev had threatened him over Berlin. In his earthy language, the Soviet leader was fond of saying that the way to make capitalist politicians pay attention was to "pull their testicles" on Berlin. He had presented Kennedy with an aide-mémoire, setting December 1961 as the deadline for agreement on a Berlin peace treaty. If the United States did not agree to Communist control over access to that city, the Soviet Union would proceed unilaterally to dominate the routes from Western Europe to Berlin. The president felt this amounted to an ultimatum, and replied that the United States would fight to maintain access to its garrison in Berlin if necessary. The summit meeting ended on that ominous note.

Kennedy reported this to me quite calmly. He thought he knew, he said, why Khrushchev had taken such a hard line. He felt sure Khrushchev thought that anybody who had made such a mess of the Cuban invasion had no judgment, and any president who had made such a blunder but then didn't see it through had no guts. Now, said the president, we have a problem.

Nothing could be resolved with the Soviets, he added, if they thought we would not insist on our rights and would not fight for them. He had tried to convince Khrushchev of U.S. determination but had failed. It was now essential to demonstrate our firmness, and the place to do it, he remarked to my astonishment, was Vietnam! I don't think I swallowed his hat, but I was speechless. If he had said he was going to run the Communist blockade into Berlin, I might have understood, but the reference to Vietnam baffled me. I finally asked him to explain, but he had to leave at once for a meeting with the British political leaders and the queen in London, so our conversation ended abruptly. On June 10, the Soviet government published the aide-mémoire, indicating that the Soviet demands were not negotiable.

When Kennedy returned to Washington, he gave orders to send another U.S. division to Europe and to triple the number of U.S. military advisers in Vietnam. Officers were assigned to the Vietnamese army at the battalion and regimental levels to advise in combat, as well as in training. They were instructed to accompany the South Vietnamese troops into battle and to fire if fired upon. He approved National Security Action Memorandum 52, which said that the objective of the United States was "to prevent Communist domination of South Vietnam." This led to more wasteful horrors, but he was fascinated by the new trickery of guerrilla warfare as practiced by Mao Tse-tung in China, whose works he had read, and he took a personal interest in building up the Green Berets, a so-called elite force, which was said to be effective in counterinsurgency.

Fearing intervention by China or the Soviet Union, he did, however, reject the advice of his more militant advisers who wanted open intervention by larger U.S. forces. He had serious doubts about Vietnam; in fact, he had doubts about many other things. Once he remarked, "Before my term is ended, we shall have to test anew whether a nation organized and governed such as ours can endure. The outcome is by no means certain."

But Khrushchev had treated Kennedy with contempt, even challenged his courage, and whatever else Kennedy may have lacked, he didn't lack courage. He felt he had to act. He sent Vice President Johnson to Saigon to check out the increasingly disturbing battle reports, and when Johnson returned insisting that success in the war depended on the determination of the United States, the president ordered even more advisers to the battlefront.

This, I always thought, was a critical mistake. Once Kennedy had over fifteen thousand "advisers" engaged not only in giving advice but also in giving support on the battlefield, United States power and prestige were thought by many officials in Washington and in the Asian capitals to be committed. And when Kennedy, alarmed by the inefficiency of the Saigon government under Diem, cooperated in approving Diem's murder, he was all the more convinced that he had to carry on the war.

No doubt, as president, Johnson was more responsible for committing the United States to that struggle (he eventually had 500,000 Americans in the war), but in my view Kennedy started the slide.

Robert Kennedy, eager to protect his brother from blame, always denied that the president intended to increase the nation's commitment to Vietnam, and also denied that the Kennedy-Khrushchev meeting in Vienna had anything to do with it. But he didn't hear what his brother said to me in the Vienna embassy, and I did.

Once back in Washington, the president held a series of emergency meetings with his principal aides. He included in the discussions former Secretary of State Dean Acheson, who thought Khrushchev's demands on Berlin were outrageous and recommended mobilization of U.S. and NATO forces. Secretary of State Dean Rusk, McGeorge Bundy, head of the National Security Council, and ambassadors Adlai Stevenson and Charles Bohlen disagreed with Acheson, and Henry Kissinger, then a private citizen, was brought into the debate and thought Acheson's proposals were bellicose and provocative.

Kennedy compromised. His decision was to keep talking to the

Soviets without concessions on Berlin, to stiffen the American military presence in Europe, and to raise the commitment in Vietnam while keeping it more limited than the Pentagon desired. Maybe Robert Kennedy was right in saying that the president did not intend after the Vienna summit to get deeply involved in Vietnam, but he went along with past commitments as he had done in the Bay of Pigs fiasco, and after his death the policy of intervention got out of hand.

What was ironic and even tragic about this was that Kennedy got out of the Berlin crisis not by military action, but by talking it to death. Also, by the masterstroke of his foreign policy, he solved the Cuban missile crisis by forcing Khrushchev to turn back the Soviet nuclear weapons on the high seas and take the rest of them out of Cuba. Thus, in the most dramatic way, he demonstrated his courage and his determination to defend the nation's interests by risking a nuclear war. But by then, the involvement in Vietnam, designed to prove American willpower and strength, began to prove precisely the opposite.

There is something about being president that inhibits even the most intelligent of them from admitting mistakes. They seem to think the people expect them to be infallible. Kennedy could have said the Bay of Pigs plan was a dumb idea and gotten away with it. Nixon could have admitted his blunders at the Watergate and saved his presidency. Lyndon Johnson plunged deeper into the rice paddies of Vietnam with the silly and, as it turned out, inaccurate cry, "I'm not going to be the first president to lose a war." And President Reagan wouldn't cut his losses in Iran or Nicaragua. Senator William Fulbright of Arkansas, one of the wisest men on Capitol Hill, called it "the arrogance of power" and that isn't a bad description.

No doubt Kennedy's decisions on the Bay of Pigs and at the Khrushchev summit in Vienna were the result of inexperience. They came in the first months of his administration before he was well acquainted with his principal advisers, who in turn knew little about him. Maybe his first mistake was to retain the services of Allen Dulles, the head of the CIA, and J. Edgar Hoover, the director of the FBI. They were his first two appointments. They believed in the worst possible interpretations of the Communist conspiracies at home and abroad. Hoover had been in office for years and had files on everybody, no doubt including the Kennedys, and Bobby Kennedy, who had served on Senator McCarthy's staff, preferred to have Hoover as an insider rather than as a vindictive and well-informed outsider.

Also, Allen Dulles, who had presided over the Bay of Pigs plans during the Eisenhower administration, not only recommended support for the anti-Castro brigade but also told Kennedy that reversing the "Eisenhower plan" and abandoning the Cuban freedom fighters would be a powerful argument against him in the next presidential election. I went to see Dulles at his house in Georgetown and asked him about the rumors of invasion, and he said the CIA didn't know anything about it.

Kennedy was more skeptical of his advisers after that, and he improved with experience. He was tested as no other president had been, during the Cuban missile crisis, and his masterful handling of that crisis was the greatest achievement of his administration. I heard that the president was moving planes and ships and men into the southeastern ports, apparently to blockade the Soviet ships then approaching Cuba with nuclear missiles. I called Mac Bundy at the White House for confirmation. He acted as if he had never heard of Russia, but he told the president, who immediately called me back. Kennedy didn't deny what was afoot, but said that if I printed what we knew, he might get an ultimatum from Khrushchev even before he could go on the air to explain the seriousness of the crisis. He was worried that premature disclosure that atomic missiles were en route to Cuba could, as Secretary of State Rusk said later, "lead to panic and confusion, and even to a mass exodus from our cities." I said I understood his request but only the responsible editors of the *Times* could decide whether or not to print. A few minutes later, Max Frankel, then covering the State Department, said we'd look foolish if the navy intercepted the Soviet ships before the president addressed the nation, and a sea battle ensued. I called the White House again, and Kennedy said he could assure me that no action would be taken before his announcement. He was calm and candid in a very sticky situation, and the *Times* spiked the story. Kennedy got out of this jam by rejecting the advice of those who advised an air strike on the missile bases in Cuba, and by accepting the counsel of those who favored a naval quarantine, but during this White House debate, Secretary of Defense McNamara was so alarmed that he wondered whether he would "live to see another Saturday night."

Camelot was never my favorite legend, but the more I saw of Kennedy after that, the more I trusted him. He seemed increasingly steady in adversity, maybe because he had to deal with so much of it in his private life. He was in constant pain with an ailing back, and for a time in 1962 had to go around the White House on crutches. His father had a stroke in December of 1961 and was never able to talk to him thereafter. An infant son, Patrick, died a few days after a premature birth in August of 1963, but none of this interfered with his work or his ability to handle the accidents of life.

He was so busy during his short term in office that he never seemed to think about or plan for the future. Once I visited him at his house in Hyannis Port and tried to get him to tell me what he wanted to achieve before he rode down Pennsylvania Avenue with his successor. He was embarrassed by the question and finally said he had never thought about that. I don't think he had a presentiment that the future was not something he would have to handle, but he had so many day-to-day problems that he didn't think much about what lay ahead. Maybe this was all to the good.

I have been recalling in these pages my luck at being on hand when big news was breaking, but I wasn't in Dallas or even in Washington when Kennedy was shot. I was having lunch with Governor Terry Sanford of North Carolina in Winston-Salem when we got the news. I cannot remember a day when the *Times* or any other newspaper did a better job of covering a major event. When it was over, Harry Reasoner of CBS said on the air: "I don't recall in my lifetime ever seeing the profession of journalism carried on at a higher level. All the facts—the exhaustive, accurate news of events, the careful study of implications in allied areas, the authoritative special comments, the wise counsel of the editorial page—were so shining and splendid that you would think the *Times* had been planning its coverage for years."

I flew at once to Washington and filed a story, not always quite seeing the keys on my typewriter: "America wept tonight, not alone for its dead young president, but for itself. The grief was general, for somehow the worst in the nation had prevailed over the best. The indictment extended beyond the assassin, for something in the nation itself, some strain of madness and violence, had destroyed the highest symbol of law and order."

A week later, I received a letter from John Finley, the master of Eliot House at Harvard. He expressed with his usual sensitivity and grace a feeling that was widely shared. He wrote:

I felt suddenly old without Mr. and Mrs. Kennedy in the White House. Not only by ability, but by sheer verve and joy, the Kennedys imparted their youth to everyone, and put a sheen on our life that made it more youthful than it is. Mr. Johnson now seems Gary

Cooper as President—*High Noon,* the poker game, the easy walk and masculine smile. But even Gary Cooper is growing older, and the companions and adversaries around the poker table reflect a less fresh, if no doubt practical and effective mood. All will be well, I feel sure, but it is August, not June.

The Kennedy "style," of course, was important . . . the handsome good looks, the lovely wife and children, the soaring speeches, most of them as carefully contrived as they seemed spontaneous. I was never quite able to determine where the genius of his speech-writer, Ted Sorenson, left off and the graceful delivery of Kennedy picked up, but I never doubted that the combination contributed to, if it was not decisive in, his victory over Nixon in the 1960 election.

Still, the more I thought of it over the years the more I felt that this emphasis on his personality tended to minimize the historic importance of his handling of the Cuban missile crisis. There were, I felt, three critical presidential decisions in my time: Truman's action in moving American power into the eastern Mediterranean when the British could no longer face the Soviet threat to Greece and Turkey; Eisenhower's success in getting the Republican party to support a nonpartisan foreign policy; and Kennedy's blockade of the Soviet missiles en route to Cuba.

Between Kennedy's success in the missile crisis and his death, I had a talk with Prime Minister Harold Macmillan of Britain. He recalled that twice in this century, the leaders of the free world had been confronted by the menacing power of a totalitarian state. From 1912 until 1914, and again from 1935 to 1939, Germany made a series of moves that clearly threatened the balance of power and even the peace and order of the world, but both times Britain, France, and the United States failed to raise enough military power or to show enough willpower to avoid the two most terrible wars and tragedies of the twentieth century.

"Kennedy did not make the same mistake," Macmillan said. "If he never did another thing, he assured his place in history by warning Khrushchev that this time the United States would not stand aside. He did what we failed to do in the terrible days of hesitation before the two German wars."

After the president's death, attention turned to his brother Robert, but I write about him with caution, for I never seemed to get to know him. I think it was because I had implicated President Kennedy in the Vietnam disaster. Bobby naturally protected the memory of his murdered brother, and felt somehow that my report of the Kennedy-Khrushchev meeting in Vienna was inaccurate or unfair. I offered to show him my detailed notes of the Vienna interview, but he said he wasn't interested and I never saw him after that.

His murder left Teddy as the sole survivor of the four brothers. I felt then that surely so much sorrow in one family would somehow be repaid in the promising career of Teddy. This childish name diminished him, but he seemed more solid and more in touch with the liberal principles of his party than any other member of the clan. He was the youngest of the lot and always lived in their shadow. I always thought he was a much better legislator than Jack, whose record in the Senate was distinguished mainly by his absenteeism. Edward Kennedy was only twelve years old when his eldest brother, Joe, was killed on a bombing mission against a Nazi submarine base in the English Channel. He was thirty-one when President Kennedy was assassinated, and thirty-six when Robert Kennedy was killed in California. I was skeptical about him at first, writing in the *Times* that "one Kennedy is a triumph, two Kennedys at the same time are a miracle, but three could easily be regarded by many voters as an invasion."

Politically, they were all quite different. Joe was even more conservative than his father. Jack was a moderate. Robert was in motion, running away from his liaison with Senator Joe McCarthy on the right toward the center. Edward was an unabashed liberal, even when in the eighties the Republicans tried to give that distinguished tradition a bad name. In the afterglow of his brother's administration, the road to the White House seemed open to him, but he took one wrong turn after a party on the island of Chappaquiddick, and as the poet Robert Frost remarked about life itself: the road taken and the road not taken make all the difference.

I happened to be at our family newspaper on the Vineyard during that weekend and looked over the scene in the morning. It was not the sort of turn on Chappaquiddick a man was likely to make by accident. The hard road ran from the party house on that island to the ferry, but with a young woman in the car, he took a quick turn to the right onto a sandy road leading to the Dike Bridge. I know that old wooden bridge very well, and, whatever his condition or intentions, it's easy to imagine how a sober man could drive off in the dark into the water.

The first part of the bridge—no more than a few yards—rises

steeply, so that the lights of a car at night are tilted toward the sky, leaving the bridge in darkness. Then the bridge veers sharply to the left and levels off. This time Kennedy didn't turn but plunged straight ahead into the deep and swirling channel. He managed to get out and tried to liberate the girl but failed and left her in the car. The islanders never forgave him for that. "We don't know what he was doing, but you never leave a body in the water," they said.

The rest of the story is well known—his swim from Chappaquiddick across the harbor to the main body of Martha's Vineyard, his secrecy and deceptions during the official inquiry, his weak explanation of how he took the wrong turn—but all the rest of his political career was blighted by that night.

I went straight from my desk at the *Vineyard Gazette* to the police station in Edgartown that morning, after a woman called from a house next to the bridge to say there had been a terrible accident and she thought Senator Kennedy was in the car. I asked for Chief Arena. "He's in conference," an officer said, but police chiefs in little towns are seldom "in conference," so I insisted on seeing him. "Senator Kennedy's in there," the officer said. Knowing Kennedy wouldn't want to talk to me in the police station, I sent in a note to the senator suggesting we meet at my house in the next block, assuming that he'd show up and talk in private, but of course he didn't. I never made that silly journalistic mistake again.

Somehow, I was never able to have a useful conversation with him after that. On an anniversary of President Kennedy's death, I went to his house above the Potomac and took down his reflections on the past and future, but the tape might as well have been blank. I think his memories were just too painful. He talked mainly about his children.

His bid for the presidency in 1980 was a calamity. He made it because the polls were saying Democrats preferred him to President Carter 59 to 16, and he blundered because he lost his temper and forgot his manners. He did not have a high opinion of Carter, but his assumption that he could defeat a president and then win with a divided and embittered party was preposterous. His organization for the campaign was as poor as his judgment, and while he made the best convention speech I had heard since Adlai Stevenson in 1952, he was soundly defeated, mocked by the Republicans, and resented by many Democrats for years thereafter. Had he waited until 1988, his service in the Senate might have overcome the memories of Chappaquiddick, but even he had decided by that time that there are some things voters never forget.

Washington tried to make amends. While it was still arguing about raising a monument to Franklin Roosevelt forty-five years after his death, it built for President Kennedy a handsome center for the performing arts on the banks of the Potomac next to the Lincoln Memorial. It was a tribute to his possibilities rather than to his achievements, and seemed to say, as he said often himself, "Life is unfair."

# CHAPTER 34

# Lyndon Johnson

When you come into the presence of a leader of men,
you know you have come into the presence of fire;
that it is best not incautiously to touch that man;
that there is something that makes it dangerous to
cross him.

—Woodrow Wilson

LYNDON JOHNSON OF Texas was a good example of Woodrow
Wilson's point, but in a tragic sense, for he was so shamelessly
intimidating that most of his colleagues hesitated to cross him, even
when they knew he was stumbling into trouble. This may have been
his strength as majority leader of the Senate, but it was a weakness
in terms of his Vietnam policy, and it diminished his otherwise
distinguished career. He could forgive his enemies, particularly when
he felt they were wrong, but never his friends, especially when he
knew they were right. The obit writers had an easy time of it when
he died, because there wasn't a politician or a reporter in Washington
who didn't have a story or two about his remarkable achievements
or stubborn blunders. He was not only available to reporters but
unavoidable. He devoured newspapers every morning in the sure
conviction that the entire press corps was conspiring with his enemies to defeat his policies, mock his character, and even vilify his
family.

He was, by nature, a suspicious bully. He saw conspiracies everywhere. He doubted everything, including members of his own staff, most of them held over from Kennedy. But the paradox of this was that he didn't question the Vietnam policy he inherited in his first days in the White House, or, in his preoccupation with domestic issues, think much about foreign policy. He later explained to me that he thought giving the nation a sense of continuity after the Kennedy assassination was more important than anything else, and that he wouldn't feel free to insist on his own ideas until he had been elected in his own right.

This was understandable, but it meant that the policy of reinforcing the American garrison in Saigon was continued, each new commitment justified as essential to the protection of previous commitments, until Johnson felt he couldn't withdraw without admitting he was wrong. He had never shown much enthusiasm for confessing error, and when he was vice president he had made some reckless promises of aid to the South Vietnamese. He even described South Vietnam's feckless Diem as "the Churchill of Asia," but there was little support in the country for more adventures in Southeast Asia.

I followed him all over the country in the 1964 campaign against Goldwater, and at every whistle-stop I attended he was loudly cheered when he said over and over again that he wasn't going "to send American boys to Asia to fight a war Asian boys should fight for themselves." But he did, and at first there was no outcry against it.

I wrote after the 1964 election: "Both the period of mourning for Kennedy and experimentation by Johnson are over. Washington is like a girl settling down with her old boyfriend. The mad and wonderful infatuation with the handsome young stranger from Boston is over—somehow she knew it wouldn't last—so she's adjusting to reality. Everything is less romantic but more practical now, part regret and part relief, beer instead of champagne. . . . The lovers of style are not too happy, but the lovers of substance are not complaining."

Johnson, of course, didn't like these comparisons, and suspected they came from the old Kennedy staff. They didn't know what to make of him. He was in turn magnanimous and petty, recklessly bold and insecure, eloquent and funny, but crude and vulgar, cautious and headstrong and wickedly sarcastic; wise in the political ways of his own country, but ignorant of the mysteries beyond our shores. He was to the politics of America what Texas is to the rest of the Union:

he was a whopper. When you interviewed him, he wound up with your life story. Anything you said, he could usually neutralize with something else on the other side. If you said he was from the South, he would say he was from the West or the other way around. If you didn't tell the precise truth about him as he saw it, he said you were dishonest, and if you did tell the truth about him, he said you were disloyal and mean. He regarded the press as a conveyor belt that should carry, without question, any baggage he wanted to dump on it.

I. F. Stone complained in his newsletter that it was almost impossible to get an objective view of Johnson because the politicians and the Washington correspondents "were outdoing themselves in flattery of the new monarch," but I didn't join them. At the end of his first year in office I wrote that he was "tyrannical with his personal staff, disorderly about administration, thin-skinned about the press, and inclined to regard criticism not as a duty in a free society, but a crime." Stone thought I would be banished from the White House for these remarks, but Johnson never mentioned them, and never shut me out.

Nobody in Washington I talked to could ever remember such a contradictory character. He didn't persuade his political opponents, he knocked their brains out. His admirations didn't last long but his resentments endured. He found it hard to believe that truth varied occasionally from his own opinions, and of course he denied that any such observation was justified. Nevertheless, the stories he left behind provide at least some clues to his character.

Shortly after he took over the White House, there were a few articles in the papers wondering how a man who had spent most of his life in the public service had managed to get so rich. The implication was not that he was crooked but that he had used his political influence to get hold of a television station, a big ranch in Texas hill country, and other expensive playthings. This tickled the gossip scribblers for a couple of weeks, and I finally wrote a column saying why didn't he sell the TV station and let's get on to more important things.

My telephone rang shortly after seven the next morning and the White House operator said the president was calling. Then, typically, there was a long silence before he came on the line, and when he did, his voice was very soft. "Where are you?" he asked. I said I was home. "You mean you've got a telephone out there?" I said I did. Then his voice raised a couple of notches. "Didn't I tell you when

I took this job that if you wanted to know anything about me all you had to do was call up?" I said he had, and then he let me have it, shouting now. "Then why do I have to get up and read this garbage in *The New York Times* about selling the television station? Don't you know that station belongs to Lady Bird? She's the one who went to college and worked for that station, and now you come along and tell me to ditch it and break her heart."

On he went for forty-two minutes (I clocked him), telling me all about his poor boyhood struggles, and how rich he'd really be if he had stayed in Texas; all about his wife's sacrifices for that station and her dreams for its development; and, anyway, who was I to go around giving him advice about how to run his life? In this entire time, I said little more than "Yes, sir" and "No, Mr. President" until finally he said, "I've got to go now but I'm not finished with you yet. You come over here at four this afternoon and see Walter Jenkins. He'll open up the books on that television station, how Bird bought it, and how much money it took in, every damn cent!"

Bang went the receiver, and sure enough, when I got to the White House, Jenkins was there with the books, the bill of sale, and other legal mysteries I have long since forgotten. But I didn't forget the barely controlled ferocity of Johnson's voice. Maybe he felt he'd been a little too rough on me, or maybe he was just giving me the treatment, but while I was going over the books with Jenkins, he came in and insisted I have dinner with him and his wife, so she could tell me the whole story about the television station. At dinner, I laughed at his pride in a new battery-operated pepper shaker he showed off. He gave it to me as a present when he finally liberated me late in the evening.

This was vintage Johnson. The obstacle before him, no matter how small, took precedence for the moment over all other things, no matter how large. He studied the FBI files on his opponents, rejoiced at the pornographic gossip contained therein, and used it to inspire more fear than trust. When on the rampage, which was often, his vicious remarks wounded friends and foes alike. He analyzed governments in terms of the individuals who led them, a dangerous procedure, but he was, in the estimate of those who worked with him and against him in the Congress, the most effective legislator of his time, and would have been one of the great presidents if the Vietnam War had not destroyed him.

He paid little attention to foreign policy history. He was always saying Roosevelt "was like a daddy to me," but he wasn't in the least influenced by Roosevelt's long battle to end France's colonial domination of Southeast Asia and allow the people there to establish their independence. He was convinced, however, as Truman and Kennedy were before him, that Korea and Vietnam were just the first targets of Moscow's campaign to dominate Asia, so he just kept saying, "Let us continue."

On domestic affairs, he added to his legislative gifts all the fervor of Roosevelt's New Deal and Harry Truman's Fair Deal—a gigantic figure calling for the completion of the liberal moral agenda the murdered president had barely started. "Do it for Jack," he told the Congress, launching a "war on poverty," and demanding justice for the American blacks. "Their cause must be our cause, too," he declared, "because it is not just Negroes but really it is all of us who must overcome the crippling legacy of bigotry and injustice." No doubt the national grief over the young president's assassination contributed to Johnson's success, but Johnson put over the Kennedy program with a combination of eloquence and cunning unseen in Washington since Franklin Roosevelt's first hundred days.

I tried to figure out how he did it, and Senator Henry Jackson, the Democrat from Washington, gave me the best explanation. "Lyndon knew every card in the deck," Jackson said. "He knew the senators personally, and their wives and their prejudices and their voting records and what they wanted for their constituencies and precisely how and where to get their votes.

"For example," Jackson added, "Kennedy knew as well as Johnson whose vote he needed. He would have his secretary call the senator down to the Oval Office, and he would explain precisely why the bill in question was so important and how much he needed the senator's support. If, however, the senator said his people wouldn't go along, Kennedy would finally say he was sorry they couldn't agree but he understood.

"Johnson's way with the same senator would be quite different," Jackson explained. "He would call up the senator personally and say, 'Lady Bird and I haven't seen you and Miss Mary for weeks, why don't you both come down and have dinner with us upstairs alone tonight?' At dinner, surrounded by the majesty of the White House and the intimacy of the small Johnson dining room, the president would see that the senator was well fed and lubricated, recall all their pleasant times together in the past, then recount in great detail all his troubles with other world leaders, including secrets that should not have been disclosed, never mentioning the real purpose of the evening, and letting things run on as if he had nothing else in the world to do. Only at the end, when the president was seeing his visitors off for the night, would he put his arm around the poor man's unsteady shoulder and tell him: 'I really need your help.' And he'd get it. That was the difference. He could charm you or knock your block off, or bribe you or threaten you, anything to get your vote."

He loved surprises, always covering his hand until he produced the winning card, and anybody in his administration who leaked his decisions was subject to instant dismissal. I once published his decision to make an important appointment, and he withdrew the appointment just to embarrass the *Times,* and appointed somebody else. The day before the Los Angeles convention that nominated Kennedy, he said, "I wouldn't want to trade a vote for a gavel, and I certainly wouldn't want to trade the active position of leadership [in the Senate] for a part-time job of presiding." But when friends of both Kennedy and Johnson, particularly Phil Graham, then the publisher of *The Washington Post,* argued that Kennedy couldn't win unless he carried Texas, Johnson accepted Kennedy's last-minute offer and switched, to the surprise even of his wife. I was not only surprised but embarrassed, for Kennedy's friend Senator Abe Ribicoff of Connecticut had assured me the day before the announcement that Kennedy had in fact decided on Johnson, but I couldn't believe it and didn't print it.

He was supremely confident that he could do better than Kennedy—a constant objective—but he was haunted by the contrast between his own craggy edges and Kennedy's sophisticated good looks and ties to the eastern intellectual establishment. Paradoxically, he failed in Vietnam in large part because he followed the advice of the intellectuals he inherited from Kennedy.

George Ball, the under secretary of state, tried to persuade him to cut his losses in Vietnam. Ball recounts in his memoirs that Johnson heard him out but wouldn't agree, and was deeply suspicious that Ball or anybody else would act in his name without his permission. Once Ball did so in approving a coup in Brazil, and he tells of the president's profane rebuke: "Don't ever do that again," Johnson warned him. "I don't give a damn whether you're right or wrong. I don't give a fuck that it was three in the morning. I want to know what's being done whatever time of night it is."

Shortly after Johnson took the oath of office in a plane returning from the Dallas tragedy, and before he made his first State of the Union message, Senator Barry Goldwater announced that he would oppose Johnson for the presidency in 1964. Sally and I went out to Arizona to interview Goldwater at the time, and while I was there, Bill Moyers, Johnson's press secretary, called me and said Johnson wanted my wife and me to come to the ranch in Texas the following day. He didn't particularly want to see me, but he wanted to know how the press had reacted to Goldwater's announcement.

When we got there, he was worried, not only about Goldwater, but also about all the appointments he would have to make and the first budget he would have to present to the Congress in a few days. "Here I've been in Congress all these years," he said, "but how am I to fill all these jobs? I don't know anybody in the Northwest or the Midwest. Nobody! And I don't know that I dare bring in a budget of over a hundred billion dollars."

This was said when we were all halfway through breakfast. During the meal, he wolfed down his food, and then, apparently to prove how democratic he was, he reached over and ate the remains on my plate. Then suddenly, he said, "Let's get out of here and go see John Connally." So he hurried everybody into a helicopter, telling us all who should sit where, and he put the budget question to Connally, who, dangling one of his children on his knee, gave him instant advice. "A hundred billion's a big fat figure," he said. "You don't want to come in like a big spender. Make it ninety-seven billion or thereabouts." And that's what Johnson did. (The *interest* on the debt at the start of the nineties was much higher.)

He flew us back to Washington the next day, but wouldn't let us go home. "Come on to the White House," he said, "I want to show you something." He led us to the president's bedroom upstairs in the White House and kneeling, pointed to an inscription on the keystone in the fireplace. It said: IN THIS ROOM LIVED JOHN FITZGERALD KENNEDY WITH HIS WIFE, JACQUELINE—DURING THE TWO YEARS, 10 MONTHS, TWO DAYS HE WAS PRESIDENT OF THE UNITED STATES—JANUARY 20, 1961–NOVEMBER 22, 1963. Johnson nodded to it, looked at Sally and me, and raised his eyebrows but didn't say a word. Then he let us go. The stone has since been removed. By whom, nobody seems to know.

Johnson had strong views on almost everything, but often there were no connections between his contradictory opinions. In many ways he was typical of the majority of his fellow countrymen in the sixties. He thought all men were more or less alike even in "all them little-bitty countries," as he called them. Yet he not only believed in Roosevelt's Good Neighbor Policy, but also could talk with the utmost sincerity of the day when all the nations of the Western Hemisphere would be bound together in a common market. I followed him to a meeting of the American states in Uruguay and complained that in order to telephone the *Times'* office in Chile, the call had to go through New York. One day, he reassured me, all that would be different. Modern communications would bring all these states together. Even in "the little coves and valleys of the Andes," he said, the children would learn by radio and television all about the big world outside.

He was eloquently hopeful about the future of his own country. "For a century," he said in a speech at the University of Michigan, "we labored to settle and subdue a continent. For half a century we called upon unbounded invention and untiring industry to create an order of plenty for all our people. The challenge of the next half-century is whether we have the wisdom to use that wealth to enrich and elevate our national life, and to advance the quality of our American civilization . . . for in your time we have the opportunity to move not only toward the rich society and the powerful society, but upward to the Great Society."

The words came from Richard Goodwin, one of Kennedy's speech-writers, but the melody was undoubtedly Johnson's, and he put the words into action by persuading the Congress to tackle the long-neglected problems of poverty, inadequate education, urban blight, and racial injustice. "Just give the Negroes the vote," he said to me one day, "and many of these problems will get better."

He boasted constantly about getting consent for his Great Society programs, but as my friend and colleague Tom Wicker observed, he was haunted by the ghost of his murdered predecessor, and convinced that the press and universities of the North were prejudiced against his southern background. Early in 1964, he agreed to see me in the Oval Office about the upcoming presidential election. In the previous week, an article had appeared in the Scripps-Howard newspapers saying that he had been driving his car on a lonely Texas highway at reckless speeds while drinking.

When Jack Valenti, one of his aides, interrupted the interview to show him a copy of *Time* magazine repeating this story, he was angry and sad. He turned to me and said very quietly, "I know why you came to see me. You wanted me to tell you whether I thought Bobby Kennedy was going to run against me this year. Well," he added, "you've got the wrong question. The question is not whether he will run but whether I'll run, when they print things like that. I don't know that a southern president can ever unify this country. These big-city folk in the national press are against me. They're trying to make a hick out of me." (This was when he had been in the White House for only a few months.)

It was a sad incident, so much so that I was moved emotionally by the urgency of his voice and finally said he had to let me disagree. He had problems with the press, I agreed, but not because of where he came from or how he looked or spoke. Besides, I insisted, the most prominent reporters and bureau chiefs in Washington actually came from the sticks themselves. I mentioned Catledge from Philadelphia, Mississippi; Wicker, David Brinkley, and Vermont Royster from little towns in North Carolina; Eric Sevareid, Walter Cronkite, Elmer Davis, Russ Wiggins, and Ed Murrow, among many others, from the land grant colleges just like himself. "You've got it all wrong," I said. But he shook his head in disagreement, and he wouldn't stop. I thought maybe he was out of control, but he wasn't. He could see I was affected by his pressure, and he just kept it on.

When I thought about this later, I put it down to his anger over the drinking and driving incident, or just to one of his calculated tantrums to put me on the defensive. But even after he left the White House, he retained this conviction and resentment against the press. "One reason the country could not rally behind a Southern President," he wrote in a book of memoirs called *The Vantage Point,* "was that the metropolitan press of the Eastern Seaboard would never permit it. I was not thinking just of the derisive articles about my style, my clothes, my manner, my accent, and my family . . . I was also thinking of a more deep-seated and far-reaching attitude—a disdain for the South that seems to be woven into the fabric of Northern experience. . . . Perhaps it all stems from the deep-rooted bitterness engendered by civil strife over a hundred years ago."

President Reagan could tell stories, most of them one-liners out of Hollywood, but he was no match for Johnson, who was a natural mimic, and whose stories were vivid with the memory of the South. He would talk about a man who was "as wise as a tree full of owls" or "as busy as a man with one hoe and two rattlesnakes" or "as noisy as a crazy mule in a tin barn."

While he told funny stories, he couldn't take a joke. He told his guests at the White House one night that he was going to give up alcohol and take up golf. Considering all his other problems, I wrote, with mock alarm, he should have been doing the opposite. As every Scotsman knew, golf inevitably added to man's sorrows while "a wee nip o' the strong stuff" was intended as a relief. Did the president not know, I asked, that the Scots invented golf as a punishment for man's sins, and that they invented whisky as a consolation so that he could suffer another day? He was outraged. Who was I, he asked, to tell him how to run his life? Nevertheless, he compromised: he neither took up golf nor gave up whisky.

Johnson took the nation deeper into the Vietnam War by stealth, exaggerating if not inventing a North Vietnamese attack on U.S. warships in the Gulf of Tonkin to get authority for bombing attacks on the north. This resolution passed 504–2. He carried it around in his pocket, calling it his "504–2 Resolution" and read it to all who expressed reservations against the widening war. He would say, "That language, just as a reminder to you, said, 'The Congress approves and supports the president as Commander in Chief to take all—all, ALL—necessary measures to repel any—any, ANY—armed attack against the forces of the United States.' "

Accordingly, he not only increased his air and ground attacks but also took command of the war room and decided on strategy and even on specific targets to be bombed, and when the bombers were out on these missions, he would roam the White House in the middle of the night until the cables came back that the boys were safely home. At least one of his aides, Richard Goodwin, later wrote that after Johnson sent another 100,000 men to Vietnam without any sign of victory, "he experienced certain episodes of what I believe to have been paranoid behavior."

Doris Kearns, Goodwin's wife, refers in her excellent study of Johnson *(Lyndon Johnson and the American Dream)* to his "obsessional, delusional thinking," his belief that he was being sabotaged by the intellectuals, the liberal newspapers, and even by some members of his own staff. He allowed her to tape his ramblings apparently in the belief that they would confound his enemies, but they merely dramatized the conspiratorial state of his mind.

"Two or three intellectuals started it all, you know," Johnson told her. "They produced all the doubt—they and the columnists in *The Washington Post* and *The New York Times, Newsweek,* and *LIFE.* And it spread and it spread until it appeared as if the people were against the war. Then Bobby [Kennedy] began taking it up as his cause, and with Martin Luther King on his payroll he went around stirring up the Negroes and telling them that if they came out in the streets they'd get more. Then the Communists stepped in. They control the three networks, you know, and the forty major outlets of communication. It's all in the FBI reports. They prove everything. Not just about the reporters but about the professors."

As Kearns noted, he dismissed the evidence he couldn't suppress by discrediting the source, and he saved his hardest hits for the columnists. "They turned against me on Vietnam," he told Kearns, "because it was in their self-interest to do so, because they knew that no one receives a Pulitzer Prize these days by simply supporting the President and the Administration. You win by digging up contrary information, by making a big splash. Truth no longer counts so long as a big sensation can be produced. . . .

"They're like a bunch of sheep in their own profession and they will always follow the bellwether sheep, the leaders of their profession, Lippmann and Reston. As long as those two stayed with me, I was okay. But once they left me in pursuit of their fancy prizes, everyone else left me. . . . Isn't it funny that I always received a piece of advice from my top advisers right after each of them had been in contact with someone in the Communist world? And isn't it funny that you could always find [the Soviet ambassador] Dobrynin's car in front of Reston's house the night before Reston delivered a blast on Vietnam?"

The facts are that the two Pulitzer Prizes in my name were awarded in 1944 and 1956, long before he ever came into the White House, and in all my years in Washington, neither Ambassador Dobrynin nor any other Soviet official was ever once in our house. The significant thing about all these tragic imaginings is that they came from the mind of the man who had directed the war, yet we're told that reporters shouldn't be so nosy about looking into the character and characteristics of candidates who seek the presidency.

I thought then and retain the conviction that the Vietnam tragedy—which finally took the lives of over fifty thousand Americans—resulted, at least in part, from the interventionist policy he inherited from Kennedy, from the anticommunist atmosphere of the country, from the "domino theory" that defeat in Vietnam would be followed by the collapse of American authority in the Pacific, and from a combination of ignorance, vanity, and booze—increasingly from booze as his disappointments mounted. First, he knew little or nothing of the enemy or the guerrilla war he was fighting. Second, he had supreme confidence that the United States could do anything it set its mind to, and thought money and machines were the answer to any test of power, and third—a touch of racism here—that America was superior and that "these little brown men," as he called the Vietnamese, would run into the rice paddies at the sight of American troops and modern weapons. The drink didn't improve his judgment, and he turned surly even to Jim Rowe, one of his closest and wisest friends, who urged him to knock off the booze.

Like Nixon later on, he was obsessed with the Kennedys, only more so. He felt sure he would be opposed by former Kennedy aides—Rusk, McNamara, Rostow, and McGeorge Bundy—if he didn't persevere with Kennedy's Vietnam policies. He was convinced that Robert Kennedy would not only lead this charge but also was peddling stories against him and planning to challenge him for the presidency in 1964. In addition, he thought it would be said that he didn't have the courage to fight in Vietnam, and the irony of this was that later on it was indeed said that he had neither the courage to fight nor the courage to quit.

Finally, in saying he wasn't going to be the first American president to lose a war—an unfortunate phrase President Nixon repeated—he was committing a common failure of thinking he was personally what he merely represented, considering his personal rather than the national interest, or confusing the two. As public opinion turned against him for doing precisely what he said he wouldn't do, and critics of the war took to the streets in protest, he withdrew into the White House or went around the country from one secure military base to another. None of us could see him in those turbulent days, but, tormented and desperate as he was, at least he didn't make things worse by using all the weapons at his command to obliterate North Vietnam.

In the end, McNamara and his successor as secretary of defense, Clark Clifford, finally broke with Johnson's policy. In a meeting in Secretary of State Rusk's office on February 27, 1968, according to an account in Clifford's memoirs (*Counsel to the President*), McNamara opposed the proposal of increasing the bombing and sending another 205,000 men to Saigon. The air force was already dropping more bombs on North Vietnam, McNamara said, than the United States had dropped on Germany during the Second World War, and it was not changing the course of the war.

"We simply have to end this thing," McNamara said, and while the president wouldn't take this advice from McNamara, he finally listened to Clifford, who had come to the same conclusion. Accordingly, on March 31, 1968, the president slipped a final handwritten paragraph of a speech into his pocket to make sure nobody would scoop him on his decision: "I shall not seek, and I will not accept, the nomination of my party for another term as your president."

I was in the middle of a speech of my own that night in Kansas

City when a note from the *Times* informed me of his decision. I read it out to the audience, which exploded with applause. In the worst days of his despair, Mr. Johnson would call for his limousine late at night and drive to St. Dominic's Roman Catholic Church in southwest Washington, where his daughter Luci had been converted to Catholicism, but when he retired to his ranch, he apparently felt that he had lost everything. He certainly lost his caution about drinking and smoking, and apparently even his will to live. I felt sorry for him then, and still do, but even sorrier for his lovely and loyal wife, Lady Bird, who stuck with him to the end, and finally said to him, "Lyndon, it's time to go home."

# CHAPTER 35

# The Reporters of Vietnam

Boys, elevate them guns a little lower.
—General Andrew Jackson
at the Battle of
New Orleans, 1815

ONE OF THE happy thoughts I had about retirement was that I'd never have to write about Vietnam again. From first to last, I felt that war involved so many lies, cost so many lives, divided so many friends, and raised so many questions about the judgment of our officials that I hated to think about raking through the rubble one last time.

I take a last reluctant look anyway, however, because I want to say a few words for the American reporters in Saigon, who, more than anybody else, brought the facts of that slaughter to the attention of the Congress and the people, and helped bring it to an end. They were vilified for their pains, denounced by the government, sometimes mistrusted by their own editors, condemned by some of their own colleagues in Washington, and even blamed by some officials for the nation's final humiliation and defeat. I thought this was unfair and still believe that these reporters, including the men with their television cameras on the battlefield, did a better job under more difficult circumstances than any other band of war correspondents in my time.

They didn't have to be geniuses to know that Vietnam was a hard place for modern armies. I went to Saigon for the first time in July of 1953, and found the reporters there, long before the United States was involved, recording the facts on how the French were swallowed up in the jungles, and warning against the weakness of the South Vietnam government and the strength and cunning of the Communist guerrillas.

At that time, the British had a military mission in Saigon, headed by a spunky little brigadier named Spear, who explained the military problems to me in terms that even I could understand. Vietnam was "not an ideal place to fight a war," he said mildly. In the past, he noted, the French had had complete control of the air and were safe enough in the cities during the day, but couldn't find the Communists in the villages most of the time, and had lost 150,000 men in the last eight years of the war. There were other problems, he said.

Ho Chi Minh and General Giap had a formidable Communist army reserve in the north. It was well supplied by the Chinese. It could, if threatened or trapped, retreat into the privileged sanctuaries of neutral Laos and Cambodia. It was supported by guerrillas in the south, where it was difficult to know the difference between friendly and hostile Vietnamese.

The brigadier went on with this tale of potential disaster, and I finally asked him if there was any way for the French, with supplies from the United States, or even U.S. intervention, to win such a war. Perhaps, he replied, there was one way. "If we gave tanks and other military vehicles to the Communists instead of to the South Vietnamese, then maybe we could get them up on the roads where we could find them and fight them on our own terms." He did not regard this wholly as a joke.

I asked him if it wasn't necessary to stop this Communist expansion as Fascist aggression had finally been stopped in Europe, but only after a world war. That was an "interesting analogy," he said, but there were two things wrong with it. First, this was essentially a civil war, and second, it was silly to think about it as if Vietnam were Nazi Germany and Ho Chi Minh another Hitler. I reported the substance of this interview to my colleagues in the *Times* Saigon bureau. "That's exactly what we have been reporting for months," they said.

The top officials at the U.S. Embassy conceded the validity of Brigadier Spear's pessimism, but feared that a Communist conquest in Indochina would be followed by more alarming Communist advances elsewhere. The trouble, they added, was that the Congress and the American people might not be enthusiastic about another war after their experience in Korea, and there was also the danger that even if we seemed to be defeating the North Vietnamese, China might enter the war. I then went to see Premier Nguyen of South Vietnam, who didn't cheer me up. The villagers in South Vietnam, he said, thought they had a better chance of getting a better life and an independent country from the Communists than from his own government.

When the United States did begin to intervene in 1961 and soon ran into trouble, Washington's reaction to the depressing military news was to blame the reporters. On October 22, 1963, at a meeting in the White House, Kennedy suggested to Arthur Ochs Sulzberger and Turner Catledge that David Halberstam, one of our men in Saigon, should be transferred. "Don't you think he's too close to the story?" Kennedy asked. But Sulzberger said he had no intention of transferring Halberstam, and Kennedy's intervention merely assured that David and his colleagues would continue to have the support of their publisher.

Halberstam's stormy talent was that he was not only "close to the story" but on top of it. This is why he had also usually been ahead of the competition in his coverage of the civil rights struggles in the South and in his reporting from the Congo. It was precisely because he and his colleague Neil Sheehan cared so deeply and personally about the pointless excesses and deceptions of the war that Lt. Col. John Paul Vann, who was exposing the lies of the official communiqués, leaked the ugly facts to them for publication in the *Times*.

Halberstam was a human lie detector, with an explosive temper, a profane vocabulary, a talent for getting into brawls, and the physique to muscle out of them. Sheehan was a gentler sort. His tours of the blasted Vietnam villages on either side of the line reduced him to tears, and he was so admiring of Colonel Vann's courage and determination to tell the truth that he spent seventeen years after the war writing a book about him—*A Bright Shining Lie,* which won the Pulitzer Prize. Kennedy was not the only one who complained about Sheehan and Halberstam.

For example, I had a letter from Joseph Alsop, one of the bravest and most opinionated columnists of his time, denouncing Sheehan's reporting of a battle in the Ia Drang valley. "Sheehan," he wrote me, "has plenty of competitors for the title of worst war reporter in Saigon, but the tone of his look-at-me-I've-got-the-big-story-about-our-losses, was a bit too much to take.

"I think I'm fairly familiar with this country's military history. I can recall few performances by seasoned, battle-hardened American troops to equal the performance of our decidedly green troops in Vietnam. I write you this, not with any hope of reforming the *Times*—that would be too presumptuous—but because I think I should say to your face what I feel bound to say when you are not present. I did not much admire Halberstam's performance, and although I know you disagree, this business of nothing but casualties, and no mention of the astonishing successes, is somehow enraging."

This lecture on the importance of objectivity from Joe, who seldom allowed the facts to interfere with his prejudices, was itself enraging, but I liked the guy, and wrote him: "I wish I could share your confidence that our magnificent fighting at Ia Drang, and our 'brilliant victories,' were symbols of decisive victories to come, but a few more 'victories' like Ia Drang and we're likely to be undone. In the face of North Vietnam's uncommitted troops and their indifference to the loss of life, I can't share your estimate of the war or of Sheehan and Halberstam. Even if we were to base our policy on your confidence and boldness, and risk all to save all—which would be a policy but not a policy Johnson will follow—history and geography would still be against us, and in the end, this may be the heart of the news." (Before he died, Joe changed his mind about Sheehan, a rare occurrence on that or any other subject.)

Since there was no way in Washington to pass judgment on the contradictory official and unofficial reports out of Saigon, I suggested that the *Times* print both, side by side under a two-column headline. Nobody was quite satisfied with this fifty-fifty display. The officials in Washington complained that we were questioning their judgment, which of course we were, and even members of our own staff thought we couldn't make up our minds. I listened to these complaints in Washington during the first half of the sixties, and finally went back to Saigon in 1965 for another look.

In 1965, the "American presence," as it was called, with a few hundred advisers in 1953, had grown to an army of over 200,000. They were all over the place. So were the nightclubs. They resounded with American country music—mainly laments from some lonely western troubadour, who always got his man, but for some mysterious reason always seemed to have lost his woman.

The *Times* office was on the second floor of number 46 Tu Do, a street of shops, bars, and subsidiary services. In the daytime, it was full of happy squealing kids, newsboys, pedicabs, and Jeeps. At night,

Tu Do was deserted after the eleven o'clock curfew, except for roving military police cars and bats, which wheeled in alarming numbers through the trees on either side of the street.

Halberstam was off on leave somewhere when we were there, but Sheehan and his resourceful bride, Susan, were there, and so was Johnny Apple, who didn't invent war but taught a whole generation how to cover it, and Charlie Mohr, who preceded Apple as Saigon bureau chief. Charlie had quit as *Time* magazine's chief correspondent in Saigon because they wouldn't print his stories about the government's lies, and I hired him. He was lame for a while that summer when hit by shrapnel, but Charlie wasn't the sort who could be benched by conventional weapons.

The working quarters there were not as cushy as ours had been in the Savoy Hotel during the big war. The place reeked of disinfectant and the vague seeping odors disinfectant is expected to banish. It had no air-conditioning, but it had a couple of lazy fans that often took the night off. It had a refrigerator full of beer, which was good, and a toilet that I will not describe. All the reporters had rooms at the air-conditioned Caravelle and Continental hotels, but they weren't there much.

They were out with the troops much of the time, and one of them was always around to cover the official evening military briefings, known as the "Five O'Clock Follies." These were presided over by Harold Kaplan, an intelligent and amiable official with a long Filipino cigar in his teeth. The briefings usually produced between twelve and fifteen single-spaced pages of reports on the day's events, for this was not one war but sixty-three different wars in different provinces and offshore in the China Sea. Kaplan permitted some ragging questions for about fifteen minutes, all ending at about six o'clock in a scoreless tie. Then began the tedious task of checking the reports and trying to transmit the stories to New York over a communications system that, in the opinion of the reporters, justified the Vietnamese rebellion against the French.

After clearing censorship, an exercise in subversive warfare, dispatches headed for New York went first to Japan, from there to London, and thence to Times Square in New York. Since Saigon was twelve hours ahead of New York, they landed when the editors on Forty-third Street were wide awake and the reporters in Saigon were half dead, waiting for the inevitable and reasonable but unanswerable questions on why our men were saying one thing and the government was saying the opposite.

Two things impressed me about this routine. First, the liberal military policy of allowing the reporters to get to the scene of the battles, providing choppers and planes for the purpose, and second, the invincible patience and even cheerfulness of the reporters. They won the trust of many officers in the field, who did not hesitate to give them a fairly honest account of the fighting, even when it was different from the official version, and most of them had contempt for Gen. Paul Harkins, the top U.S. commander. They even made up a mocking song about him, which they sang to the tune of "Twinkle, Twinkle, Little Star":

> We are winning, this we know,
> General Harkins tells us so.
> In the Delta, things are rough,
> In the mountains mighty tough.
> But we're winning, this we know.
> General Harkins tells us so.

I have tossed a few slurs at television in these pages, but I have to say that its cameras brought the human tragedy of the Vietnam War home to the American people more vividly than the newspapers could describe it. They showed the brutality of the Communists in the villages, but it was left to Morley Safer of CBS to show on film U.S. Marines setting fire to the thatched peasant houses of the villagers. This dramatized what was happening not only to the enemy but also to our own men, and it raised such an uproar at home that the marine command ordered a stop to the practice.

Naturally I know more about the reporting of the *Times'* men in Saigon, particularly the long and brilliant service of Halberstam, Sheehan, and Apple, and also of their colleagues, Homer Bigart, Gene Roberts, Eric Pace, Malcolm Browne, and Joe Treaster, but many others did distinguished work, including Peter Arnett, a New Zealander on the AP, Edward P. Morgan of ABC, Ward Just of *The Washington Post,* and Frances FitzGerald of *The New Yorker.*

The longer I stayed in Saigon, the more depressed I became. I admired and respected the officers in the field, who had been given an assignment to clear the Communists out of the south, but not the means to carry it out. I talked to Gen. Lewis W. Walt, the commander of the Third Marine Division, and he took me on a helicopter ride over the scene of a recent battle with the Vietcong at Chulai and explained how difficult it would be for any modern army, limited by political considerations, to win such a war.

He had captured one of the enemy headquarters. It was dug thirty feet underground, with long tunnels spacious enough for men to walk upright, and with entrances and exits cunningly concealed by branches from the piney woods. The headquarters were deserted when we arrived, except that in one passage we found 130 women and children huddled in the mud.

The war in Vietnam was so alien to the American experience and such a tangle of conflicting cultures, interests, memories, religions, and personal, regional, and tribal ambitions that it defied precise definition and was almost beyond comprehension.

Even the words normally used to describe a war were misleading. It was not a war in the usual sense. It was a series of violent actions, some rather like Al Capone's gang raids in Chicago, some like the frontier skirmishes in the French and Indian War, still others like the savage encounters between the Americans and the Japanese in the Pacific island caves of 1945—all this with the Strategic Air Command, of all things, bombing guerrillas, of all people, in tunnels in the Vietnamese forests, of all places.

It really needed a new vocabulary. Vietnam was not a nation but a physical and strategic entity broken into conspiratorial families, clans, sects, hamlets, and regions by many generations of Mandarin, French, Japanese, and religious influence.

The prime minister in Saigon was not prime. Nothing was as it seemed. Buddhists and Catholics bore little relation to Western notions of either Buddhism or Catholicism, and we even had some Chinese mercenaries fighting on our side, one of whom was a bodyguard for Ambassador Henry Cabot Lodge.

In that situation, it was almost impossible to perform the reporting function of reducing diversity to identity. All you could do was try to illustrate just how complex human political and military relations were in that part of the world.

How was it, then, under such circumstances, that the prudent advice of so experienced a military commander as Eisenhower was later amended by President Kennedy and reversed by President Johnson? The journalists and the historians argued in vain about this for twenty-five years, maybe because it was a job for the psychiatrists. Some suggested that the explanation lay in the arrogance of power, others in the valor of ignorance, or maybe a little of both.

My favorite explanation came from George Ball, under secretary of state in the Johnson administration. Kennedy and Johnson just didn't ask the giraffe question, he observed mysteriously, and then clarified it with a story. A man took his little boy one day to the zoo and, pointing to a long-necked spotted creature, said, "That's a giraffe." And the little boy said, "Why?" That was the problem, concluded Ball. "We didn't ask the little boy's simple question: Why, *why,* WHY did we get into that mess in the first place?"

It isn't quite true that they didn't ask why. All the top decision makers thought they had good reasons for getting in, at least just a little bit in. Most of them, Ball excluded, agreed the expansion of Communist power and influence had to be opposed even if it resulted in no better than a truce, as in Korea. That was the lesson of appeasement at Munich in the last world war, wasn't it? they asked. That was the promise of the Truman Doctrine—to oppose the Communist conquest of all free peoples; that was the commitment of the United Nations Charter—to deter direct or indirect aggression anywhere in the world.

Secretary of State Rusk, a minister's son, had additional moral reasons. The thought of standing aside and allowing over 14 million South Vietnamese to be conquered by the North Vietnamese Communists affronted his sense of honor and decency. He was very cautious about committing American troops to the fighting, but he had served in the China-Burma-India theater in the last world war and was convinced that the Chinese were even more eager for expansion than the Soviets, and argued in private and in public that if we failed to save South Vietnam, Communist influence would spread to India, the Middle East, and eventually to Latin America.

I left Vietnam in 1965 under circumstances I did not plan. I spent a couple of days on the aircraft carrier *Independence,* marveling at the skill and bravery of these young American fliers returning from their raids and roaring onto the deck in the dark. On August 30, 1965, I catapulted off the *Independence* in a Grumman C-1A naval plane along with former Assistant Secretary of Defense Eugene Fubini and two senior military officers.

We were headed for Saigon, but shortly after takeoff the hydraulic system developed a leak, and the pilot veered off toward the closer military airbase at Da Nang. We almost made it. The plane gradually lost altitude until, when we were in sight of the airport, the pilot lost all control and we crashed in a suburban housing development.

"Get out before she burns," shouted the pilot, and we crawled out through the roof, badly bruised but not seriously injured. President Johnson got word of the accident and called Tom Wicker. "Tell Sally Scotty's all right," he said.

. . .

When I got home, I heard the same complaints from administration officials about "negative reporting" out of Saigon, and did everything I could to defend the integrity and accuracy of my colleagues in Saigon. I wrote that the Johnson administration might finally get over its agony in Vietnam, but it would probably never regain the people's confidence in its judgment and veracity. With the bombing of targets on the outskirts of Hanoi and Haiphong, it had now done almost everything it said it wouldn't do, except bomb China. It said it was not seeking a military solution to the war, and it was obviously seeking precisely that. It said it was there merely to help a legitimate government defend itself, and it ended up by supporting a military clique that was not a government, not legitimate, and not really defending itself.

The president called me to the White House and gave me "the works." He denounced my colleagues in Saigon in terms I could hardly bear after my trip, and he asked me, "Why don't you get on the team? You have only one president." I had heard it all before and said I thought he was trying to save face. He stood up and showed me to the door. "I'm not trying to save my face," he said, "I'm trying to save my ass."

# CHAPTER 36

# *The* Times
# *and National Security*

NOTHING GAVE US more trouble during my years on the *Times* than the conflict with the government over what should and should not be published during periods of war or threats of war. In 1941, when I started working in Washington, President Roosevelt was denouncing the press for reporting his hidden efforts to aid the Allies without the consent of the Congress, and fifty years later President Bush was still complaining about those in the press who were exposing his devious politics and diplomacy before the outbreak of the Gulf War.

This was not exactly a new problem. The first great newsmaker in the history of the human race was Adam, and the accounts of his creation—including whether it was a good idea—have been a source of controversy ever since. At the beginning of the American republic, Thomas Jefferson was saying that fearless independent newspapers were indispensable, but sometime after he read them, he was saying they were intolerable. The Cold War, however, with its emphasis on propaganda and subversion—the Age of Deception—embittered this conflict and raised some new questions for the press.

For example, what to do when the government, often with the best of objectives, waged war on the sly. Specifically, what to publish or not publish about past official mistakes; how to deal with the U.S. spy planes over the Soviet Union, or the Central Intelligence Agency's gun-running and other underground deals in the Middle East and Latin America. Also, how to gather information in closed Communist societies, and display information in a crisis, when the government in Washington was saying all was well in Vietnam, for example, and our own reporters in Saigon were saying the opposite.

We debated these questions endlessly with the government and didn't always agree among ourselves on the *Times.* We tried unsuccessfully to define a general principle to guide our decisions on how to deal with these sensitive subjects, but finally decided that we had to handle each case separately in accordance with what facts we could gather. This wasn't easy, for we couldn't always be sure we had all the facts, and like the government, we made our mistakes. I was involved in many of these "national security" controversies and recall some of them here in case the reader chooses to put himself in the editor's chair.

For example, in May of 1948, shortly after the United States had joined the North Atlantic Treaty Organization, and just before a critical meeting of the Council of Foreign Ministers in Paris, George Kennan and his State Department policy planning staff drafted a proposal for the reduction of U.S. and Soviet military forces in Germany as a means toward the reunification of that country. I wrote about this secret proposal at the time, and caused considerable controversy within the Alliance and with the Soviets.

As Ambassador Charles Bohlen wrote in his memoirs, "The article raised a good deal of hell in Europe. The suggestion had been opposed by the Joint Chiefs of Staff, who pointed out that the United States would have to withdraw forces more than three thousand miles, whereas the Soviets need only withdraw theirs a few hundred miles. Someone—not Kennan—leaked the contents of this paper to Reston . . . The French and British were alarmed that the United States was going to reduce its commitment in Europe only weeks after the signing of the NATO treaty."

I thought at the time that this was an odd and risky proposal, and after it appeared in the *Times,* and the ensuing controversy in Paris, the proposal was withdrawn, but should it have been published in the first place? Kennan and Bohlen thought it was an interference with the requirements for secret negotiation, and they had a point, but I thought then that anything so important and controversial as the withdrawal of U.S. forces from Europe justified wide discussion. In retrospect, I'm not so sure that I was right.

I mentioned earlier the decision of the *Times* to report the sinking of the British cruiser *Belfast* early in the Second World War in defiance of our written agreement to abide by the rules of wartime censorship. This was clearly a mistake.

The *Times* was under no such wartime commitment, however,

when the CIA was sending its U-2 spy planes over the Soviet Union in the fifties, even on the eve of the Eisenhower-Khrushchev summit meeting in Paris on May Day of 1960. As mentioned earlier in this book, we had known on the *Times* for months about these flights over the USSR, which began in 1956.

The *Times* never printed a word about it before the U-2 piloted by Gary Powers was hit while the Soviets were rejoicing in their annual May Day festival.

We were preoccupied then with a more favorable turn in U.S.-Soviet relations, after Khrushchev, in February of 1956, had astonished the 20th Party Congress with his denunciation of the Stalin regime and its crimes. Having interviewed Khrushchev in Moscow in 1957, and having followed him through the farms of Iowa in 1959, I was feeling that despite all Khrushchev's wild talk, maybe Ike was right in thinking that he had a last chance to reduce the tension before he left the White House in 1961.

Was the *Times* right in withholding what we knew about the U-2 flights? I thought so at the time, but now I am not so sure. Ike himself, though he insisted on approving every flight, had his doubts about the whole exercise and once said, "The Soviets . . . might misinterpret the overflights as being designed to start a nuclear war." But he knew that the Soviet leaders were aware of the flights, that Moscow had actually protested formally against them on several occasions, without doing anything more about them, and besides, since the U-2 was equipped to destroy both the plane and the pilot if the plane was intercepted, it was assumed in Washington that the Soviets would have no evidence to prove their case.

Eisenhower concluded that covering up mistakes in government was usually more dangerous than the mistakes themselves, but Kennedy didn't learn that lesson until after the Bay of Pigs, Johnson ignored it in Vietnam, Nixon defied it when Watergate was discovered, and even in the eighties, Reagan was still trying to conceal the misuse of public funds in his proxy war against Nicaragua.

We had an awkward time in 1961 when Kennedy succeeded Ike and inherited a plan to train and supply 1,400 Cuban exiles for the overthrow of the Castro government. The *Times'* handling of this disaster was for years a subject of controversy among journalists, and especially within the *Times* itself. Much has been written about the military aspects of the fiasco, so I deal here mainly with the conflict within the paper.

The *Times* wasn't first with the story about the CIA training anti-Castro Cubans in Guatemala. *The Nation* magazine broke the story on November 19, 1960, before Kennedy was inaugurated. I was then head of the Washington bureau and was involved in sending Paul Kennedy, our correspondent in Mexico City, to Guatemala to check the facts. He wrote a long story in the *Times* of January 10, 1961, confirming that the CIA was indeed training Castro's opponents with U.S. advisers, planes, and weapons. We were particularly interested in Guatemala, for earlier the CIA under Allen Dulles had managed to overthrow the government of that country, and Dulles had tried to get rid of our correspondent there for asking too many embarrassing questions about what the CIA was doing.

Accordingly, the issue at the *Times* was not whether the activities of the CIA and the Cuban exiles should be reported. (We had published the facts of the Guatemalan training base in detail.) The issue arose later, when, on April 6, 1961, Tad Szulc, one of the *Times'* designated scoop artists, filed a two-column story from Miami saying that the invasion of Cuba was "imminent." This one word was the central issue. The editors in the bull pen, where the front page was made up, were two of the best we had in all my years on the *Times*— Ted Bernstein and Lew Jordan—and they were accustomed to laying out the paper without the advice of the managing editor. They had every reason to trust Szulc, a big experienced investigative reporter of Polish descent, who had spent many years in Latin America, knew the Cuban exiles well, and had been in Miami for days talking to them and watching exiled Cuban officers and doctors leaving, as he was told, for the invasion takeoff areas.

But Turner Catledge was concerned about the word *imminent* and even more concerned about Bernstein's dummy of the first page. Bernstein had the Szulc story leading the paper under a four-column headline, which, in the *Times'* cautious tradition, was an alarm bell. Catledge conferred with the publisher, Orvil Dryfoos, and they telephoned me in Washington and asked for my reaction. I said the word *imminent* suggested that the invasion would take place in the morning, and my information was that it was at least a week off. I had no trouble with printing the facts of the situation but *imminent* was a prediction and not a fact. Besides, if the story and headline remained as written, and Szulc's information proved to be right, I said, we would hit the streets the night before with the news and be accused of warning Castro and blamed for whatever happened when the exiles landed. It was one thing, I thought then and still do, to repeat that the anti-Castro legions were mobilizing (Castro had his own agents in their ranks)—but quite a different thing to inform Castro of the timing of the invasion.

Catledge eliminated the *imminent* and the references to the CIA, and cut the headline down to one column, and Bernstein and Jordan were furious. They asked the publisher why their judgment and authority had been challenged, and even five years later they were still denouncing Catledge and me for what they regarded as the "humiliating changes."

They were encouraged in their anger when Kennedy later remarked to Catledge that if we had made more of the story maybe he would have avoided what he called his stupid mistake. But that, I felt then, and still feel, was a cop-out. He had always said—and the official record confirms it—that he would insist on his authority to call the whole thing off even within the last twenty-four hours, and he still had eleven days to think about it between the Szulc story and the actual invasion. During this period he was not lacking in advice. I wrote and the *Times* published a couple of columns a week before the landings, denouncing the whole affair.

I assumed that the invasion would take place in a week or so and pointed out that this would be a clear violation of our treaty commitments to the United Nations and the Organization of American States, and one more demonstration of Washington's "big bully policy" in Latin America. How could we base our policies all over the world on the sanctity of treaties, and lecture the Soviets on their threats and use of force, if we did the same ourselves? I went to see Allen Dulles at the CIA, and he denied that his agency had anything to do with it, though he later accepted personal responsibility for goading Kennedy into the disaster.

Nevertheless, even E. C. Daniel, when he was the *Times*' managing editor, was insisting at the University of Minnesota years later that if the *Times* had stuck to its story and its four-column headline on the assumption that the invasion was imminent, maybe Kennedy would have come to his senses. Maybe he would and maybe he wouldn't, but anyway I wondered and still do whether it is the job of a newspaper to make up its front page in such a way as to influence decisions of the president.

The editors in the bull pen and Daniel apparently thought it was and were sore about being overruled. If Catledge made any mistake, it was, I believed, that he didn't make clear to his men in the bull pen often enough that the job of a managing editor was to manage and edit, and that the job of a publisher was not to influence the president but to protect the paper's reputation for accuracy and responsibility.

Occasionally I felt the *Times* was too inclined to cooperate with the government. For example, in the 1950s, when neither our government nor our press had any access to the news in China, the Chinese government invited the *Times* to send a reporter to Peking, as it was then called, but our government opposed the move and even threatened to prosecute us under the trading-with-the-enemy act if we accepted. I thought this was an interference with the right and duty of the *Times,* but the paper refused Peking's invitation, and the news blackout continued.

In the 1970s, the publisher of the *Times,* Arthur Ochs Sulzberger, worried by the CIA's attempts to use *Times* reporters, was still writing to George Bush, then head of the CIA, demanding to know whether the government would back off. "Would you be prepared," Sulzberger asked, "to make your letter of February 24, 1976, conclude with the sentence: 'The CIA will not use full-time American journalists or stringers for *any* intelligence purposes'?" He asked this in protection not only of the reporters of the *Times,* but *all* American correspondents.

Bush finally replied on May 27, 1976: "You asked whether I would be willing to conclude my letter of February 24 with the following statement: 'The CIA will not use full-time American journalists or stringers for *any* intelligence purposes.' The answer is in the affirmative, subject to my February 11 directive to the effect that contact is permitted with American or foreign national journalists employed by American news-gathering organizations who voluntarily seek contact with the agency at home or abroad for the purpose of transmitting on a confidential basis intelligence or counterintelligence security information without financial remuneration or other favor." Whether this promise was kept by other intelligence agencies of the government or ensuing administrations I have no way of knowing, but I have my suspicions.

Sometimes during the Vietnam War, when U.S. officials were putting out information our own correspondents knew to be false, the *Times* tended to display the official version more prominently than our own. Joe Alsop and Marguerite Higgins of the *Herald Tribune* were writing that David Halberstam and Neil Sheehan in the *Times'* Saigon bureau were carrying on a vendetta against the war, and the *Times,* by tradition opposed to crusading reporters, was constantly questioning their reports. As mentioned, when I went to Saigon and talked to our officials at the embassy and officers at headquarters and in the field, I was convinced that our reporters were far more accurate than our officials, and former Secretary of Defense Clark Clifford, among many others, confirmed this judgment. I look back on the paper's decisions during this period with respect. Sometimes it was right and sometimes wrong, but it was never in my experience careless or indifferent to the claims of national security or its duty to report as much of the truth as it could find.

The *Times* drew a clear line between military security and diplomatic and political security. It opposed the government, for example, when Roosevelt tried to block publication of the Dumbarton Oaks papers on the formation of the United Nations; when Eisenhower opposed our publication of the defense of Robert Oppenheimer, who was drummed out of the government as a "security risk"; when Nixon tried on grounds of "national security" to cover up the Watergate scandals; and when Reagan opposed disclosure of his administration's secret funding of the war in Nicaragua.

The most famous conflict between the government and the *Times,* however, was Nixon's attempt to block publication of the Pentagon Papers, which were an official study of the mistakes that had led years before to the disaster in Vietnam. This study had been ordered by Secretary of Defense Robert McNamara back in the Johnson administration in the hope of avoiding similar blunders in the future. The papers had been copied illegally by Daniel Ellsberg, an opponent of the war, when he was serving in the Pentagon, and passed on to Neil Sheehan of the *Times.* There then ensued not only a legal battle with the government, but also the most bitter controversy of my days on the paper between the editors and the lawyers of the *Times.*

Louis Loeb had been the *Times'* chief counsel and also a close friend and legal adviser to the Sulzberger family for more than a generation. He was a big, ruddy, cheerful man, firm in his judgment of the law, and it was his proudest boast that in twenty-three years under his guidance the *Times* had "never lost six cents in a libel suit." He was opposed to publication of the Pentagon Papers, because, as he saw it, the *Times* was in possession of stolen goods officially classified as top secret. We should not, he insisted, publish them but return them and ask that they be declassified. He thought his job was to keep the *Times* out of trouble. James Goodale, the in-house lawyer of the *Times,* disagreed. He thought that it was the duty of the *Times* not to stay out of trouble but to defend the First Amendment, and he believed the paper could win if the government took the case to court.

Arthur Ochs "Punch" Sulzberger, the new publisher of the *Times* since 1963, listened to all these arguments. He was not amused when Loeb told him that previous publishers, Punch's father, Arthur Hays Sulzberger, and his grandfather, Adolph Ochs, would not even have considered publishing the papers, and that Loeb's firm (Lord, Day and Lord) would not represent the *Times* in court if it did. Punch then called the lawyers and editors together and each was asked for his opinion. Most editors were for printing a summary of the papers, but some were opposed to printing the documents. When my turn came, I said I was for printing everything, that if we didn't somebody else would, and if nobody else did, I would print them myself in our little family weekly, the *Vineyard Gazette.*

"Then you'll go to jail," Loeb told me.

A team of reporters, including Neil Sheehan and Ned Kenworthy of the Washington bureau, holed up in the New York Hilton Hotel so they could prepare the material away from the bustle of the *Times'* office; a new team of lawyers, including Alexander Bickel of Yale and Floyd Abrams, an expert on the First Amendment, agreed to represent the *Times*; and the publisher, who had to go to Paris and London at the height of the controversy, finally gave the order to print over the transatlantic telephone.

The first article appeared in the Sunday paper on June 13, 1971, and the next night Sulzberger received a telegram from John Mitchell, the attorney general: FURTHER PUBLICATION OF INFORMATION OF THIS CHARACTER WILL CAUSE IRREPARABLE INJURY TO THE DEFENSE INTERESTS OF THE UNITED STATES, it said. ACCORDINGLY, I RESPECTFULLY REQUEST THAT YOU PUBLISH NO FURTHER INFORMATION OF THIS CHARACTER AND ADVISE ME THAT YOU HAVE MADE ARRANGEMENTS FOR THE RETURN OF THESE DOCUMENTS TO THE DEPARTMENT OF DEFENSE.

The *Times* then gathered its lawyers and editors together and drafted a statement for Mitchell, to be printed the following morning, "respectfully declining" to obey the request of the attorney general. By coincidence, Sally and I happened to be dining that night with Robert McNamara, the initiator of the Pentagon Papers, and the *Times* called me at his house and read me the proposed statement. I wrote it down and asked them to wait a minute. I then showed the statement to McNamara, who thought it did not make clear that the *Times* would obey an order from the Supreme Court—not just any court. I passed on this observation to New York, but the *Times* still agreed to abide by the order of "the courts" and was duly closed down for a few days.

After we lost the first round in the case of *U.S.* v. *The New York Times Co.,* however, the Supreme Court, by a vote of 6–3, denied the government's plea to prohibit publication. I was delighted, but told my associates that the thought of publishing this "world scoop" in the *Vineyard Gazette* was so funny that I almost, but not quite, wished the *Times* had taken Louis Loeb's advice.

My questions to Stalin and his reply on Christmas Eve of 1952 illustrated the conflicts within the *Times* itself over how to cover the Cold War. When it was obvious during the presidential election of that year that General Eisenhower was likely to win, I asked the Polish ambassador in Washington, Jozef Winiewicz, how he thought the Soviet Union would react to an Eisenhower victory. He said he didn't know, but he thought he could find out and told me to check back later. Just before the voting in November, he gave me a surprising reply. His Communist associates in the Soviet Embassy in Washington had said Stalin would regard an Eisenhower victory as the equivalent to the rise of General Kurt von Schleicher in Germany, and this view, he said, had been confirmed by the Polish ambassador in Moscow.

I had never even heard of General Schleicher, but I looked him up when I got back to the office and discovered that he had preceded Hitler as head of the German government. I hurried back to the Polish Embassy. Did this mean, I asked, that Stalin thought Eisenhower would introduce fascism in the United States? Surely, I suggested, this was too preposterous, even for Stalin. The Polish ambassador stuck to his story. Accordingly, when Ike did win, I drafted the questions to Stalin, cleared them with Arthur Krock, my boss as the Washington correspondent, and arranged to send them through the U.S. diplomatic pouch to Moscow.

I had tried this dodge before with other world leaders, usually without success, so Sally and I went off to Florida for a brief vacation. On Christmas Eve, while we were celebrating our seventeenth wedding anniversary, Arthur Krock called me from Washington to say that he had been called to the Soviet Embassy on Sixteenth Street and handed Stalin's replies. Instead of confirming his fears of Eisenhower, Stalin said that he had "a favorable view" of an Eisenhower-

Stalin meeting, and was willing to cooperate on a new diplomatic approach looking to the liquidation of the Korean War. The story dominated the front page of the *Times* the following morning and Secretary of State Dulles said that concrete proposals by Stalin would be seriously and sympathetically received.

Others were not so receptive. Henry Luce at *Time* magazine led his next issue with a sharp attack on the *Times* and me for giving Stalin a platform for Soviet propaganda. We had, *Time* said, "walked, eyes open, into a trap," and much to my surprise even the publisher of the *Times* and his principal editors were sharply critical of the whole incident. I wrote to the publisher, not exactly in the Christmas spirit.

I said that both Krock and I regretted that we had not consulted New York before submitting the questions to Stalin, for while we had never asked permission in the past about how to gather news, the publisher obviously had the right to decide whether to seek information from Stalin. I said I hoped we hadn't decided not to print propaganda out of Moscow, since that was about the only thing that came out of that capital. I pointed out that no Republican administration since the Russian Revolution of 1917 had ever made official contact with any Soviet government, and I thought it important, in light of the Polish ambassador's report, and even in the anticommunist atmosphere of the moment, to find out as much as we could about Stalin's approach to the new administration.

"I assure you," I wrote to the publisher, "that I did not think that you or anybody else in authority on the *Times* questioned my integrity. I don't want to be an Eagle Scout about this, but I think you know that if that had been the case, I would have resigned at once. . . . But I am left with the impression that you and Turner still think, after reading my reasons for sending the questions, that it was a bad idea to submit them in the first place, and this naturally disturbs me because it raises the whole question of the function of a reporter and of a newspaper's obligation to seek information on fundamental questions.

"It is true—and in the present atmosphere of the country inevitable—that such inquiries will produce a storm of criticism, which is—I freely admit—why there must be consultation before anything of the sort is done. It is also true that the easy course is not to submit such questions or get involved in such controversies. But it seems to me that if we are—as I believe we must—to live up to the noble precepts of your speech at the Waldorf the other night, we must search for answers, even if we get back nothing but propaganda. . . . This is an unpleasant way of saying bon voyage before your vacation, but if we don't say to each other what is in our hearts, the whole basis of our professional relationship, and what is more important, our friendship, will be gone."

This frosty incident was not without its ironic and sunny side. For when the Soviet Embassy spoiled Arthur Krock's Christmas Eve festivities with Stalin's answers, we were so close to deadline that Krock and I could merely discuss on the telephone how it was to be handled, and Arthur Krock wrote most of it under my byline. Thus, I was in a way scooped on my own scoop, but it improved my relations with Krock, if nobody else, and that had an important bearing on the rest of my days on the paper.

My main regret about all these controversies over the press and "national security" was that that term was seldom defined and too narrowly applied. It was applied to military security but not in the same degree to nonmilitary matters. I thought the lamentable condition of our schools was a threat to the national security, but while the government agreed there was a problem, it tossed the burden mainly to the states. Washington declared war on the spreading use of drugs, but spent more money on a few bombers than it did in fighting the drug problem.

I didn't think the invasion of millions of illegal immigrants was a threat to the national security, but I did think that inadequate education of their children in the English language was raising an even larger generation of laborers unskilled for a world of computers. I admit to being slightly paranoid on this subject, but regional security if not national security is at stake in this neglected but looming problem.

Pollution has become a recognized issue in the nineties, but not political pollution or moral pollution. Officials have agreed in principle to clean up our waters but not our politics. The government accuses the press of threatening the national security by printing the truth, but sees no such threat when the government itself tells lies. The deceptions and losses of the housing and savings and loan scandals of the late eighties made the Teapot Dome scandals of the twenties seem like innocent pranks, and nobody could praise the press for uncovering them, for we missed the theft of hundreds of millions of dollars for years.

Everybody denounced the trickery of the Cold War, its lies and deceptions and broken promises, but when it was over I could think of no greater threat to the national security than the atmosphere of distrust that increased during and after the Vietnam War, for if a people loses confidence in the truthfulness of its leaders, nobody can feel secure.

# Part Twelve

# THE CHANGING OF THE GUARD

# CHAPTER 37

# *Death and Transition*

IN THE SIXTIES Sally and I were in our fifties, at the middle age of life, when our parents were failing and our children were leaving home. On May 30, 1960, my father died of cancer at age eighty-six in Santa Cruz, California. Sally's mother died on January 17, 1961, and her father, Judge Fulton, followed two months later. That left of the old generation only my mother, who came back from my father's grave conceding at last: "Now Jimmy's gone. He was a good man."

That was no exaggeration. He was not only good but also kind, wise, and cheerful. He had no fear of death. He never thought of life as anything but a hard passage to a heavenly rest. He believed with the utmost confidence, as did my mother, that we would all meet again on the other side. I was at his bedside when he regained consciousness after a four-and-a-half-hour operation. "Where are we, Jimmy?" he said. "Are we in heaven?" I was never able to achieve his redemptive faith, though I tried, but he has lived every day in my memory. I wake sometimes in the night, hearing his voice, or when walking alone, particularly at Fiery Run in Virginia, suddenly I think I see him at my side.

Sally's memories of her early life were more varied than mine, with all the intimacy of village neighbors and teachers and close ties to a large extended family. Her parents and their brothers and sisters wrote to one another in a family circular letter for over forty years, and while the Fultons were more concerned with the politics of the world than were my mother and father, they shared many of my parents' convictions about faith and discipline.

When Sally's father wasn't riding his judicial circuit in Illinois or sitting on the Illinois Supreme Court, he was often holding court on his front porch with neighbors who came to him with their troubles. There was no doubt at 103 Alma Street in Sycamore about whose judgments would be obeyed. When Sally thought of going on to law school, her father objected that he didn't want her to live in the quarrelsome and often depressing atmosphere of the courts. When her brother Bob devoted more time to playing bridge than studying at the University of Illinois, acquiring some modest debts in the process, the judge thought he should take a menial job in the Anaconda Wire and Cable Company's factory in Sycamore. Bob worked hard in various branches of that prestigious company all the rest of his life, and ended up as president in its New York headquarters, with a chauffeur and a private airplane at his disposal, and a retirement house in Florida.

That vanishing world of the old generation bore little resemblance to the America of the nineties. In the thirties, over 30 million Americans lived in villages smaller than Sycamore, with their simple routine of school, church, and work. Judge Fulton didn't sit on the bench for forty years, sometimes in Chicago, without knowing something of the brutality and corruption of city life, and he was, I think, wary of the way the world was going when I first met him.

He knew there would be wars and depressions and bank failures—he spent many years meeting the obligations he acquired as a board member of the Sycamore bank when it failed—but he didn't really believe in the nightmare predictions of atomic war. He had complete confidence in the nation's ability to defend itself, but he didn't think Uncle Sam should be running around trying to stamp out communism and poverty all over the world. No doubt he hoped each generation would be better educated and maybe even better behaved, and that there would be a greater respect for the law, but he passed no judgments without evidence. The only reckless prophecy I ever heard him make was that his favorite baseball team, the Chicago Cubs, would one day win the World Series.

It was only after our parents died, I think, that Sally and I really understood the power of their influence on us. They did not believe in complete freedom for young children, but thought that good habits were acquired through discipline and an ordered routine. They took an intense interest in our schoolwork and our early flutterings, but they did not allow us to imagine that the world was made for us or that it would provide every object of our desires. They were also aware that outside influences would compete for our attention against their teachings, and monitored the company we kept with sleepless vigilance.

I like to believe our faith in the teachings of our parents had something to do with bringing Sally and me together in the first place. We talked a lot about their beliefs, which became our beliefs, before we were married. And fortunately, we lived long enough ourselves to discover that their principles were not only relevant but a constant and reliable guide to us even in the strange, insecure world they left behind. We grieved in the sixties when they were gone, but were proud of their sturdy high ideals and tried to pass them on to our children.

At least we were prepared for the deaths of our parents, but not for the tragic and unexpected deaths in the early sixties of two of our closest friends, Orvil Dryfoos, the publisher of the *Times,* and Philip Graham, the publisher of *The Washington Post.* Dryfoos, worn out by a 114-day strike on the *Times,* died in 1963 of heart failure at age fifty, and Graham committed suicide that same year at age forty-eight. These two men played an important part in the *Times* and the *Post,* and incidentally, in my own life.

I was in charge of the Washington bureau of the *Times* at that time, but I had another responsibility. I was asked by Arthur Hays Sulzberger to work closely with Dryfoos, his son-in-law, then just taking over as publisher of the paper. This was an agreeable and useful assignment. Dryfoos was an intelligent and attractive man, but modest about his limited news and editorial experience. He had come out of Dartmouth College, and had had a seat on the New York Stock Exchange before marrying Sulzberger's eldest daughter, Marian, and joining the *Times.* He brought to that job not only a winning personality but a good supply of business brains, then in short supply on the *Times.*

Sally and I thought of Orv and Marian Dryfoos as our best friends on the *Times* in New York, and Orv called me from time to time about his problems. We shared a common interest in recruiting the best talent available. For example, it was Dryfoos who insisted, against the opposition of the editor of the editorial page, on starting Russell Baker's column, which was one of the best decisions he ever made. He was also a force in giving the reporters more scope to explain and analyze the news, expanding the reach of the paper with a West Coast edition, and even during the strike trying, unsuccessfully, to save the failing *Herald Tribune* by sharing costs and facilities with the *Times*.

He had been publisher only a short time when he ran into the worst labor union strike in the history of New York journalism, at the end of 1962. The issue for the *Times* and the other New York newspapers was the right to set type by modern photocomposition, and eliminate featherbedding, which was a favorite resting place for the printers. The issue for Bert Powers, the feisty head of the typographers' union, was keeping all the jobs he could and giving his men control over the new printing techniques. The printers in those days even regarded their jobs as personal property that they could pass on to their sons.

I wasn't involved in these negotiations, which were left mainly to Amory Bradford, the general manager of the *Times,* a tall, well-educated preacher's son, whose vanity was matched only by his belief in his own effortless superiority. At first, I tried to be optimistic and even lighthearted about the strike and wrote a column about it for the *Times* News Service on Christmas Eve of 1962:

> Dear Santa: All I want for Christmas is *The New York Times.* I don't ask for any of these new fur bed sheets, or electric socks, or automatic spaghetti winders, but a man is entitled to have old friends around at a time like this. When everything else is changing, the *Times* remains the same, typographical errors and all. So please do what you can to get the papers back. It's hard enough on the public, Mister, but think of the poor reporter. I've been fielding the *Times* on the first bounce on my front stoop every morning now for 25 years, and it's cold and lonely out there now. Besides, how do I know what to think when I can't read what I write?

I was increasingly worried and angry as the strike went on and finally wrote another column suggesting we publish and be damned, but Dryfoos called me on the phone to say he thought he was on the point of an agreement and would I mind spiking that column. It was the only time in fifty years that I was ever asked to change or withdraw a column, and I agreed. The strike went on for months, however, and ended, appropriately enough, on April Fools' Day of 1963. Dryfoos's death soon after was a painful shock to everyone, and certainly to Sally and me. I tried to pay my respects to him in a eulogy at his funeral, which is printed in the Appendix at the back of this book.

. . .

Like Dryfoos, Phil Graham got into newspapering by marrying the publisher's daughter. On June 5, 1940, the main news on the front page of *The Washington Post* was Churchill's famous "We shall never surrender" speech, and on the society page an announcement that Eugene Meyer's third daughter, Katharine, twenty-two, had married Philip Leslie Graham, twenty-four. He had come out of Harvard Law School the year before, tenth in a class of four hundred, and had just completed a year as clerk to Mr. Justice Reed of the Supreme Court. He was an attractive, intelligent, almost recklessly witty man. He was not deterred by lack of newspaper experience, or modesty, and before long was not only running the *Post* but also telling me how we should be running the *Times*.

We had a long, bantering, happy relationship, marked by common agreement on most political issues, and amiable disagreements on others. He joined the army air corps after Pearl Harbor and went off to the Pacific, but returned after the war and took over as publisher of the *Post* in 1946 when President Truman appointed Eugene Meyer to be the first president of the World Bank. Two years later, Meyer turned over the majority voting stock in the paper not to Katharine Graham but to Phil. It was not, at that time, much of a bargain. In the war years of 1942–45 it showed for the first time a profit amounting to only $249,451.

Sally and I developed a warm friendship with the Grahams in the venomous days of McCarthy. We went on vacation together, talking shop and nonsense most of the time, and when Herbert Elliston, the editor of the *Post*'s editorial page, had a heart attack, Graham asked me in 1953 to take his place. I told Phil at once that I could never leave the *Times,* but this merely provoked his combative instincts. He got out a big yellow pad and jotted down a long catalog of figures, doubling my salary, and adding offers of stock, family insurance, and other inducements. He was no tightwad. "Add them up, you dumb Scotchman," he said. "The *Times* is not a profit-making business, it's satisfied if it breaks even." "That's why I like it," I said. "I'll be back," he said, and he was, several times, with more alluring offers, but with the same result.

This made no difference to our friendship. On vacation with Kay, Sally, and me, he would propose outrageous propositions for debate. "Tonight," he would say, "we'll discuss the abolition of Congress, or why the South should have won the Civil War." One of his favorite topics, always directed at getting me to join the *Post,* was how Scotchmen could be so smart and dumb at the same time. He could forgive Scotland, he said, for imposing whisky, golf, and Calvinism on the world, but why did it have to send its people over here to add to America's miseries? He was the founder, president, and sole member of an organization he called Athletics Anonymous, created to oppose all forms of physical exercise. He explained the system by saying that whenever anybody picked up a golf club or a tennis racquet, or talked about jogging, he always put a drink in the poor man's hand and talked him out of it. He seldom missed an opportunity to demonstrate in the evening how his system worked.

I really liked the guy. This delicious nonsense covered up a deeply serious character. He was born in Terry, South Dakota, grew up in Florida, and came out of the University of Florida with intense sympathy for the poor in the depression. This was what attracted him to Washington and Roosevelt's New Deal experiments. But he was a king-maker, addicted to politics. He wasn't satisfied to analyze them or write about them, but had to get involved with them personally. He overdid everything. He was in constant touch with candidates and presidents, giving them advice, writing their speeches, and collecting a stable of political heroes and villains. He backed Eisenhower in 1952, but was viciously critical of Ike at the end, and he was uncritically partial to Kennedy and Johnson. He told Kennedy during the 1960 election, "Your problem is simple. You pick Johnson for vice president, take Texas, and win. Or you don't take Johnson, and you lose." I thought we should stay out of the smoky room, but he thought detachment was a cop-out, and I never had any doubts about whose views would prevail if I joined him at the *Post*.

Ironically, it was his compassion that started his physical and mental decline. During the crisis to integrate the public schools in Little Rock, Arkansas, in 1957, he thought it was his "Christian duty" to support the blacks, and that the United States would lose the Cold War if it continued its racial prejudices. In this campaign, he wrote Joe Alsop, the columnist, he spent sixteen hours a day on the telephone urging his views on officials in Washington and Arkansas. His brother, William, thought Phil's "disillusionment after Little Rock was the first step toward the manic-depressive."

He was seldom in the office in the last months of 1957, and in and out in 1958 and 1959. It was at this period that he asked Sally and me, with the agreement of his wife, to take responsibility for their children "if I don't make it, and Kay needs help." We agreed to this arrangement, and on several occasions when he was deeply depressed, he would appear at our house and talk about religion. He seemed to think that I could provide some spiritual guidance, but I'm afraid my faith was not strong enough to help.

He recovered somewhat at the beginning of the sixties until a further collapse in 1963, when he left his house and ran off with an Australian girl who worked in the Paris office of *Newsweek* magazine. At that time he took to calling President Kennedy, who liked Phil, understood the problem, and gave orders always to put Phil's calls through. Once when Kennedy differed with him on the phone, Graham said to the president, "Who do you think you're talking to?" Kennedy replied, "I don't think I'm talking to my old friend Phil Graham."

He was drinking heavily then and retreating to Chestnut Lodge, a Maryland rehabilitation center, with Kay always at his side, but on August 3, 1963, when he seemed better, she took him to Glen Welby, their farm outside Marshall, Virginia, and there he slipped away from her and killed himself with a 28-gauge shotgun.

When Kay recovered from this shock and had to face the office for the first time, she wondered how to proceed. "Take the joint over," I suggested, and she did with remarkable courage. Shortly thereafter, she revived the question of my joining the *Post,* without quite defining what my job would be. She noted that my doubts of working happily under Phil no longer existed. She appealed to both Sally and me, knowing that we would decide together, and finally wrote to us in 1964.

Dear Scotty and Sally: I have thought hard about our talks. They have been indefinite only because I wanted to work out what was best for you, since what is best for us is to have you here advising me and advising us, and being part of *The Washington Post.* My hopes are that you can consider coming to us at this point in your lives. I fully realize your close ties and emotions binding you to *The New York Times.* They have meant a great deal to you and you have meant as much or more to them. . . . You have given up a lot of the world's goods already as proof of what they meant to you, and of your loyalty to them. . . . I am arguing hard that you can be with us; that we have always wanted you and want you even more now that we are without Phil.

Walter Lippmann then talked to me about this, I think at Kay's request. He argued that the *Times* had long since been established as the foremost newspaper of the nation and that there was little I could do there except help carry on the tradition, whereas the *Post* was just on its way to becoming a great newspaper and I could make a larger contribution by accepting Kay's offer. I explained to him that I had left executive work in New York primarily because I wasn't very good at it, and preferred the freedom of writing on my own—precisely as he had done when he left the New York *World* to concentrate on his column.

Sally and I talked all this over at length. She said, "Forget everything but where you will be most happy in your work." I then wrote to Kay: "You are right, your offer has touched all kinds of human feelings—my own about what I want to do with my life, my affection for you and Phil . . . but I just can't do it." Shortly thereafter, I asked Kay's son Donald to join me in the *Times* Washington bureau, and the consolation of these sad stories about Dryfoos and Graham was that these two newspapers went on under Kay Graham and Arthur Ochs Sulzberger to their most successful years, their sons in line to carry on into the new century.

# CHAPTER 38

## Arthur Ochs Sulzberger

THE DEATH OF Orvil Dryfoos in 1963 changed many things on the *Times*. When he was followed by Arthur Ochs Sulzberger as publisher, a new generation came to the fore, more decisive, more orderly, more interested in business. It also affected my own future on the *Times*. Orv and Marian Dryfoos were of Sally's and my own generation and while Dryfoos was somewhat more conservative than I, we thought alike about the *Times* and he had talked a lot about our working together in the future. Now that he was gone, I was in the middle, a generation younger than Arthur Hays Sulzberger and a generation older than his only son, Arthur Ochs Sulzberger, who took over at the age of thirty-eight, and for more than a quarter of a century presided over the most successful period in the paper's history.

Punch, as he was called, didn't start under ideal circumstances. Soon after he became publisher in 1963, the country was in an uproar over the Vietnam War. There were antiwar demonstrations in New York City and racial violence in Alabama, Mississippi, North Carolina, Virginia, and Maryland. Unemployment was rising, and President Johnson was saying, "come, let us reason together"—and sending more troops to Saigon.

There was an awkward situation on the *Times,* too. The paper's West Coast edition was losing money. Though the long labor strike that had frustrated Orvil was over, the settlement was expensive and the negotiations for some kind of partnership with the *Herald Tribune* were dragging on. Punch's father, at seventy-two and in ill health, favored the deal. "He hated to see a good newspaper die,"

Punch said. But the lawyers and accountants on the *Times* were less romantic.

More important, there was an embarrassing delay in deciding how the new management of the paper should be organized. Amory Bradford, the general manager, for some reason thought that his mismanagement of the strike entitled him to manage the paper as publisher, or at least as president of the company. His good looks were matched only by his bad judgment, but the elder Sulzberger, then chairman of the board, thought Punch should share his responsibilities with Bradford and asked my opinion of such an arrangement.

I said I thought it was a bum idea. I reminded him that he had not been very happy when Mr. Ochs had insisted that he share the direction of the *Times* with Julius Adler, and I added, "If you don't trust Punch now, you'll never trust him, and you'll cripple him." He didn't like this opinion, and he then sought the advice of George Woods, the former head of the World Bank, who was the most influential member of the *Times'* board of directors. Woods came up with an equally silly idea. On May 27, 1963, he wrote to Punch's father:

> Dear Arthur: I have thought a good deal since we talked yesterday. I am still hopeful that some alternative to making Punch president and publisher may emerge. The risk about proceeding on this route that troubles me most is that he will have too much responsibility too soon—and possibly to his future detriment.
>
> So I write to say I favor a team of Punch and Scotty; Punch should be No. 1 and Scotty No. 2—one as president and the other as publisher—with their duties divided as they may decide between them with the chairman's approval. . . . I am not writing to cast a vote as a trustee or a director must. I am simply advising you, as a friend, and I feel I must in good conscience express my judgment. If you and Iphigene decide otherwise I will understand it and nevertheless will tell you what I think about future questions if you ask me. Warmest regards—George.

I knew nothing about this at the time; the chairman never mentioned it to me, but he finally decided that Punch should be publisher, with Bradford as his assistant, and it was then that Punch demonstrated that he had learned something in the marines. He told his father that he would take the job without conditions or he wouldn't take it at all, and the moment he said this, the job was his. He soon took charge.

Punch was the Harry Truman of the *Times*. He was undertrained and underestimated. He didn't worry about problems, he decided them. Like Harry, he was not too gentle with some of the people who thought they were indispensable, and replaced them with his own team. He didn't waste much time on alluring outside projects that were losing money but tidied up the *Times* itself. In short, he dealt with the obvious.

First, he killed the West Coast edition. It had met its circulation targets, but its readers were scattered over several western states, and the local advertisers weren't interested in readers far from their stores. I was disappointed in this, for I thought the *Times* should be available nationally early each morning, but the economics were against it until satellite transmission became available years later.

Only a few weeks into his job, he turned his attention to the question of a merger with the *Herald Tribune* in New York. I liked the idea of getting the *HT* out of the morning and Sunday fields and giving the city two serious morning and afternoon papers (the Scots don't mind spending other people's money), but it was a complicated and dicey business and Punch didn't like the odds.

So on July 8, 1963, he called his principal assistants to his office and decided not only that a joint operating agreement was "not in the *Times'* interest" but also that negotiations with the *Herald Tribune* should be stopped at once. He did approve, however, an agreement with the *Herald Tribune* and *The Washington Post* for a combined paper in Paris, and this was a success from the start.

After the morning *Herald Tribune* and the afternoon *World-Journal-Tribune* failed, he flirted with the idea of starting a New York afternoon paper and even had it dummied up, but his associates were divided about it and he finally spiked it.

It was said that the family never expected Punch to be publisher, but that was only partly true. His father once said to me that maybe one day the *Times* should be owned partly by its employees, and he thought that Punch should get some training on such an employee-owned paper. I suggested the *Milwaukee Journal* and Punch reported there for a while, reaching the conclusion that what worked in Milwaukee probably wouldn't play on Broadway.

He was trained on the *Times* under the direction of his father. He worked away almost invisibly for years from the basement to the attic, and he went to Paris and Rome as a correspondent, but his success as publisher came mainly from his personal characteristics rather than from his experience. He had none of the qualities usually attributed to publishers. He didn't think the world was a Punch and

Judy show. He wasn't an opinionated intellectual. He didn't hobnob with the politicians and publicity saints in Washington. Unlike the McCormicks or the Reids or the Pulitzers, or even some of his own editors, he didn't think he knew more about running the country than the president. But he proved that common sense and a little humanity go a long way, and he knew how to listen, and when he had heard enough.

It was the editors who gave him the most trouble. Over the years, the *Times* had become an editors' paper. They were inclined to believe that the publisher's job was to make money, handle outside complaints, represent the *Times* at civic functions, and leave them alone. They conceded that it was all right for him to back a certain candidate for president, governor, or mayor, but otherwise his authority should be delegated to the managing editor on the daily paper, the Sunday editor at the weekend, and the editorial page editor on most questions of opinion. Punch Sulzberger didn't think this was such a hot idea.

Accordingly, he decided to put both the Sunday and the weekday *Times* under an executive editor, and appointed Turner Catledge to this unprecedented job. He didn't discuss the move with Lester Markel, who had been running the Sunday paper with great success since the days of Adolph Ochs. He simply told Markel what he had decided. Fortunately, Catledge was the sort of man who could unify the army, navy, and air force, but unifying the *Times* wasn't easy and it wasn't always successful. It left nobody in doubt, however, that henceforth things would be different on the *Times.*

Even the union bosses eventually got the point. For with the assistance of Walter Mattson, who became president of the company, the *Times* decided to buy other newspapers, magazines, and television stations that enhanced its earnings and ensured its independence in dealing with the unions. When Punch became publisher of the *Times,* its daily circulation was 772,048, Sunday circulation 1,416,838. After he was on the job for twenty-five years, the circulation in 1991 was 1,209,200 daily and 1,762,000 on Sunday, both record highs. Like Truman, he had the last laugh and in the confusion even had the foresight to produce a son and a namesake to carry on the old tradition.

# CHAPTER 39

# *The* Times' *New Executive Editor*

> When you come to a fork in the road, take it.
> —Yogi Berra

IN 1968, FIVE years after he became publisher, Punch Sulzberger asked me to replace Turner Catledge as executive editor. Aside from the fact that Turner was irreplaceable, this was, in many ways, an odd decision. Punch was planning for the future, but I was almost sixty at the time; it had been twenty-four years since I had served as his father's assistant, and therefore, it seemed to me, the more logical option was to choose a successor not of my generation, but of his own. The publisher conceded this, but said it would be a temporary assignment and reminded me that I had promised his father years before that I would do anything I could to help with the transition to younger men. Arthur Hays Sulzberger, then in ill health but chairman of the board, also recalled the promise, and I moved to New York in 1968.

There was very little rejoicing among the editors on Forty-third Street about this decision. Catledge didn't want to step down and he was, with good reason, highly popular with the other editors, who had almost unlimited freedom under his direction. They thought, with some reason, that I might limit their authority and change the system that had produced the finest newspaper in the country. Besides, I had gone through a troubling controversy with the editors in New York, not only over the *Times'* handling of the Bay of Pigs invasion, but also over the direction of the Washington bureau.

The controversy over Washington occurred during the presidential election campaign between Nixon and Humphrey in 1968, when the *Times,* as usual, was considering what changes, if any, should be made for covering the new administration the following January. After running the Washington bureau for eleven years, I had asked to give over my administrative duties, so I could concentrate on my column, and I had been replaced by Tom Wicker, who became Washington bureau chief. Tom was highly regarded, then and ever since, as one of the most able political reporters of his generation.

However, a decision was made by Catledge, with the approval of the publisher, to replace Wicker with Jimmy Greenfield, who had come to the *Times* from *Time* magazine and was a close friend of Abe Rosenthal, one of Catledge's principal assistants. No announcement was made; Wicker was simply told that Catledge and E. C. Daniel, the managing editor, were not satisfied with the Washington bureau's performance. News of the proposed switch was soon widely discussed in Washington, to the consternation of the staff and the delight of Ben Bradlee, the executive editor of *The Washington Post,* who never cried much over the *Times'* troubles. Punch Sulzberger then called me to New York for a talk with him and Catledge and told me what they intended to do. I said I thought it was the dumbest idea since Eisenhower chose Nixon as his vice president. Since they hadn't even explained why they had chosen Greenfield, I asked them how they intended to explain this to Wicker, and also, if they were determined to make a change, how they would explain to Tony Lewis and Max Frankel that they were being passed over as bureau chief in favor of Greenfield, who was comparatively new on the paper and whose qualifications to take precedence over Lewis and Frankel were not apparent to me. Catledge said he would suggest sending Frankel to Paris, and offer Lewis the opportunity to serve as assistant to Francis Brown on the Sunday *Book Review.*

I mention all this not only to explain why my reception later as executive editor in New York was not exactly popular but also to indicate that the *Times,* like most other big institutions, occasionally pays more attention to who's doing the job than to what job it's trying to do. I made no impression on Sulzberger and Catledge, and the publisher said he would go to Washington and tell Wicker what had been decided. He asked me to join him in that meeting and I said, "You'd better do it in private because it will be a rough night and things will probably be said that a third person shouldn't hear."

After that meeting, Wicker came to see me and said that he was going to quit before he was shoved, and he so informed the publisher, who then reflected on the consequences, ordered a cease-fire, and called the whole thing off. Catledge, Daniel, and Rosenthal were humiliated and angry about this public reversal of their plans, and Greenfield resigned. When Punch asked me to replace Catledge as executive editor, he said he had put the whole Washington incident out of his mind, but his editors obviously had not.

My first impression as executive editor was that there was more talent around the place, more experts on everything from the inner cities to outer space, than had ever been gathered together in any newspaper office. I understood better then than ever before what an impressive instrument of public information had been built since the days of Ochs. My second and more fanciful impression was that the tradition of the paper was so strong that, with or without an executive editor, indeed even if no reporters or editors at all showed up one night, the *Times* would, by some combination of habit and magic, come out anyway.

I thought at the beginning that the executive editor should sit out in the city room near the reporters, where I could be closer to the staff, hear the gossip, and handle the gripes. Daniel felt this was carrying democracy too far. I also had the equally silly idea that I could apply to the very large staff in New York (over seven hundred reporters, editors, and assistants) the chummy informality that worked with the much smaller staff in Washington.

In Washington, we had a skull session almost every working day, attended by everybody but the janitor, on what we missed yesterday and what we intended to do to the opposition tomorrow. These sessions were lively, funny, and often productive, but obviously we couldn't do the same thing with the battalions in New York unless we hired Carnegie Hall. I respected the judgment of the editors, but believed then, and still do, that the critical question is not how editors direct reporters, but what kind of reporters and copy they get to direct.

This view, naturally, was not shared by the editors in the bull pen. I had never wholly understood the dominance of the bull pen on the paper. It was staffed at that time by two competent editors—Ted Bernstein and Lew Jordan—and while they were assistants to the managing editor, they really decided what news was fit to print and where it should fit on the front and other pages.

The advantage of this procedure, originally devised by Jimmy

James, when he was managing editor, was that it enabled him to get home for dinner, but one of the disadvantages, or so I thought, was that the bull pen editors seldom had time to read the stories they put on the front page, let alone the other pages. Other editors read the copy and made their recommendations for page one, and the bull pen then decided what recommendations to accept and what to reject.

My subversive reservations about the bull pen were not well received, but I had a little better luck with a suggestion that we organize a continual search for good young reporters and especially for good young writers. Such was the prestige of the *Times* that we got more talented applicants unsought than we could hire, but even so there was general agreement that maybe we could find others even better if we watched the papers all over the country for promising recruits.

Considering the temporary nature of my assignment in New York, I insisted on continuing to write my column three days a week, because while there was no noticeable demand for my opinions, I wanted to go back to the column when the great transition was over. If I had had the foresight to invent the forty-eight-hour day, I might have been able to keep in touch with Washington, preside over the daily and Sunday papers, referee all jurisdiction disputes between the various departments, reward the winners and console the losers, and still write wise and witty columns three times a week, but I carried the column and my executive duties, to the detriment of both.

I was preoccupied with the news, for just as I arrived in New York—I think it was just a coincidence—the country had the equivalent of a nervous breakdown. By mid-June of 1968, Vietnam had become the longest war in the nation's history, with military deaths totaling 33,641. I had no sooner moved the family to New York when an antiwar crowd shut down Columbia University, and the demonstrations and sit-ins spread to other campuses, requiring the services of the National Guard at particularly ominous gatherings.

Mayor Richard Daley of Chicago didn't help things much by ordering his cops to shoot to kill in extreme cases of arson and rioting, and the presidential election of 1968 got off to a violent start with the murder of Robert Kennedy, just after he had won the Democratic primary in California. The presidential nominating conventions in Miami and Chicago were a disaster if not a disgrace. There was rioting in Miami, where the Republicans dumped Nixon on the country, and not being satisfied with that, added for bad measure Spiro Agnew of Maryland as vice president. But the Republicans were positively meek compared to the Democrats in convention in Chicago.

There the demonstrators were not only numerous but frantic, and while the gentle mayor and his minions didn't shoot to kill, they gave the impression outside the hall that they might, and the disorder inside the convention was almost as bad. In the end, the delegates nominated Hubert Humphrey, and later, in trying to analyze how on earth he ever lost to Nixon, I concluded that the voters watching this outrageous Democratic party performance on television had decided then and there that if the Democrats couldn't govern themselves, why take a chance on them governing the country?

When the election was over and Nixon had won with the slimmest margin of any election since 1912, I was invited to make a speech at New York University, which I titled "The Problems of the New Administration," and I made the mistake of accepting. It should have been entitled "The Problems of the New Executive Editor," for just when I had started talking to four hundred people in the Eisner and Lubin Auditorium about what Nixon was up against, there was a roar outside the auditorium. There was then a crash as one locked door was battered down with a sofa, and my audience was immediately augmented by about a hundred "students" yelling, "Ho, Ho, Ho Chi Minh!"

For an instant I thought this lunatic cry was funny, and being in possession of the microphone at that moment, I said, "He isn't here." I then invited the new guests to sit down, or, if they preferred, to take the microphone and explain their message and their manners. Instead they dismantled the loudspeaker system and ran up and down the aisles shouting obscenities until the audience, feeling more concern for their present safety than for Mr. Nixon's future, crept away without any physical damage. This incident did not encourage my future efforts at public expression.

Two happy events, however, relieved this doleful period. Lyndon Johnson announced that he was retiring to his Texas ranch at the end of his term, and the government, apparently despairing of the state of the terrestrial world, announced that our astronauts were going to the moon. When the moon project was announced, I called up Archibald MacLeish, my Georgetown neighbor during the war, and asked him what was the point of having an American poet laureate if he didn't celebrate the landing on the moon in poetry and in the *Times*. He replied that they hadn't landed yet. I said we'd like to publish his reflections on the front page the morning after they did, and I gave him a deadline. He said he'd try. He not only produced the poem but also went over our galley proofs and made numerous suggestions about the selection of the type and the staggering of the lines. It was the only poem ever printed on page one of the paper, and I still retain our merry correspondence on the marriage of poetry and journalism.

I also have among my souvenirs of those years in New York one or two thumping ideas I tried to impose on my colleagues. First, I thought the page numbers in the paper were too small and managed to get them set in a larger type. That was triumph number one. And second, it was my firm conviction that the readership of the *Times* could be greatly increased if we printed it in ink that didn't come off on the readers' hands and clothes, or if that proved impossible, if we provided a washcloth with each copy of the paper. My colleagues didn't think this was practical or even very funny.

In short, I was not a successful executive editor. Like my earlier stint in New York as the publisher's assistant, this one involved constant controversy with the other editors, and necessary but painful changes. Sally and I were living in fancy quarters in the United Nations Plaza, which were too elegant for our taste, and for the first time in years I felt like an outsider again, and I asked to be relieved of the job.

Before returning to Washington, Sally and I went to Italy and spent a few days at the Villa Serbelloni on Lake Como. At that time, our son Jim was teaching creative writing at the University of North Carolina, but was wondering about giving it up to devote all his time to writing books. I wrote him as follows:

"Our situation is not entirely different from your own, for Mother and I have to see the realities of our lives clearly if we are to be useful and happy in the coming years. Like you, I prefer writing to all else. I insisted on giving up the most important news position on the *Times* because I was overextended and would have ended by being a bad editor, a poor columnist, and probably a sick man." I'm sure I was right about this.

I was conscious at that time of the passing of the years, not only because our sons were well launched, but also because the young reporters were treating me with uncharacteristic courtesy, and the British government made me a Commander of the British Empire. My mother, despite her lifelong reservations about the monarchy, was pleased about this, but when I asked my old friend Leonard Miall of the BBC what this decoration meant, he said, "I understand the CBE is particularly useful for eliminating warts on the back of your neck."

This period in New York as executive editor was useful in one or two important respects. At the *Times,* as in the government in Washington, it's never easy to tell where the new ideas begin and how they develop. Things don't *happen* at the *Times,* they *emerge* by slow growth like flowers from the seed. The incubation of the op-ed page—making room on the page opposite the paper's editorials for outside opinion—illustrates the point. This was not a new idea. The New York *World* had introduced something similar in the twenties. I had argued for it with the publisher between our gin-rummy games on our trip to Moscow in 1943, but the editors couldn't agree on who should direct it, so the project was filed for future consideration.

This long internal controversy was finally resolved on instructions from the publisher on September 26, 1970, and he ordered it to begin under the able direction of Harrison Salisbury, but not without one last difficult debate. E. C. Daniel felt that the *Times* was not under any obligation "to present a forum for people who disagreed with us." ("They have the 'Letters' column, don't they?" he remarked.) An op-ed page, he argued, would put the paper in a "ridiculous position," and would not only be expensive, but would also take the place of a whole page of news.

I said I thought we were not paying enough attention, either in the news columns or on the editorial page, to the news of ideas. If some assistant secretary of state or two-bit senator denounced the Soviets for the hundredth time we'd be sure to print it, but if some thoughtful citizen made on the same day an original analysis on the critical importance but neglect of Mexico, we might easily ignore it. Nobody was suggesting that the op-ed page replace a page of news, I insisted, and I hoped nobody was suggesting that the insiders on the *Times* were wiser than the best of the outsiders. I argued that the thing that set the *Times* apart was the unmatched quality of its readers in the universities, governments, and multinational corporations of the world, and that it was a unique opportunity to make a page available every day for their ideas and opinions.

The issue, I insisted, was simply whether the *Times* would be a better paper with the addition of the best thoughts we could gather all over the world, or worse. Punch Sulzberger finally decided it would be better, ending a debate that had gone on for more than a quarter of a century. The idea has since been copied by almost every other serious newspaper, and I like to think I had a part, along with many others, in getting it started. The other thing I feel I helped accomplish is in giving the reporters more freedom to write and explain the news to the limit of their abilities.

All told, however, the last two years of the sixties, as I approached my own sixties, were the worst of an unhappy decade that ended with the death of my boss and dear friend, Arthur Hays Sulzberger. I saw him whenever I was allowed to visit, during his final illness, and the last thing he asked me to do was to say a few words for him when he was gone. These words are included in the Appendix of this book.

# CHAPTER 40

# Hough and the
# Vineyard Gazette

THE SIXTIES WEREN'T all bad, for at the end, as usual, I got another lucky break. It was Sally's conviction that I could do a good year's work in eleven months but not in twelve, so she arranged a vacation in Martha's Vineyard off the coast of Massachusetts, and there we met a remarkable man who added a new dimension to our lives. He was Henry Beetle Hough, a hand-cranked Yankee, who for half a century had owned and run the *Vineyard Gazette,* one of New England's famous weeklies. He distrusted the world beyond his island, and seldom went there and hated to print a word about it. He had none of the trappings usually associated with successful journalists: he wasn't rich, famous, or even notorious, and he deplored the invention of automobiles, and other modern "inconveniences." He was, as he said, "just a country editor," one of the last of the old pamphleteers, who turned his back on a promising newspaper career in New York and worked all the rest of his life with his wife, Betty, on the *Gazette.* It still looks, after 144 years of uninterrupted publication, almost as old-fashioned and substantial as Ben Franklin's almanacs, with spread-arm sheets and ads on the front page, and a line of poetry above the masthead.

In the days of my youth, some restless reporters, usually when they were tipsy or sore at some editor for mangling their copy, would damn the big cities and babble about retiring to edit or even own a little country paper. This longing for the simpler life was based on the fantasy that village editors all lived like William Allen White in Emporia, Kansas, dispensing wisdom on the front porch in the evening and loafing or glorifying the bucolic arts the rest of the week.

The truth is that not since the abolition of slavery has anybody worked harder or longer hours than country editors. I admired but didn't envy their lot and was surprised and perplexed when, shortly after I had met Henry Hough, he wrote and asked if my wife and I would be interested in buying the *Gazette.* He was at that time depressed by the death of his wife, who had been his partner on the paper for half a century. He had no children, and while he had several prospective buyers, he said he had come to me "because I want it to go into a newspaper family and you have writing sons."

I hesitated about this. I thought he was not ready for retirement and never would be, but he had been thinking about it for years. Seventeen years before I met him, he had written in one of his twenty-eight books (*Once More the Thunderer*):

> How to resign the duties of a country editor—that is what we should like to know now. . . . How to sweep the papers from the desk that have been there so long, and leave the heap of exchanges unopened, and hear the telephone ringing but let it go unanswered, as one steps through the door as an editor for the last time into a street of mellow twilight. . . . Apparently there is no way to taper off as there is in some worldly occupations. It is all or nothing until the end.

He was wrong about this, as it turned out. The more we discussed his proposal, the more I came to respect him and his philosophy of journalism as a public service. He talked about the *Gazette* as if it were his only child, which in a way it was, and about the island as if he were its caretaker, which indeed he was. He knew every old house in Edgartown, and who had built it and who had lived in it and what sort of folks they were. "You have to know what went before," he told Sally. He was a gentle scrapper for the public good, an unselfish man of unusual ability and unsleeping integrity.

He and Betty had been given the *Gazette* by his father as a wedding present when they were graduated from Columbia University in 1920. It was then a struggling little adventure above a grocery store on the main street of Edgartown, with a hand-cranked Fairhaven press and a circulation, some of it paid, of 600 eight-page issues a week. They had devoted their lives to it, and now that she was gone, he felt abandoned without her.

"We have been on a country newspaper," he wrote on one of his melancholy days, "long enough to know the disillusioning lesson that most worthwhile battles must be fought over and over again.

The winning of them once—for some we have won—was more than comforting, it was sustaining, but to face the same struggle for the same victory after almost thirty years finds us more irritable than is good, and sometimes with weariness that is poor armor even for the smallest crusade."

Sally and I talked this all over, feeling it was wrong for him to make such a decision when he was depressed, and we finally proposed a compromise. I explained that I was at that time just taking on the responsibilities as executive editor of *The New York Times*, and suggested that he stay on with a binding legal assurance that we would buy the paper when he did finally retire. This he refused to do because, he said, he had lived a long time and had seen many of his old friends in good health one week and hopelessly incompetent the next. He agreed to continue writing for the paper but insisted that we buy it or forget it. Accordingly, since we had always played our hunches and accepted the accidents and opportunities of life, we signed the contract, and my son Richard and his wife, Jody, eventually assumed direction of the paper and worked with him happily until the day he died.

Along the way, he took us with his collie to all his secret walks on the island, along the silent shore in winter and down the sandy up-island lanes where he had a hideaway next to his father's house, which was called Fishhook. He was a spare, active man, quick of foot and speech. Every prospect reminded him of something or somebody, usually of the old days, and he talked and wrote a lot about the old editors who had gone before him.

There were only three of them in over a hundred years. The first, whom he always identified as "Mr. Sampson's great-uncle," started the paper, he would say, "the year Herman Melville's *Typee* was published." It began with a proclamation that the *Gazette* "would be tied to no party, nor bound to any man's opinion" but would "furnish the latest news, both foreign and domestic, and in our selection we shall endeavor to unite the agreeable with the useful, and if possible to please the taste of the business man and the man of leisure." A part of the paper, he added, would be devoted to moral and religious reading.

This venerable founder with long whiskers and a cape billowing in the wind was fiercely independent. Once he published in italic: *"We print today 8,960 copies of the Vineyard Gazette. We ask for no patronage. We have all we want."* He was an unreconstructed Democrat after the Civil War, though most voters on the island were staunchly Republican, and in the contested presidential election of 1876, he announced in black boxcar type the "victory" of Samuel Tilden over Rutherford B. Hayes. Tilden had more popular votes than Hayes but lost in the electoral college. The old editor didn't wait for the final result but elected Tilden: BLOW YE THE TRUMPET! his headline roared, and under that was a cut of the American eagle, and then another line: THE EAGLE SCREAMS OVER A LAND REDEEMED FROM MISRULE AND CORRUPTION . . . A REIGN OF BENEFICENCE, EQUALITY AND JUSTICE ASSURED. The only thing that was assured after that was the laughter of the island.

The old original owner did not take kindly to criticism. Once he wrote to a complaining reader: "We will here say that we have never inserted in the *Gazette* a line, either in our editorial or advertising columns, which 'dying we would wish to blot' nor never will we." Then he explained to the reader the burdens of an editor:

> Alas! How little is known of the ceaseless toil and thousand annoyances that make up the daily routine of his duties. . . . He is a man of all work. He knows or should know everybody and a little of everything. He is in the world and out of the world, and lives in the past, the present, and the future. He must sometimes see and not seem to see, hear and not seem to hear. . . . Indeed, an editor must be all things to all men, or all men will be nothing to him.

This was not a bad description of Henry Hough's problems. When he took over the *Gazette* in 1920, type was set one letter at a time, by hand. It was printed on an old hand-cranked press on sheets cut with a butcher knife and fed and retrieved by hand. He printed six hundred papers a week at the start, which, as he explained with a shrewd smile, was not the same as *selling* six hundred.

The subscription price in 1920 was $2.00 a year, soon raised by Betty Hough to $2.50, and with advertising selling at ten cents a column-inch, Betty figured that if they sold every inch in the paper, leaving out all news, total revenue for the year would amount to almost $12,000. Accordingly, while they made adjustments and did most of the editorial and mechanical work themselves, they did not live extravagantly, but somehow survived the depression and developed the paper into one of the best weeklies in New England.

By the time we came along in 1967, forty-seven years after Henry Hough took it over, he had moved the paper into a plain but lovely old house in Edgartown at the corner of Summer Street and Davis Lane, but by then even the linotype age was drawing to an end, and

Henry didn't think he could face one more major transition to photocomposition and the new offset presses.

Sally and I then tried to lend a hand. We couldn't find a linotype operator who was willing to come to the island from the mainland, so we imported Leslie Baines, a bright young operator from London. We invested in a new offset press, computerized the typesetting, and built a second story above the pressroom, being careful to be faithful to the old shingled house, to modern photocomposition copies of the old fonts of type, and especially to the lines of poetry by Joseph Story above Henry's desk:

> Here shall the press the people's right maintain,
> Unawed by influence and unbribed by gain;
> Here patriot truth her glorious precepts draw,
> Pledged to religion, liberty, and law.

Fortunately, as Henry said, we had sons, and Richard, our eldest, after years on the *San Francisco Chronicle* and more years on the *Los Angeles Times* as its State Department, Moscow, and London correspondent, volunteered to make the switch to country journalism. On the business side, he had the help of his wife, Jody, who, as they say on Madison Avenue, could sell ice to the Eskimos. These two took over, and under their direction, the *Gazette* was honored in 1990 by the New England Press Association as the best New England weekly of the year.

Henry explained the difference between big-city and country journalism: if you make a silly mistake in the columns of a metropolitan paper, a common occurrence, you are likely to get an angry letter from some offended reader, but if you do the same on a little weekly, you may get a punch in the nose. It was Hough's opinion that this threat of instant physical retaliation was by far the best way to encourage accuracy, courtesy, and respect for neighbors.

He also explained the advantages of an island: being cut off from the mainland by five miles of salt water was, in his view, a blessing, but it had one or two complications. On Martha's Vineyard, there are six towns, each with at least sixty different ideas about what was best for all inhabitants. It was, he insisted, the most beautiful island in the world, covering about one hundred square miles, with a year-round population of ten thousand who are invaded in the summer by the entire population of Boston, Providence, and New York combined—or so it seemed.

This invasion from Memorial Day to Labor Day naturally pleased the merchants, but irritated many of the permanent residents, some of whom wanted to ban motorcycles, limit automobiles, restrict housing construction, and if necessary secede from the Republic. Henry felt that it was the job of the *Gazette* to report their battles while preserving their unity, without getting clipped by all parties. "No easy trick," he said. He added, in illustration, that the *Gazette* was careful to record the vital statistics of birth, graduation, marriage, sickness, and death, but not divorce or other family difficulties. On an island where people lived so close to one another, it was, he believed, not his job to see everything, but to keep the unavoidable personal conflicts from becoming intolerable.

In sixty years, he left the island only a few times, usually to attend meetings of the Thoreau Society in Boston. One of his young reporters asked him one day if he ever got the urge to see the world. "Once in a while," he replied, "but when I do I just go upstairs, put my feet in a bucket of water, and read old copies of the *National Geographic.*"

He emphasized that it was often harder to write about the homely, intimate things than about the big battles and conflagrations of the world, but that it was often more important to do so. For the *Gazette* was trying to give a picture of life on the island as a whole, and not just the unusual aspects of it, a process we forget all too often on the big papers. Also, unlike his predecessors, whose neighbors were whaling captains, he didn't think we should pay attention to world events. He did, however, break this rule the week World War II started on September 1, 1939. He explained the exception as follows:

> Ordinarily, the *Gazette* has no concern with outside news, but because this was an occasion that weighed heavily on our hearts, we wanted to take some notice of it. So I set on the linotype a few paragraphs about how the residents of our community had heard that morning on their radios of Warsaw and the invasion of Poland. By now, the last clouds of a northeast storm had drawn away in the unveiling of a crystal-gilded morning, so I put in what kind of day it was in order that future generations might know, if they cared to look back in the files, what things were like on our island when the world went mad.

Like Sherlock Holmes, he examined and found surprises in ordinary things and made us respect the uses of the past. Like Sally's granny, he was careful not to fuss over secondary things. To make things last was one of the admonitions of his forebears, and he enjoyed the wear and tear of time. "The companionship of a house," he once wrote, "is nourished by mellowing and shabbiness; otherwise you must always be on guard, must never drop anything on the floor, must never put your feet up, and must eye your guests while they eat their soup."

He had an endless collection of stories about the paper and the island people. Once a woman came to the *Gazette* office on a Friday morning when the press was running. She said her husband was desperately ill, and if he read in the paper that their son had just been convicted of drunken driving, she didn't know what would happen to her man. There was no way, she added, that her husband would miss this sad news, for he had read the *Gazette* carefully all their married life. Henry listened and told her to wait a few minutes. He then went out into the back shop, stopped the press, eliminated the offending article, ran off one copy of the paper without it, then put the original story back for the rest of the press run, and gave the one special copy to the boy's mother for delivery to her husband.

That was typical of Henry Hough. He always managed, somehow, to reconcile the personal with the professional, maybe because he didn't stay in the office writing about the glories of objectivity, but mingled with the people and knew a lot about their personal struggles. It seemed to me that he had learned some of the secrets of life, which is why, ever since, he has been a model and a memory I will always cherish.

There was a unity and purpose to his life. The personal and professional benefited from the constant companionship of his wife. Like Jean Monnet, he knew that concentration of thought and energy produced clarity in his work. In the print shop, he enjoyed the craftsman's satisfaction in skilled physical work, and at his typewriter he could forget his worries in his hunt for just the right word and rhythm of a good English sentence.

All this inspired a fierce loyalty among members of his staff, whose talents would have brought much higher financial rewards elsewhere. Bill Roberts, by some magic, overcame every potential disaster in the print shop, Joe Allen covered the waterfront in a column called "The Wheelhouse Loafer," and Phyllis Meras wrote descriptive prose that would have graced the columns of *The New York Times,* as indeed it did for some time.

I never thought of Henry Hough as a happy man, though paradoxically, he had many qualities usually associated with happiness. His life wasn't cluttered up with a lot of possessions or unachievable ambitions, but was devoted to things outside himself, particularly to the preservation of the environment of the island. Maybe he wasn't happy, because he longed for a simpler world that was gone, but he felt himself part of that world and believed that in the development of the paper he had left something behind.

I thought, when he died, that as the American people had moved off the land into the cities, they had forgotten the old country editors who had played such an important part in the infancy of the Republic and didn't even know that a few such characters still existed. So now that Henry was gone, I tried to pay my respects to him in a column in the *Times,* and part of what I wrote is the following:

> One of the most interesting things about journalism in America is that so many of its memorable characters have been country editors. From Tom Paine to Mark Twain, William Allen White of Kansas and Elmer Davis of Indiana, and the Baltimore crowd from Henry Mencken to Russell Baker, it was, in a funny way, the hicks from the sticks who took over the big-city crowd.
>
> Henry Hough is, in my mind, a symbol of the country journalism that has been the school where many of these modern reporters got their training. He worried about death and retirement. "I suppose," he wrote in *Country Editor,* "that death is the most characteristic of all the forces in a country town, because there are always so many old people living there, and the passing of an individual is so much more important than it is in the city. Besides, a town has time to mourn."
>
> It amused Henry Hough when one of our old buddies on the Vineyard, Red Smith of the old *Herald Tribune* and the *Times,* made a speech saying, "Death is no big deal—almost any of us can manage it. Living is the trick we have to learn." Henry Hough learned that trick very well. He thought the main thing was to concentrate on simple things—his family, his paper, his community, and nothing else.
>
> He went on until just a few days ago, when he wrote his last editorials. Then he did at eighty-eight what was very typical of him. He was always a punctual man, and he died at four o'clock on a Thursday afternoon just before deadline on his Friday paper. He always said he would get his copy in on time, and that's precisely what he did.

# PART THIRTEEN

# WRITING AND TRAVELING

# CHAPTER 41

.........................................................................................

# In Defense of
# Columnists

> I pray Thee make my column read,
> And give me thus my daily bread.
> Endow me, if Thou grant me wit,
> Likewise with sense to mellow it.
> —Don Marquis

AFTER MY ASSIGNMENT as executive editor, I joined the ranks of the vice presidents of the *Times*, served on the board of directors for five years, and was free to concentrate on my column and look around the world with Sally. I had heard all the gossip about the executive-suite shenanigans of big business, but the *Times* board was as correct and exciting as an assembly of church deacons. It concentrated on budgets, acquisitions, and other mysteries beyond my competence, but in my experience it didn't cut any corners or even tell many jokes. I obeyed the new boy tradition of silence most of the time. Once, when some member proposed raising the price of the paper to twenty cents, I did say they might as well make it a quarter, but this was regarded in those far-off days as a reckless proposal, so I said little thereafter and devoted myself for the next twenty years to writing columns and defending this peculiar American practice from readers who thought it carried freedom of the press too far.

It pleases a columnist to blow off two or three times a week about how to save the human race, but it obviously irritates a lot of people. How, they ask, did you get so smart about so many things, and so critical of officials who have so much more information than you do? I usually admitted, in reply, that there was something arrogant and even comical about a choleric old geezer preaching atop a column with no other visible means of support, but I didn't apologize.

In a big country like the United States, I thought the syndicated newspaper columns were a useful if controversial public service. They were created not by popular demand but by economic necessity. Few newspapers could afford to establish their own bureaus in Washington, or, as world affairs increasingly affected their own communities, send qualified observers abroad. They could, however, buy syndicated columns of analysis and opinion as cheaply as they bought comic strips, picking and choosing between liberals and conservatives, or even better, giving their readers the opinions of both. This not only saved money but also enabled newspaper owners to avoid thinking for themselves, and to drop columnists who began writing a lot of nonsense, a common occurrence.

There are, of course, many kinds of columns. Some are a stimulant to make readers think, others a sedative to put them to sleep. The most popular are those that give advice to the lovelorn or explain how to cook a seven-course meal in fifteen minutes or where to get a good French dinner for $3.95. In contrast, political columns, puncturing official windbags, are not welcome, particularly in Washington, the windmill capital of the universe.

I thought of my column as a letter to an absent friend. Since he couldn't be around to sort out all the mysterious contradictions coming out of Washington, I was his self-appointed legman. And since it wasn't always easy to tell when the administration was telling the truth and when it was watering the milk, I consulted the best-informed characters I could find about the latest lies and exaggerations in circulation, and sent along their conclusions to my imaginary friend.

I wasn't permitted to name my "well-informed officials" or even my "high-level quarters," so many columns were a form of compulsory plagiarism. I could tell on my own that Vice President Quayle was not, as advertised, "the best man qualified for the job," and that President Kennedy didn't hire a talent committee before choosing his brother Bobby to be attorney general, but most of the time I had to rely on officials who knew more of the facts than I did, and were more truthful than their superiors. Many readers didn't like unattributed information, but in my experience, they either had to accept it or swallow whatever mush the administration put on their plate.

In defense of early-warning or lie-detection columns, one remembers the misleading official accounts of how the administration was winning the Vietnam War, balancing the budget by cutting taxes and doubling the Pentagon's appropriations, regulating the savings and loan institutions, and defending the security of the nation at the Watergate. The columnists were not alone and were not first in exposing these scandals, but some of them helped.

Occasionally, they helped to expose corruption inside the government. It is not easy for officials to go to their boss and accuse his department of harboring crooks or overcharging the government, but they can leak the facts to the press. Criticizing governments, however, is not always popular with the readers. When I wrote in defense of some liberal decision of the day, I was denounced by the conservatives. When I defended the conservatives, I was scalded by the liberals, and when I wrote from the right one day and from the left the next, both sides agreed that I couldn't make up my mind.

My column changed as the problems and mood of the country changed, and as I changed over the years. In the fifties, I was writing most of the time about the transition of the two political parties from isolation at home to leadership abroad. In the sixties I was preoccupied with the conflicts of the Cold War, but with the arrival of Nixon in the seventies, I dealt increasingly with the decline of integrity in the conduct of private and public affairs, not only in Washington but elsewhere in the country.

I never thought that either political party had the key to the Promised Land, but that much depended on a few simple things: maintaining trust between the president and the Congress; keeping a balance between the nation's commitments and its resources; nominating and appointing the most qualified people to the top executive positions; and seeing that they were consulted adequately before major decisions were made.

After World War II, there was a kind of anything-goes attitude in the political and commercial life of the nation, dramatized by misleading political propaganda and foreign, domestic, and personal scandals that made the moral squalor of the twenties seem almost innocent. In the conduct of the Cold War and the Persian Gulf War, the executive and legislative branches of the government often treated one another not as partners but as opponents to be overcome for advantage in the next political election.

Accordingly, I wrote much of the time, as did many other columnists, about the difference between the nation's ideals and its performance, and the rising trickery of political campaigns, but with little effect. No doubt these appeals for plain speaking and honest dealing were the result of my early teachings and my advancing years, but actually they were the oldest themes of political journalism in the United States. The pamphleteers of the eighteenth century during the struggle for independence were the first of the American columnists, and they wrote with their fists. They were constantly insisting that they were trying to create not only a secure nation but a moral nation. In fact, from Tom Paine and Ben Franklin to the abolitionists in the days of slavery, they were preaching that a nation couldn't have security without morality, and that this New Jerusalem, as they called it, depended on respect for the people and the Constitution, and even in the closing years of the twentieth century I don't think their convictions are out of date.

In the seventies, politics were dominated by salesmen who applied all the techniques of commercial advertising and television to the conduct of public policy. I thought it was the duty of the press to try to keep the record straight, but the reporters on the beat were better at this than the columnists. It was the reporters and not the columnists who exposed the official trickery in Vietnam and the Watergate. In fact, the more prominent the columnists became, the more time they spent on television and the lecture circuit and the less time they devoted to digging out the facts.

Accordingly, there was much contention, particularly during the Cold War and thereafter in the Gulf War, between the presidents and the press, between the optimists and the pessimists, and between officials who thought expediency should govern their decisions regardless of questions of morality, so I wrote a great deal on these two subjects.

### PRESIDENTS AND COLUMNISTS

Columnists like presidents—they are our favorite topic—but this sentiment isn't mutual. Presidents don't mind praise, they wallow in it, even from sources they don't like, but when we write on leadership or the lack thereof, they think we're an arrogant bunch, and they are often right. Lyndon Johnson always seemed to be singing "Nobody knows the trouble I've seen, nobody knows but Jesus." Nixon thought we were a disgrace to the First Amendment, and Reagan tolerated us only because he seldom read what we wrote.

Over the years, I changed my mind about political leadership. I started out with some romantic notions about the indispensability of "great men," probably as a result of watching Roosevelt in the depression and Churchill in the Second World War. They had succeeded, whereas Hoover and Chamberlain had waffled and failed. Also, my history books had glorified the men who had led the people instead of waiting for a safe majority. I concluded that if General Washington had waited for the doubters, he'd still be crossing the Delaware. Later, some farsighted character like Thomas Jefferson or William McKinley or Teddy Roosevelt was always buying Louisiana or building the Panama Canal, or picking up an empire in the Philippines when nobody was looking, so I was sure great men made history and not vice versa. For example, Winston Churchill, looking the wrong way, was hit by a car in New York City in December of 1931, and fourteen months later, an assassin named Zangara took a potshot at Franklin Roosevelt in Miami, Florida, but missed and killed the man next to him. Surely, as the historian Arthur Schlesinger, Jr., observed, the history of our times would have been quite different if these two men had been killed before their great achievements.

Unfortunately, the "age of the giants" also included Hitler and Stalin, who didn't wait for a safe majority, but tore the world apart on their own, so I had some second thoughts about the great man theory, partly because I didn't see many of them around Washington, and began to think that maybe they weren't even necessary. And just when I reached *that* conclusion, along came Gorbachev and liberated Eastern Europe all by himself.

One of the first things I did when I arrived in Washington in 1941 was to go to the Treasury and buy a set of the official steel engravings of all the presidents. I then treated myself to a big mahogany frame, and placed these right honorable gentlemen in regimental rows, leaving five empty spaces for presidents to come. I figured that, with luck, I might last that long, but I ran out of spaces with Nixon, and the big picture remains in my den upstairs with Ford, Carter, Reagan, and Bush on the side.

"The men upstairs," as I call them, have been my constant companions ever since. I don't have to call up to see them now. When I get up to write in the middle of the night, they look down on me from my old rolltop desk, and I look up at them with wonder and respect, sometimes with pity but usually with affection. Except for Bush, I know the end of their stories now, and see their surviving wives and children and grandchildren, and even their stories seem different. For their struggles with decisions that usually seemed half right and half wrong are over, and what remains in my mind are not so much their falterings and failures, but their yearnings and, taken together, their achievements under the hardest circumstances since the Civil War.

The ones I wrote about in my column were not remarkable men, with the possible exceptions of Roosevelt and Eisenhower, but they did some remarkable things. They were not prepared—no way could they possibly have been prepared—for the collapse of the old world order or the wars and revolutionary conflicts of science, weapons, economics, and politics that replaced it. But they also inherited from the founders a remarkably resilient political system that helped the best of them and got rid of the worst, and there wasn't a Caesar among them.

With the invention of the atom bomb and that other explosive device called television, it seemed to me that the power of the president increased substantially in the last half of the century, particularly on questions of peace and war. The nation was entangled in two protracted wars, Korea and Vietnam, and in various subversive wars, without any declaration of war by Congress, and often without even adequate consultation with congressional leaders, or explanation to the people, but usually on the decision of the president alone. For that reason, they had to be watched.

"His [the president's] is the only *national* voice in affairs," Woodrow Wilson once observed. "Let him once win the admiration and confidence of the country and no other single force can withstand him. His position takes the imagination of the country. His is the vital place of action in the system." Sometimes this authority was useful, especially in the anxious days of the great economic crash of the thirties, when Roosevelt, in his Sunday night fireside chats, explained like a reassuring uncle how we had gotten into the mess and how we were all going to pull ourselves out of the ditch. But while Roosevelt raised his voice to rescue the needy, Reagan used his power to defend the greedy.

I didn't share the fears that the modern presidents were too weak or that Congress, despite its wayward ways, was too strong. This may have been true when the isolationist impulse prevented Roosevelt from taking effective action to deal with the early aggressions of Hitler, but it seemed to me that many of our postwar follies resulted from impulsive presidential actions in Cuba, Vietnam, Latin America, Iraq, and elsewhere in the Middle East.

I didn't notice that presidents had all that much trouble getting the support of the people for essential legislation, despite our constant criticism. If it was true, as I believe, that my generation of Americans could have done more than it did to understand the tangles of foreign affairs, it was also true that the people did almost everything they were asked to do, sometimes too much. People are naturally more concerned about their private interests than about the general interest, so if a man is offered a choice between no more taxes and a swift kick in the pants, we shouldn't be surprised if he doesn't bend over. What were the people asked to do that they refused to do in the last half-century?

They were asked to restore the broken economy of Europe, and they helped bring that continent, within a decade, to the highest level of prosperity in its history, meanwhile transforming the economy and reducing the tensions between the races at home.

They were asked to accept higher taxes and military conscription after Pearl Harbor, and they not only obliged but also helped police the world from the North Cape of Norway to Japan, and from Jerusalem to Korea, and even, alas, to Vietnam.

They were asked to maintain a standing army in Europe, and they did so for forty-five years, with scarcely a word of protest from any responsible body of politicians. They did a lot of wondering and grumbling from time to time, but these were not the actions of a slack or decadent people. In fact, I know of nothing in the history of free peoples to compare with it, and all the presidents of my time, with the cooperation of both political parties, made some major contribution to the result.

Roosevelt pulled us out of the depression, assisted the Allies as best he could until Pearl Harbor, and began the organization of the United Nations. Truman ordered the first military moves against Communist expansion in Greece, Turkey, Korea, and Berlin. Eisenhower brought the Republican party into a bipartisan foreign policy, ended the Korean War, and avoided the swamp of Vietnam. Kennedy turned back the Soviet nuclear missiles from Cuba in perhaps the bravest naval action of the postwar period. Johnson, despite his disasters in Vietnam, strengthened the voting rights and the civil rights of all the people at home. Nixon ended the long diplomatic stalemate with China. Ford held the country together after the follies and scandals of Washington. Carter gave new meaning to human rights in the conduct of the nation's foreign policy. And Reagan not only rearmed the country but also made more progress toward the control of nuclear weapons than any of his predecessors.

No doubt the historians will put all these presidents into better perspective, but I'm not writing history but memoirs, and prefer to think that these achievements will be remembered long after Vietnam, Watergate, Iraq, the budget deficits, and the political corruption and financial scandals are forgotten. If any general charge is to be made against them, it will probably be not that they did too little but that they tried to do too much; not that they hesitated to use military force to defend liberty and democracy, which was the tragedy of the isolationist era, but that they used it too often and sometimes preferred to fight rather than negotiate.

In general, the most successful of them, I thought, were the cheerful optimists, who appointed competent advisers and listened to them: Roosevelt, Truman, and Eisenhower. The least successful were the pessimists, who assumed the worst in everybody and didn't listen to anybody: Nixon and Johnson. And the only trouble with this conclusion, as with most of my generalizations, was that there was always something to be said on the other side. Reagan, for example, laughed at everything, listened to everybody, and gave optimism a bad name. Kennedy, who smiled a lot and appointed many intelligent people, was basically pessimistic and even skeptical about whether the American political system would work. Carter added to my puzzles. He was probably more intelligent and he certainly worked harder than any of them, but he had no sense of humor and thought the people really wanted to hear the unvarnished facts—a dubious assumption.

Nobody, however, could accuse them of doubting the power and superiority of America or questioning its missionary mission. In this, they were following the precepts of the founders, who insisted that it was the duty of the United States to "extend our vision to all mankind." Tom Paine, in one of his many exuberant moods, declared, "My country is the world; my countrymen are all mankind." But General Washington was the first isolationist, and the people followed his doctrine from the days when it was indispensable until the twentieth century, when it became insupportable. I wrote a lot about this conflict between the desirable and the attainable, which tormented all the presidents of the last half of this century.

Despite all the tricky political propaganda, however, despite the casual way we chose our presidents and vice presidents, appointed cabinets, and made important executive decisions, I counted not on great leaders, important as they are in establishing goals for policy and models for personal conduct, but on the system of divided powers and challenging debate. Washington was, it seemed to me, a noisy playground for demagogues and extremists, but I liked the wrong-way signs and speed limits on Capitol Hill, and believed that, in the clash of debate, the moderates had triumphed most of the time.

## OPTIMISTS AND PESSIMISTS

All through my working days, public opinion seemed to me to go through long periods of excessive optimism and pessimism, and I devoted my column much of the time to appeals for moderation and hope. I worried during the Cold War debates about the constant domination of politics and the press by the pessimists, roaring about Communist military superiority, Communist subversion, imagined missile gaps in the Pentagon, and the need for civilian bunkers to guard against atomic attack. I didn't question that the Soviet Union, with its military power, its unholy trinity of envy, self-pity, and cruelty, and its messianic mission, was a serious menace to the United States and the whole free world, but as the leaders of those days now concede, the politics of fear was used, perhaps justifiably at first, to get more and more weapons out of the Congress, and the more the Pentagon got, the more the Kremlin got, and so on and so on.

In fact, I thought, and still do, that these bristling reveries about Soviet intentions and capabilities, which tended to dominate the TV and the front pages, distorted our priorities, and turned the serious but manageable East-West split into a wider unbridgeable chasm, encouraging the McCarthyite witch-hunts and creating the atmo-sphere of a religious war.

Accordingly, long before Gorbachev came to power, I tried to define the case for optimism and moderation in a speech at the University of Minnesota on February 22, 1955, when I said, "I have no doubt whatsoever about the outcome of the Cold War. No hand-ful of men in the world are smart enough to run this vast Communist empire. The thing is against human nature, and its inner contradic-tions will change it or bring it down if we are strong, vigilant, and patient. But this is a marathon and we're running it like a hundred-yard dash.

"We need to develop a philosophy about our country's place in the world today, a way of looking at the endless scare headlines. Other-wise, I fear, the constant press of events will drive us into a state of indifference, which is a menace to democratic government, or into a condition of constant anxiety, which destroys both a tolerant public opinion and private tranquillity."

This was mocked at the time by many serious and thoughtful people, and may have seemed even silly during the Vietnam War and the U.S.-Soviet confrontations over Cuba and Berlin in the sixties, so the pessimistic arguments for more and more military weapons prevailed, apparently on the assumption that if two martinis made you feel good, five would make you feel even better.

There was, I argued, great turmoil in the nation because it was finally grappling with the most fundamental questions of human life. It was struggling, probably more seriously than ever and probably more actively than any other nation on earth, with the problems of war, the contradictions of great wealth and poverty, with the selfishness of powerful factions and nations, and with the perplexities and hypocrisies of human relations in the church, the university, and the marketplace. My objection was merely that the politicians were even more pessimistic than the people, most of whom were just going on with a hope that was too deep to be lost in a generation.

Early in the eighties, when President Reagan was not satisified with the policy of containing the Soviets but talking about rolling them back, I wrote, to the hoots of the pessimists, that "we've won the Cold War and don't know it." But I never imagined the counterrevolution of 1989, and the liberation of Eastern Europe, which in many ways was the greatest triumph of hope in the twentieth century, and led in turn to false assumptions of an enduring reconciliation between Washington and Moscow.

It was received in Washington with neither excessive optimism nor pessimism but with prudent approval. There was no silly rush to disarm, as there was after World Wars I and II. Nobody knew what would happen if Moscow's experiments with limited freedom at home and cooperation abroad threatened Moscow's control over the restless nationalities within the Soviet Union, but at least it became possible to write about peaceful coexistence without the old charges of being soft on communism.

I don't believe, however, that this reduction of tension has been brought about by the optimists, but by the clash of hard and honest debate between the pessimists, who led the fight for rearmament, and the optimists, who believed in the possibility of reconciliation. It has been, I think, a triumph of the democratic habit of free discussion, and I like to think that radio and television, penetrating the Iron

Curtain with the news, and the newspapers and even the columnists have contributed something to the more hopeful world in the last decade of the century.

## EXPEDIENCY AND MORALITY

I never thought a government could be run by saints and moral philosophers, but I didn't find that the militarists and the Machiavellians were very good at it either. Public opinion was usually on the side of those who, like Mao Tse-tung of China, thought that "peace comes out of the barrel of a gun," but it seemed to me that the ideals of the United States were usually a fairly reliable guide to policy even during the Cold War. I don't mean moralistic posturing, an unfortunate pastime in Washington, but honest dealing, plain speaking, and generous thinking.

In fact, I decided Washington was most successful in the past fifty years when it acted on its better instincts in areas that were really vital to its security: reconstructing Europe after the Second World War, creating an alliance for the defense of freedom, making peace with its former enemies, and easing the tension between the races. And that it was least successful when it ventured into areas beyond its control, broke its treaty commitments, and relied on military power or subversive warfare in Vietnam, the Bay of Pigs, Iran, Iraq, Nicaragua, Panama, and the Watergate.

Kennedy didn't get into trouble by facing up bravely and openly with his own forces to the menace of Soviet missiles in Cuba, but he got in a mess when he tried to run a sneak operation at the Bay of Pigs, and his brother Bobby monkeyed around with amateur plots to assassinate Castro. Johnson lost his way in Vietnam and Nixon lost his presidency at the Watergate by following their worst rather than their best qualities, whereas Eisenhower, after considerable wavering, stuck to the simple objective of unifying the parties and the Allies, and stands higher in the nineties with the historians than he did in the fifties with the journalists.

The evidence against this view that good prevails in a wicked world was, of course, monumental. The British didn't build an empire by following the precepts of the Church of Scotland, and the American pioneers didn't expand the Union to the Pacific and on to the Philippines in accordance with the Golden Rule. Even Thomas Jefferson thought expediency sometimes had to take precedence over morality or even legality.

"A strict observance of the written laws," he said in 1810, "is doubtless ONE of the high duties of a good citizen, but it is not the HIGHEST. The laws of necessity, of self-preservation, of saving our country when in danger, are of a higher obligation. . . . To lose our country by a scrupulous adherence to written law would be to lose the law itself."

It was on this understandable ground that Roosevelt justified misleading the Congress to help the Allies before Pearl Harbor, and Truman, right or wrong, ordered the atom bombing of Hiroshima and Nagasaki. But Jefferson was talking about the gravest of all crises, when the life of the nation was clearly at stake, not about using illegal means to save the Republic from Fidel Castro in Cuba, or the Communists in Nicaragua, or Noriega in Panama, or Saddam Hussein in Iraq.

What happened under the stresses of the Cold War was that presidents of both parties sometimes applied Jefferson's life-and-death pragmatism to limited civil wars or distant uprisings, and *called* them threats to the life of the nation. They pretended they were saving the country, when much of the time they were thinking mainly of saving themselves from the consequences of their blunders. Johnson and Nixon were not the first, nor would they be the last, to fail in Washington because they were thinking about themselves rather than the country. And Reagan painted the most alarming picture of the United States being threatened by invasion from Nicaragua and defended his lawbreakers as heroes—not, however, with great success in Nicaragua.

One thing that reassured me was that the United States wasn't very good at the cloak-and-dagger business. Government by dirty tricks went against the American grain. The Congress didn't like to be ignored or deceived, the press didn't like to be lied to, and some official, outraged by the deception, was always giving the game away. No doubt many crooks succeeded, but from the days of McCarthy to the days of the bank scandals, housing scandals, and even church scandals in the eighties, I rejoiced in how many of them were caught.

Much of the confusion in the popular discussion of morality and security came, I believed, from a failure to define the two words, and from the vaporings of politicians who talked the most about morality and did the least to act on it. There were those, for example, who believed that peace could be achieved only by total military security, forgetting that no such thing had ever existed and, in any event, could be achieved only by making other nations insecure and hostile.

In writing about personal morality in relation to public policy, therefore, I meant acting decently, candidly, and honorably as best we could under difficult circumstances, rather than deceitfully or treacherously. And by referring to the security of the nation, I meant not only military security, but that wider essential security that comes from trust among the people that their government was not only defending them abroad and at home but also treating them fairly and honestly.

I was certainly not talking about Sunday-school morality, for while religion encourages restraint on deceit and human brutality, few things have been more damaging than the tendency of priggish moralizers to turn wars over material things into theological conflicts that can seldom be stopped short of annihilating the heretics. Examples were Saddam Hussein's alliance with God in the Persian Gulf War of the nineties, Chamberlain's refusal to make an alliance with "Godless" Russia against Hitler in 1939, Dulles's sermons on the importance of every human soul combined with his threats of "massive retaliation," and Reagan's characterization of the Cold War as a conflict with the evil empire of atheistic Soviets.

The great advantage of the free nations over their adversaries in the Cold War, as I saw it, did not come primarily from their military weapons, which the Soviets produced in equal if not superior numbers. It came from their ideas of individual liberty, fair play, free trade, the right of dissent, and a decent respect for the truth. It was only after the spectacular collapse of the Soviet empire at the end of the eighties that the influence and power of these ideas were recognized. But even then the principle of open dealing was often defied.

For example, when President Bush resorted to war in Panama to get rid of a two-bit dictator named Manuel Antonio Noriega, it was, as he knew, in clear violation of the nation's treaty commitments to the United Nations, where he served for years as ambassador. And the irony of it was that while Bush invaded Panama to "save American lives," he lost more than he saved, didn't know what to do with Noriega when he caught him, and even then gave himself an ultimatum to go to war by a certain date in Iraq.

No doubt the politics of sedation and duplicitous diplomacy often succeeded, but not for long. The American experiments with subversive warfare in Vietnam, Iran, Iraq, Cuba, and Central America led to death and destruction, and while Richard Nixon's trickery carried him twice to the White House, he was finally trapped by his own deceptions, disgraced, and virtually run out of the capital. The Founding Fathers believed in what they called virtuous government, and while virtue and morality were not popular subjects for columnists when I was in Washington, I found that they were more popular with the people than with most of the men in the White House.

# CHAPTER 42

## China, Israel, and Mexico

DURING THE THIRTIES and forties, the main news was in
Europe, but just when I got the map of that continent into my mind,
the headlines switched in the sixties and seventies to Asia, the Middle
East, and Latin America. Accordingly, Sally and I explored these
areas whenever we had an excuse. We went to China by accident at
the beginning of the seventies just when Henry Kissinger, then head
of Nixon's National Security Council, was on a secret mission to
restore diplomatic relations with that country. Some reporters
thought this was a shrewd bit of timing on my part, but it was merely
another instance of my dumb luck. We went there because China had
been closed to American reporters for years and much to my surprise, I had a message from the Chinese ambassador in London in
June of 1971 saying I could have a visa, and I asked for two.

At that time, the Vietnam War was declining from calamity to
disaster, or vice versa, and I wanted to know what the Chinese were
thinking about it. In the process I had more adventures than Marco
Polo. I missed Kissinger and lost my appendix in an operation by
acupuncture, but I got a couple of good stories and discovered that
China was a very big place with a lot of people.

I had some fun with Henry at the beginning of this trip, and he
had a lot of fun with me at the end. He regarded his "opening to
China" after years of Sino-American hostility as a major diplomatic
effort to weaken the Soviet-Chinese alliance, and he planned it with
gleeful cunning. After he disappeared from Washington and the
reporters noticed his absence, it was announced that he was off to
Vietnam, Thailand, and India to appraise the course of the war,
which was both true and misleading.

For when he arrived at Rawalpindi in Pakistan, it was said that the poor man had gone to bed with a "stomach ailment" when actually he had gone to Peking on a private Pakistani plane and landed at a remote airfield outside the Chinese capital. This was on July 9, 1971, and on that same day, Sally and I, knowing nothing of the above, crossed the little iron bridge from Hong Kong to the customs station at Lo Wu on the China mainland.

Upon hearing that I had proceeded to Canton and would be in Peking the following morning, Kissinger informed his hosts that the one thing he didn't want to see in China was a reporter from *The New York Times*. Accordingly, my wife and I were told that our plane to Peking was not available, and we were snookered into a little hilltop inn, spent the next day at a nearby commune, and were put on a slow train to Peking a couple days later. It arrived in the capital after Kissinger had flown back to Pakistan. That is one of the many things I always admired about Henry: he paid attention to details.

I mention this incident partly to illustrate the games officials play in their preoccupation with leaks. This one was innocent enough, and Kissinger and I often laughed together about his dodge, but most of the time officials overestimate the investigative talents of the press. Of course he had to protect the secrecy of his mission, but he didn't have to travel a couple of thousand extra miles to do so. In Peking, I didn't know anybody and nobody knew me. I couldn't even find my hotel, let alone find Henry.

Despite the loss of Kissinger, however, I did manage to see Premier Chou En-lai on that trip to China, and it came about under unexpected circumstances. While I was at the Foreign Office explaining what a boon it would be to Sino-American relations if I could have a little talk with Mao Tse-tung, an official handed me a communiqué saying that Henry had been in town and arranged for President Nixon to arrive before the month of May. I wasn't scooped, I was skewered. It was then, I think, that I felt the first stab of pain in my groin. By evening I had a temperature of 103, and in my delirium I could see Henry floating along my ceiling and grinning at me out of a hooded rickshaw. The following morning, my wife and I checked into the Anti-Imperialist Hospital under a big sign reading: THE TIME WILL NOT BE FAR OFF WHEN ALL AGGRESSORS AND THEIR RUNNING DOGS IN THE WORLD WILL BE BURIED. THERE IS CERTAINLY NO ESCAPE FOR THEM. At that moment this sounded all too true.

However, hearing that I was about to be operated on for appendicitis, Chou En-lai appeared at the hospital, anxious not to lose the first journalistic running dog since Kissinger's visit, and assured me that with the blessings of acupuncture, I would soon be well. On that assumption, I asked for the interview and he promised me it would be arranged. Meanwhile, I meditated on this acupuncture business.

I was in considerable discomfort if not pain during the second night after the removal of my appendix, and Li Chang-yuan, doctor of acupuncture at the hospital, with my approval, inserted three long, thin needles into the outer part of my right elbow and below my knees, and manipulated them in order to stimulate the intestine and relieve the pressure and distension of the stomach.

That sent ripples of pain racing through my limbs and at least had the effect of diverting my attention from the distress in my stomach. Meanwhile, Doctor Li lit two pieces of an herb called "ai," which looked like the burning stumps of a broken cheap cigar, and held them close to my abdomen while occasionally twirling the needles into action.

All this took about twenty minutes, during which I remember thinking that it was a funny way to get rid of gas on the stomach, but there was a noticeable relaxation of the pressure and distension within an hour and no recurrence of the problem thereafter. Having nothing else to report from China, I wrote a long account of this needling, which the *Times* played on the front page. This brought two messages from home.

The first was from a few of my amiable colleagues in Washington, accusing me of faking the whole illness to get behind the official Chinese Curtain. This overestimated my store of imagination, courage, and self-sacrifice, for while there were many things I was prepared to do for a good story, getting slit open in the night in China and offering myself as an experimental porcupine wasn't one of them. The other message or messages—there were quite a few of them— were rather sad, because they came from people back home suffering from various incurable illnesses, and wanting to know if acupuncture could possibly revive their hope. Sally and I did see numerous acupuncture experiments on patients suffering from paralysis, mental disorders, and even blindness, but we were mystified by all this, including the faith of the patients clinging desperately to Mao Tse-tung's *Little Red Book* of political proverbs, without the relief of painkillers.

All I knew was that everybody was kind to me. They bathed me with towels to relieve the intense heat. They checked everything I had that moved or ticked. They took blood out of the lobe of my ear. They took my temperature constantly, measured pulse and blood pressure, and worried over a cardiogram showing a slightly irregular heartbeat. I felt like a beached whale at a medical convention, but was soon able to sit up in a quiet perfumed room and ask questions about acupuncture and politics.

After a few days, I paid my bill ($27.50) and left the hospital with a feeling of relief and gratitude. Despite its name and all the bitter political slogans on the walls, it was an intensely human and vibrant institution. It was not exactly what the Rockefeller Foundation had had in mind when this vast establishment was founded as the Peking Union Medical College, but like everything else in those days, when Maoism was an infectious disease, it was on its way toward some different combination of the very old and the very new. As Sally and I left the hospital, we noticed that the "running dog" sign had been removed.

I have said elsewhere in these pages that interviews with Soviet officials were usually an unrelieved exercise in propaganda, if not an insult to human intelligence, but Chinese officials were different. Even in those days of the Cultural Revolution, while they took us to all their showplaces and babbled on about Mao's maxims, they always left time at the end of each performance for questions and even for critical observations. For example, Sally and I spent a day at Peking University, and when we were asked what we thought of it, I said that in my eyes it was not a university but a propaganda factory. They were not affronted by this candid insolence, but discussed the philosophical question calmly and politely, suggesting that, after all, our universities emphasized the glories of capitalism. When the students demonstrated for freedom in 1990, however, the government didn't hesitate to slaughter them in Tiananmen Square.

The interview with Chou En-lai, as promised, took place in the vast Fukien Room of the Great Hall of the People and lasted, including dinner, for five hours. He was an austere man, highly intelligent, with disobedient bushy eyebrows, cool and inquisitive brown eyes, and very white expressive hands. He said he was looking forward to President Nixon's visit, but added that while war was quick, peace took a long time. He was calmly critical of U.S. policy in Vietnam, and said we were trying to "make over" that country as we had tried to change China, but no such policy would work. He did not, however, dwell on the differences between our two countries, but showed great interest in the history and progress of the United States.

He praised the great men who had founded the American republic, noted that it was not Mao Tse-tung who had invented guerrilla warfare, but General Washington, and said he was pleased to hear of the progress of the blacks in the United States. He inquired about John Stewart Service and John Carter Vincent, two China experts in the U.S. Foreign Service who had been vilified by Senator Joseph McCarthy, and he was intensely interested in the fact that the English language now dominated the diplomatic and commercial intercourse of the world.

China had many problems, he conceded, of which one was overpopulation, another was Taiwan, and a third was the Soviet Union. He was remarkably curt but frank about Moscow. "We Chinese are not afraid of atomic bombs," he said. "We are prepared against their attack. That is why we are building underground tunnels, not only in Peking but all over the country."

His questions were in some ways more interesting than his answers. Looking back on the clash of arms between the U.S. and Chinese armies in Korea, he asked repeatedly why President Truman and Secretary of State Acheson had ignored his warnings at that time. He mentioned this almost casually but seemed genuinely puzzled. What he referred to was that he had repeatedly warned the United States not to move into North Korea and threaten China's border, and that on October 3, 1950, he had summoned the Indian ambassador in Peking, Sirdar K. M. Panikkar, and informed him that if the U.S. armies moved across the 38th parallel, China would enter the war in defense of its neighbor, North Korea. There would be no Chinese intervention, he told Panikkar, if the South Vietnamese crossed, but if MacArthur's troops did so, the Chinese would certainly oppose them. He had assumed, Chou En-lai added, that Panikkar would convey this message to the British and thence to Washington.

That is precisely what happened. Around five o'clock on the morning of October 3, 1950, a cable was sent from the Indian government to the State Department with instructions that it be delivered to Acheson regardless of the time of day or night. Acheson informed Truman and the Joint Chiefs of Staff, but, under pressure from MacArthur, who thought the war would be over in a month, the warnings were ignored. "Why?" the Chinese premier insisted. I said I didn't know but assumed they thought he was bluffing, which was interesting, if true, for at that time, the Soviet Union was obliged by treaty to assist China if that country were engaged in war.

Chou En-lai shook his head, and deplored the decline of "the old diplomacy." In previous years, he noted, governments knew how to convey solemn warnings to other governments while maintaining an atmosphere of calm. Before the "curse" of propaganda—I was astonished at his use of these words—statesmen had mastered the art of understatement and could send messages indirectly so as not to provoke hostility. There was, he recalled, a well-recognized code of diplomatic phrases so that if a government said it could not "remain indifferent to" such and such an action, this clearly meant that it intended to intervene. Or if it expressed "grave concern," this foreshadowed future action, without creating public excitement. But these carefully measured but serious warnings had now been discarded, he said, and even though China's decision to intervene in Korea had been worded in plain English, it had been dismissed as propaganda in Washington. I made no comment about this, but I never forgot it, even in the nineties, when President Bush gave not only the Iraqi government but also his own government an ultimatum to make peace or face war after a certain date.

After this polite remonstrance came the dinner, during which Chou En-lai stopped talking business and insisted that the tape recorders be turned off. He raised his glass repeatedly to toast the United States and all guests present, without swallowing a drop.

I asked him if he had kept a diary or journal of his revolutionary days, and indicated that the *Times* would be interested in publishing it, but he said none of the Chinese leaders had kept any personal record of these events. They were making history, he observed, not writing it. When dinner finished after midnight, and he led my wife and me to the door (which couldn't have been less than a quarter mile away), I thanked him and said I would like to come back, "But I have only one appendix to give to my country." Never mind, he said, "come back anyway."

Before leaving Peking, I discovered, or thought I did, China's solution to America's problem of overeating. Having unsuccessfully tried every slimming formula from Lenten repentance to Joe Alsop's drinking man's diet, I reached the scientific conclusion that it is impossible not to lose weight if you rely on chopsticks. I saw few fat folks in China. We were told this was because their diet staple was rice, and that they worked hard in the countryside and walked or rode bicycles in the cities. But after a few days of desperate experimentation with chopsticks, my problem was not how to lose weight but how to avoid starvation.

The food was said to be excellent and plentiful. It was tastefully served on high tables and could, in an emergency, be slid or shoveled into a business position if the victim was sitting on a low chair. But eating Chinese food properly with chopsticks, which is to say delicately and in reasonable silence, was a challenge that defied not only me but also the law of gravity.

I naturally started with the overlapping grip. This was supposed to give me good control, but in my case it seemed to put spin on the bamboo shoots. I got good distance but developed a wicked slice to the right. I then switched to the interlocking grip, without noticeable success and, in frustration, finally tried stabbing with the business end of the stick. But stabbing with these slippery utensils, I was firmly told, was cheating, so there I sat, like a blind dog in a meat house—eager, panting, and helpless.

The Chinese, of course, were as sympathetic as they had been in the hospital. Innumerable amused but compassionate waitresses, Foreign Office officials, and understanding strangers gave me lessons, and I practiced in secret with easy items like dried beef. I studied the sayings of Chairman Mao, but neither finger gymnastics nor Communist philosophy did much good.

Meanwhile, the Chinese all around Sally and me used their chopsticks with the agility of a lobster, and added a little more food to my undiminished mound. Much to my embarrassment, Sally was as dainty and nifty as usual, but my only consolation was the soup and the beer, for even when I looked around in desperation for a slice of bread I discovered that this was the only item in the whole spread that wasn't available.

Incidentally, we had almost as much trouble getting out of China as we had had getting in. We asked for Soviet visas so that we could travel by trans-Siberian railroad from Peking to Moscow, but were first told to apply for Chinese exit permits. There we were told to apply at the Soviet mission for Soviet visas in Hong Kong. In Hong Kong we were instructed to apply at the Soviet Embassy in Tokyo, but when we got there, we were refused again. However, said a Soviet official with two steel front teeth, since we were going to London via British Airways, and the plane stopped in Moscow, no doubt we would be permitted to get off there. This we were able to do, but only to get into the airport, and later it was explained to me that since the foreign ministry didn't like my interview with Chou En-lai, as published in the *Times,* it would be "inconvenient" for officials to receive me in Moscow.

## ISRAEL AND THE DOMINION OF FEAR

We must not imagine that all is well if our armaments
make the enemy afraid; for it is possible that it is fear
more than anything else that is the cause of war.

—Herbert Butterfield

Wherever we wandered in the troubled areas of the world, we
found that fear, while often justified, also contributed to excessive
tension and even to wars that might have been avoided. Extravagant
fear undoubtedly led to the two disastrous world wars that were
really a civil war within Western civilization; fear was at the root of
the Cold War, and of Japan's mad lunge at Pearl Harbor, and of the
enduring Indian-Pakistani conflicts, the Holy War in Iraq, the terrorist war in Ireland, and the racial wars in South Africa. But nowhere was the dominion of fear more evident than in the wars
between Israel and the Arab states, where Israel's arms prevailed but
brought no peace.

Israel's few millions of Jewish survivors were no threat to the
so-called Arab nation, and certainly their religious faith was no
threat to Islam—it was even a declining force among the Jews—but
the Arabs threatened Israel's destruction and helped create a military state in Jerusalem that the Arabs couldn't tolerate or defeat.

I discovered that it was not easy to cover this ironic tragedy of
wars over holy places without arousing even fear of the truth. In my
experience, there were two sure ways of my getting into trouble: one
way was to write about Israel, and the other was not to write about
it. If I praised it, which I did most of the time, I was denounced by
the Arabs; if I criticized it, I was condemned by many Jews; and if
I ignored it, I was accused by my colleagues of ducking my responsibilities.

It was one of my duties in Washington to report on the U.S.
government's policy toward the Middle East conflict. It was obvious
in doing so that U.S. interests were not always identical with Israeli
interests, but most efforts to point out the differences were inevitably
followed by a torrent of abuse from the supporters of Israel. This was
unpleasant but unavoidable. For I believed that a principle clearly
stated in President Washington's Farewell Address was as valid for
the United States at the end of the twentieth century as it had been
at the beginning of the Republic.

He warned that it was a mistake for the United States to hold a passionate and permanent attachment or hatred toward another country. "The nation," he said, "which indulges toward another an habitual hatred or an habitual fondness is in some degree a slave. It is a slave to its animosity or to its affection, either of which is sufficient to lead it astray from its duty and its interest."

It was easy to support Israel when it was fighting for its life, even when it resorted to preventive war, but at other times it seemed to me that the Israeli politicians would rather fight than think, and that they were often unfaithful to the spirit of Jerusalem, which they claimed as their capital, and to the principles of democracy they claimed to represent at home. My personal fear was that their fears of the past might keep them from taking advantage of the changing nature of world politics.

One of the advantages of living for a long time, however, is that you learn from experience that many problems that once seemed unmanageable somehow yield to patience and common sense. Dictators, whether in Germany or Russia, Iraq or Syria, have a great talent for making fatal mistakes, and ordinary people don't tolerate the mismanagement of their affairs forever. In fact, so many of the "hopeless" conflicts in my own lifetime were solved or at least diminished—the division of Europe for example—that I came to believe in miracles, even in the possibility of peace in the holy places.

My fear for many years was that this tragedy in the Middle East had gone on for so long that it was accepted by many as a way of life—inevitable, interminable, and insoluble—but in the rapidly changing world of the nineties, I could not believe, despite Saddam Hussein's madness in Iraq, that the coming generation of Israel and the Arab states would continue the deadlock as before, or that the children of Israel, now on the West Bank and the Gaza Strip, would always deny to the Palestinians the same self-determination sought by the founders of Israel.

I had no such hopeful reflections so long as the United States feared that the Soviet Union was determined to dominate the oil in that strategic hinge of the continents, but when these two nuclear giants began working together to end rather than to provoke regional conflicts, my nightmares changed to brighter dreams. For example, the Soviet Union could have vetoed the U.S. resolution in the United Nations to oppose the aggression of Iraq in Kuwait, and though Israel didn't like Moscow's efforts to settle that dispute without war, it benefited from the Soviet Union's original decision to condemn Iraq. Much, of course, would depend on whether Moscow continued a policy of cooperation or reverted to the imperialism of the Cold War days, but I couldn't believe that even the Soviets would be that stupid, or that the United States and the Soviet Union, while reducing their own Cold War tensions and military budgets, would continue to pour expensive modern weapons into the Middle East at past levels. Nor could I believe that the old warriors in Israel, who had been invaluable in the thirties and were intolerable in the eighties, would prevent their children from taking a less fearful view of the changing world. In fact I even dared hope that one day Yasser Arafat, the PLO tyrant, would get a shave.

I assumed that the Israelis would feel safer after they had U.S. Patriot missiles that could defend the state from the modern missiles of their enemies. I also felt confident that they could deal with a few hundred Palestinians throwing stones on the West Bank and the Gaza Strip. But what would they do if the Arabs, always favored by geography and fertility, gathered by the hundreds of thousands in Tel Aviv, like the dissidents in Eastern Europe, to demand self-determination and a Palestinian state?

My thought was not that the Israelis would lose a clash of organized armies, but that if they went on as before they would lose the clash of ideas and their support in the world, and eventually be overwhelmed by the multitudes of the Arab peoples. In short, I did not believe in the continuing superiority of Israel's military power, but I believed in their intelligence and in their remarkable capacity for self-preservation. I have to admit, however, that I had been wrong about them many times before.

I followed their struggles and yearnings for many years. One of my first assignments in Washington and at the United Nations in the 1940s was covering the movement to establish a homeland for the Jews in Palestine. President Truman was for it, but Dean Acheson, under secretary of state, Secretary of State George Marshall, and most of the State Department's Middle East experts had serious doubts. I had long talks with Acheson about this in 1945. He shared the president's concern for the homeless Jews displaced by Hitler, but feared that building a Jewish state in Palestine would create great instability in the region and imperil U.S. and other Western interests. He even talked to me about the possibility of establishing a refuge for the Jews in Brazil. He remarked in his memoirs:

"From Justice Brandeis, whom I revered, and from Felix Frankfurter, my intimate friend, I had learned to understand, but not to share, the mystical emotion of the Jews to return to Palestine and end the Diaspora. In urging Zionism as an American government policy they had allowed, so I thought, their emotion to obscure the totality of American interests. Zionism was the only topic that Felix and I had by mutual consent excluded from our far-reaching talks." Acheson was not so inhibited in his discussion of this subject with me. He referred to it repeatedly, often in brutal terms, and his influence on Truman was so strong that I was inclined to believe that his views would prevail.

I overestimated Acheson's influence, however, and underestimated Truman's determination. The president was deeply moved by the catastrophe of the Holocaust, and impressed by the appeals of his close friend and former business partner, Eddie Jacobson, a Zionist from Kansas City, and in the end the British, needing U.S. help on many other problems of their own, finally but reluctantly agreed with Truman. Accordingly, the state of Israel was finally proclaimed on May 14, 1948. On the same day, it was recognized by the United States and invaded unsuccessfully by the armed forces of Egypt, Lebanon, Syria, Jordan, and Iraq.

Since then, Israel has won three wars against the rejectionist Arab states. I admire its bravery. A nation has to save its life before deciding what to do with it, but, as of this writing, it has been in a state of war for forty-three years and, like the Arab states, it approaches President Bush's promise of a new world order with many of the same policies that have eluded peace in the past.

I was in Israel during the Six-Day War of 1967, the cause of all the Arab-Israeli disputes over territory ever since. On the way there, I stopped in Cairo and spent a day with Mohammed Hassanein Heikel, the editor in chief of *Al-Ahram,* and an intimate adviser to President Nasser. He spoke fatalistically about the coming war. Egypt didn't want war, he said, but the United States was using Israel as "a base of Western culture and military power, and that is intolerable." He understood the longing of the Jews for a homeland, he added, and he also understood the sympathy of the Western world for the suffering of the Jews, but, he reminded me, the Holocaust was committed not by the Arabs but by the Nazis.

He was obsessed by fear. He spoke of the Jews in Israel as "a foreign substance," as a "wedge" separating the Arabs in the west from the Arabs in the east, as a "barrier" to the unity of the Arab nation, and though the Israelis had won the last war and might win again, he concluded, the Jews in Israel would always be surrounded and rejected unless they abandoned their "Western beliefs in the dominion of power."

I took the last commercial plane into Tel Aviv, and by the time we landed the war had started. I drove at once to Jerusalem, seeing it for the first time, and hearing at once fear of a violent Soviet reaction, and the much more justified fear that unless the enemy air power could be destroyed within the first few hours, Israel might be overrun by the combined forces of its enemies. There was, however, no lack of courage in the barracks among the soldiers, as I reported in the *Times* after the first day of the fighting.

They went to war, I wrote, with remarkable calm and élan. Other modern armies, once they gave up marching and took to the trucks, also gave up singing, but not the Israelis. This was a singing army, not polished but rumpled, as if it had been in battle for months, not all young but all mixed up, with the young and the middle-aged waving to the youngsters at the side of the road and singing like Hemingway's heroes at the start of the Spanish Civil War. By evening, civilians were making a long detour downhill through the stony valleys over a one-lane road to Tel Aviv, and by the time we got there the city had changed.

The Hilton, normally brighter than Times Square on a Saturday night, was as dark as a coal mine even before the air raid sirens sounded. The streets were empty, and running copy to the telegraph office was an obstacle race, with perky instant commanders at every corner. Thus in a single day all the symbols of a country at war were in place: the wildly contradictory and uncheckable official reports from the different warring capitals; the charges of aggression and claims of victory on both sides; the censors eliminating facts the enemy obviously knew—all so reminiscent of past wars but with one saving grace, the thoughtfulness of simple people caught in a common predicament.

By the middle of the week, it was clear that Israel had swept the skies of enemy planes and the war would soon be over, but fear remained. The battle over what to do with the captured land was just beginning, and in the middle of the week, General Moshe Dayan, the new defense minister and instant hero of the war, was saying in Jerusalem, "We have returned to this most sacred shrine of shrines, never to part with Jerusalem again."

But by the end of the week, Israeli officials were expressing anxiety about the reaction in the other capitals of the world that regard

Jerusalem as something above the sovereignty of any nation. What would the United States think about the new and enlarged Israeli borders? What Israel wanted then was a U.S. political and military guarantee of the security and integrity of the nation.

"We realize," one official told me, "that you do not give foolproof guarantees except to nations where you are obliged to put your own men and do most of the fighting, but even so, with such a guarantee from the United States, all questions [of territory] would be negotiable."

I thought then, and continued to write much later on, that such a guarantee, not of the expanded borders but of adjusted borders, might have produced a negotiated settlement, and I never thought it was fair for the United States to press Israel to trade land for peace unless we were prepared to back them if they gave up the land and then did not get peace but war. Yet the United States never took that risk, and even Israel preferred vague promises of U.S. aid that would not limit its ability to take whatever military action it liked, even to wage "preventive war" if it chose.

Fear of Soviet intervention, fear of being abandoned by the United States in a crisis, even fear of a U.S.-Soviet agreement to force a settlement at Israel's expense have in all the ensuing years never been entirely absent from the Israeli mind and the nation has lived as a garrison state ever since, often following brutal policies in defiance of its spiritual heritage, and building a nuclear arsenal Washington ignored.

During this long period, my responsibilities lay primarily in Washington, and I reported and commented on it primarily from the American point of view, not always with excessive admiration. It seemed to me that the United States had one clear and vital interest in that part of the world and that was to prevent the Near and Middle East from being dominated by the Soviet Union, and that in turn meant (1) reducing or ending U.S. reliance on the oil of the Arab nations, and (2) making clear that the United States would not tolerate the destruction of the state of Israel, and that could be done, I believed, only by a clear guarantee that the United States would not tolerate the destruction of Israel.

No U.S. government in these past fifty years has dealt effectively with the oil problem, but has kept selling vast quantities of military arms to the Arab states in exchange for their oil, even sending to Saddam Hussein in Iraq weapons that were used against the U.S. expeditionary force in the Gulf War of 1991. This thoughtless export of American arms had happened before. For example, during the Nixon administration, we sold $1.28 billion of arms to Iran between 1969 and 1973, and an additional $11 billion between 1973 and 1976, while saying that neither the Soviets nor the Israelis should worry about this. This did not diminish the dominion of fear, and one could imagine what we would have said if Moscow had made similar shipments to Mexico.

Every time Sally and I went back to Jerusalem or other Middle Eastern capitals, we heard the same litany of complaints, the same fear of unacceptable demands on both sides, the same opposition to compromise. In February of 1970, I interviewed Premier Golda Meir at her little house in Tel Aviv and found her irresistibly appealing and intelligent, but she was saying that Moscow was the cause of all her fears, and she was contemptuous of President Gamal Abdel Nasser of Egypt.

"So he's humiliated and frustrated," she said. "Well, what's he frustrated about? Because he tried to throw us into the sea and didn't succeed? So I must have sympathy with him for his frustration? Are we supposed to sit on the canal and take his shelling?"

She complained that Nasser was getting more modern weapons from the Soviet Union than Israel was getting from the United States, but conceded that Israeli planes were ranging over Egypt without serious opposition from Nasser's Soviet MiGs. She rejected the concept of a Palestinian state next to Israeli territory. When I asked her what would happen if Nasser fell, she replied that his successor "couldn't be worse."

As I left her, she took me out to the gate of her modest house and spoke almost in despair of any resolution of the conflict. "The hardest thing for me," she remarked, "is when a young man and wife come to this gate and ask me what lies ahead for a Jewish family in Israel—could they risk having children?—and I have no answer."

I went away to Cairo and interviewed Nasser, who depressed me even more. In fact, I wondered about the wisdom of these interviews, for the Egyptian president had read an account of my Meir interview in the *Times* and clearly resented her personal remarks about his "failures." He said he was trying to get new MiG-23 fighters from Moscow, and more technical aid (but not Soviet pilots) and added that if Washington countered this by giving more Phantom aircraft to Israel, the United States would lose its economic relations with the Arab world within two years.

He could not accept, he said, giving Israel "one inch" of Arab territory; he wanted peace but peace meant complete evacuation of the Israeli-occupied territories, including Jerusalem, a solution of the Palestinian refugee problem, and the creation of a nonfanatical multireligious Israeli state. He died soon thereafter and was replaced by Anwar Sadat, who talked more hopefully when I interviewed him in Cairo at the end of 1970, and seemed to change the basis for negotiation by going to Israel and later to Washington in 1978 to see President Carter and Prime Minister Menachem Begin of Israel.

I began then to believe in the possibility of a compromise settlement when these three men got together at Camp David. President Sadat had made a difference by going to Israel and President Carter made a difference by approaching the political problem from a philosophical and even a religious point of view.

He proposed that they concentrate on their ultimate objectives rather than their immediate differences; on the end of the road rather than on the roadblocks; on the things that united them rather than the things that divided them; and then work backward from the goal to the barriers. This was typical of the the missionary Carter, and he turned their meeting at the White House into a revival meeting.

That was a great day for plowshares and pruning hooks. Not since William Jennings Bryan had there been such a torrent of rhetoric about church and state, faith and politics. Carter, Begin, and Sadat clearly differed on the terms of the Egyptian-Israeli peace treaty they had signed. But they agreed on the tragedy of human life, and came together in the hope that their own doubts and the nightmare predictions of their political opponents were wrong, and that by some kind of confidence in one another and by some undefined religious belief, they might produce a compromise and avoid another war.

In the afternoon ceremony on the White House lawn, Mr. Carter quoted from the Koran: "But if the enemy inclines toward peace, do thou also incline toward peace? And trust in God." We pray, he added, that these dreams will come true. Mr. Sadat praised Mr. Carter as a man of faith and compassion who was "armed with the blessing of God." And Prime Minister Begin recited the soaring words of Psalm 126: "They that sow in tears shall reap in joy."

All this, I said at the time, put quite a burden on God, who must by that time have grown weary of the Middle East, and when this remarkable experiment in moral diplomacy was all over, the great expectations were disappointed, and there were more tears than joy.

.   .   .

By the beginning of the nineties, however, I did not believe that this deadlock could continue in the face of so many fundamental changes elsewhere in the world. If the Soviet Union would not intervene in Eastern Europe to save its empire, what would justify the fear that it would intervene in Israel? With Moscow and Washington beginning to cooperate in the settlement of regional disputes, why would they remain at odds in the Middle East? This question was answered when Presidents Bush and Gorbachev cooperated to reverse Iraq's invasion and annexation of Kuwait, but before long, the United States was at war with a half-million soldiers in the battle.

All this transition of economic and political power would no doubt take a lot of time, I thought. I was not confident that Yasser Arafat would change his mind, but I felt sure that the old Israeli warriors, who had been so necessary for a time, were not immortal and that Israel couldn't live forever in a state of war. I was never able to forget something Mrs. Meir said to me in that talk at her house in Tel Aviv: she was afraid not only of Soviet intervention, but also of what was happening to the people of Israel under the tension of endless war. "Twice before," she recalled, "we had sovereignty. Twice before we were occupied by foreigners. When we were occupied, we were never allowed to remain on the land but were dispersed, and though our people roamed around the world for two thousand years, somehow they had the faith and the tenacity to come back."

But if the Jews were dispersed again, she wondered, would they have the reservoir of religion, of culture, of the deep Jewish life to come back once more? "I have to tell you," she said, "that has gone. And I would not be honest if I told you that I have no doubts as to whether if we were dispersed again and our sovereignty destroyed, it would ever be restored again, because that reservoir of undiluted Jewishness has been destroyed."

"Peace cannot be kept by force," Albert Einstein said. "It can only be achieved by understanding." At the beginning of the Second World War, Roosevelt and Churchill made "freedom from fear" one of their major objectives, and as the tensions of the world diminish at least for a time in the nineties, it is my hope and belief that Jerusalem, the holy city, will become once more a symbol not of strife and fear, but of reconciliation and peace.

## MEXICO: OUR NEGLECTED NEIGHBOR

We acquired in our wanderings a special interest in Mexico, our yearning and struggling neighbor to the south. Sally went there alone in 1943, when I was working at the U.S. Embassy in London during the war, and we went back together every few years thereafter. Every time it seemed more interesting and disturbing. Everything threatened it—the sun-baked stony land, overpopulation, unemployment, inflation, debt, and corruption—but nothing conquered it. It worked and in many ways it prospered, but it never seemed to catch up with its human burdens.

For over forty years, I wondered about its children, full of innocence and fire—children producing more children. My dream was that one day Mexico would grow up, and my nightmare was that one night it might blow up, with alarming consequences for the whole hemisphere. However, by some combination of perseverance, political manipulation, religious faith, and a backdoor escape hatch to the United States, it managed after the revolution of 1920 to avoid the violence that tormented most other Latin American countries in the last half of the century.

It tolerated one-party government for sixty years, but its economic growth and political stability were more impressive than that of any other major country below the Rio Grande. In the forties and fifties, it increased agricultural production by 223 percent, devoted 21 percent of its budget to education, and wiped out malaria, which had killed twenty thousand people a year. But the paradox of this was that while it tried so hard and made so much progress, it never got off the treadmill of debt, unemployment, and overpopulation. Even when it struck oil in the south, the earnings from this bonanza were not quite enough to service the interest on its national debt.

I went to Mexico City for the first time in 1944 to cover the preliminary negotiations that led to the formation of the United Nations. The population was then just under 20 million. I went back a generation later, and the population had more than doubled. In the sixties, I spent a few days with President Echeverría of Mexico and Fidel Castro in Cuba, and on the flight back to Mexico City, I suggested to Echeverría that the population of his country would, at present rates of growth, be 100 million by the end of the century. "Oh, no," he replied, "by the end of the century it will probably be over 125 million!" I have worried about these statistics ever since.

So have many officials in Washington. Roosevelt had his Good

Neighbor policy and Kennedy his Alliance for Progress, but even they never imagined that by the 1990s the United States would have lost control of its southern border and would be dealing with millions of illegal Mexican aliens. Even the Justice Department doesn't know how many millions.

This may provide one clue to Mexico's survival without violence. For Washington has tried to keep illegal Mexican aliens out of the United States, and if this policy had been effective, the pressure on the most resourceful and rebellious of the Mexican people, without an escape hatch, might have been intolerable. This is the only case in my experience where the failure of a U.S. foreign policy has contributed to peace.

I went back to Mexico every few years after World War II, and interviewed every president there in the process, but never lost either my dream or my nightmare. Always the goodwill of the United States government was obvious, but I wondered whether Washington gave "the Mexican problem" the priority it deserved.

"If we really had a Communist problem," President de la Madrid said to me one day in Mexico City, "maybe Washington would pay more attention, but we had our revolution and our problem is not political or military but economic." As usual, I brought up the population question. The rate of growth, he said, had dropped from 3.5 percent to just below 3 percent in the eighties, but the outlook was still for more than 100 million people by the year 2000. I mentioned that in India, the government had reduced the birthrate by introducing electric lights and television in the villages. I asked him if this would help in Mexico. "I'm afraid not," he replied, "the commercials are too long!"

History is also a problem. Even in the nineties, Mexican children are still taught that the present boundaries of the United States were achieved by war at Mexico's expense. None of the Mexican presidents blamed Washington for Mexico's problems. All conceded that U.S. loans and tourism eased their economic difficulties, but they obviously thought Washington could do more, considering what it had taken from Mexico in the past.

Maybe Washington would if the press, radio, and television in the United States paid more attention to this ticking bomb in the south. Mexico, I wrote for years, was probably the most important and neglected area of the underdeveloped journalistic world, and "the American people would do anything for it but read about it." This is not as true in the nineties as it was in the forties or fifties, but we have written more about Afghanistan, Nicaragua, Panama, and Iraq in recent years than about Mexico. No shooting, no communism, no news! President McKinley fought what was called "a splendid little war" with Spain over Cuba and picked up the Philippines for $20 million on the side. But while this began the imperial chapter in our history, the thing was done, like President Kennedy's adventure at the Bay of Pigs and President Reagan's proxy war in Nicaragua, without much thought about the consequences.

Mexican officials are invariably courteous in their talks with U.S. reporters, always saying relations with Washington are improving, but usually their private doubts come out. President Echeverría insisted that the alternative to war in the world was a new social and economic charter between the industrial and the underdeveloped nations. He had proposed such a charter at the United Nations, he recalled, and it had had the support of 120 nations, but the United States had opposed it. "I believe," he said, "that conditions exist in the American continent that would permit the transnational corporations, for example, with their large production and scientific research capacity, to cooperate in the development of our countries in terms of mutual and equitable convenience, but this requires a change of mentality."

Nothing in my time has changed the resentment in Mexico against U.S. military policy in Latin America. President Adolfo López Mateos told me he even blamed the United States for its "clumsy handling of Cuba." Castro, he said, was in deep economic trouble after replacing Batista. He was, said the Mexican president, like a drowning man in a pool who sought help from the American side, but the United States "stepped on his fingers." There was also a time, he added, when the Cuban revolution could have been saved without communism, but when Mexico, Brazil, and Canada tried to mediate, the Eisenhower administration refused to cooperate.

Even in the eighties, President de la Madrid was repeating many of the arguments of his predecessors. He deplored the expenditure of $930 billion a year by all the nations on military arms while half the human race was going to bed hungry every night. The industrialized countries, he said, cannot live in security in such a world, and military intervention is no answer to the problem. He condemned the Reagan administration's military intervention in Nicaragua. "We cannot accept the United States as the supreme judge of our political systems, to say who is good and who is bad."

His successor, Carlos Salinas de Gortari, said much the same thing when I interviewed him in Tabasco. "I think governments should not interfere in the affairs of other governments. I don't find it acceptable to fund a rebel movement in a country with which you have diplomatic relations. I believe the Central American governments have the capacity to solve their own problems through political means and not with foreign means." He quoted an old Marxist maxim: "Mexico is too far away from God and too close to the United States."

The Mexicans, of course, don't say they can handle their economic problems without U.S. help, and their sleeping grievances, justified or not, don't vanish just because we neglect them. I mention them because, with tensions between the nuclear powers decreasing, the attitudes and problems of the underdeveloped nations are likely to take priority as the expenditure on arms decreases.

Fortunately, the improved relations between the United States and the Soviet Union has opened up new prospects for relieving the suffering of the underdeveloped nations. So long as they were in debt themselves with vast military budgets, their aid to these countries had to be limited. President Eisenhower, over and over again, proposed to the leaders in Moscow that both the nuclear powers make substantial cuts on military expenditures and transfer the savings, or at least a large part of them, to assist the poor countries of Latin America, Africa, and Asia, and with the ending of the Cold War, this suggestion, always rejected by Moscow, has become a practical possibility.

However, this requires not only the change of attitude Echeverría and de la Madrid spoke about, but also means the transformation of the American economy from military to civilian production, and the abandonment of the practice of minimizing problems until they become violent and intolerable. The Great Depression, the wars of the century, and more recently the troubles in Central America illustrate the point. All the warning signs were ignored or minimized until they became unbearable.

Maybe my dream about Mexico will come true, for in the nineties President Bush is talking again about a free market with Mexico, but a nation can endure Mexico's birthrate, 40 percent unemployment, 100 percent inflation, and staggering debt for only so long without an eruption. The problem illegal aliens pose for the United States is how to help create conditions that will enable them to make a living at home. Whenever I go to Mexico, I see lush pastures of green in the vast expanses of brown earth. The prospect of expanding the fertile growth by the use of atomic energy to desalinate the bordering Mexican sea water, and of increasing production by U.S. companies in Mexico, as in Korea, Taiwan, and elsewhere, is fairly obvious. But this is not likely to be done until Mexico's possibilities and dangers are viewed in Washington as a top priority.

# PART FOURTEEN

## THE SEVENTIES

# CHAPTER 43

# The Man Who
# Trusted Nobody

Radical insincerity was regarded in the post-war years as
the only practical politics. The effects were devastating.
The public man himself became so preoccupied with
maintaining his public personality that he tended to lose
what personality and what personal conviction he may
have had. He became so interested in the "reaction" to
what he was doing that he lost sight of what he was
doing.

—Walter Lippmann

I THOUGHT OF Nixon and the 1970s as a tale of petty betrayals
and massive deceit, and also as the great testing time of American
democracy. I was by then in my sixties and I had seen a lot of
political deception in Washington, but the corruption of the seventies
was different. For it was clear then that we were dealing not with the
normal personal duplicity of politicians, but with calculated efforts
at the very top of the government to corrupt the political system
itself—that is to say, to deceive the Congress, the press, and the
people, and to evade the safeguards of the Constitution.

The personal hanky-panky of money and ambition were common
throughout my other decades in the capital, but no threat to the
government's integrity. Even the trickeries of subversive warfare in
the fifties and sixties had been accepted as distasteful but essential to
deal with Communist conspiracies abroad, but now these same tactics
of subversion and manipulation were being applied at home against

the critics of the Vietnam War. By the end of 1970 that war had taken the lives of over forty-four thousand Americans.

Sally and I went to Capitol Hill to listen to President Nixon's inaugural address in January of 1973 and were reassured. "The greatest honor history can bestow [on a president]," he said, "is the title of peacemaker. We find ourselves rich in goods but ragged in spirit; reaching with magnificent precision for the moon, but falling into raucous discord on earth. . . . We are torn by division, wanting unity. We see around us empty lives wanting fulfillment. We see tasks that need doing, waiting for hands to do them. To a crisis of the spirit we need an answer of the spirit. . . . We cannot learn from one another until we stop shouting at one another. . . . For its part, the government will listen."

Now, we thought, his better instincts had been restored by his reelection, and he began pulling troops out of Vietnam and ending the long separation from China. But before long he was giving orders to invade the neutral state of Cambodia, increasing the bombing raids on North Vietnam, compiling a list of his enemies in the press, tapping the telephones of reporters and even of members of his own staff, taping the conversations of his visitors in the White House without their knowledge, and finally losing his presidency after the burglary of Democratic party headquarters at the Watergate.

The significance of the seventies, however, was not that Nixon destroyed the political system but that it destroyed him, not that he fooled the people but that the people turned against him and forced the end of the carnage in Vietnam. I never did figure out how a man with so much intelligence and experience could be so deprived of judgment or even common sense, but I discovered that he was a stranger even to his closest associates.

The real cover-up of the Nixon seventies was not Watergate but President Nixon himself. He even covered up his good qualities, which were many. He was thoughtful and industrious. He had a shrewd concept of world affairs, and finally learned how to compromise with China and cut his losses in Vietnam. But he trusted nobody and lost the trust of everybody. I thought his greatest weakness was that he tried to govern the country, as he had won the election, by deception and manipulation. He lived a life of pretense, faking a personal confidence and security he didn't have, manufacturing his place in history with tape recordings he didn't need, and destroying an otherwise competent presidency in the process. He wasn't the first president and unfortunately he wasn't the last to concentrate on the appearance of things rather than the reality of things, but he was more vulnerable than the others and had to quit before he was fired.

Over the years, I followed him through his various phases, good and bad. Unlike Ronald Reagan, he was a poor actor, and always seemed false in whatever role he was playing. He knew that freedom in the world depended on the leadership of the United States, but he thought leadership was a conspiracy, and couldn't even lead himself. He was a sensitive man, personally shy and even generous, but he hid these appealing qualities behind a mucker pose of profanity and vulgarity. He was called Tricky Dick, and few would say he didn't earn the name.

I saw the young Richard Nixon, and the new Nixon, and the old Nixon, but I don't think any reporter ever saw the real Nixon. He always gave the impression that he was hiding something, some insecurity or fear that he would be found unequal to the job. It was not a wholly unjustified anxiety. He inherited some good instincts from his Quaker forebears but by diligent hard work he overcame them. By the time he rose to prominence in Washington he had assumed the guise of a bold and self-confident battler against the Communists. Unlike Eisenhower, his running mate for eight years, he didn't unite people but divided them. He blamed the "procommunist" Democrats for the wars in Korea and Vietnam, and with this appeal to fear of Soviet expansion and subversion, he was elected president twice, which said more for the indifference of the people than for their judgment.

At least, that's the way I saw him. He was no handsome young Lochinvar like Kennedy or movie star like Reagan. He had a scowling face and a fidgety smile. Kennedy beat him, mainly on television, by only 118,000 votes in the 1960 election. He lost the race for the governorship of California in 1962 and promised his wife he would never run again. "You won't have Dick Nixon to kick around anymore," he told the reporters. But he was a political addict, persistent and clever, and as usual he didn't keep his promise.

I often thought of him as Joe McCarthy's revenge. He tidied up McCarthy's tactics but retained many of Joe's vicious themes, exploited the fear of Communist military power, and overcame the doubts of his party and the criticism of the press. He was fascinated by the new instruments of communication that could sell things at more than their worth, and the irony of it was that he was brought down in the end by television, and by tape-recording the evidence of his own administration's blunders.

There were other ironies. When he finally captured the White House, he preserved in office many of the opposition policies he had denounced to get there. For example, he had condemned Truman as an appeaser for abandoning the Chinese Nationalists and losing China, and then announced as a triumph his decision to restore normal U.S. diplomatic relations with Mao Tse-tung and Red China. But there was intelligent pragmatism behind this switch and it didn't bother him. "I didn't change," he explained. "The world changed."

Likewise, once in the White House, he increased the presidential power he promised to reduce, and even dramatized "the imperial presidency" he had condemned by dressing up White House servants like musical comedy palace guards until this produced laughter and mockery, two things he couldn't bear. He was painfully self-conscious, always looking at himself and his policies in the mirror of the press, seldom liking what he saw, and often imagining slights that weren't intended.

When President Eisenhower suffered a heart attack at the end of his first term, I criticized Ike's chief of staff, Sherman Adams, for pushing Nixon aside during the president's convalesence, but Nixon insisted that the eastern press was invariably hostile to him. This was odd, for almost every head of the Washington newspaper bureaus of his time was a conservative. During the honeymoon period, when an aide observed that the press was supporting him 90 percent of the time, he remarked, "But, oh, that other ten percent!"

He wasn't of course, the first president to be apoplectic about the press, but he was the most clumsy. He wasn't the first president to crusade against communism either, but he was so successful at it that it became standard Republican strategy for a generation.

Tricky tactics became common for a very simple reason: they worked. The voters didn't like Communists and they weren't very hot on reporters either, so Nixon bashed both. Truman and Acheson had persuaded the Congress to restore and defend Europe by anti-communist appeals, and after Nixon applied this theme to domestic politics, the Republicans won four out of five presidential elections. Nixon's mistake was that he expanded this policy to extremes in Southeast Asia, in the belief that bombing North Vietnam in what I called at the time "war by tantrum" would bring peace.

Unable to stop the infiltration of Communist guerrillas in Vietnam, he pushed the war into Cambodia, a neutral country, and tried to conceal this adventure from the Congress and the public. It was not the unavoidable battles of policy and politics that led to his downfall but his avoidable stupidities. His fight with *The New York Times* over publication of the Pentagon Papers was another case in point. These papers were merely a study of the mistakes that had led, years before the Nixon administration, to the war in Vietnam. But he insisted that they were a threat to national security and a boon to the Communists, and pursued the issue all the way to the Supreme Court, where he lost.

On June 15, 1971, he sent this memorandum to his chief of staff, Bob Haldeman:

In view of *The New York Times'* irresponsibility and recklessness in deliberately printing classified documents without regard to the national interest, I have decided that we must take action within the White House to deal with the problem. Until further notice, under no circumstances is anyone connected with the White House to give any interview to a member of the staff of *The New York Times* without my express permission. I want you to enforce this without, of course, showing them this memorandum. I want you particularly to bring this to the attention of Kissinger, Peterson, Rumsfeld, Finch, Safire, Ehrlichman, Ziegler, Klein, and anyone else on the White House staff who might be approached by *The New York Times* for information or for a special story.

Under absolutely no circumstances is anyone on the White House staff on ANY SUBJECT to respond to an inquiry from *The New York Times* unless and until I give express permission (and I do not expect to give such permission in the foreseeable future). This is a delicate matter for you to handle, and all the orders, of course, must be given orally. It is vital, however, that there be absolutely no deviations within the White House staff because if there is the message will not get through. I realize that you will have a number of objections raised that we are hurting ourselves by this policy. However, I have made the decision because of the national interest and the decision is not subject to appeal or further discussion unless I bring it up myself.

He had a persecution mania and saw himself as the victim of unfair criticism, ingratitude, and even treachery. He entertained all sorts of comfortable falsehoods about himself and others, and thus had to endure endless self-imposed tortures. When he moved into the White House, he had a large table put by his bedside to accommodate two tape recorders and he dictated into these night and day, a constant stream of observations, orders, and suggestions. Every day he received a detailed report of what was said in the press and on the television, and each morning his staff was under orders to analyze and prepare answers to any criticism. After his resignation, these were made available against his wishes by the courts. They revealed not a self-confident president but an anxious character, full of self-doubts and self-promotion.

He organized outside the White House a team of private political supporters to write letters to the papers and television stations defending or praising his actions. He referred to himself in his memoranda as "R.N.," who wants this or demands that. One such memo, addressed to his two daughters, suggested that, when speaking to reporters, they tell about his encounters with Churchill and de Gaulle, how he played the piano by ear at family gatherings, and how much time the private R.N. spent on the telephone comforting simple people who were in trouble.

Another went to Henry Kissinger, then his national security adviser, just before Nixon was going to China in 1971. It read, in part, as follows:

One effective line you could take in your talks with the press is how R.N. is uniquely prepared for this meeting and how ironically in many ways he has similar characteristics and background to Chou En-lai [the Chinese premier]. I am just listing a few of the items that might be emphasized:
1. Strong convictions. 2. Came up through adversity. 3. At his best in a crisis. Cool. Unflappable. 4. A tough, bold, strong leader. Willing to take chances where necessary. 5. A man who takes the long view, never being concerned about tomorrow's headlines but about how the policy will look years from now. 6. A man with a philosophical turn of mind. A man who works without notes—in meetings with 73 heads of state, R.N. has had hours of conversation without any notes. 7. A man who in terms of his personal style is very strong and very tough when necessary—steely but who is subtle and appears almost gentle.

There was something almost pathetic about this, for he was in some ways better than the image he tried to create. He had some chivalrous instincts and occasionally a kind of lunatic bravery, but he had trouble looking people straight in the eye and needed, even demanded, constant reassurance. We in the press knew about his preoccupation with his image, but not enough about this Walter Mitty self-portrait of the "strong . . . gentle . . . man who was never concerned about tomorrow's headlines." His fatal last stand at the Watergate was not only avoidable but also unbelievable. Those who bungled the burglary of the Democratic National Committee's head-quarters were supposed to be searching for incriminating evidence of Communist associations, but the Democrats were notoriously unable to keep files even on themselves, let alone the Communists, and Nixon's attempts to conceal his part in this stupid and shabby affair were even more clumsy than the crime itself. Even amateurs don't keep tape recordings of their own misdeeds.

"The farmer," said Ralph Waldo Emerson, "imagines power and place are fine things. But the president has paid dear for his White House. It has commonly cost him all his peace and the best of his manly attributes." Nixon learned the truth of this. Inevitably, the Vietnam and Watergate scandals created an uproar in the country. University students led the rage. There were vast demonstrations in Washington against the Cambodian invasion and the killing of four students by the National Guard during an antiwar protest at Kent State University in Ohio. But even when Nixon decided to get out of Vietnam he did it on the installment plan, complaining and bombing all the way.

Even sixteen years after he was run out of Washington, he was still blaming his downfall on the liberal Democrats and the liberal press. The Republicans on the House impeachment investigating committee joined in demanding that the incriminating tapes be turned over; the Republican leaders of the Senate and some of his own White House staff finally advised him to resign; and the conservatives on the Supreme Court insisted that the tapes be admitted in evidence. Also, it was the darling of the Republican conservatives, Senator Barry Goldwater of Arizona, who passed a harsher judgment on him than anybody else. "He was," Goldwater wrote, "the most dishonest individual I ever met in my life. President Nixon lied to his wife, his family, his friends, longtime colleagues in the U.S. Senate, lifetime members of his political party, the American people, and the world."

Nevertheless, when he resigned and President Ford pardoned him, the good Quaker side of his character, so evident in his first inaugural address, revived. He didn't, like so many of his predecessors, give up and give in. He didn't retire back home in California but settled down among his old enemies in the East and wrote some sensible books and gave some good advice to his Republican successors.

But for years he managed to avoid assuming any basic responsibility for his record. He treated the Watergate fiasco as sort of an accident of nature, like an earthquake, beyond his control. But in the end he did write a book called *In the Arena*, in which he conceded one important personal flaw: "In retrospect . . . I should have set a higher standard for the conduct of the people who participated in my campaign and administration," he said. "I should have established a moral tone that would have made such actions unthinkable. I did not. I played by the rules of politics as I found them. Not taking a higher road than my predecessors and my adversaries was my central mistake."

I understood his dilemma over leaving Vietnam. He clearly believed that a defeat there would make the United States look, as he said, like "a helpless, pitiful giant," but his failure to denounce immediately the Watergate burglary as a stupid blunder, and his failure to destroy the incriminating tapes of this conspiracy, were almost as incredible as the crime itself. We were pretty stupid ourselves at the *Times* when the burglary took place. At first, we brushed it off as a minor incident, carrying only a few paragraphs inside the paper, until *The Washington Post,* sensing the magnitude of the crime, splashed it all over the front page.

Nixon's last days in the White House were pathetic. He stayed up all night in the Lincoln sitting room after he resigned, and Al Haig found him in the morning surrounded by volumes of the biographies of past presidents. He had inserted a slip of paper at passages he found comforting in his predicament. "He was seeking solace," Haig later wrote, "from the only men who could truly know what he was feeling—his kinsmen in history, the other presidents."

Even then the historians, who had more time than the reporters, couldn't figure him out, and his closest aides were puzzled and embarrassed. Milton Eisenhower, Ike's brother, liked him personally but was baffled by him. "In private," Milton Eisenhower wrote in his memoirs, "Nixon was gracious, warm-hearted, friendly, humorous, and devoid of pretense. In public, he appeared to be austere, remote, given to self-praise, and for reasons I have never understood, a pictorial affirmation of the 'Tricky Dick' syndrome. I did not, to the disappointment of President Eisenhower, reach the conclusion that he would be a good president."

Bryce Harlow, one of Nixon's strongest supporters, speculated that maybe he had been deeply hurt as a child by some family rejection. Elliot Richardson, upon being appointed Nixon's attorney general, recalls saying to him: "Mr. President, there's one thing I've been wanting to say to you for a long time. I wish somehow, down inside yourself, you could come to believe that you've really won. If you could only bring yourself to reach out with magnanimity toward your former opponents. . . ." But the president did not respond.

After his second victory in 1972, Nixon's friends thought that he would finally feel that all his struggles had been justified and that he would be content, but instead he declined into a mood of depression and demanded the resignation of many who had helped him win. When it came to firing Haldeman and Ehrlichman over the Watergate scandals, he couldn't face them and asked Bill Rogers, his best friend and secretary of state, to give them the bad news. When he decided to get rid of Rogers, he asked Al Haig to tell him, but Rogers insisted on facing him and handing him his resignation.

The tough guy, the foul language, the mucker pose were all, according to Kissinger, "a kind of fantasy in which he acted out his daydreams of how ruthless politicians acted under stress." Nobody quite knew what he would do when his presidency was collapsing, and I was told at the Pentagon that certain "precautions" were taken lest he give dangerous orders affecting the national security, but in the end all his defenses collapsed. The night before he resigned, he called Kissinger to the Lincoln Room in the mansion and dropped to his knees in prayer. In their book *The Final Days,* Bob Woodward and Carl Bernstein of *The Washington Post* described the tragic scene, with Kissinger trying to comfort him and the president asking, "What have I done? What has happened? How has a simple burglary done all this?"

It seemed clearer to me at the end of this human tragedy that personal character affected public policy more than I had ever imagined. How many lives had been lost in Vietnam through personal vanity, fear, ignorance, and illusion? How many lies had been told, how many petty betrayals or even timid silences had been committed in the cabinet room? Nixon was not the only president to deceive the country, but he also deceived himself, and kept going, not by facing the truth, but by nourishing his alibis and polishing his illusions.

I saw no evidence after all this, however, that the American people made this connection between personal characteristics and public responsibilities, and thought accordingly that the press should be especially careful to investigate the character and tendencies of candidates long before they reached the White House. In fact, even after Nixon, many regarded such investigations as an intolerable invasion of privacy.

What baffled me then, and still baffles me almost twenty years later, was how such a man ever reached the White House. His record of trickery was well publicized in the press. His colleagues in the legislative and executive branches of the government had made no secret of their distrust of his devious ways. The television cameras not only exposed but magnified his most unpleasant personal characteristics, and in the end it was left to the Constitution, which he tried to evade, to put an end to his astonishing career. I found that the most consoling event of the seventies.

# CHAPTER 44

# Henry Kissinger

> If I had to choose between justice and disorder on the
> one hand, and injustice and order on the other, I would
> always choose the latter.
>
> —Kissinger, quoting Goethe

NOTHING IN MY experience was ever quite as good or as bad in Washington as the fashionable opinion of the day, and my favorite example of this proposition was Henry Kissinger. People were always giving him more credit or blame than he deserved—for discovering China or destroying Cambodia or being too nice or too beastly to the Communists—but I hate to think of what might have happened if he hadn't been around Nixon during the slaughter of Vietnam or the scandal of Watergate.

No doubt I was influenced in his favor by some of the men who preceded and followed him at the State Department. Some of them (Hull and Stettinius) were chosen because they merely looked like secretaries of state; others (Byrnes and Baker) because they were clever politicians; and still others (Rusk and Haig) because their presidents thought foreign policy should be operated from the White House.

But Kissinger was different. He not only knew a lot about foreign affairs, he *was* a foreign affair. He was a refugee from Hitler's Germany with a suspicion of all governments, including Nixon's. He had a philosophy of history; he thought progress was made by a few exceptional men who had maintained the peace for a hundred years after Napoleon, and whose examples he sought to follow. He knew more about Castlereagh, Metternich, and Bismarck than he did about the leaders of Congress.

I met him for the first time in 1951, when he invited me to address his seminar on international affairs at Harvard. On that occasion, I sounded off on the glories of a free press, but I don't think he was impressed. I admired him then and later, however, because he applied the lessons of the past to the future, could say clearly what he thought, and poked fun at all human pretensions, including his own. He had some other qualities that were useful to me at the time.

For one thing, he thought my tendency to equate personal morality with political morality was unrealistic if not ridiculous. All nations, in his view, were greedy and selfish in varying degrees, and officials, unlike private individuals, usually had to choose between policies that were part good and part bad. He was not inhibited by modesty or undue regard to moral scruples, but despite what his many critics said against him, I didn't think he was indifferent to the conflict between morality and justice. He simply believed that in the inevitable clash between the forces of chaos and the forces of order, stability was the main objective, that diplomacy backed by power was the main hope of avoiding a third world war, and that deterring such a catastrophe was the highest moral objective.

Unlike most of his predecessors and successors as secretary of state and assistant to the president as head of the National Security Council, he began with a clear definition of this principal objective and then tried to reconcile the day-to-day decisions with that goal. His aim was a balance of power between the nations that had the capacity to wage nuclear war. If this meant reaching compromises with the Communists for that purpose, or fighting them in limited wars, as in Korea and Vietnam, he would do either. Without stability there could be no peace and without at least some cooperation with Moscow, there could be no stability.

Since both the United States and the Soviet Union had enough nuclear weapons to destroy each other many times over, he was impatient with those who demanded superiority over Moscow in the acquisition of nuclear weapons. What did "superiority" mean, he once asked me, when each side had enough nuclear weapons to blow up the world twenty times over? He thought it was a mistake to make demands on other countries that we wouldn't accept ourselves. For example, he didn't believe the United States would allow the Soviets to interfere with our immigration policy; therefore, he didn't think we could get the Jews out of the Soviet Union by lecturing the Kremlin on human rights. And he believed good relations with China were so important that he could minimize if not ignore that country's vicious treatment of its youthful opponents.

Unfortunately, he was impatient with many other things—particularly colleagues who didn't equal his intelligence or share his convictions. He favored the invasion of Cambodia even though four of the five members of his National Security Council staff opposed it. One of them, Anthony Lake, argued that this "incursion," as it was politely called, would extend the war in Southeast Asia and produce a bloody upheaval in the streets at home. But Kissinger approved when Nixon declared that the United States would seem like a pitiful helpless giant if it did not oppose "the forces of totalitarianism and anarchy."

I found this particularly puzzling in a man so proud of political realism and so contemptuous of romantic diplomacy. For he was as critical of adventurism in Vietnam during the Kennedy days as he was in defending it when he came to the White House. When I wrote in opposition to Kennedy's decision to send 16,000 "advisers" to Saigon, Kissinger called to praise this criticism. He thought it was absurd to think that 16,000 advisers could achieve what France had failed to achieve with over 200,000 combatants, and when President Johnson increased the U.S. intervention to half a million men, Kissinger prophesized, quite accurately, that it would be a disaster.

But once in office he had a different concept: to withdraw with so large an army on the battlefield would mean breaking a solemn commitment, which may have been unwise but had to be kept. The "credibility" of the United States was at stake and so was his favorite doctrine of the balance of power. He approved withdrawal on the installment plan in order to get peace with honor, but he got neither.

Nevertheless, one of the remarkable things about the Nixon period is that so much progress was made in other critical areas of foreign policy despite the crises of Vietnam and Watergate. For this, much credit must be given to Henry Kissinger, and also to Nixon for putting Kissinger at the head of the National Security Council and later appointing him secretary of state. They were an odd couple, the historian and the politician. It sometimes seemed that the only thing they had in common was their unpopularity, but while everybody was blaming Nixon for getting into Watergate and not getting out of Vietnam, a start was made in controlling nuclear weapons, Nixon eased the tension in the Middle East after the 1973 October war, and Kissinger went to China and helped change the balance of power between the United States and the Communist world.

Nixon didn't usually reach out to his political opponents for help, and, unlike Kennedy, he was no fan of the intellectuals at Harvard. But though Governor Nelson Rockefeller of New York had opposed him for the presidential nomination in 1968, and Kissinger had been Rockefeller's principal foreign policy adviser in that campaign, Nixon, when he won, brought Kissinger to the White House.

It was one of the boldest moves he ever made. In its weakened condition the Nixon administration was even vulnerable to any hostile maneuvers by its potential enemies; but Nixon and Kissinger not only moved adroitly in the foreign field but also for a time used diplomacy to divert attention from the disarray on the home front.

The United States got involved in the Korean and Vietnam wars because it feared that the alliance between the two major Communist powers, dominating the Eurasian continent from the Sea of Japan to the Baltic Sea, threatened the security of all the free nations. The rift between Nikita Khrushchev and Mao Tse-tung, however, marked the greatest shift in the balance of power since the end of the Second World War. It forced the Soviet Union to divide its military manpower and missiles between the European and Asiatic fronts, and offered new diplomatic opportunities for the United States.

Kissinger, on the urging of Nixon, seized the opportunity. He believed that the restoration of U.S. diplomatic relations with China could be achieved without creating a deeper crisis in U.S.-Soviet relations; it was a risk not widely approved at the time. His analysis proved to be correct, and his trip to China in 1971 proved to be as significant a switch in U.S. policy in Asia as the Truman Doctrine and the NATO alliance had been in Europe.

He had a few habits not common in Washington. He had a philosophy of peace and a conviction of how to achieve it. He thought nations acted in relation to power rather than principle. He wasted no time on Wilsonian dreams of making the world safe for democracy, or threatening to destroy the evil empire in Moscow. He didn't think Washington could expect nations to cooperate if it threatened to destroy them. Accordingly, he sometimes seemed to pay more attention to the concerns of the nation's adversaries than its allies, and he was not deterred by self-doubt.

He didn't reach these conclusions by accident. As a Jewish refugee from Germany, he brought to the United States a brooding sense of the tragedy of life, and from his studies of European history at

Harvard, he was more interested in power politics than in the romantic dreams of Roosevelt or the appeasement tactics of Chamberlain. The lack of historical background among presidents and secretaries of state contributed more to the misconduct of U.S. foreign policy in my time than almost anything else. It was exceeded if possible only by the general ignorance of foreign affairs in the Congress. But Kissinger was a historian of a very special kind. He had studied not only the history of Europe but also the intrigues of European statesmen, and Washington was full of intriguers when he arrived. He was a student of history and of strategy. That is to say, he concentrated on the relationships of history, military power, and domestic politics. He was no genius on the mysteries of the latter, but being something of an intriguer himself, he was well prepared to take advantage of the changing policies in Peking and Moscow.

He once explained to Tony Day of the *Los Angeles Times* his approach to such problems. "What a national leader has to do at such a time," he said, "is to take his society and the world, insofar as the issues are international, from where it is to where it has never been. This means he cannot prove the destination is desirable until the society or the world gets there. The great leaders—I think of Churchill, de Gaulle, Lincoln, or Roosevelt—had that sort of vision. That was their elemental quality.

"In government, somebody finally has to say, I've now heard all this talk and we are going here. Nobody can lift that from the shoulders of the president. But he cannot avoid the curse of giving a sense of direction by hedging. That's the most important lesson I learned in government. The tendency is to try to do a little of everything. Once you've decided, you pay the same price for doing the thing properly as for doing it halfheartedly."

Kissinger learned this the hard way. His whole life had been a series of battles. He had overcome the difficulties of education in a new language, endured the snobbery of the Harvard Yard, and prepared for Rockefeller's Special Studies Project a serious and massive analysis of the problems facing the country at the end of the sixties. In fact, one of the many ironies of this strange relationship was that some of Nixon's best statements on foreign policy were originally written by Kissinger for Rockefeller. Nixon himself was no amateur in this field after eight years as Eisenhower's vice president, but Kissinger had analyzed the influence of nuclear weapons on modern foreign policy, and this gave Nixon something to hold on to when everything else was falling apart.

Kissinger was a difficult man, inconsiderate of his staff, intolerant, often contemptuous of less brilliant but more practical men, and devious in his relations with the Congress and the press. But in any summary of this historical period, it was his judgment, not widely shared, rather than his abrasive personality that deserves to be remembered. He risked bringing China and the Soviet Union into the war. He moved in the midst of the U.S. bombing raids on North Vietnam, which were sharply condemned by both Moscow and Peking. Also, increasingly at that time, he was dealing with a president who was fighting to avoid impeachment, and not thinking clearly, if at all.

I had no means of knowing what role Kissinger played in trying to save Nixon's presidency, but whatever he did, he was attacked more severely than any other secretary of state since Acheson. He remains a controversial figure, subject to the slights and jealousies of many he trampled on his way to the top, the victim even of private anti-Semitic slurs. No doubt his advice was sometimes no better than his manners, but in my view, he was one of the most intelligent, imaginative, and effective public servants of his time.

Before he left office, he reflected on these days. He said we should never have gotten so involved in Vietnam in the first place, and that he was a casualty of that war. And in a long interview I had with him in the *Times,* he summarized his own conclusions.

The historian and the statesman, he said, tend to see the world in different ways. As a historian, he had to recognize that most civilizations of the past had ultimately collapsed. History, he observed, "is a tale of efforts that failed, of aspirations that weren't realized, of wishes that were fulfilled and then turned out to be different from what one expected."

But, he added, while the historian had to live with "a sense of the inevitability of tragedy," the statesman "had to act on the assumption that problems could and must be solved." In foreign policy, he believed, the most difficult issues were often those whose necessity could not be proved when decisions were being made. He often had to act on assessments that were guesses. Measures to avoid catastrophe could almost never be proved. For that reason, it was essential for leaders to have a certain amount of support from the people.

"There is undoubtedly a profound disillusionment in America with foreign involvement in general," he said. "We have carried the burden for a generation. Most programs have been sold to Americans with the argument that they would be the end. Now we have to convince them that there will never be an end to exertion. That's a very difficult problem."

He even seemed in this interview to have some second thoughts about morality and security. For years, he said, the annual foreign policy reviews in the State Department had concentrated on the defense of "our interests," but, he added, while he was no fan of naïve American idealism, "pragmatism unrelated to a purpose becomes totally destructive."

It was this sweep of his mind, so often lacking at the top of the government, that I admired the most. He shared my admiration for Jean Monnet, but unfortunately didn't follow Monnet's belief that it was more important to do something than be somebody. Henry wanted both. He wanted to "do something" but sometimes his insistence on "being somebody" minimized his influence at a time when his brilliant talents were most needed.

# CHAPTER 45

# Missionary in the White House

AFTER RICHARD NIXON'S fakeries, the voters were apparently looking for just any honest man, the plainer the better. They found him in James Earl Carter, a former governor of Georgia, who looked and sounded a little Sunday-schoolish and thought of himself as sort of a southern Harry Truman. I write of him with caution, for I was sure he couldn't possibly win the presidency in 1976 or lose it so soon thereafter, and I was wrong both times. He disproved my theory that a good, intelligent, moral man would be a good and popular president, but he always seemed to be running up the down escalator. He had a tendency to say precisely what he thought about people and issues in Washington, a reckless and unusual experiment in those parts, and was surprised to discover that his candor was not always welcome. He was not a politician, certainly not of the Truman stamp, he was a missionary, but he is the best ex-president I ever saw. In fact, his whole career seemed to be a preparation for elder statesmanship.

He was a throwback to the old log-cabin tradition. Of the first nine postwar presidents, seven of them came from poor families, but Carter was nearer the soil than any of them. He still had the mud of Plains, Georgia, on his boots when he came to town, and could run a man-of-the-people campaign without makeup. He insisted on calling himself Jimmy, probably his first mistake. On inauguration day, he walked to work down Pennsylvania Avenue. When he moved into the White House, he sold the president's yacht and got rid of the cabinet's limousines.

I liked this common touch, but a lot of people thought he overdid it, and denounced him as a stiff-necked moralist. He hadn't even had time to find his way around the White House before they were criticizing him for wearing a sweater, working in his own Georgia peanut patch, and carrying his own garment bag over his shoulder. This sort of thing worked fine in the primary elections, but didn't suit the public fancy after he moved into the gracious surroundings of the White House.

During the campaign, he said he wanted to have "a government as good as the American people," and promised them, "I'll never lie to you." After he was elected but before he was inaugurated, I had a talk with him at the L'Enfant Hotel in Washington. "Suppose," I asked him, "that you find out that the American people are not all that good but selfish and don't respond to your moral philosophy?" He gave me an intimidating smile and said, "Why do you ask me a question like that?" I said because my own mother always assumed everybody was good, but when they turned out bad, she was absolutely unforgiving. He brushed me off, but later I thought he felt the American people had indeed brushed him off, and if he forgave them for defeating him in 1980, I never noticed it.

I admired Carter but learned, not for the first time, that the good personal qualities I respected weren't always good politics for a president. Also, that the personal deceit I detested in other presidents was sometimes highly successful. Carter was far from the innocent yokel his enemies denounced. Unlike Nixon, he was self-confident. Unlike Reagan, he was a worker. He devoured not only the texts of legislation but also the footnotes. But this led to the charge that he couldn't see the forest because he was counting the trees *and* the leaves. Even his closest friends and associates agreed that he spent so much time studying the details on little things that he often missed the big things, like how to peddle his policies to the Congress.

He seemed to think that unless he mastered the footnotes he couldn't understand the whole book. He didn't exactly cook every meal and wash every dish, but he did decide who could use the White House tennis court. Sol Linowitz, who helped him negotiate the Panama Canal treaty, among other things, comments in *The Making of a Public Man* on Carter's meticulous habits:

> He learned by gathering details and putting them together, but there wasn't always time to learn that way. . . . He lacked the sure-footedness he thought he should have, and he was uncomfortable about relying on others for things he thought he should know and be

able to do himself. He had an unusually strong grasp on what he wanted to accomplish but an uncertain hold on how to go about it.

His idealism, particularly his compassion for the poor, was apparent from the day he appeared on the national scene. I tried to praise it in a talk at Miami University in Ohio early in his administration. "There has," I said, "always been a missionary strain in the American people, looking beyond their own selfish interests, always trying to help, always seeking to comfort the afflicted and afflict the comfortable. Carter is good at this, but he came along at a time when the appearance of things was more important than the reality."

I've spent a good deal of time in these pages denouncing the trickery of TV politics and the elevation of personality over substance, but Carter didn't even try to present his attractive side, and Congress was not always impressed by his idealism and generosity. He was more conservative than his party, and his budgets didn't always match his sermons. Unlike most presidents who advertise their religiosity, Carter was a true believer and thought, with some justification, that his religious faith contributed to his successful Middle East negotiations with the Israelis and the Egyptians at Camp David.

I asked him one day at the end of his third year in office about his negotiations with President Sadat of Egypt and Prime Minister Begin of Israel, and whether he believed that history was influenced by religion. "Yes," he replied, "I found that one of the common things that Begin and Sadat and I share is a deep religious conviction. Begin and Sadat frequently refer to it in public and so do I. I think the fact that we worship the same God and are bound by basically the same moral principles is a possible source for resolution of differences. I was always convinced that if Sadat and Begin could get together, they would be bound by that common belief."

He undoubtedly felt that he had been raised from comparative obscurity to the presidency by the will of the Lord, and many observers were inclined to believe that nothing less than divine intervention could have gotten him to the White House. Whatever the source of his strength, he was sure he could do the job without flattering the elders on Capitol Hill or pretending to agree with them when he didn't. He was accessible to the committee chairmen and to most congressmen who had a grievance. At one time early in his administration, he even proposed that he have an office on Capitol Hill in order to be closer to the legislators, but he felt above the wheelers and dealers in the Congress, and they never really felt quite comfortable with him.

For while he was an attentive and patient listener, his eyes, like headlights, had a way of suddenly switching from dim to bright at any sign of danger, and he hit the brakes. He was actually much more persuasive in small gatherings than on the platform, but his soft-spoken arguments often ended without satisfying his visitors. He had no time for the small talk, pork-barrel trading, or congenial after-work "visiting" that marked such legislative wizards as Lyndon Johnson, and his modest platform manner left many audiences feeling he lacked the dash and force they expected in a president. Occasionally, though he was a naturally courteous man, he was insensitive even to his guests. It was not unusual for him to leave official dinners early in order to get back to his work. He was at it late at night and up at five-thirty every morning, but in Washington he found that honesty as he saw it, and "early to bed, early to rise" did not necessarily constitute the best policy.

During my years in Washington, no president ever had a more admirable family life than Carter. Rosalynn Carter was more than a loving wife, she was his partner, as she had been in their Georgia business. She sat quietly in back at cabinet meetings. She had strong views on policy and politics, and while I have no personal knowledge of how much influence she had on his decisions, I would be surprised if it were not considerable. Certainly he preferred her company to all others'. I found this both understandable and admirable, but again my reactions were not shared by those who were left behind when he abandoned meetings to go upstairs.

Early in his administration, he thought his main job was to try to bring people together after the bitter divisions of the Nixon era. He told me in an interview at the end of 1977: "This country has been through such an ordeal in the last five to ten years that it is still in a healing stage—Vietnam, the CIA, Watergate. This really shook the American people and their confidence in government. I don't think there will be a complete restoration of their confidence until proof is not only complete but extended over a period of time."

He was intolerant of nightmare predictions and pessimistic advice about the problems of reaching a compromise with the Soviet Union on the control of nuclear weapons. For example, he invited Paul Nitze, who had more experience in this field than anybody else, to discuss the question at a private conference in Plains between his election and his inauguration, but when Nitze presented a bleak picture of the prospects, Carter decided he didn't want him in his administration. Nitze later proved during the Reagan administration that this was a mistake.

It was said that Mr. Carter was too lenient on the Soviets and that he was too tough on the big spenders in the Pentagon—and compared with Reagan this was true—but actually he began the rearmament program in the seventies, and he was responsible for committing the United States to use any means, including military force, to keep the oil fields of the Persian Gulf out of hostile hands. (This was, of course, called the Carter Doctrine, because for some mysterious reason most presidents didn't really feel they were in the big time unless they had a doctrine.)

In dealing with the Soviets, however, Mr. Carter tolerated the divided counsels of his secretary of state, Cyrus Vance, and his head of the National Security Council, Zbigniew Brzezinski, perhaps longer than he should. Vance was inclined to believe that the Soviets were members of the human race who preferred life to death and might even compromise with the United States, but Brzezinski wasn't so sure, and wasn't elaborately discreet in expressing his dark forebodings inside and outside the government. Carter never really resolved this honest difference of opinion, and when he decided on a military raid to rescue the hostages in Iran without consulting his secretary of state, Vance resorted to a remedy long neglected in Washington: he resigned on principle.

Carter, of course, was hurt more by the prolonged captivity of the hostages than anything else. He put up with it until the United States was humiliated. He then ordered a sudden military lurch on Teheran to liberate them, but it was bungled, and while he could say at the end that the hostages came home alive, he never recovered from the charge that his administration was weak and indecisive.

Unlike Nixon and Johnson, however, he didn't blame the press for his failures and misfortunes. He usually said in public roughly what he was saying in private. He thought the American people were too impatient, and excessively anticommunist, and there, he added, a malaise in the country. This undoubtedly was true, but the people didn't hire him to tell them they were down in the dumps. He was widely criticized in the press for this unfortunate remark, and he followed it by the uncharacteristic and politically damaging decision to fire some members of his cabinet, but he was philosophic about the ensuing criticism.

"There is in the press, as there is in politics," he told me at the end of 1977, "some irresponsibility, and some absence of integrity, some deliberate distortion. But I have said many times truthfully that my overall relationship with the press is good and my respect for the press is high. What sometimes impresses me on a day-to-day transient basis is the aberration and the misreporting of something about which we know the facts. I think some of this may stem from an overemphasis in reporting on the mechanics and politics of policy-making as opposed to the substance of policy. In my experience, so-called inside stories on policy-making are usually more wrong than right. But I would say in general the press has treated my administration fairly. They and I are trying our best, but we all make mistakes, not because of evil intent, but because we're human."

He brought Hedley Donovan, the editor of *Time*, to the White House as a personal adviser and he made good use of experienced men such as Ellsworth Bunker, Sol Linowitz, Lloyd Cutler, and Clark Clifford on special diplomatic assignments, and most of them, like the members of his cabinet, respected his intelligence and good intentions even when they questioned some of his personal judgments.

Donovan, in a perceptive book of memoirs called *Roosevelt to Reagan,* thought he was "a man of decency and compassion, yet also capable of petty and vindictive behavior . . . a tendency to impute unworthy motives to those who crossed him . . . almost meek in his public style but inside there was a steely determination bordering on arrogance . . . with a surprising weakness for hyperbole and an odd lack of a sense of history."

I learned from all this to be a little more canny about passing snappy judgments on presidents. Reporters, particularly of the Scottish variety, have a tendency to be a bit self-righteous, but Carter helped me see that most presidents, like the rest of us, are full of contradictions. Nixon got into trouble because he was too insecure, too concerned with the appearance of things, while Carter was almost too sure of himself, and almost indifferent to the public reaction to his attitudes and actions.

I never, however, lost my respect for his character. He came about as near to living by his principles as any man I met in public life, and about as close to an approximation of the truth as any president dare, and he helped to establish a standard of decency, industry, and integrity which wasn't always appreciated or copied.

When he left the White House, he was broke. His peanut business, which had been in a blind trust when he was in the White House, was over a million dollars in debt when he got out, but he never took refuge in the many jobs that were offered him. He continued his concern for the homeless and even went out on construction sites and helped build houses for the poor. He was asked to help resolve many conflicts in the poor countries of Africa and Latin America and finally achieved in retirement the popularity that had eluded him in office.

Also, he developed a warm personal friendship with Gerald Ford, whom he had defeated for the presidency, and these two former presidents worked together to assist their successors whenever they were called upon to do so. I don't know where the historians will rank Carter with the presidents, but for my money he deserves better marks than he got when he was in the White House. For he tried to apply moral purpose to his decisions, and set a standard worthy of the presidency, but he never really learned to say hello until it was time to say goodbye. The people wanted style, and that's what they got with Reagan in the elections of 1980 and 1984.

# PART FIFTEEN

## THE REAGAN YEARS

# CHAPTER 46

# Hollywood Comes to Washington

It's better to have loafed and lost than
never to have loafed at all.
—James Thurber

AFTER CHASING POLITICIANS for forty years, I thought I was
beyond surprise, but I didn't count on Ronald Reagan. He made
more friends, had more fun, fooled more people, presided over more
sustained prosperity, incurred more debt, controlled more nuclear
missiles, encouraged more individual freedom at home and abroad,
and escaped responsibility for more scandals than any president in
the history of the Republic and was more popular at the end of two
terms in the White House than he was at the beginning. It was the
best theatrical performance of my days in Washington and the greatest triumph of television politics.

Of all the fantastic success films produced by Hollywood, few, if
any, compared with Ronald Reagan's own true story of the poor boy
from Illinois who was twice elected president of the United States.
His record as governor of California and in the White House was
controversial from start to finish. His intelligence and diligence were
questioned, and his pretensions were mocked, but nobody doubted
that his personal magnetism created one of the memorable legends
and mystery stories of American politics.

He presided in an unsettled and unsettling time, but didn't seem
to notice he was a bundle of contradictions. He denounced the cen-

tralization of power in Washington, but increased the influence and authority of the presidency and the military. He was endowed with more confidence than knowledge, but despite his woolly vagueness, he negotiated more compromises with the Soviets and the Congress than any other president of the Cold War period. It was a triumph of personality, of charm, guile, and good luck. His only bad break was that he was reelected for a second term, when the bills came in for his many extravagances.

During his two terms, over 18 million new jobs were created and total production of goods and services amounted to $30 trillion—a record expansion. But in the same years the United States borrowed more money than had all previous administrations combined. His arithmetic wasn't very good, but his timing was perfect. His administration coincided with the fall of communism, and he didn't hesitate to take credit for its collapse. The country was in a psychological slump when he took over, but he never stopped smiling. His personal appearances were an intoxicating delight. He calmly assumed the truth of everything he said, without bothering to provide any evidence in its support. Carter had told the people what was wrong with America and taken them to the woodshed; Reagan told them what was right and took them on a joyride. "Fly now, pay later," he seemed to say, "and spend your troubles away."

It wasn't hard to understand his popularity. The country had been through a long period of war and humiliation, and he cheered it up. Most people liked his carefree style. He announced when he arrived that it was morning in America, but he didn't like to get out of bed. Unfortunately, when he wasn't looking, which was not unusual, some of his own officials assumed that they had a license to steal or break the law. It wasn't only that he was absent from Washington more than most presidents but that he was often so absentminded when he was in the capital that he had the most expensive banking and housing scandals on record and didn't even notice them.

Still, he did some very good things. Like any good actor, he understood the power of both words and the heroic pose. He increased the defense budget for six straight years—twice the length of any previous peacetime buildup—and doubled the military appropriations between the fiscal years 1980 and 1986. He strengthened the strategic forces and expanded the power and reach of the navy and the air force, all of which undoubtedly contributed to the success of the United States in the Cold War and the Gulf War of the nineties.

At the beginning of his term in office he denounced Gorbachev for presiding over an evil empire that would do anything to further its interests, and at the end he compromised with him and decided he wasn't such a bad guy after all. He had many critics but few enemies. He seemed to regard the presidency as if it were just another movie. Every day was a new performance—the warrior one day, the peacemaker the next, the supply-sider or the backslider, and he was good at them all. And one of the appealing things about him was that, unlike many presidents, he didn't pretend that he had the answers to everything or even that he was running the show. He played the role of the president precisely as he could play the role of King Lear, but it never seemed to occur to him that he was actually the king.

Every new administration is as welcome to the reporters in Washington as the cherry blossoms in April. The new boys usually come to town, giddy with success, assuming that nothing happened before the November election, and if anything did it was probably wrong. Carter saw life as a predicament; Reagan saw it as an entertainment from the day he took the oath of office.

On a score of one to ten, we rated Reagan's first inauguration, with its fun and glitter, at about twelve. They danced until they shook the Washington Monument, and after Jimmy the preacher, their promise of a Reagan revolution sounded delightfully sinful. He didn't claim that everything was perfect, but blamed all imperfections, such as the deficit, on the Democrats.

Even before we knew all the names of the cabinet members, the Reaganites, as they were called, had cut the individual income tax rates to levels that hadn't been seen for sixty or seventy years, and even his opponents were wondering how Reagan had done it. At least part of the answer, I always thought, was that the American people liked him because, in many ways, they were like him: cheerful, optimistic, patriotic, inconsistent, and casually inattentive. His jokes were funny but they were expensive.

When he took over the White House, the federal debt was less than $800 billion; when he left, it was $2.2 trillion. The annual interest on the debt in his first year was $69 billion, and in his last year it was $169 billion. And when, as the oldest president in history, he left the White House in his seventies, having survived the Cold War, the ridicule of the press, and even an attack on his life, he looked almost as young as when he came in.

He handled the attempt on his life early in his first term with such courage, grace, and even humor that he acquired a kind of political immunity, and thereafter his political opponents and even the press treated him with unaccustomed gentility, and even in the second term, when his shortcomings were denounced, he never seemed to mind.

As most presidents and all good actors know, first impressions are critical and sometimes decisive, and Reagan's were a joy. On inauguration day, he didn't walk down Pennsylvania Avenue like Jimmy Carter and the rest of the folks; he put on a costume party and rode with his resourceful wife in a limousine as long as a freight car. He made every cliché sound profound. His acceptance speech had just the right befuddling mixture of hope and corn, and he read it off the TelePrompTer as if he had just thought it all up.

Equally important, he had a clear simple message. The people were the hope of the country, and he was going to give them more for less: big armies and small taxes and a balanced budget. He didn't get it all, like Roosevelt, in one hundred days, but in two hundred he got most of his economic program through the Congress. The Democrats said all this was baloney, but they swallowed it. Some of us wrote that increasing the defense budget and cutting taxes was a dizzy way to balance the budget, but the people endorsed it, and as all newspapers know, attacking popular presidents, especially at honeymoon time, is no way to increase circulation.

He arrived in Washington full of fairy tales and nursery stories, but the movie moguls never ventured to produce a story as fantastic as Reagan's. He not only proved that nice guys finish first—Hollywood's favorite theme—but he also made bad government popular. He thought the government was "too big" but presided over the biggest government in the nation's history. He recommended religion, but seldom went to church. He was divorced and not close to his children, but preached family values. If it hadn't been for his indolence, his ignorance would have been intolerable, but as a politician he was better lazy than many of his opponents were working forty-eight hours a day.

This was partly due to the fact that, unlike Carter, he didn't take on too many things. He didn't tinker with details, he ignored them. He had a few strong convictions, and at first they dominated the issues for discussion. He didn't drive the money changers out of the temple, he drove them into it and lost over $200 billion in the savings and loans in the process. He was against inflation, high interest rates, and unemployment, and thought the country could borrow its way to prosperity. Fortunately, he had Paul Volcker at the Federal Reserve to save him from the worst of his financial follies.

In some ways he was more honest than his immediate predecessors. In the economic depression of the thirties and the wars that followed, the people naturally turned to the president for relief and guidance. Even in the conduct of domestic affairs, most presidents were expected to have the answers to all the increasingly complicated and dangerous problems at home as well as abroad. Most presidents of the postwar period accepted this daunting and improbable assignment of knowing everything about everything, but not Reagan. He made no such pretense. Even when he was governor of California, he had an aversion to hard work and didn't bother much with the nuts and bolts of the state machinery. Thus, while he was constantly criticized for indifference and even ignorance of many important issues, it couldn't be said that he deceived the people with claims of superior knowledge.

I interviewed him for the first time on March 3, 1968, in the state capital Sacramento, long before he took over the White House. He looked and sounded back then about the same as he did later in Washington: cheerful, imprecise, and personally irresistible. His answer to the mounting tragedy in Vietnam was "leave it to the generals." All the people needed, he said, was "a banner to follow." He added, "I still have a great deal of faith that government can't possibly match that great body of citizenry out there as to genius and ability and power to get things done, if you just mobilize them and turn them loose on a problem." He had a joke about leadership as about almost everything else, and liked Groucho Marx's wisecrack about it: "Only one man in a thousand is a leader of men—the other nine hundred and ninety-nine follow women." The Republicans didn't buy his formula in 1968, but he followed it and expressed it almost in the same words when, as he was fond of saying, he "lived up above the store" on Pennsylvania Avenue.

His faith in decentralized government might have worked better if he had delegated his authority to a distinguished cabinet and White House staff. But he had his own idea of what a president's staff should be. He told me on November 10, 1980, just after he was elected and while he was picking his cabinet: "I want people who are already so successful that they would regard a government job as a step down, not up." So he selected Ed Meese, his own chummy lawyer, as attorney general; Cappy Weinberger, another successful California lawyer and businessman, as secretary of defense; James Watt, who loved to cut down trees and build up the oil companies, as secretary of the interior; Donald Regan, a Wall Street wizard, as chief of staff; Samuel R. Price, Jr., a second-rate politician, for the

Department of Housing and Urban Development; and William Casey for the CIA. Fortunately, he also had George Shultz at State and James Baker at the Treasury and in the White House, or he might have made even more mistakes than he did.

Nevertheless, he did what a conservative government is supposed to do: he challenged the policies of previous opposition Democratic administrations; he put a brake on the welfare state programs that he felt had gone too far; he tolerated what worked, and cut out or cut down what didn't. He really believed the country could spend its way to peace and prosperity without going broke. The Democrats said he was a phony, but at least he was an authentic phony. He didn't mind the store, but he didn't pretend. He was both hearty and unconsciously heartless. He had mastered the arts not only of Hollywood but also of Madison Avenue. He never remembered anything that was inconvenient, but he never forgot how and when to make news. He set a record for presidential press conferences: that is to say, he held fewer of them than any of his predecessors.

What was worse in a way is what he did to the mind of the country, to its sense of fairness, its priorities, its better instincts, its belief in the president as a model of personal behavior. He had no time to denounce inefficiency or even dishonesty within his own government, and even after he retired saw nothing wrong in taking $2 million from a Japanese press lord for a couple of twenty-minute speeches. All this was denounced by the press but he laughed at our feebleness. One night he began his speech at the Gridiron Club by saying, "Before I refuse to answer your questions, I have a statement."

He didn't ask many questions either. When his chief of staff, Donald Regan, handed him a budget as thick as the Los Angeles telephone book, he reports that the president glanced at it and said, "That's fine, Don." And when a delegation of senators came back from a mission to Moscow and a long session with Gorbachev, he listened to their report but showed no curiosity about their observations. In these private sessions, he was a great storyteller, but everything serious seemed to remind him of something frivolous.

The Democrats blamed the press for their defeat in the 1984 election. Reagan had won, they said, because the newspapers had been too easy on him, but that was not entirely true. Never since the days of H. L. Mencken had so many reporters reported and even mocked the shortcomings of a president and influenced so few voters. He dealt with the newspapers by ignoring them. In a switch from Jefferson's famous remark, he said in effect, "Were it left to me to decide whether to have a government without newspapers or news-papers without a government, I would choose TV every time." When the bills began to come in he was roundly criticized, but by then he was headed home to California.

It wasn't that he had no ideas, but there were no connecting rods between them. He had a few strong conservative beliefs about private enterprise, free trade, the superiority of the United States, the wick-edness of communism, and the dangers of a strong federal executive government, but he didn't always let his ideology get in the way of his popularity. He was not only "the great communicator," but much to the despair of the Republican militants, he was also the great compromiser. He was defiantly opposed to new taxes, but when necessary he went along with "revenue enhancement." He demon-strated that politics is a performing art, and he was good at symbols. He called his MX missile the Peacekeeper and his allies in Central America freedom fighters. (Incidentally, in 1844 President John Tyler called a new twelve-inch gun the Peacekeeper, but when he demonstrated it on the *Princeton* during a cruise down the Potomac, it blew up, killing both the secretary of war and the secretary of the navy.)

In a way, Reagan was a visionary. He didn't trouble much about other people's individual troubles, but he was all for putting a nu-clear shield over the whole human race. He called it the Strategic Defense Initiative. Others who were more interested in jobs, poverty, clean water and air, and houses for the homeless called it Star Wars. He couldn't hear or see very well, and seemed to live much of the time in the blur of his own imagination.

Nevertheless, despite his casual and contradictory ways, or maybe even because of them, he made more progress toward an accommo-dation with the Soviets than any president since the beginning of the Cold War. A more consistent man with stronger intellectual and analytical qualities might easily have felt that he had to defend everything he said in the past, no matter how irrelevant to changing circumstances, but Reagan wasn't that sort of man. He dealt with things one at a time and balanced the books every day.

On August 21, 1983, during his first term, I wrote that "the Soviets are without doubt the most spectacular failure of the century. The Russian people don't believe in them. The Communist parties of Western Europe no longer regard Moscow's economic theories as a model for their societies. Every year in this advancing computerized world, they fall farther behind and try to keep up by borrowing and stealing Western technology. . . . I think we have won the Cold War and don't know it." The president scoffed at this at the time, but by the end of his second term he not only agreed with this theme but also talked as though he had invented it.

It was fun covering Ronald Reagan, sort of like going to the movies. Sitting there in the dark, you didn't believe much of what you saw and heard, but it took your mind off the facts. And the cast of characters was almost as diverting as the leading man—a national hero running his own foreign policy out of the basement of the White House; a vice president who was "out of the loop"; and a First Lady who consulted an astrologer about the president's schedule.

Back out in the bright daylight, however, when the glitter faded and the interest debts got bigger than the first Johnson budget, all this didn't look so good. In his second term, he was involved in scandals in Iran and Central America, and his relations with Congress and the press declined. Part of the reason for this was that many other political leaders copied Reagan's tactics, and the debates became more personal and divisive. "Everybody does it" became not an indictment but an excuse, yet while his popularity fell when the economy and Wall Street slumped, he was usually resilient enough to handle it.

One reason for this was that he was lucky in his opponents. The Democrats thought that if a thing was worth doing it was worth doing expensively, and they talked about raising taxes to pay for their extravagances. To nobody's surprise, the voters preferred Reagan's policy of leaving the bill to the next generation in the next century. Whether he was right or wrong, he usually dominated the news, and if the Reaganites got their facts wrong, you could always find them on the Sunday morning TV shows saying they were misunderstood or misquoted. Tension with the press, however, didn't bother Reagan. Unlike every president from Roosevelt to Nixon, he never got mad at the reporters. In fact, after I had spent eight long years criticizing him, he sent me a mash note when I retired.

He was also lucky in his Kremlin adversaries. In his first term, three of them were frail or dying—Leonid Brezhnev, Yuri Andropov, and Konstantin Chernenko—but he undoubtedly contributed to ending the Cold War with his massive rearmament program that made negotiations seem wiser and cheaper than confrontation. He may not have changed history but he stage-managed it and encouraged the development of a powerful network of think tanks and political manipulators that greatly strengthened the conservative cause for the last two presidential elections of the century. When he left Washington for California and was asked how he liked the life of retirement, he replied as usual with a joke. It wasn't all that different, he said, from his days in the White House.

Even after he left Washington, however, even his friends couldn't explain him. He seemed so open to everybody, but his intimates testified that they didn't really know him. He seldom mentioned his family or his Illinois roots. He talked about his war record but he had none. In many ways, he was almost recklessly brave, but he was for many years afraid of flying. He took refuge from a drunken father in boyhood fantasies, divorced his first wife, began his political life as a Democrat, saw no inconsistency in his policies, and tolerated his critics with an understanding smile. All the amateur psychiatrists in Washington tried to figure him out and failed, but by his own lights he was a great success, and he left behind a Supreme Court with a majority favorable to his conservative philosophy. On his eightieth birthday, he shared a last laugh with about a thousand friends, including former British Prime Minister Margaret Thatcher. As he said, "Not bad for a country boy!"

# PART SIXTEEN

## JOURNEY'S END

# CHAPTER 47

# Bush and the
# New World Order

SALLY AND I have come to the last lap of our journey in the 1990s, and spend a lot of time counting our lucky stars. After my old friend Mark Childs died, I was referred to, not unkindly, as the "dean" of the Washington press corps, and was called on occasionally by obit writers and other students of ancient history for reminiscences of the past and predictions of the future, but the more I thought about the unpredictability of history, the more I decided that prophecy was a risky business.

The last decade of a century is a tempting time for presidents, journalists, end-of-the-world preachers, and other dreamers. Presidents in particular begin meditating on their place in history, and wondering how to make it look a little better than it was. George Washington made his famous Farewell Address in the last decade of the eighteenth century, and foresaw safety and prosperity for the new Republic in isolation from the quarrels of the world. In the last decade of the nineteenth century, President McKinley was not thinking of isolation (or of his sudden death soon to come), but planning a new American empire, and leading the country into the Spanish-American War. And at the beginning of the last decade of the twentieth century, George Herbert Walker Bush, the forty-first president, was proclaiming the dawn of a "New World Order," and starting it with a war against Iraq in the Middle East.

After studying the fortune-tellers of the past, I admired their bravery more than their judgment. In the 1890s, the best of them were writing confidently about a future world of inevitable progress. They were convinced that there was something in the nature of the universe, or maybe in the economics of supply and demand, or in the spread of knowledge and education, that would surely lead to the golden age. By the time I arrived on the scene two world wars later, however, the pessimists had taken over, with books deploring *The Decline of the West* (Spengler), *The End of Our Time* (Berdyayev), and *The Fate of Homo Sapiens* (H. G. Wells).

Most of the events that determined the history of the twentieth century were not foreseen. In its first decade, when I was born, the leaders of the world did not even imagine the First World War or the Communist revolution in Russia or the rise of Nazism in Germany, or the Great Depression. Even at the start of the Second World War, nobody counted on the invention of the atomic bomb, or the collapse of the old empires, and at the end of that conflict, the world was surprised again by the Cold War, the Korean and Vietnam wars, the economic challenge of Japan, the rise of Islamic fundamentalism, and the turmoil in the developing nations of Africa and Asia. In fact, it was not generally realized even in Washington and the other Western capitals that from the end of World War II until the end of the Gulf War of 1991, over 17 million people lost their lives through war and starvation in these so-called underdeveloped nations.

All the guesses of the past were interesting but most of them were wrong, for the world changed faster than they could change their minds. Some chalky genius, monkeying around in a laboratory or a garage, was always discovering how people could fly like birds, or send messages, pictures, and even the music of Beethoven through space, or extract more food from the bounteous earth, or wipe out disease, or go to the moon. These thinkers and tinkerers not only invented a better mousetrap but a better mouse named Mickey, who went into the movies and made children happy. They also developed new ways to kill more people with atom bombs, but the human race just went on producing more children by the same delightful old-fashioned process. For example, the population of the United States in 1800 was 5,308,483, including 896,849 slaves; in 1900, it was 75,994,575; and in 1991, it is over 250 million, with almost that many different opinions about how to run the most powerful, generous, and influential nation on earth.

I admired the optimistic spirit behind President Bush's New World Order, but I couldn't find much new in it other than his war in the Middle East. He talked about ensuring "for ourselves and for future generations" an age of peace, "where the rule of law governs the conduct of nations." I was all for George, but thought this sounded very much like the pronouncements of other presidents who thought not only that America could change the world, but also that it had a moral duty to do so.

Woodrow Wilson saw the first great catastrophe of the twentieth century as a "war to end war" and make the world "safe for democracy." After the Second World War, Franklin Roosevelt said just before he died that henceforth the world was to be governed not by the old "outmoded" and "discredited" balance-of-power politics, but by the noble principles of the United Nations charter. Harry Truman didn't limit his military aid to Greece and Turkey in 1945, but promised to help any nation anywhere threatened by Communist expansion. And President Kennedy, in a more poetic and heroic vein, promised in his inaugural address at the beginning of the sixties that the American people would "pay any price and bear any burden" in defense of liberty all over the world.

There was, I thought, something both wonderful and arrogant about all this persistent American determination to reform the world. It reminded me of the little signs that used to hang in some of the service stores in Dayton when I was a boy. I forget the exact words, but they promised to do anything "possible" by tomorrow but conceded that the "impossible" might take a few days longer. This was the spirit that had conquered the American continent, survived the Great Depression of the thirties, helped restore Western Europe and Japan after World War II, and survived the Cold War with the Soviet Union for almost half a century.

But before you could say Saddam Hussein or even Yasser Arafat, President Bush had sent half a million Americans to the Middle East battlefield when the Congress wasn't looking, and chased the Iraqis out of Kuwait in four days. It was a perfect American war: quick, flashy, and all on television. More Americans were murdered at home during those four days than were killed in that war. President Bush called it, without undue modesty, the greatest military victory in the history of the Republic and scarcely mentioned the 150,000 Iraqis who were slaughtered in the process.

Accordingly, I began to wonder about these wars to end war, and think that maybe John Quincy Adams had a better idea. Adams said on July 4, 1821, that America should always try to help other nations in trouble, but he added that we go "not abroad in search of monsters to destroy." In my years in the capital, however, we were finding monsters all over the world, not only big-league monsters in the Soviet Union and China, but bush-league monsters in Korea, Vietnam, Cuba, Nicaragua, Panama, Iraq, and various other places that didn't want our advice about freedom and democracy or even know what the words meant.

I don't doubt that there will be continuing violence in the future, requiring a substantial but modified U.S. military establishment, but I don't think we can outlaw war any more than we were able to outlaw booze after World War I, and I don't think the nation has adjusted to the disorder left behind by the hot and cold wars of the last half of the old century.

No doubt the Gulf War served several useful purposes. It put future aggressors on notice that they could not assume American neutrality. It made clear that the United States regarded the oilfields of the Middle East as vital to its security and would not permit them to come under the control of any hostile power. It put an end to the self-doubts that had plagued the nation after its defeat in Vietnam, but this Vietnam syndrome was followed by a kind of Iraq swagger of boasting that Uncle Sam was number one and would now at last redeem the optimistic visions of Woodrow Wilson and the other prophets of eternal peace.

My optimism doesn't go quite that far. I think the long nightmare of an atomic war is over for the foreseeable future, but I have more modest dreams. I don't believe in New World Orders that rely on fighting wars rather than deterring them, or in United Nations resolutions that "authorize" the United States to do most of the fighting. I believe in collective, not selective, security, and I think we need to ask ourselves some questions.

What areas are really vital to the security of the United States? Will our schools and slums be high on this list? When are we going to make the United States independent of Middle East oil and how? How can we have a New World Order without cooperation between the United States and the Soviet Union? When are these giants and the other industrial nations going to control or stop the shipment of advanced military weapons to the shaky gangster nations of the world? In short, where is the end-of-the-century threat to U.S. security anyway—abroad or at home?

So every once in a while I have mounted my old pulpit at the *Times* and suggested that the time has come not for another New World Order proclaimed, financed, and policed by the United States, and started with a war, but for a New American Order beginning with a reappraisal of our commitments and resources, and a reform of our priorities and decision-making procedures. I'm not throwing off the old disorder—it made so much news!—but I feel it can be improved with a little less fighting and a little more patience, common sense, and diplomacy. I may be wrong about this, but I don't think it would hurt to review our commitments, keep them in balance with our bank balances, pay our debts, and prepare our children for the new problems of the coming century.

I had thought I knew George Bush fairly well, but I didn't recognize his warrior pose. I longed for years that some gentleman president would come along and set an example of calm thinking and honest talking, and I felt that George Bush was precisely that sort of man. The one I knew had promised a "kinder America" in "a gentler world" and I admired his record. His whole career seemed a preparation for the presidency. He had more personal experience in Congress, business, military intelligence, war, and diplomacy than any other president of my time. He was not an ideologue, but, like his father, came out of the old Teddy Roosevelt and Colonel Stimson progressive nonpartisan tradition. I followed his career in the House of Representatives and at the United Nations. Sally and I flew around with him during the 1980 presidential election when he was mocking Ronald Reagan's voodoo economics, and I felt sure he would bring a more pragmatic spirit to the White House.

In many ways he did. On most things, he consulted the leaders of the Congress. He abandoned his silly campaign promise of no new taxes. He tolerated dissent, and he held almost as many press conferences in his first eight months in the White House as Ronald Reagan had in the previous eight years. But something happened to him on his way to the White House. He campaigned like Richard Nixon and talked like Lyndon Johnson, saying publicly that Saddam Hussein was worse than Hitler, and vowing publicly to "kick him in the ass." And when it was said that maybe he was a bit of a wimp, he disproved it by plunging into two wars in his first two years in office.

He defied the principles of the United Nations when he went to war in Panama to get rid of another dictator named Noriega (again the personal military approach to foreign policy), then relied on the UN principles when he went to war against Iraq, and defended both as a moral contribution to good over evil and right over wrong. More important, he talked about "the next American century," and said it was the purpose of the United States to ensure the stability and security of the Middle East. "Among the nations of the world, only the United States of America has had both the moral standing and the means to back it up," he said. "We're the only nation on this earth that could assemble the forces of peace."

The Republicans used to call this sort of thing "globaloney." Whatever it was, I thought it aroused excessive expectations that would be followed, as usual, by excessive disappointments. There was no doubt that Hussein's brutal aggression deserved to be punished, but there were many places in the world where war might be morally justified but politically unwise. My fear was that this interventionist policy would eventually produce a negative reaction in the United States, weaken the Western alliance, revive the spirit of American isolationism, and provoke racial tension among the blacks, who made up a disproportionate percentage of the American ground forces.

His one-hundred-hour war against Iraq, however, was highly popular. It was short and dramatic. The armed services demonstrated more military foresight and skill in waging the war than the civilian diplomats had shown in preventing it. Like the president, the American press rejoiced in how few casualties there were on the allied side, but when I added up the cost, I felt a little Kurdish.

Before the Gulf War started, I wrote that saying "my president, right or wrong," was like saying "my driver, drunk or sober," but once the bombs started falling on Baghdad and Tel Aviv, the debate ended, and the president's popularity increased, as it had at the beginning of the Korean and Vietnam wars. Accordingly, I worked on my own idea, not of a New World Order, but of a New American Order, which, in my dreams, would be planned in the last years of the nineties and put into operation with a fixed deadline of January 1, 2000.

I found, to my delight and the despair of my younger friends, that the older I got and the less information and energy I had, the more dogmatic I became. Sally greeted this with a melancholy sigh, but I went ahead anyway. The New American Order of my imagination didn't contain anything that was not both reasonable and achievable. For example, it would have in place by the first day of the new century an energy program that didn't depend on the oil of the Middle East. I thought this was essential even if we had to rely on the sun, the wind, atomic energy, taxes, and horses. I didn't think this was ideal, but it seemed to me more realistic than counting on peace and sanity in the Middle East.

In my New American Order the world wouldn't be peopled by phantoms, and the objective would be to settle political disputes by negotiation, even with scoundrels, and not by proclaiming another American century with Uncle Sam as schoolmaster and chief of the world police. "Let George do it," I told myself, wasn't a policy but a line out of an old musical comedy, which I didn't think would be very popular when the bills came in.

By deadline 1/1/2000, under my dreamy scheme, both political parties would be in agreement that the main threat to the nation's security came from within and not from abroad; that a strong and modified defense force was essential; that even America's resources were limited, and should not be squandered on reluctant peoples who would rather fight than eat. I thought that clarity as well as charity begins at home, so we should cut our military guarantees to the essential minimum, and reduce all moral posturing by congressmen and columnists as much as possible under the First Amendment. (This would, of course, be denounced as the new isolationism, but I thought it was better to be denounced for avoiding unnecessary wars than for fighting them.)

Under my fantasy of a New American Order (NAO), the two political parties would have an official smoke-filled room, preferably the old Supreme Court chamber in the Capitol, where candidates for the parties' nominations for the presidency and vice presidency would be chosen by party leaders who know something about the character and ability required to govern the country. The political parties would, before the election of 2004, I insisted, have abolished the present disgraceful system of campaign financing, and arranged for at least six free TV debates between the candidates (minus all reporters). They would not eliminate the state primary elections but would retain the power to veto any turkey or quail proposed in these popularity contests.

On one wall of this smoke-filled room, there would be a portrait of Warren Gamaliel Harding to remind the pros not to make the same mistake again, and on another wall there would be a portrait of Teddy Roosevelt, preferably not on horseback, together with his favorite warning:

"The things that will destroy America are prosperity at any price, safety first instead of duty first, a love of soft living and the get-rich-quick theory of life. This country will not be a permanently good place for any of us to live unless it's a good place for all of us to live."

I had some other dandy, if not original, ideas: I thought it would help if presidents and other leaders told the truth, and mentioned the word "sacrifice" once in a while. I didn't think we should amend the Constitution to conform to every popular whim of the day, or try to police the bedrooms of the American people. I thought it was unwise to corner dictators and other wild beasts, and since presidents are not immortal, I favored vice presidents that were as reliable as a spare tire. I was for a longer school year because I was more interested in smart kids than smart bombs; for voluntary national service by young people to help in the overburdened, overexpensive hospitals; and for a national anthem that anybody could sing, drunk or sober.

Nobody listened to these fantasies, of course, but that's one of the nice things about being over eighty. You don't care whether they listen, and even when they do, you can't quite hear what they say.

# PART SEVENTEEN

## SUMMING UP

# CHAPTER 48

# *What Happened to the World?*

> As I grow older I grow calm. . . . I do not lose my hopes.
> . . . I think it not improbable that man, like the grub that
> prepares a chamber for the winged thing it never has
> seen but is to be . . . that man may have cosmic
> destinies that he does not understand. . . . And so
> beyond the vision of battling races and an impoverished
> earth, I catch a dreaming glimpse of peace.
> —Oliver Wendell Holmes

AT THE END of this long journey, I share Judge Holmes's hopes and think there is some evidence to justify them, but I also have some doubts. I don't expect to see "the new heaven and the new earth" of my dreams, but I think the major nations are gradually adjusting to a few brutal facts that threaten them all. They have learned that even war with conventional weapons is an expensive and unpredictable business. They are frightened of nuclear war, and considering the havoc they have wrought in this murderous epoch, they are even frightened of themselves.

"We later nations, we too now know that we are mortal," Paul Valéry observed. "We had long heard tell of whole worlds that had vanished, of empires sunk without a trace, gone down with all their men and machines into the unexplorable depths of the centuries. And we see now that the abyss of history is deep enough to hold us all."

This seems to me the haunting lesson of our wanderings in the world: out of suffering and fear, at least the major nations, weary of war, deprived of faith, and baffled by freedom, are pausing at the end of the century to reflect on the past and look with different eyes on the new century to come.

Accordingly, though I was raised by the pessimistic Calvinists, I check out with the optimists for several reasons. Most of the spectacular scoundrels of the century have not only been defeated but also died in their bunkers or were strung up by the heels. In the nineties, there is a new balance of power in the world, and the dominant nations are not the dictatorships that fought their way to oblivion, but the democracies that preserved and expanded personal liberty. I listened to Nikita Khrushchev proclaiming in the fifties that capitalism would collapse by its own "inner contradictions," but by the nineties the inner contradictions of communism produced the greatest political failure of the century.

Many of the dogmatic political theorists of the past have vanished with their dreams. Those who believed that ideology was the sure and simple answer to the economic needs of the people have found that unfettered capitalism, socialism, and communism had to adjust to the changing realities of a computerized and interdependent world. And by the end of the century, it is widely recognized at last that polluted wind and water pay no attention to national boundaries, and that a general atomic war threatens the tolerable existence of the entire human family.

There are still, of course, other nations that would rather fight than think, and even in the nineties literally millions of people are dying in regional and tribal wars or by avoidable slaughter, famine, and disease, but the idea is beginning to get around, at least in the major capitals, that spending over a trillion dollars a year for a world of military arms is an extravagant investment, and that maybe more progress can be made by cooperation than by military confrontation.

Also, the world at the end of the century is no longer an impenetrable network of nationalistic barriers to trade, but gradually becoming one vast trading area, with a common market developing among the United States, Canada, and Mexico, and an emerging unified Western Europe with open borders, common manufacturing standards, and even a common currency.

All this has sustained my hopes, but the fear of nuclear war has been replaced by other anxieties. The world hadn't even had time to celebrate the end of the Cold War in 1990 before the endless struggle for control of the Middle East erupted in the invasion and conquest of Kuwait by Iraq, and the dispatch of over 500,000 American troops into the Arabian desert to punish aggression and ensure the safety of over 60 percent of the world's oil reserves in that tormented region.

Meanwhile, the industrial nations are still exporting increasingly explosive and accurate military weapons to shaky terrorist nations that can't even feed their own people, and the world is full of refugees, seeking security in unfamiliar countries and cultures. For example, the population of the rich industrial world has stabilized at about 2 billion, but in the last decade of the century, the population of the poor nations is over 4 billion and doubling every generation and migrating into the northern industrial nations faster than they can be controlled or absorbed.

Also, it is not clear how the peoples of the Soviet Union will adjust to freedom, or even avoid the kind of civil war that followed the cries of secession in nineteenth-century America. The world has more questions than answers. Has a unified and increasingly powerful Germany learned the terrible lessons of the two world wars? Can the nations control the spread of nuclear weapons? What is to be done about the endless tension between Israel and the Arab states and the racial and tribal wars of Africa? It is clear that the world is looking to the United States to deal with the wreckage of the Cold War as it dealt with the reconstruction of Europe after the Second World War.

I am not a prophet, and don't presume to guess the answer to these questions. All generalizations are risky, including the above, especially since military power and political leadership can change overnight, so I have had to go canny with predictions, having so many past misjudgments to regret.

Nevertheless, I think that science, despite all its murderous contrivances, is expanding the reach of freedom. It, to be sure, gave us the atom bomb, which we didn't need, but it has also given us a communications revolution, which is in many ways more explosive. When I was a boy, dictators could control the flow of information and imprison and warp the minds of their peoples, but radio penetrated the Iron Curtain, allowing the captive peoples to know what was happening beyond their borders, and the whole world watched the Gulf War of 1991 on television.

Thus, it is no longer easy for dictators to get away with decisive surprise attacks. Radar gave the Royal Air Force just enough warning to save London from the Luftwaffe in the blitz, and might have saved Pearl Harbor if the operators hadn't been out to breakfast. Information satellites whirl around the earth night and day and can spot the mobilization of armies in advance, and there are hot lines between the White House and the Kremlin to guard against accidents and misjudgments.

No doubt the human urge to destruction is still with us, and our machines, if misused, can lead us into terrible temptations, but they also give us light and sound and I no longer fear the darkness of the past—the sudden crash in the night, the ignorance, isolation, the hopelessness that made the Dark Ages so dark, and the pessimistic nightmares of the Cold War so terrifying.

The balance of power, mocked by the idealists before the two world wars—though it maintained a tolerable peace throughout most of the nineteenth century—has, by the end of the twentieth, been restored, and at the end of the Cold War there was even reason to hope that the United Nations would finally be given a chance to provide collective security, as originally intended.

One of my first diplomatic assignments was to cover the opening sessions of this world security organization, held appropriately at a skating rink in Lake Success, New York. But there was little success, for it was operating on thin ice, with the Soviet Union and even the United States using their veto to block any action they didn't like. Now that the Cold War has ended, however, and the United States and the Soviet Union are cooperating (for a change) to maintain the peace, there is finally just a chance, or so I believe, that this organization can be more effective in dealing with the threat or punishment of military aggression.

Is all this too optimistic? Many thoughtful people I respect think so. But I knew not one of them, always with the exception of Monnet, who imagined at the end of World War II that our enemies would become our allies; that the nationalistic barriers of a divided and warring Europe would be falling; that the United States would be presiding over the most effective military alliance ever organized, with an army still standing guard in Europe over forty years later; or that the United States and the Soviet Union would be not only negotiating the control of nuclear weapons but also beginning to destroy them.

This isn't exactly a New World Order, but it seems to me that the old order defined in the principles of the United Nations Charter back in 1945 would work if the Soviet Union, the United States, and the new developing European Community finally gave it a chance. They have all needed a long period of peace to deal with their internal problems, relieved of some of the financial pressure of excessive military budgets, so I turn to the question of what happened to America during the long period of the Cold War.

# CHAPTER 49

# What Happened to America?

> Ours is a story mad with the impossible. It began as a dream and it has continued as a dream down to the last headlines you read in a newspaper. And of our dream there are two things above all others to be said, that only madmen could have dreamed them or would have dared to, and that we have a considerable faculty for making them come true.
> —Bernard De Voto, in letter to Catherine Drinker Bowen

IN THE NINETIES, the United States has emerged as the richest and most powerful military nation in the world, but it is deeply in debt and divided over how to finance its new problems abroad and its old problems at home. This is not surprising. For over two generations, its mind, its budget, its policies, its research and development, its industries, and its politics have been dominated largely by the threats of a third world war. In the process, it has triumphed over fascism and communism, and rescued its civilization in what seemed to me one of the greatest chapters of American history, but in the last years of the century it has to deal with the consequences of its success, and it faces two questions: first, what is it going to do with all this power and wealth? And second, who will make these critical decisions in the changing world of the future, and how will they decide?

The United States has a vast military establishment that is disproportionate to dealing with any remaining hostile nation. It is leading a North Atlantic alliance designed to protect Europe from the nations of the Warsaw Pact, which has collapsed. But the Soviet Union still has thirty thousand nuclear weapons with nobody clearly in charge, and the administration in Washington, long accustomed to assuming the worst about Moscow's intentions, has hesitated to reform a military system that was so successful in the Cold War and the war in Iraq.

This too is understandable. Yet many people, I among them, think we are holding on too long to militaristic policies, as we clung too long earlier in the century to the policies of isolation. I believe that the threats to the nation's security after the Cold War are coming not from abroad but from the neglected problems at home. No country has ever been so rich, but at the beginning of the nineties the bipartisan National Commission on Children reported that America's infant mortality rate was higher than those of twenty-one other industrial countries; that one fourth of all births in the United States were to unmarried mothers; that one in every four children was being raised by a single parent; and that 40 percent of all children in school were in danger of failing. In the last half of the century, the United States has doubled its population, largely by accident. It has lost control of its southern borders and is trying to absorb millions of new aliens. For example, more immigrants, many of them illegal, entered the United States in the eighties than in any other decade of its history, and most of them came not from Europe, as in the past, but from Latin America, Asia, and Africa.

The larger the nonwhite population becomes, the more it is likely to resent its unequal economic handicaps and challenge the dominant white political and cultural power. In the eighties and early nineties at least some black leaders, who previously fought for political integration, have been emphasizing not the unity of all Americans, but the differences between the races. Precisely at the time when progress is being made toward a more peaceful and integrated world, we are hearing demands in America for more education in other languages. I sympathize with the blacks who resent the enduring racist prejudices of segregation, and I don't like to think about a future America separate, unequal, half white and half nonwhite. I think we need to know more about the cultures of all our ethnic minorities, and I admire my Scottish "roots," or at least some of them, but I don't want to go around wearing the tartan kilt or playing the bagpipe or boasting of the Scottish clans. In fact, I think clannishness is one of the major problems of the world, and like the historian Arthur Schlesinger, Jr., who has fought most of his life for racial integration, I don't want to trade the melting pot for the Tower of Babel. This, however, is clearly a rising problem.

The plight of what has been called the underclass has generally been realized, and much has been done by the federal and state governments to deal with it, but at every census it seems worse. The cost of federal welfare programs more than tripled between 1965 and 1987—from $141 billion a year to $520 billion (in 1988 dollars). In the nation as a whole, two thirds of black babies are born to unmarried mothers, and unemployment among blacks was 10.5 percent at the beginning of the nineties, twice that for whites. Though there is a developing black middle class, almost half of the black teenagers in Chicago fail to graduate from high school; in Washington, D.C., four times as many blacks are jailed as graduated from the public schools. As an indication of the continuation of racism, the Democratic party declined in popularity in the eighties and early nineties at least partly because it was generally regarded as being more sympathetic to the condition of the blacks than the Republican party is. While the Democrats still had a majority in the House and Senate, the Republicans controlled the White House and had a clear conservative majority of 6–3 on the Supreme Court.

Meanwhile, the United States is being challenged for the industrial leadership of the world by Japan and the new developing Economic Community of Europe. It has moved from being the world's leading creditor nation to being the world's leading debtor nation within a single decade, and it cannot agree on how to raise and spend the necessary funds for the health and well-being of its own people. In short, it has, by historic exertions, transformed the world, and is talking about a New World Order and spending vast sums on the exploration of outer space before bringing order into its own slums, schools, homes, industries, and politics.

It has borrowed extensively abroad to meet its debts, and owes more money to other nations than all the other debtor nations combined. Its interest payments alone in the nineties are larger than the entire federal budget at the beginning of the Cold War. It has had to find hundreds of billions of dollars to deal with the safety of its savings and loan institutions, its nuclear energy wastes, and the pollution of its atmosphere. In some ways, it is acting in the nineties like a colonized nation, selling its raw materials to its industrial rivals, importing their high-priced technological products, and buying more from abroad than it sells abroad. It has built houses it can't sell, and has more homeless people than it can handle. It has gone to the moon at immense expense and shortchanged its children, its health, and its old folk. It is addicted to credit cards and other drugs. It talks more about family values and education than any convention of preachers and teachers, but has more divorces and illegitimate and illiterate children than any other country in the free world. Considering its triumphs in the second half of the century, it should be rejoicing, but it is worried about its economy, its crime, its politics, and even itself.

Even this doesn't suppress my hope. It takes time to turn a great ship around or change the political habits or thinking habits of a vast nation, but America has a great talent for fixing things that don't work, usually by deadline or a little later. It corrected itself and showed great foresight in handling the Communist menace without a major war, and in the nineties it is beginning at least to debate its priorities once more under difficult circumstances. The people are concentrating on their freedoms and their rights. They are on the move again: into the cities and into the sun, restless, violent, living in an atmosphere of noise and watching television an average of over six hours per person per day. They were told in the eighties not to worry about things, but they worry anyway. There is, in short, a different atmosphere in the nation, a rise of factionalism, a rejection of taxation and regulation, much of which is being blamed on the leadership in Washington.

# CHAPTER 50

# What Happened to Washington?

The whole history of civilization is strewn with creeds and institutions which were invaluable at first and deadly afterward.

—Walter Bagehot

IN THE DEPRESSION thirties, Washington was regarded as the nation's refuge and its strength, and it even had a major league baseball team, but by the nineties, despite its triumphs abroad, somehow its popularity has gone, and so has its ball team. According to its detractors, it is not the answer to the problems of war, unemployment, inflation, illiteracy, illegitimacy, and financial and moral bankruptcy, but the cause. Even candidates for the presidency, noting the popularity of this indictment, have flown around the country proclaiming that the muddle of our political affairs either started or ended on the banks of the Potomac.

This isn't exactly new. New York and Philadelphia blamed General Washington for stealing the capital in the first place, and moving it close to his house at Mount Vernon for his personal convenience. The South blamed it for the Civil War. The populists blamed it for ruining the farmers. Everybody blamed it, at one time or another, for doing too much or too little, and concluded that it was not a great city like London or Paris, but a petty and quarrelsome "company town" that couldn't add and subtract or balance a budget.

I think this was a little stiff. In fact, I think Washington has often saved the people from themselves. It certainly didn't rescue the free world by popular demand. There were only twenty years between the two world wars when the great capitals of London and Paris were supposed to be maintaining the peace, whereas Washington helped bring those two wars to an end, and avoided a third world war with the Soviets for over forty-five years. It is, to be sure, excessively gabby, but the founders never expected it to be a cheerleader or errand boy for the loudest majority of the people.

In the era of television politics, all the techniques of commercial advertising are applied to the sale and packaging of candidates for high office, and even to the conduct of public policy. The tactics, strategy, and negative propaganda of the campaigns are increasingly determined by a new breed of "political consultants," who raise the funds, poll the people for popular themes, and write the speeches that promise more than they can deliver. The candidates themselves are probably as honest as their predecessors—in some cases more so— but in the last third of the century, television campaigning has cost more and has been more effective in spreading doubt about the character and policies of the opposition. All this has given Washington a bad name.

The main charge against it has been that it isn't like the rest of the country, not really representative of the majority of the people. My complaint is that it has often reflected the worst qualities in the American character instead of the best. It has been flighty, extravagant, boastful, and woefully ill informed about the rest of the world. But it seems to me that it has usually woken up before the rest of the country. Most Americans were against fighting against the British for independence in the first place; most were against a strong federal government in Washington or anywhere else; most favored slavery until Lincoln abolished it; and, even after Hitler had conquered the continent of Europe, most were against fighting in the Second World War until Pearl Harbor. It wasn't until the people opposed the Vietnam War that they showed themselves to be smarter than Johnson and Nixon, which wasn't all that hard.

One of the reasons why Washington has gotten such a bad name is that it is so noisy, quarrelsome, divided, and slow, and while this is tiresome and often maddening, it was precisely this deafening clash of debate that brought it out of isolation to the leadership of the free nations. I covered the House of Commons in London before I ever saw Washington, and I admired for a while the power of the British prime minister to limit debate and enact his program into law, but the thought of a President Johnson or Reagan having authority to impose his party's policies on the opposition made me grateful for the loud palaver and speed limits on Capitol Hill.

Here I confess to some professional prejudice, for all this noise at least made news, and that made my day and bought my baby's shoes. But when you ask what has happened to Washington in these fifty years, the answer is that, despite its win-at-any-cost politics, it has led the people against the enemies of freedom, and helped establish a little more sanity and order in the world.

In the first place, both political parties abandoned many of their old isolationist, protectionist, and racist policies to deal with the threats of poverty, illiteracy, and war. The country needed reform both at home and abroad, and their representatives differed fundamentally about these things in the thirties. Accordingly, they argued endlessly and often aimlessly over these issues for decades, and are still at it in the nineties, but I love the racket, the exaggerations, the outrageous roguery of it all, for it is our natural way to compromise, and I haven't noticed any other system in any other country that has worked any better or as well.

In this last half-century, the Republicans and the Democrats have each held the White House for twenty-five years. They have both had good presidents and poor presidents, and they have fought like scalded dogs, but each has moderated the other's wilder swings, and the people, like the Founding Fathers, have seemed to like this skeptical system of sharing power and responsibility. In fact, they have seemed able to tolerate almost any kind of president, and to get rid of the worst if they couldn't.

My main complaint about what has happened in Washington is that it overdoes everything. It either goes to sleep, as at Pearl Harbor, or goes crazy, as in Vietnam. It was late in recognizing the menace of Hitler, but then thought every other tin-pot dictator was another Hitler and hurried into war to get rid of him, even if this meant sending armies into rice paddies and deserts on the other side of the world. It was by turn too optimistic—"Who would dare attack the United States?"—or too pessimistic—"If we don't hold Vietnam, America will become a helpless, pitiful giant." It compromised under pressure, but in the eighties it was almost as extreme in its economic policies as in the twenties.

But even in this cynical age, when Washington has experimented with subversive warfare, there has been something in the American memory or character that has tugged Washington back to its roots. In the first place, it isn't very good at the dirty tricks of subversive warfare. Even presidents blame their failures on somebody else in this era of no-fault policies, but some official or nosy reporter always exposes their lies, evasions, and other deceptions.

"What did you make of it?" my father always asked me after the latest controversy in the capital, and often I didn't know what to make of it, or even what to make of myself. For I was always rejoicing at Washington's successes after grumbling about its follies, but I liked Washington for many reasons. I thought it was the most interesting city in America. There was no problem or reform that didn't end up on Capitol Hill or in Foggy Bottom or at the Supreme Court for decision. It was always talking about what could be done to improve the chances of a more decent life, which was admirable even when many of its ideas were silly.

I especially liked most of its officials, even when they were talking rubbish. They always had stories to tell, some of which were occasionally true. I thought it had the most intelligent and least appreciated civil servants in the world. During and after the Second World War, most countries sent to Washington their most accomplished diplomats, whose conversation was even more nourishing than their dinners. And the Congress still made room for eccentrics, a fast-vanishing American breed, whose preposterous antics and outrageous proposals were fun.

I did complain, however, about the way it shortchanged its women. Most First Ladies in the White House paid dearly for their fine position. They were photographed more than the Lincoln Memorial, often seen and seldom heard. They were eulogized, patronized, and analyzed on the style pages of the newspapers, but silenced by love or loyalty, they knew more and said less than all the other players in the play.

Maybe in retirement they found relief in obscurity, for onstage they were condemned to a life many of them hated. They gloried in the great man's successes and suffered with his failures and extracurricular activities. They looked upon him in public with frozen, adoring smiles, laughed at his feeble jokes, and applauded the punch lines they had heard a hundred times. It seemed to me that this was a form of cruel and unusual punishment, probably unconstitutional, and more often than not, they inherited at the end—if he lived—the wreckage of a restless and embittered old man.

One other thing: some of them were accused of influencing their husbands, but I thought they didn't do it often enough. I decided soon after arriving in Washington that the wives of presidents should be authorized and even encouraged to ask their husbands at least once a month: "What on earth did you think you were doing?" And on occasion to tell him what nobody else would, namely, "I love you, but sometimes think you're a certified fathead."

Some First Ladies were rewarded, or at least remembered. My favorite was Lady Bird Johnson, who devoted her life to the hopeless tasks of civilizing her husband and beautifying the federal capital. She was always holding things together. When President Johnson quarreled with his old friend Senator J. William Fulbright of Arkansas and refused to see him, Mrs. Johnson didn't intervene. She just sent a bunch of flowers to Betty Fulbright once in a while to indicate she was sorry and understood.

Eleanor Roosevelt was an influential adviser in the White House, but came into her own as a formidable political force only after her husband died. Julie Nixon, who married President Eisenhower's grandson, wrote an appreciative book not about her father but about her mother. Nancy Reagan wrote a book about her life in the White House, and later wished she hadn't. Bess Truman was wiser. She just went back to the old house in Independence, Missouri, and listened to Harry playing the piano.

In some ways, the wives of senators and congressmen had to endure many of the same problems without the glory. A few of them did useful work, running their husbands' offices, but most of them were relegated to work below their capacities. They had to keep the children from being spoiled by the limelight—no easy task. They had to maintain a family house in Washington and another back home in the state or district, and they had to wonder what the right honorable gentleman was up to when he was roaming the country. For while politicians are no more interested in sex than other goats are, their opportunities and temptations are greater.

Women have gotten more top jobs in Washington during the second half of the century than they did during the first. A few of them have made it to the cabinet, and one got a seat on the Supreme Court, but mainly they have been restricted to supervisory work, carrying out men's orders, presiding over the cabinet offices, keeping the boss on schedule, and keeping his secrets. Roosevelt without Missy LeHand, Eisenhower without Ann Whitman, and Acheson without Barbara Evans would have been as helpless as children. No doubt these big men thought they could run the world, but they couldn't run an office, keep their appointments, or even whistle up a ham sandwich without external assistance. So what would have happened to Washington and the government without the women, who make up 48 percent of the 300,000-strong official work force, I can't imagine.

In sum, I think even more nonsense has been talked and written *about* Washington than *by* it. I don't understand why it has always tried to save the world with its second team, but I love it anyway and have never flown into it without a happy sense of coming home. I glory in its parks and trees and its pretentious official buildings, and have even learned to tolerate its maddening circles and traffic jams. What I like about it most is that for all its changes in these fifty years it looks almost the same, without a single skyscraper towering over the White House. It is extravagantly beautiful in the spring with its flowering shrubs, and it is close to the mountains and the sea. In fact, if only it had a ball team, I think it would be the perfect spot for an old man's retirement, and defend it even for its sins.

# CHAPTER 51

# What Happened to
# the Press?

LIKE MANY OTHER American institutions in these fifty years, the newspapers have paid more attention to how they looked than what they did. With the help of advanced offset presses and color photography, they have had their faces, if not their minds, lifted, and they look a lot snappier. Most of the big-city dailies, I think, are also better written, better edited, and more accurate and inquisitive than in my cub-reporting days, but in a time of hot wars, cold wars, and subversive wars, they have peddled more bad news than the people have wanted to swallow, and they haven't been very popular. Part of the reason for this is that, while we are in the communicating business, we have done a poor job of communicating to the people what the responsibilities of a newspaper really are, and how our work has changed as the world has changed.

In these fifty years, I feel that the balance of power has shifted in favor of the government and against the efforts of the press to report what the government is doing. The latter-day presidents have increasingly dominated the news with the help of anonymous political and advertising advisers. Reporters had far more access to the news during the Vietnam War than they had during the Gulf War of the nineties, and in my experience, the people have tended to approve this official management of the news.

A small incident illustrates the point. After the nomination of President Eisenhower at the 1956 convention, my wife and I returned from San Francisco by train and sat in the dining car with a minister from the Fourth Presbyterian Church in Chicago. He was a warm supporter of Ike and thought I had written too negatively about the president. As we were leaving the dining car, he surprised me by asking if I still read my Bible. I said I did, occasionally. Well, he said, when you get home, look up the nineteenth chapter of the Book of Luke, the first to the third verses. "What's your point?" I asked him. "Never mind," he replied, "just look it up!" So when I got home I did so and then understood his meaning, for the passage read:

"And Jesus entered and passed through Jericho. And, behold, there was a man named Zacchaeus . . . And he sought to see Jesus . . . and could not for the press."

Still, with the development of worldwide television and daily newspapers that can be produced simultaneously in many capitals, the media has played an increasingly important role in world affairs. The television cameras on the battlefield during the Vietnam War, and on the refugees after the Gulf War, aroused public opposition to the death and suffering, and undoubtedly persuaded the government in Washington to amend its policies.

Diplomacy, which was once regarded as a written art, depending on documents and agreements that could be verified, became a verbal art with the development of radio and propaganda, and eventually it became a visual art with the spread of television. The results were varied. During the Gulf War, President Bush and Saddam Hussein were not talking to each other personally but watching each other on TV and trading personal insults in the next day's TV replies. This new megaphone diplomacy was not widely regarded as an improvement over the old diplomacy, but in some cases it produced positive results. For example, most observers credit television with informing the people of Eastern Europe of the superior results of democracy in Western Europe and leading to the revolts against communism in the Soviet empire.

Thus, while officials complain that reporters—to use their mildest term—are not "helpful" to the conduct of public policy, they occasionally (and usually in times of crisis) turn to reporters for help. For example, I went to see President Kennedy at his house in Hyannis Port, Massachusetts, at the beginning of September of 1961, when he felt that the Soviet Union underestimated his willingness to go to war, if necessary, to maintain the U.S. military garrison and political headquarters in Berlin. He assured me that he would not be forced out of there by Soviet pressure, but did not want to make the crisis worse by making a personal declaration to this effect.

It would, however, be "helpful," he said mildly, if I wrote in the

*Times* on my own authority that this was his clear intention. Accordingly, with the knowledge of the *Times'* responsible editors, I wrote: "Any action that closes U.S. access to Berlin will certainly lead to counteraction by the West, first in the UN, then in the field of economic countermeasures, then, if necessary, with an airlift or conventional military action on the ground to force the passage of supplies." These words were approved by Kennedy, and so were the following in a column I published:

"Any assumption that the United States would acquiesce in the defeat of its command on the ground without resorting to the ultimate weapons of nuclear power would be highly reckless. For nuclear war in such circumstances is not unthinkable. It is, in cold fact, being thought about and planned, and Mr. Khrushchev, unless he wishes to preside over a Soviet wasteland next door to 800 million Chinese, would be well advised to take this into account."

Frankly, I am not happy with this selective cooperation between officials and reporters, but the days of the old secret diplomacy are obviously over, and besides, the old diplomacy of secret arrangements secretly negotiated did not prevent, and may even have contributed to, the outbreak of the two world wars.

We assumed in the thirties that newspaper circulation would increase with the increase in the population and the spread of public education, but in the last decade of the century, circulation has leveled off, and many old geezers of my generation have complained that reading is going out of style.

I haven't joined this melancholy chorus, but obviously the newspapers have taken some hard knocks. The first of these was the decline in the popularity of the American front porch. In the thirties, when Father came home from the factory on the streetcar, he could read the paper on the way and then settle down on the front porch to study Roosevelt's latest rescue operations. But in the nineties, he is driving home from work, which makes reading awkward, and usually when he gets home he has no front porch.

Obviously, the place of the daily paper in American life has changed. In my early days, we were the first purveyors of the news, but radio and television changed all that, and when the old man checks the next morning's newspaper for the latest locker room gossip on the baseball game he watched on television the night before, it merely says "Late Game" and doesn't even give him the score. What is more ominous for the future, the children are no longer picking up the newspaper habit by reading the comic strips, but find the latest TV murders much more exciting than "Little Orphan Annie" or even "Peanuts."

None of this has been improved by the editorial writers, who are always "viewing with alarm" or saying "it is sincerely to be hoped" that the government will do what the editor thinks best—not forgetting the columnists, some of whom are telling the people that everything is wonderful while others are moaning that everything is terrible. In the labor union wars of the fifties and sixties, several famous old dailies folded—the *Herald Tribune* in New York, the *Bulletin* in Philadelphia, and the *Evening Star* in Washington, for example—but with the invention of photocomposition and new color presses, many papers covered the day's news with more foresight and hindsight.

Also, these new cheaper printing methods have spawned a lively press in the suburbs, where most Americans live, and with the development of satellite transmission, some of the giants like *The Wall Street Journal* and *The New York Times* print national editions and deliver them all over the country before breakfast time. So I don't agree with those who think the newspaper is in decline, and I don't notice much red ink on their balance sheets.

In fact, I think we are witnessing the greatest expansion of information since the invention of movable type. On the three hundredth anniversary of America's first newspaper (Benjamin Harris's *Publick Occurrences Both Foreign and Domestick,* published in Boston on September 25, 1690), there were 1,625 U.S. dailies with a circulation of over 62 million, and it was said that many of them were hauling in an average of 20 percent in profit before taxes—a record matched by few industries.

The other side of this is that the death duties have forced many family-owned papers to sell out to the chain gangs, with varying results. For example, when I started in this business we were reading Walter Lippmann's *Preface to Morals,* and when I retired, the most prominent newspaper book on the best-seller list was *Confessions of an S.O.B.* by Al Neuharth, the presiding genius of *USA Today.*

There are, however, some reasons for rejoicing. The old dictator-publishers of my youth, who polluted their papers with their prejudices, are as scarce in the nineties as linotype machines, and the one-party newspapers have vanished along with the old political bosses to the general benefit of the Republic. Fortunately, their successors are more independent. They provide more access to outside opinion, and they have brought a new generation of reporters to the fore and given them more freedom to analyze the news.

I like this new generation on the beat. For one thing, they are better educated. Unlike my contemporaries, they know the difference between Iran and Iraq, especially after the Bush war of 1991, and they speak foreign languages and can even understand the federal budget. They are better paid, and move over on the sunny side of the tracks, which doesn't improve their understanding of the poor, but even so they produce more scoops and expose more corruption than the old-timers. In fact, their fascination with scoopery sometimes leads them into snoopery, which I don't always enjoy, but they aren't intimidated by presidents, as old-timers often were, and they have helped rid the capital of many certified scoundrels. Also, in this public service, they have had the cooperation of the most talented group of newspaper cartoonists in the history of American journalism, led by the best of them all, Herbert Block of *The Washington Post.*

Officials, of course, don't like these journalistic investigators and mockers. "Who elected you?" they ask. "Why don't you leave us alone instead of nosing around like a bunch of suspicious cops?" I don't mind these questions and try to answer them, without noticeable success. I think we print bad news because the news is bad. We don't leave officials alone because, while they are no worse than the rest of the human race, they are no better, and will, I feel sure, make off with the Treasury unless they are watched. "Leave them alone" was a popular cry when the abolitionist press was trying to get rid of slavery, and I didn't think it was very good advice during the scandals over Cuba, Panama, Vietnam, and the Watergate. Who elected us? Nobody, but the Founding Fathers didn't expect politicians would be saints or that reporters would be cheerleaders.

It has never occurred to me that the people would or should like us. We're in the service business. We deliver a commodity every day like the mail, and also like the mail, a lot of what we deliver is junk. Like most people we rattle along about the bad and the unusual and, I confess, ignore a lot of good news that happens every day. I believe, however, that the American newspapers are adjusting to their new challenges, and will undoubtedly survive in the next century, although maybe a little skinnier and poorer. Meanwhile, they have learned to pay more attention to subjects that are really popular: the latest developments in education, the arts, fashion, and health, including the latest tips on such mysteries as how to make mashed potatoes.

Fortunately, they have had the assistance of new inventions. The new tape recorders, for example, are a boon to accuracy. My old one was often a crutch for my wobbly memory. It was invariably reliable in recording the preliminary and personal irrelevancies at the beginning of interviews, but unfortunately, my tape had a habit of running out, unnoticed, just when the great man got down to the main point.

Other inventions, while useful, have had unexpected influences on news and the government. The telephone, while handy, has contributed more than its fair share to misunderstanding between reporters and editors. The TelePrompTer, most unfortunate invention of all, has enabled presidents to fool more people more of the time than any other modern gadget, and I have come to have my doubts about the jet airplane. For while reporters find it convenient, it is a temptation that has become an addiction for presidents and secretaries of state. These opulent contraptions have comfortable beds, well-stocked kitchens and bars, and intelligent and obedient servants. They have elaborate secret communications that enable the president to issue orders without having to answer questions, and they arrive and depart to the sound of bands and the clicking of cameras.

All this is seductive stuff, and has obscured more news than it delivered. For officials, it is obviously easier and more pleasant than fussing with members of the Ways and Means Committee over the budget, or greeting the shouters for and against abortion, but summitry has its disadvantages. When lesser officials make a mistake, they can always be repudiated, but when presidents promise what they can't deliver, there is no higher authority to remedy the damage.

When I am asked what has happened to the press, one of my favorite answers is the invention of the photocopying machine. In the old days, when an ambassador sent a particularly important cable to the secretary of state or even to the president, marked "eyes only," the chances were that it actually did go to the secretary or the president and nobody else. But as events became increasingly complicated, and the big-shakers had to rely on experts who knew what the ambassador was cabling about, even these sensitive documents had a way of going first to the photocopying room, from which they emerged in flurries for distribution and analysis. This infuriated the security officers but delighted the reporters, who are as partial to leaks as plumbers, and think that most leaks do more good than harm.

My own experience was that governments usually got the voluntary cooperation of the media when secrecy was essential to national security. It was when governments were addicted to secrecy and used it to cover up their mistakes and protect their political and personal interests that representative government and a free press came into conflict. I have yet to meet a top official, including many moral philosophers, who wouldn't mislead me in a pinch or lie to me when in serious trouble, or try to wheedle out of difficulties by saying the press had misquoted him or her or taken remarks out of context. In fact, I have come to believe that blaming the press is really the last refuge of a scoundrel, and in saying so I am amazed at my moderation.

Accordingly, my main concern has not been that the newspapers would fail but that in their success they would become too complacent, too influenced by their prominent political and social friends, too likely to accept corruption on the ground that "everybody does it," and too forgetful that they were protected from censorship on the assumption that they really would "comfort the afflicted and afflict the comfortable."

Now for the commercial. As may already be apparent, I make no modest claims for newspapering, maybe because it's kinder to the reporters than to the readers. The main thing is that it gets a man out of the house and the office, and surprises him almost every day. In a world of increasingly repetitive and boring specialized labor, this gift of variety more than doubles a man's pay. There are other bonuses.

Many writers in other fields live a lonely life and often die before benefiting from the masterpieces that kill them, but solitary dead geniuses don't have much fun. Others devote ten years to a novel, and after reading the reviews, wish they hadn't. But newspaper writing, like liquor, is quicker, and while what we write today may be condemned tomorrow, at least somebody has noticed that we're alive, and we can start all over the next day.

We are often told we meet such interesting people, which is true, and a great many of them are other newspaper folk. Our bunch may be no smarter than any collection of accountants or real estate agents, but on the whole they are good companions: intelligent, outrageous, energetic, cocky, funny, and full of the latest gossip, some of which may actually be true. The only handicap to this is that we are so busy that we don't leave as much time for friendship as we should.

It is not a popular opinion, but I think honest reporting cuts a man down to size. Out on any important story, he soon learns that truth is a scarce and slippery commodity and that there are not two sides to every problem but maybe ten, held with genuine conviction by serious people who probably know more about the facts than he does. This occasionally makes us consider that maybe sometimes we have been wrong. Also, we have to get our copy past our editors, and while these anonymous lifeguards are regularly denounced as willful tyrants, I think one of them should get the Pulitzer Prize every year.

Finally, if you write for fifty years about the casualties of wars and politics, and about broken lives and promises, you count your blessings and don't expect to be popular. I don't want the press to be popular, just to deserve to be believed, and in the past fifty years I have come to the not wholly objective conclusion that it has earned more respect than it gets.

# PART EIGHTEEN

# RETIREMENT

............................................................................

# CHAPTER 52

# Love and Hope

We will not weep that Spring be past
And Autumn shadows fall;
These years shall be, although the last
The loveliest of all.
                                    —Alfred Duff Cooper

---

WHEN I RETIRED, one of my buddies gave me a useful present. It was a pair of socks with a bright green thread on the right side and a bright red thread on the wrong side. He explained that if I kept the green or "go" thread on the outside, I could get out of bed with complete confidence. This has proved to be correct. Before breakfast, I also find it useful to tune in on the weather and traffic reports. Listening to accounts of the coming storms and the traffic jams in the Washington streets, I sit back with my first cup of coffee in the blissful knowledge that neither gridlock nor glassy streets can interfere with a day without deadlines.

I then read the *Times* and play Walter Mitty. I can tell at first glance that all the bad habits of writing and editing I banished from the paper years before have been faithfully restored; that President Bush is still appointing dummies to important jobs, and more seriously, tossing armies at bush-league dictators.

None of this, however, interferes with my repose. I turn to the obit page, and even this doesn't depress me. For I have discovered that, while many of my friends and acquaintances died in my seventies, fewer of them are left for the obit writers in my eighties. I read about the wages of sin, as recommended by my mother, and about the collapse of the last of the empires in Eastern Europe, as predicted by Monnet, reassured from time to time that, despite the sleeping sickness of years gone by, maybe the human race is beginning to wake up.

It seems to me that, just as I started to work in the thirties, precisely when the world was made for reporters, I quit at just the right time. Many modern inventions are a boon to retirement. I can watch the football games on television, calling every play and denouncing every fumble from my armchair. When I am away somewhere, I can capture the good programs on my VCR and play them back when I get home. I have listened to the singing at the Berlin Wall on my shortwave radio and to perfect reproductions of the music of the ages on my CD player, always reflecting on how my father would have enjoyed all this if it had been available as he slipped into his eighties.

I like particularly the inventions that shut things off. It gives me immense pleasure and even a sense of power to silence the beer ads and singing commercials with the touch of a button. I have decided that America has become a nation of hypochondriacs, but when the patent-medicine hucksters begin telling me on TV about how to live forever, and the legal eagles start explaining my right to die, I can cut them off from across the room.

During my working days, I wrote a lot about collective security, but in retirement I am concentrating on personal security, and I've found that the telephone answering machine is a great boon. "Mr. Reston is busy right now," it says, which isn't exactly a lie, for I am probably wandering around the house looking for my specs, or listening to the latest disaster in the news.

Lately, I have been working on a campaign to make junk mail expensive for the senders who bury me every day with shiny pamphlets that make things look better than they are. I think it would relieve us of a lot of trouble, reduce the cost of a first-class stamp, and wipe out the postal deficit if we could just stamp this unwanted junk RETURN TO SENDER at the sender's expense. Unfortunately, I haven't yet figured out how to get the support of the Congress for this obviously desirable reform.

I have come in retirement to regret my many nasty cracks about television, for I have learned to use it selectively, and I have discovered that each day's menu usually offers something delicious or nourishing. The sports events on the weekends are especially satisfactory, for unlike the clash of politics and foreign policy that dominated my working days, they punish dirty tricks and put a time limit on filibusters.

I have retained my interest in politics, sort of, and one of the interesting things about this is that so many of the problems that seemed insoluble in my earlier years now seem so much easier and even correctable in my old age. For example, it now appears obvious to me that many of the problems in Washington could at least be minimized simply by appointing and electing people who know something about them. Since even the official stenographers in the government have to pass certain intelligence tests and demonstrate that they are fit for the job, why not ambassadors, cabinet members, and even vice presidents? I can find nothing in the Constitution requiring a president to appoint his brother or his buddy, regardless of qualifications, to be attorney general, and all it would take to produce this revolution in our affairs, I have concluded, is the abolition of human selfishness.

I have been warned that it is a great danger in retirement not to "keep up with things"; this, I have been told, would indicate that I am giving up. But there are so many things I don't want to keep up with that I have ignored this advice. Like Sally's granny, who said she managed to raise nine children by "not noticing everything," I don't notice many of the latest books and movies and other things dramatizing the violence and nastiness of life. Sally and I read together at night, concentrating on things amiable and of good report, and while this undoubtedly deprives me of many juicy items, I enjoy what I miss.

Having plenty of time to spare, I often turn my attention to education, and I have reached some thumping conclusions. I have decided I am for it. George Bernard Shaw argued that it is a pity to waste education on children, but I disagree, and I have hit on a number of useful reforms. I have decided that teachers should be paid as much as plumbers; that the content of schoolbooks should not be determined by politicians; that all children in all states, especially my grandchildren, should be given the same rigorous course in world history; and in defense of homework, I have concluded that all television should be banned nationwide for two hours after the evening news, by constitutional amendment if necessary. It has also occurred to me that to assist with these reforms it would be useful to have both a father and a mother in every house.

As to the problem of balancing the federal budget, which seems to baffle the leaders of both parties, it seems to me that there is a fairly simple solution. Like preachers and the heads of other institutions, the president could admit he was broke and pass the hat. If this voluntary appeal doesn't wipe out the debt, say by the end of the century, he could then by executive order impose a capital levy on all the people in accordance with their ability to pay. Unfortunately, I never figured out how to get the consent of the Congress and the people for this admirable scheme, but if you read my lips you'll see what I have in mind.

Retirement has some benefits dear to a Scotsman's heart. As a certified senior citizen, I can ride downtown on the bus for a quarter and go to a really good movie, if I can find one, for a dollar or two. It seems a shame not to take advantage of these bargains even if I don't want to go downtown, and I can also rent some funny old movies at cut-rate prices and show them to my grandchildren on my VCR.

Some of my Golden Pond plans, however, haven't worked out as expected. I never have gotten anywhere with that kitchen garden at Fiery Run. Too much bending over. When I'm there, it rains too much or too little. My tomatoes contract spotted fever, same with the apples in the pasture, and even my turnips grow no bigger than radishes. I have concluded it is more satisfactory to sit on the porch and watch the grass grow.

There have, of course, been the inevitable sorrows. On February 26, 1990, Iphigene Sulzberger died at the age of ninety-seven. Sally always said every family should have at least one elderly friend who is an inspiration, and Iphigene was ours. She was not a deeply religious person but lived by her favorite biblical injunction "to do justice, and to love mercy" and she was wise in the ways of the world. Once when her son Arthur came back from a private luncheon with the president, the vice president, and the secretary of state, she was pleased by his report but not overly impressed. "What did they want?" she asked. When I reflect on what holds families and institutions together, I think of the intelligence, goodness, and forbearance of this remarkable woman.

When I'm not too busy with all this, I play "What if?" What would have happened if the Japanese hadn't bombed Pearl Harbor? If Kennedy hadn't been murdered? If Gorbachev hadn't come along just in time? If Hitler had won the race for the atom bomb? If I hadn't met Sally?

. . .

As to writing, I haven't gone along with Graham Greene's gloomy advice. He said that writing in retirement was a form of therapy; he wondered how old people who didn't write managed "to escape the madness, the melancholia, the panic fear which is inherent in the human condition."

Well, I'm not mad, or melancholy—at least I don't think so. I am a little scared going downstairs or navigating traffic around the Washington circles, but I don't write for therapy, as Greene suggested.

I write for the record and for fun, and because I want to say a few things about the influences on my life. I mean by this the discipline of my parents, the example and love of my wife, the tradition of the *Times,* the advantages of the depression in the thirties, and even, as I look back on it, the thing I hated most—the fear of being rejected, of being ridiculed as an outsider, different, and even absurd. My mother and father made me feel, through the church, a sense of things beyond and above myself. I learned to work during the depression and didn't go around wondering whether I should go into law or business or something other than what I was doing. Being a loner was a spur to prove I could make it, even if this meant just hitting a golf ball a little straighter than others, and when Sally accepted me that made all the difference. In my eighties, I'm not even troubled by the thought of death, because as long as Sally lives, I feel connected to my family, including those who went before and those who will be around when I'm gone.

I enjoy writing about these things and I write when I please—in the middle of the night, for example. Most of the ideas I have ever had have come to me in bed. I can sit at my computer for hours during the day, watching the cursor blinking and saying "Hurry!" without writing a paragraph, but half asleep in the dark I can often find under my pillow just the right word or connection. Then, wide awake and elated by the discovery, I creep upstairs before I forget it and peck away in the silent house.

This book, for example, is a product of my nocturnal wanderings, no doubt explaining the sleepy passages, but I wrote it not to escape but to relive the happy days with Sally and reflect on those past experiences that might have some relevance to the future. So what happened to the Restons?

Sally and I have kept our promises and found that love at last sight is even better than love at first sight. There are, I have come to believe, a few personal things that endure in a dizzy world. The longer I live, the more I respect the teachings of my parents, not only as ideals but also as practical guides to life. All their tips about getting up early, working hard, and punting on third down have stood up fairly well, but it was Sally who banished my early fears of being alien and alone, and gave me a life of love and thought beyond my dreams.

We have walked the long plank together for fifty-five years, hand in hand to keep them from trembling, and I still can't think of a better formula for the pursuit of happiness. I look on these years as a joyful adventure and as an intellectual privilege, for I have constantly been in touch with a faithful, generous heart and a quick and independent mind. Sally not only married me but also educated me. She kept up with the news and also kept reminding me there were other things in life, partly because her education gave her a wider view.

For while I was focusing narrowly on journalism in college, she was studying and taking the highest honors in philosophy and literature and thereafter regarded life as a postgraduate course in these subjects. I didn't read books, I gutted them in search of something specific and relevant to my work; but we read our favorites aloud to each other in the evening and there were few awkward silences. We were often separated during the wars but never apart. I have never quite been able to share my parents' unquestioning religious faith, but I have found my salvation in the love and companionship of my wife.

It is one of old love's many blessings, and saves a lot of increasingly precious time, to discover together that you never have to finish sentences but understand with a blink or a nod. We have often canceled out each other's votes, but outside of politics, we usually agreed about most things and most people we met in our wanderings. I disagree with her habit of putting one foot on the brake and the other on the gas at the same time. Being a canny Scot, I love bargains, but Sally is inclined to believe that anything on sale is no bargain at any price. But we have laughed a lot and haven't cried much.

On the old folks' problem of memory, I never have been able to remember the name of the guy I met last Tuesday, whereas Sally can remember what was said at the junior prom. She has a remarkable talent for losing keys and eyeglasses but remembers everything else. This has been especially helpful to me in the production of this interminable book, and she helped me with my column for over thirty years. The idea of a husband and wife combining their personal and professional lives is supposed to put a strain on the family tie, but it hasn't on ours, even when we wrote magazine articles together. Once a young reporter asked me if Sally and I had ever "collaborated" on anything. I told him, "Yes, we have three sons."

Sally knew my Scottish weakness for preaching. I always knew she would spot any malicious or mischievous phrase in one of my columns and ask me in a gentle way whether I thought that jibe was necessary. So I always waited and listened.

In our house, I field the newspapers every morning when they hit the basement door, and we settle down and devour them. Over the years, they have become an addiction: give us this day our daily disaster. On the mornings when my column appeared, I turned at once to my favorite author and then fidgeted until Sally got around to it.

I pretended to be reading but watched her cannily out of the corner of my eye. If she got to the end and then turned the page without saying anything, I knew (for she always tried to say something nice) that it was another loser. If she mumbled "hmmm" halfway through, I had to wonder whether she thought that point was interesting, inaccurate, or just plain stupid. If she said, "I like your ending," I had to guess either that she didn't think much of the rest of it, or even worse, that she was relieved to have reached the end. But every once in a while I heard a delicious giggle, and that always made my day.

One of the blind spots of reporters is that after a while we are inclined to forget that officials are people. Preoccupied with issues, we come to regard them as liberals or conservatives, honest or crooked, but seldom as ordinary folk who have wives and children and cry when they're hurt. Sally was always saving me from this folly. She knew a lot of these official families and knew also when their kids were sick or flunking out of school or fiddling with drugs. Thus when some political luminary seemed to be in a slump, talking more nonsense than usual, she would say maybe he was worrying about the family or, as I was inclined to believe, about his own wandering and wayward habits. Still it was useful to be reminded that these headline characters have things to worry about other than the national debt—their own debts, for example.

There was another tradeoff between home and the office. A reporter spends a lot of time covering other people's problems, which helps take his mind off his own, but after a while this steady diet of political argument, much of it bitter and some of it nasty, is depressing. It's not clear that life can bear all the analysis we give it, month-long, year-out, and it helps to come back to a peaceful house and watch the sun go down over the Potomac bluffs.

So our lives have gone on, the longer the happier. We have had the wonderful experience of reaching that temperate zone of life when your children become your friends, when all are free and can talk about anything with equal candor and trust. Our sons went away into the world but have drifted back and somehow seem closer to home. We have thought a lot in the gloaming about our own parents and the sacrifices they made, for it's only when life makes full circle that you appreciate what went before. "It is," said Archibald MacLeish about the nobility of old age, "when the human heart faces its destiny and notwithstanding sings—sings of itself, its life, its death—that poetry is possible."

Even in her nineties, my mother still had strong views about the pointless miseries of the human race. She's still news in my mind because, unlike most mortals, she never seemed to be plagued by doubts, and the older she got the surer she was of her answers. Her view was that all this progress was only wickedness going faster. She always knew, she said, that life would be no daisy. The great thing about the Presbyterians, she thought, was that they expected so little that they were always ahead of the game.

The trouble with the modern world, in her view, was that people were always "led into temptation" but could never resist it or handle it. There were inexplicable accidents—she lost her favorite granddaughter in a crash on the Santa Cruz hills—in which the good were struck down and the wicked triumphed for a time. But she insisted that in the end—by which she meant the dark on the other side—the books would be balanced, the good would be redeemed, and the wicked punished.

On more worldly questions, she had equally strong convictions. For example, she was not at all in sympathy with the women's liberation movement. They didn't go nearly far enough for her. She didn't want equality with men but authority over them. Most men, in her view, were spoiled and willful children who would go to the bad unless policed by some good woman and the church.

Accordingly, she was not the least surprised by all the unspeakable horrors of a world run by men. If a nation founded on religion and faith lost its faith, no wonder it felt "lost," she insisted. If it did not apply those virtues she associated with her religion—humility, pity, charity, and respect for every human soul—it was bound to be in constant trouble. "There it is," she would say, "plain as the nose on your face."

I took her one shining day in an open car along the spectacular winding road along the Pacific, and she spoke not about all her struggles of the past but about what a wonderful life she had had in America. "I'm as old as the hills," the lady said with a giggle. "I sometimes think I'll live forever."

When she began to fail in her ninety-eighth year, my sister, Jo-anna, and I thought she should stop trying to take care of her house and go into a rest home, but we feared she would oppose it. On the contrary, she was happy sitting in a sunny window by a garden and getting her hair fixed once a week. "I've looked after people all my life," she said, "and now everybody's looking after me." When we buried her alongside my father in Santa Cruz, I thought of one of her favorite Burns poems:

> John Anderson my jo [sweetheart], John,
> We clamb the hill thegither,
> And mony a canty day, John,
> We've had wi' ane anither;
> Now we maun totter down, John,
> And hand in hand we'll go.
> And sleep thegither at the foot,
> John Anderson, my jo.

From my parents, my wife, and my work, I came to believe in a number of simple things that were old-fashioned long before I was born. I think it's better to take things with gratitude rather than for granted. I'm not sure what I believe about the ultimate questions of life and death but I believe in believing. I think the world is too complicated to be governed by ideology and that there are many roads to the Promised Land and many sides to truth. Therefore, I prefer courtesy to dogmatism and patience to judgment. For example, I'm not at all sure how I would have managed if I had been "led into temptation" and confronted by the evil of the latter generations. In short, I believe, thanks to Sally, in love and hope, for it's the first that leads to the second.

Thus, while I fear our inevitable separation, and hope that, like Sally's parents, we will go together, I do not fear death itself, for I find consolation in feeling a part of the life that has gone before and in the lives of our children and our grandchildren that will continue when we are gone.

In a way, the life of a reporter carries one into the larger life of the world and encourages self-forgetfulness. For one shares in the eternal pilgrimage of the human family, and at the end of this brutal century, can rejoice in the triumph of life over death. Accordingly, "in the new heaven and the new earth" Sally and I share in our dreams, there are no regrets, and no daily deadlines.

I figure when I get to the Pearly Gates I'll be asked if I have anything to declare, and like most travelers, I plan to declare as little as possible: one old typewriter, for I plan to do a little writing in my spare time; a bag of scoops to remind me of the happy days; my old steel engravings of the presidents, for I assume some of them went to "the other place"; and a picture of Sally and me on the day we were married, and of our parents and our children.

# Acknowledgments

WRITING A BOOK of memoirs with a wobbly memory requires a lot of help, and I got more than my fair share. My dear sister, Joanna, almost six years older than I, contributed many long-forgotten incidents from our Scottish years. I don't think she really approved of my "telling stories" about ourselves in a book, and I know she disapproved of my political opinions, but she remembered better than I the strictures of our parents, the paths we took to school together as children, and the names and faces of our playmates and teachers.

My wife, Sally, not only provided the story for this book but had to jolly it along for a couple of years and even help edit it at the end. I was told that such an arrangement was often a threat to both peaceful living and creative writing, but not in our case. After fifty-five years of experience, she was not unacquainted with the author's foibles and could kill a cheeky paragraph with a smile and eliminate a whole chapter with a frown. She is in no way to blame for the final result, but with no Sally, no book.

During our London years, when I was learning my craft, various famous characters gave me a hand without knowing it. I am indebted, for example, to Sherlock Holmes, who was always complaining that Dr. Watson was often at the scene of the crime but failed to notice the incriminating details. "You looked but you didn't *see*, Watson!" This encouraged me thereafter to notice the little giveaway expressions on presidents' faces and telltale gaps in their arguments. I didn't keep a diary, at least not for long, but I always read with a commonplace book at my side. I stuffed it with every joyful political jibe I found in the writings of the eighteenth-century essayists, and applied them occasionally on a bipartisan basis to some of the wayward politicians in Washington.

I look back with admiration and gratitude on the officials in Washington who advised various administrations during the Cold War and helped me understand some of the mysteries of that bitter conflict. I refer, among others, to George Ball, whose neglected advice might have avoided many tragedies in Vietnam; particularly to George Kennan, who thought with more intensity and wrote with more grace than any other Foreign Service officer of his time; Tommy Thompson; Charles "Chip" Bohlen, who also served as our ambassador in Moscow; and Paul Nitze, who spent most of his professional life on the importance of rearmament, and the end of it negotiating the reduction and control of nuclear weapons.

Also in Washington, I benefited from the knowledge and professional skills of Wallace Carroll and John Finney, the news editors of the *Times'* bureau, and from the chief correspondents who succeeded me: Tom Wicker, Max Frankel, Clifton Daniel, Craig Whitney, Hedrick Smith, and Howell Raines. Maybe some other newspaper had a more intelligent, knowledgeable, and delightful staff of companions than these, but if so, I never met them.

Jonathan Yardley, a former colleague on the *Times* and now the top book critic of *The Washington Post,* read the first draft of this book, and fortunately did not publish his observations. I not only benefited from his suggestions, but decided that all authors would be happier if critics shattered their illusions before publication rather than after.

My colleague Russell Baker not only read what I thought was the finished manuscript but went beyond the ties of friendship and spotted many silly mistakes. He didn't like the title *Deadline,* thought it "sounded like a Humphrey Bogart movie," and wanted me to change it to *Scotty,* but that would have left out Sally, and I didn't want to do that. My lifelong buddy Ned Kenworthy read the manuscript and didn't let our friendship get in the way of his judgment.

All three of our sons had a shot at the manuscript and all made their contributions, but the champion detective was Thomas Busey Reston, who caught me in more mistakes than anybody else.

When I started writing a column, I made a deal with the *Times:* I would do without a secretary if permitted to appoint one promising young reporter each year to answer the mail, find the missing facts, and review my copy. Yardley was the first of these, fresh out of the

University of North Carolina, and he was followed by twenty-five others, who contributed to my long survival on the *Times.* Most of them had nothing to do with this volume, but five saw me down the back stretch. They were Richard Coe, from the University of Michigan and Yale, Jack Steinberg, currently with *The New York Times,* Hilary Stout, now of *The Wall Street Journal,* Stewart Yerton, also with the *Times,* and Amy Wallace and James Newton, who apparently did not give me their undivided attention, for they married each other on the side, and escaped against my wishes to the *Los Angeles Times.* These young people are not only part of this book, but I think of them as almost part of my family.

The *Times* opened up its invaluable archives to me and I was able to rifle the *Times* index with my computer. This proved to be helpful, for I was constantly discovering that the articles I was sure I wrote in 1971 actually appeared in 1962 or 1984. The index also enabled me to run down and reprint here the few sensible things I had written, and suppress the rest.

I have many reasons for expressing my thanks to the Sulzberger family for their character and kindness and for the many opportunities they placed before me, and this goes as well for my old skipper in Washington, Arthur Krock. He opened the front door to me in Washington, and taught me how to keep my mouth shut and work my way out of jams.

I also want to thank my editor at Random House, Kate Medina, assistant editor Jonathan Karp, copy editors Amy Edelman and Lynn Anderson, and designer Jo Anne Metsch.

The reader may have noticed that there are no footnotes in this book. This is because I hate footnotes or pockmarks at the bottom of the page. They are symptoms of what the British call "foot and note disease," and seem to say: "If you don't believe me, look up old So-and-so." No doubt they are permissible and even essential in a work of history, but this is not a work of history—it is a work of love.

# Appendix

McCLOY ON THE A-BOMB
[The following is John J. McCloy's private account of how the United States government decided to use the atom bomb on Japan.]

When, in April 1945, it became increasingly apparent that the bomb would be successfully developed, Stimson set up a committee to advise the president and him on its use and implications. This came to be known as the Interim Committee. It was chaired by Mr. Stimson and in his absence by George L. Harrison. Its members were: James F. Byrnes, as personal representative of the president; Ralph A. Bard, under secretary of the navy; William L. Clayton, assistant secretary of state; Dr. Vannevar Bush, director, Office of Scientific Research and Development and president of the Carnegie Institution of Washington; Dr. Karl T. Compton, chief of the Office of Field Service, OBRD, and president of MIT; Dr. James B. Conant, chairman of the National Defense Research Committee and president of Harvard University. I knew these men and not infrequently had discussions with them about the use of the bomb.

In Washington, around May 10, I was present at a series of talks with the secretary, the Joint Chiefs, and Averell Harriman, who had returned from Moscow with a gloomy report about future Soviet policy. At this time Stimson discussed with General Marshall the timetable for the attack on Japan. It was scheduled for early August. Stimson, having learned from General Groves that the first atomic bomb would be ready around August 1, wondered whether it would not be feasible to hold up the attack, with its anticipated heavy casualties to American troops, until the A-bomb was ready for use.

Mindful of the various military, moral, and political questions involved, Mr. Stimson finally concluded that dropping the bomb would be the quickest possible way to end the war and the bloodshed it would entail.

For a time Stimson discussed suggestions that had been made for a demonstration explosion not against a real target but against a remote, uninhabited Pacific island to show the Japanese what was in store for them if they did not surrender. Objections were raised such as, Suppose something goes wrong, the bomb doesn't go off? Finally the conclusion was reached that the bomb should be used against a military target, with civilians in the area, if it were to create the "shock" effect required to convince the Japanese to surrender. The Interim Committee favored a military target and the Joint Chiefs were of the same mind. Ralph Bard, under secretary of the navy, who was a member of the committee agreed but a few weeks later changed his mind.

We also discussed various elements of the surrender terms to be given to the Japanese, particularly the future of the emperor, who was considered to be near divine by the Japanese. There were those who wanted to execute the emperor for his responsibility for the war. Among them were men generally considered to be liberals, who felt the emperor should be tried as a war criminal. Others believed that if the emperor was allowed to continue as a constitutional monarch the Japanese would more promptly surrender.

Sometime in mid-June 1945, Mr. Stimson advised me that the new president wished to meet with a number of the decision makers, mainly the Joint Chiefs of Staff, to determine what alternatives or options we had in order to wind up the war with Japan promptly, with as few casualties as possible. The central decision was whether or not we should attack the main Japanese islands, Kyushu and Honshu, and what form the attack should take.

As I recall, I had not talked about the bomb with President Roosevelt or with any cabinet member other than Mr. Stimson. In addition to my associates in the War Department I had talked with General Marshall at some length and with Joseph Grew, our former ambassador in Tokyo and at the time under secretary of state, whose appraisal of the attitudes of the Japanese leaders and people made a strong impression on me.

General Marshall was anxious to leave the main questions regarding the use of the bomb to the president. He treated it as a matter involving the highest form of policy for which he looked to political leaders for direction. He believed that the decision should not be left to the military leaders. He never indicated to me that he opposed the use of it, but the general is on record as favoring that warning of some kind should be given in advance to the Japanese before any atomic bomb would be dropped. He had heard of the use of such terms as *primordial* and *Promethean* applied to the force which could be generated by an atomic bomb. "I am not," he frequently said to me, "a scientist to judge how destructive the bomb will be. Nor," he added, "am I sure that even the scientists can do so." He had heard that among the scientists there were some who were seriously concerned that the program contemplated for the bombing of Japan with the chain reaction and exponential formula might produce cosmic results. The fact that this would be the first time in all human history that any such force would be released made it clear to him that more than military considerations had to be taken into account before it should be dropped.

Dr. Forrest C. Pogue, Marshall's biographer, has yet to publish his final volumes on the life of the general. When published, they may, I conjecture, contain material or documents that would throw further light on the general's attitude in regard to the bomb.

My talks with Mr. Grew were extensive. He had definite ideas about the possibility of bringing the Japanese war to a successful end without sacrificing further lives by an appeal to the more moderate elements of the Japanese government and people. He seemed to feel that it was possible to effect a full capitulation and the surrender of all Japanese forces by pointing out our overwhelming superiority and our willingness to afford them a just and fair surrender. In short, Grew persuaded me that we would have nothing to lose by warning the Japanese of the cataclysmic consequences of the weapon we possessed and indicating that we would be prepared to allow Japan to continue as a constitutional monarchy with reasonable access to raw materials so that the Japanese could achieve a viable economy, provided they surrendered their armed forces.

On June 18, shortly prior to the time when all, or most all, hands left for the Truman-Churchill-Stalin conference at Potsdam, a crucial meeting took place at the White House. As it was a meeting of such vital importance, the secretary of war, as well as the Joint Chiefs of Staff, were to be present. As I recall, the secretary of state was not present. The night before the meeting, Mr. Stimson told me that he was not feeling well and that he might want me to attend in his place. Accordingly he wanted to discuss with me the advice that should be given to the president. I am not certain whether we talked the matter over at Woodley or in his office.

I suggested that the war had reached a stage where a surrender might well be effected without any further bloodshed, notwithstanding the remaining large Japanese forces under arms. We had arrived at an overwhelming superiority in everything, there were no more large Japanese battleships to sink, it was difficult to find suitable targets from the air that had not already been saturated with bombing. We had an enormous moral ascendancy over the Japanese, who had treacherously attacked Pearl Harbor. We had moved steadily across half the world to bring the war to the very heartland of Japan. Our prestige was tremendous. In these circumstances, I said, we should have our heads examined if we did not consider the possibility of bringing the war to a conclusion without further loss of life. I felt we could readily agree to let the Japanese retain the emperor as a constitutional monarch. We talked about the possibility of a message to the Japanese government, what form it might take, and whether or not we should mention the possession of the bomb. I told Mr. Stimson that the object, as I saw it, was a full Japanese surrender or capitulation, which gave us all we had been fighting for but which would be regarded as fair to them. It was not our objective to devastate Japan any more than it had been our aim to pastoralize Germany. We had the means to force a surrender or at least to try to achieve it without an attack and without dropping the bomb. The determination to drop the bomb would be clear if Japan did not surrender on terms wholly acceptable to us. Mr. Stimson let me do most of the talking but he didn't just listen. And, as I recall, he did not demur.

I thought we had reached full agreement as to what attitude I should take at the next day's meeting and I felt I had Mr. Stimson's authority to develop with the president and the Joint Chiefs of Staff the conclusions we had reached.

### Decision at the White House

The next day I went to the White House, having heard again that Mr. Stimson wanted me to attend in his place. To my surprise and pleasure, Mr. Stimson also appeared. I asked him whether I should leave, but he requested me to remain after telling the president that, having felt indisposed, he had asked me to take part. At the last minute he had decided to attend. He said that he wished me to remain because I had been working intensively on the terms that might end the war. To this the president agreed.

The meeting was largely a military one without representation from the State Department. Full discussion was inhibited by the fact that whereas a number of people in the room knew about the progress on the A-bomb, others did not. Consequently, though a momentous decision was about to be taken, a thorough and penetrating discussion of alternatives was somewhat inhibited.

The president chaired the meeting. He summed up the purpose of it by putting to those present the question whether in their view there were any reasonable alternatives to his authorizing the attack on Kyushu to bring about the prompt conclusion of the Japanese war. He first called on General Marshall, who stressed the fact that he did not believe a surrender of the Japanese forces could be effected solely by bombing, stating that in his opinion, bombing alone had not brought about the German surrender. He called attention to the fact that there were still many Japanese soldiers under arms. They could be expected to put up a fanatic defense as they had during the entire course of the war. Photographs of some of the defenses on Honshu were available and our heavy losses on Okinawa were described. We were confronting a grim affair. The chief of staff made no mention of the A-bomb. There was talk of alternatives: a blockade of Japan and a continuation of the bombings without a landing. These suggestions were discarded as impractical or ineffective. General Marshall's recommendation was that we should first attack the island of Kyushu, the southern island, as a possible preliminary to an attack on Honshu. The chief of staff of the navy, Admiral King, made the same recommendation, and I gained the impression that there had been a caucus and a consensus reached among the chiefs of our military, air, and naval forces prior to the meeting.

At the conclusion, the president polled all present and the upshot was that no alternative to an attack on Kyushu was suggested.

I did not speak, because Mr. Stimson was there and he gave his opinion that the president's best course was to approve the attack on Kyushu. I was surprised at this, but surmised that the secretary had reached conclusions other than I thought we had reached the day before. After the polling, the president then gave the directions for the attack on Kyushu, but he repeated that no attack was to be made on Honshu until he had a full opportunity to give this alternative further thought.

As we were packing up to leave, the president noticed me and he said, "McCloy, you didn't express yourself, and nobody gets out of this room without standing up and being counted. Do you think I have any reasonable alternative to the decision that has just been

made?" I looked at Stimson and he said I should feel entirely free
to express my views. So I said, "I think you have an alternative that
ought to be fully explored and that, really, we ought to have our
heads examined if we do not seek some other method by which we
can terminate this war successfully other than by another conventional attack and landing." I then stated what I had said the night
before to Mr. Stimson.

I said that a political solution at this stage would not only be
honorable but also highly desirable in view of the heavy casualties
that would have to be contemplated if we did not at least attempt the
alternative. I said our superiority was so great, both physically and
morally, as to be almost fantastic, particularly with our possession
of the bomb. True, we had not completed our tests, but it had the
full confidence of the scientists. All the reports were to the effect that
the problems connected with the bomb had been overcome. I recall
the atmosphere that my mention of the bomb out loud, so to speak,
created even in that high circle. It was like mentioning Skull and
Bones in good Yale society.

President Truman asked that I spell out what I meant. I said I
would have him send a strong communication to the emperor describing our overwhelming military superiority and stating that we
would demand a full surrender but one that would recognize Japan's
right to continue to exist as a nation after ridding itself of the elements that had brought such destruction to the country; that this
might include the continuation of the mikado but only on the basis
of a constitutional monarchy; access to necessary raw materials outside Japan but not such control over them as they had been planning.
Then I said that if after such an offer no surrender was forthcoming,
we should notify the Japanese of our possession of a weapon of
revolutionary proportions and so devastating in its effect that it could
destroy a city at one blow; that we would be compelled to employ
it if they did not surrender. I said I was prepared to use the term
*atom bomb* but realized that there was such an air of secrecy about
it that we could use other words to describe its effect but they had
to be graphic enough to be more compelling than the threat of
Hitler's secret weapons had been.

At my mention of the bomb, there was a gasp in the room. But,
I said, I thought our moral position would be better if we gave them
a specific warning of the atom bomb. Suggestion of a political solution of the war was not popular with most of those attending the
meeting. There seemed to be a general feeling among some that it

would be taken as a sign of weakness even though the character of the bomb and our determination to use it were real.

The president indicated that what I had said was in the nature of what he was seeking. He asked me to elaborate further on my suggestion and to take the matter up with Mr. Byrnes, who was then acting as the assistant to the president. He had been the majority leader in the Senate and he was a powerful political figure. Mr. Byrnes was not present at the meeting of June 18.

I immediately called on Mr. Byrnes. He told me that he would have to oppose my proposal because it appeared to him that it might be considered a weakness on our part. Mr. Byrnes inferred he might not insist on treating the emperor as a war criminal, but he would oppose any "deal" as a concomitant of a demand for surrender.

Accordingly, the communication later sent from Potsdam demanding surrender did not specifically mention the bomb or the status of the emperor. Two bombs were dropped on Japan without any specific warning and with gruesome results. The emperor concept was in fact recognized and maintained; raw materials were certainly made reasonably accessible to Japan. President Truman, though much intrigued with the possibility of reaching a surrender with Japan without the need of an invasion or the dropping of any atomic bomb, was, typically, quite prepared to accept full responsibility for the dropping of the bombs.

At Potsdam, I did not attend the meeting at which Stalin was told of our possession of the bomb. I was told of Stalin's reaction after President Truman disclosed it to him. Stalin, apparently, simply said, "Well, that's fine. Let's use it. What's the next item on the agenda?" We thought he would be more excited about it. We had just received reports of the test conducted at Alamogordo. They were graphic, dramatic, and awesome reports of what had taken place. Whether Stalin knew all about the bomb beforehand or not, we didn't know; we were not, I believe, aware of the English defectors at that time. It was apparent that the atomic bomb would give us a significant card to play in obtaining a decisive victory. Certainly after Alamogordo the idea of pressing the Soviets to enter the war took on much less significance.

There is a small footnote. One indication that the president had been intrigued by my suggestions at the June 18 meeting, even though they were not carried out, is the fact that when the surrender document, which I had had a part in drafting, arrived from the battleship *Missouri* and was presented to the president in the presence of the Joint Chiefs of Staff, Mr. Truman held up the taking of the photograph until, at his invitation, I could get to the White House to be included in it. The president said he had taken this step because I had given him a thoughtful presentation of what his options had been in bringing about a prompt and successful end to the Japanese war. The picture was published in *The New York Times,* September 8, 1945. I'm there in the back row.

### The Question of Decision Making

I have always felt that if, in our ultimatum to the Japanese government issued from Potsdam, we had referred to the retention of the emperor as a constitutional monarch and had made some reference to the reasonable accessibility of raw materials to the future Japanese government, it would have been accepted. Indeed, I believe that even in the form it was delivered, there was some disposition on the part of the Japanese to give it favorable consideration. When the war was over I arrived at this conclusion after talking with a number of Japanese officials who had been closely associated with the decision of the then Japanese government, to reject the ultimatum, as it was presented. I believe we missed the opportunity of effecting a Japanese surrender, completely satisfactory to us, without the necessity of dropping the bombs. Whether or not we would have been better off, or the world would have been better off, if we had not used the atom bombs in conjunction with the surrender of Japan, is now a matter of speculation. What I think we can be certain of is that if the atom bombs had not been detonated over Hiroshima and Nagasaki, we would have had a radically different set of circumstances to face than now confront us.

My point also is, that in arriving at a decision, which was made to go ahead with the ultimatum, as we did, the matter was not given the thoroughness of consideration and the depth of thought that the president of the United States was entitled to have before a decision of this importance was taken. The decision was made without consideration of the implications and imponderables that the use of the bombs demanded. Before the decision was made, there should have been more thorough discussion of these aspects of the problem.

I have always been disturbed that we were not more effective in pursuing the possibility of achieving a surrender without the employment of the atomic bomb. I do not criticize the judgment, good faith, or intentions of those who were responsible for the decisions leading to our final action. I do feel strongly, however, that our decision-making process in respect of the termination of the Japanese war was an example of our need, which continues today, to improve our decision-making process in this menacing nuclear age.

I have a few additional comments to make in regard to the manner in which the Japanese war came to an end. In fairness one must recall the bitterness that the surprise Japanese attack on Pearl Harbor produced; the atrocities of the Bataan march, and the casualties we had endured in fighting the war across the Pacific. I gained the impression that certain so-called liberals among the group who were giving the matter thought were in favor of treating the emperor as a war criminal though it was apparent he was a puppet of the warlords when it came to starting the war. And, those who were in control of weapons designed for use in the war wanted to see them used. The air force wanted to use its bombers, the navy to use its ships, and the army its men and armor. It is, of course, possible to understand the president's and Mr. Byrnes's reasons for the use of the bomb as the shortest route to surrender. It could be said that the horrendous character of the bombs would never have been sensed except through their actual use on live targets. It can be argued that they would have become less of a deterrent to a future nuclear exchange than if the bombs had not been dropped. I am not convinced. I believe our influence would have been more effective in the long run if we had given warning of our coming nuclear attack. We needed drop the bomb only if our offer of an honorable surrender were rejected.

I do not wish to place myself in the class of those who, many years after an event, say that they favored a different action and consider how right I was! My desire is simply to show how some major policy decisions have come to be made at critical periods in our history. It is also to point to the need for having in place the best methods, procedures, and habits by which our thinking can be effectively composed.

Military and naval opinion are not alone sufficient even in times of crisis for ultimate decisions, nor is political opinion. In connection with the Japanese surrender I repeat that I do not think that the State Department played its full and proper role, and the same can be said of the advisers in the White House. Clausewitz was right—war and policy do go hand in hand. There wasn't enough vigorous thinking going on in the State Department or for that matter in the White House at the time. At the June 18 meeting, it should not have been left up to the assistant secretary of war to bring up the possibility of political settlement. The secretary of state should have been present and proposing such solutions. But during the war, with the military at the center of all attention, political thinking became less keen in the State Department, and the White House came to rely perhaps too heavily on its soldiers for all advice. It is most important to have, as we once had, a committee such as SWNCC, that is, the State, War and Navy Coordinating Committee. We had a hard time forming it. It was difficult to convince the State Department that it ought to be sitting down with the soldiers, and thinking in terms of policy in connection with the conduct of the war. The lesson I believe basically is that the State Department should never abandon its duty, even if it does not prevail, to think with full vigor in political terms, even in the midst of a war. And the White House should take care to see that the the ultimate decision maker—the president—is presented with a full consideration of all the plausible alternatives and options. This is what I was told he asked for and what I believe he did not get.

## MY TRIBUTE TO ARTHUR HAYS SULZBERGER

The purpose of this service of remembrance is to pause for a few minutes to think about the meaning of a life—rather than the moment of a death. We have come here to pay our respects to our dear friend and to his family. And in the process, I hope we may fortify our faith in human decency and renew our courage by trying to recall something of the magic of his personality and the quality of his work and character.

We cannot help but grieve at such a time, but we are not called upon to be morbid. For Arthur Hays Sulzberger was, among many other things, a joyous man. Five years ago, when he was already seriously ill, he wrote out the instructions for this occasion.

There were to be none of the ghoulish trappings of death, he said. No fancy casket, no mountains of flowers smelling of the grave and, on pain of eternal punishment—for some reason not quite clear to me—no Mozart. He had a thing about Mozart and he was forever chasing the poor man off the *Times* radio station.

It is not easy for a man at the top of a newspaper to be joyful these days. Those of us who report have fun but a newspaper publisher is a little like a doctor: he spends a good deal of his time listening to people who have a pain. Also, Arthur Sulzberger did not have the good fortune to lead the paper in a calm or joyous time.

He became publisher in 1935 during the economic depression and endured the tumult of three wars until the end. This was a time, first, of drift and hallucination, then of unspeakable violence and disorder, leading to the transformation of our professional life, of our national life, and of the larger life of the human family.

Still, he presided over the *Times* during this convulsive period with rare good judgment, unfailing human consideration, and a remarkable combination of seriousness and merriness. Few arguments ever became strident for long at his council table before he broke the tension with an amiable jest.

He had a wonderful compassion for the weaknesses of the human spirit and hated gossip and personal criticism or spite. Nobody ever made a silly fool of himself without being told to forget it. Was anybody sick or in trouble? Arthur Sulzberger was usually the first to help out. Were families separated in the service of the paper? He was usually the first to remember.

He kept a "calendar of kindness" and was forever sending notes or genial rhymes, or presents, to mark birthdays or anniversaries, not only to his own loved ones, but to the larger family of the *Times,* and the widening circle of his friends.

I have known a lot of good newspapermen and a lot of good family men, but not so many who were both. There is an unfailing rule of life—that news always breaks just when a man is supposed to be going home. But Arthur Sulzberger, late home or not, somehow managed to reconcile his professional and family responsibilities.

He was an incorrigible poet, cartoonist, storyteller, amateur painter, interior decorator, drink-mixer and furniture-mover.

For twenty years he moved the furniture up and down and around the old family house at 5 East Eightieth Street, and then, when he was finally satisfied with the arrangement, he sold the house.

There was an irrepressible streak of Lewis Carroll in him, and he turned his home into a wonderland of his own. Who but A.H.S. would name two of his children Punch and Judy? Who but he could sit on the stairs with the children on his way to a party, demonstrating the art of blowing out his collapsed tall silk opera hat?

He wrote and illustrated books for the children—about Ellie (the elephant) and Allie (the alligator), who turned into pigs when any of the children ate too much ice cream.

His production of illustrated letters to the family was prodigious. He always portrayed himself as Barney Google. He celebrated August 14—the date he first proposed and was rejected—by presenting

Iphigene one year with a beautifully iced cake, made entirely of wood.

When she finally did agree to marry him under a tree at Lake George, he had the tree moved to their house in Westchester County. When the eldest of his three daughters was married, he wandered around the wedding reception with a sign on his back, reading: IF YOU LIKED THE SETTING AND THE CEREMONY, REMEMBER I HAVE TWO MORE.

Though he was deeply involved in life, there was something in him that stood apart. His sense of humor was really a sense of perspective, and he used it to a purpose.

His rhymes were kisses, and sometimes they were gentle admonitions to the children, and occasionally they were editorials, but always this exuberant capering was the expression of a merry and a loving heart.

It is only fair to say that he did not pick up this quality on Forty-third Street—after all, the *Times* is not widely known as a center of puckish frivolity.

This is something he inherited, and he was obviously a poetic spirit before he was a publisher. He was the second of the three sons of Rachel Peixotto Hays and Cyrus L. Sulzberger.

His eldest brother, Leo, died in 1926. The youngest brother, David, died in 1962. Thus what is passing here is the last member of the seventh generation of a remarkable American family that started here in 1695, before there was an independent country.

From this family, too, he inherited not only a merry but a deeply serious strain, which increased as his health and strength ebbed.

He was not given to philosophic speculation and wasted little time on phantom ideas. But occasionally he scribbled his thoughts on a little black notebook that was always at hand.

"I have no personal God," he once wrote. "No one who watches over me. No one to whom I am indebted for the gift of life other than my parents, who have been dead for many years.

"My prayers are to me. I challenge myself to be good to those I love, to treat decently those with whom I come in contact. If I deserve punishment, it will be meted out by my fellow men or by my own conscience. That is ever present, and one cannot fool or mislead it."

When we come to assess his contributions to his newspaper and profession, we have to do so without any self-glorification on his part. It may have occurred to a few of you from time to time that modesty is not the newspaperman's most prominent characteristic.

But Arthur Sulzberger was a genuinely modest man. A year after he became publisher, he wrote, "I find myself not as an arbitrary wielder of authority but rather as a servant to the course of events, over which I have no control and to which I must react."

Even after he had been on the *Times* for forty years, during which he had led it to spectacular successes, he was giving most of the credit to his associates and conceding only that "the backs of my ears are not as wet as they were."

He was mortally afraid of abusing personal power, or the power of the paper. He was always reminding himself that even in private conversation what he said might carry unintended significance because of the position he held, and either hurt somebody or give one of his reporters the wrong idea that he wanted his views reflected in the paper.

Newspapering is a savagely competitive business. You have to make major changes or die. The graveyard of great newspapers, alas, is very wide and deep, but Arthur Sulzberger risked the changes and made the advances.

He combined reverence to the symbol and tradition of the *Times*—and reverence is the right word—with fearlessness of revision. This is no time or place for comparisons, but in most newspapers the owners tend to consolidate and the managers to innovate.

Maybe because Arthur Sulzberger thought of himself in terms of stewardship rather than of ownership, he managed to strike this difficult balance between the two, and my own experience with him was that he was more fearless in revision than most of us.

What is particularly interesting is how he did it. He didn't have the particular swing or melody of our craft when he joined the *Times* at twenty-seven.

He never even learned how to run a typewriter. He was not a specialist in gathering news or advertising. He was not a prophet of the coming age.

He was not full of self-confidence when he took over and he didn't even begin with the confidence of all his associates, but by any standards of excellence or commerce or ethics, he was a remarkable success.

The explanation, I believe, was simple integrity. He combined a general ease and charm in personal relations with good judgment, a belief in young men like Orvil Dryfoos and Arthur Ochs Sulzberger, and a true and natural morality of action.

He was not a moralizer, but he preserved that vanishing gift of actually listening to what other people said and then thinking about it before he answered.

The result was that men went away from him feeling that they had been heard out to the end and that they were treated fairly, for he had the gift of reminding us, by his gusto and his example, of the decencies of life.

If you have any doubt about the enduring quality of his example and character, all you have to do is look around.

The new generation of this family is already in place, with another Arthur Sulzberger at its head, and has carried the *Times* to even greater successes than ever before, and they are going to have to step lively, for the next generation is already knocking at the door.

The test of great leadership is whether it leaves behind a situation that common sense and hard work can deal with successfully.

Reverence for the symbol and fearlessness of revision—all that we have and mean to defend—all that and Iphigene Ochs Sulzberger, and her children, and their children, who will learn the art in their time.

### REMARKS ON A FRIEND: ORVIL DRYFOOS

The death of Orvil Dryfoos was blamed on "heart failure" but that obviously could not have been the reason. Orv Dryfoos's heart never failed him or anybody else—ask the reporters on the *Times.* It was steady as the stars—ask anybody in this company of friends. It was faithful as the tides—ask his beloved wife and family. No matter what the doctors say, they cannot blame his heart.

In the spiritual sense, his heart was not a failure, but his greatest success. He had room in it for every joy and everybody else's joy. This was the thing that set him apart—this warmness and purity of spirit, this considerateness, of his mother, whom he telephoned every day, of his wife and children, of his colleagues and competitors. And this uncorrupted heart, broken or no, is what is likely to be remembered of him in this great city and at Dartmouth, his other home.

The obit writers had a hard weekend with Orv because they kept hunting for him in the files and, of course, he wasn't there. He didn't make speeches, he made friends. The last time I saw him, he was breathing hard but still worrying about everybody else's worries and insisting that everybody get a good rest after the long strike.

Most of the time, it is the heart that governs understanding, and understanding was his special quality. He not only understood human frailty but also almost preferred it. He understood the sensitive pride and combative instincts of reporters and editors, which is not easy. He even understood the anxieties of the printers during the time of our troubles.

Throughout that whole ghastly period, when he wore his life away, he was again worrying about other people, this time about those who were on the street with no work, and those who were in the office with too much work. He was running the office by day and often negotiating far into the night. Even when his heart began to rebel and the doctors put him on digitalis to regulate it, nobody knew what was going on but his family. When the strike was over, he finally slipped away to the hospital and never came back.

This quality of concern for others is vital to the tradition of the *Times.* A newspaper is a very special kind of partnership. The main ingredients are not newsprint, ink, and advertising, but the more volatile human ingredients of blood, brains, pride, and courage.

This is why understanding is so important at the top, and why Adolph Ochs, Arthur Sulzberger, and Orvil Dryfoos, having understanding, were so good at it. For they saw a newspaper, as Edmund Burke saw a nation, not only as a partnership of the living, but as a partnership "between those who are living, those who are dead, and those who are to be born."

There should be some consolation for us all, believer and non-believer alike, in this thought. Orvil Dryfoos had this special sense of trusteeship to a marked degree. He thought of himself, as his father-in-law did before him, as one of a team working for an ideal larger than himself, of carrying on for a time something he devoutly believed to be important. And he not only carried it higher up the hill but also expanded its influence across the continent and planted a new edition of the *Times* beyond the Rockies. Thus he achieved his ideal much more than most men are able to do, and remains a part of an institution that will go on as long as men are faithful to its ideals.

I never thought much of the family joke that Arthur Sulzberger and Orvil Dryfoos "married *The New York Times.*" The women they married were so much better than any newspaper. Besides, it was the women who married them, and what is important now, bore them the children who must carry on.

Their fathers have given them a good lead. It is summed up for them—and I ask the children to remember it—in a quote from Robert Burns. He said: "Whatever mitigates the woes or increases the happiness of others—this is my criterion of goodness. And whatever injures society at large, or any individual in it—this is my measure of iniquity."

Orvil Dryfoos lived by this noble ideal, but knew that ideals and traditions are not self-enforcing. Somebody must decide in the newspaper business. In no other institution are so many choices offered every day of the year. In no other craft are there so many men with so many diverse ideas on so many subjects, about which so much can be said. But the tyranny of the deadline is always present, and while most of these decisions are made on the desk, the big ones have to be made at the top.

Here Orvil Dryfoos was equal to his duty. I will always remember him in the city room on election night of 1960 when he was first to sense that we had gone out on a limb for Kennedy too early and insisted that we reconsider. And again in 1961 when we were on the point of reporting a premature invasion of Cuba his courteous questions and wise judgment held us back.

He had his weaknesses, like all of us, but usually they sprang from the more amiable qualities of the human spirit. To hurt a colleague was an agony for him, and in this savage generation, when men decide, other men often get hurt. But he could make up his mind. He suffered, but he acted.

Perhaps the simplest thing to say about him—and I believe I speak for my colleagues in this—is that the more we knew him, the more we respected him. He was a gentleman. He was faithful to a noble tradition, to the family from which he came, and to the great family he joined and loved.

Martin Buber once said: "If we could hang all our sorrows on pegs, and were allowed to choose those we liked best, every one of us would take back his own, for all the rest would seem more difficult to bear."

Let us then honor Orvil Dryfoos with remembrance rather than with tears. For his children will never be able to cry as much as he made them laugh.

## My Assistants and Their Last Known Whereabouts

| | | |
|---|---|---|
| 1961–62 | Jonathan Yardley | *The Washington Post* |
| 1962–63 | Christopher Willoughby | World Bank |
| 1963 | Donald E. Graham | *The Washington Post* |
| 1964–65 | Steven V. Roberts | *U.S. News & World Report* |
| 1965–66 | Craig R. Whitney | *The New York Times* |
| 1966–67 | Iver Peterson | *The New York Times* |
| 1967 | David K. Shipler | Carnegie Endowment |
| 1967–68 | James P. Sterba | *The Wall Street Journal* |
| 1968–69 | Linda Greenhouse | *The New York Times* |
| 1969–70 | Rick Edmonds | *Florida Trends* |
| 1973–74 | William Hamilton | *The Washington Post* |
| 1974–75 | Steven Rattner | Lazard Frères |
| 1975–76 | David W. Dunlap | *The New York Times* |
| 1976–77 | Matthew L. Wald | *The New York Times* |
| 1977–78 | John Hough, Jr. | Novelist, Martha's Vineyard |
| 1978–79 | James Brooke | *The New York Times* |
| 1980–81 | Nis Kildegaard | *Vineyard Gazette* |
| 1981–82 | Philip Shenon | *The New York Times* |
| 1982–83 | Sam Howe Verhovek | *The New York Times* |
| 1983–84 | Eric Schmitt | *The New York Times* |
| 1984–85 | Amy Wallace | *Los Angeles Times* |
| 1985–86 | James Newton | *Los Angeles Times* |
| 1986–88 | Hilary Stout | *The Wall Street Journal* |
| 1988–89 | Jack Steinberg | *The New York Times* |
| 1989–90 | Richard Coe | *The New York Times* |
| 1991– | Stewart Yerton | *The New York Times* |

# Index

## ABOUT THE AUTHOR

JAMES RESTON was born in Clydebank, Scotland, on November 3, 1909, attended the public schools of Dayton, Ohio, and was graduated from the University of Illinois in 1932. He began his newspaper work on the Cox newspapers in Dayton and Springfield, Ohio, and after three years with the Associated Press in New York, joined the London staff of *The New York Times* on September 1, 1939. He won his first Pulitzer Prize for his coverage of foreign affairs in 1944, and his second for his reporting of the presidential election of 1956. He succeeded Arthur Krock as Washington bureau chief for the *Times* in 1953, a position he held until 1964, when he became associate editor of the paper. In 1968, he was named executive editor of the *Times* with principal responsibility for directing the news of the daily and Sunday papers. His nationally syndicated column appeared regularly in the *Times* from 1953 until 1987. In addition to twenty-eight college and university honorary degrees, his awards include: the Presidential Medal of Freedom; the Roosevelt Four Freedoms medal; Commander, Order of the British Empire; the Légion d'Honneur; and the Ordre National du Mérite (France).

## A NOTE ON THE TYPE

The text of this book was set in a typeface called Times Roman, designed by Stanley Morison (1889–1967) for *The Times* (London) and first introduced by that newspaper in 1932.

Among typographers and designers of the twentieth century, Stanley Morison was a strong forming influence—as a typographical adviser to the Monotype Corporation, as a director of two distinguished English publishing houses, and as a writer of sensibility, erudition, and keen practical sense.

MP 1 OW